Changing Images of the Family

CHANGING IMAGES OF THE FAMILY

EDITED BY

VIRGINIA TUFTE AND BARBARA MYERHOFF

NEW HAVEN AND LONDON
YALE UNIVERSITY PRESS

The assistance of the Robert Sterling Clark Foundation, Inc., is gratefully acknowledged.

Designed by Thos. Whitridge and set in VIP Janson type. Printed in the United States of America by Vail-Ballou Press, Binghamton, N.Y.

Library of Congress Cataloging in Publication Data
Main entry under title:
Changing images of the family.
   Bibliography: p.
   Includes index.
     1. Family—History—Addresses, essays, lectures.
2. Family—United States—Addresses, essays, lectures. 3. Family in literature—Addresses, essays, lectures. I. Tufte, Virginia.
II. Myerhoff, Barbara G.
HQ728.C42   301.42'09   79-537
ISBN 0-300-02361-8 (cloth); 0-300-02671-4 (paper)

12   11   10   9   8   7   6   5   4

to our families
who give us
fullness of being

Contents

viii

Acknowledgments

The contributors to this book discussed images of the family in two colloquia at the University of Southern California convened by the editors in April 1976 and February 1977. Although the idea for the book grew out of the colloquia, most of the essays were written or revised in late 1977 or early 1978.

Grants from the National Endowment for the Humanities, the Rockefeller Foundation, and the University of Southern California's Division of Humanities supported the colloquia. Two grants from the Robert Sterling Clark Foundation, Inc., assisted with editing and publication. Several of our colleagues at the University of Southern California sponsored us for the grants and gave aid both official and personal: David Malone, dean of the Division of Humanities; John A. Schutz, dean of the Division of Social Sciences and Communication; John B. Orr, director of the School of Religion; Karen Nichelson, director of General Education; and Barbara Gardner, director of the Joint Educational Project..

A number of other colloquium participants helped in various ways. We remember, in particular, Melinda Cramer, Sheila de Bretteville, Joan Glusman, Robert F. Higgins, Luther Luedtke, Marvin K. Opler, Ann Stanford, Carlos Velez-I, and Sherrie Wagner. Marla Knutsen and Anke VanHilst Gray gave expert editorial assistance, and Joanne Kajiyama typed the manuscript with intelligence and goodwill.

The book has benefited also from the talents and discernment of Ellen Graham and Maureen Bushkovitch at the Yale University Press.

Our thanks to all.

Introduction

Van Wyck Brooks, in *America's Coming of Age*

Brooks's remark is at once appalling and encouraging if we are setting forth yet another treatment of the family—appalling because he reminds us that it is futile to expect strong verification of any point of view, findings, or interpretations; encouraging because we are indeed embarking on turbulent waters. The family itself has long navigated these currents—a small craft hitherto seaworthy—but now, in the face of such menacing external elements, it has never looked so fragile. We can attend to the water seeping in or the water held out, but somehow we must see to it that the vessel holds, for it may be our only means for survival. Its well-being and our own are the same.

In examining the literature of the family we are immediately overwhelmed with contradictory claims and interpretations, and this applies to purportedly factual as well as artistic and humanistic approaches. If we didn't have Brooks's quotation we should have to invent it. At the very outset, we find support for sharply different definitions of the family. Some authors stress its territorial dimension, focusing on the household, that physical unit made up of kin and others living together, sharing daily life on a primary, face-to-face basis. Legal experts stress biological relationships. Other scholars and artists look at kinship and family as an attitude, a self-defined identification with or among a group of individuals who exist for each other psychologically and socially, however geographically remote they may be. Mass transportation and communication make a new kind of unit feasible, one composed of dispersed membership based on per-

I

ceived emotional proximity and interaction rather than face-to-face contact; this is now possible through exchange of telephone calls, letters, photographs, tape recordings, and the like. All of these definitions are entirely sensible.

Neither is there agreement on the family's current state of health. There are scholars who claim that the family is imperiled, shrinking, on the verge of collapse or disappearance. Others, with as much authority, assert the family is merely in flux, responsive to altered external conditions; its changes reflect its viability. It is, they say, notoriously flexible and indeed there is even reason to think the family is more important than it ever was.

Nor do we find consensus on how the family has changed (though no one seems to argue that it has remained the same). One set of studies claims that the family is growing steadily smaller, less important, and less satisfying; that before widespread urbanization and modernization, the family was extended, larger, more important, and happier than at present. Another set of studies claims that such a view is an idealization, that in the past the family was never so large as scholars once thought, nor so emotionally satisfying; indeed, these studies suggest that premodern families were characterized by emotional indifference, violence, and corruption. Still another stream of interpretation emphasizes the importance of kinship in urban settings, examines the importance and prevalence of extended families (particularly in ethnic families), and presents a contemporary picture rather like the allegedly idealized past family forms. A fourth group of investigators claims that nuclear family forms are not nearly so common in our time as once was supposed, that the current view (like our reading of the past) is idealized and sentimental. In this thicket of interpretations, reliable, extensive data and documentation are found for every view and claim. Demographic materials are cited, as are genealogical, archaeological, iconic, imaginative, and phenomenological evidence (as in diaries and autobiographies). And often logic, like evidence, is unimpeachable, yet results in quite opposite conclusions. For example, demographic materials are used in one set of studies to suggest that before the twentieth century the combination of high infant mortality rates and high birth rates created an attitude of indifference, of self-protective noninvolvement of parents with their progeny, who had small chance of surviving. If they lived into childhood (usually after baptism) they were granted the status of "people" and gradually valued and incorporated as genuine members of society. Before that crucial threshold had been crossed, infants were mere "potential." And because so many were born, neglect of them was often extreme, occasionally verging on infanticide, made morally acceptable by the infants' provisional humanity.[1]

This argument has some logic on its side, but surely it is no less plausible to argue that their fragility could make infants more precious, more fully loved rather than less. When we look for evidence on this question in different societies, we find that mere hardship and risk of early death are not a sufficient explanation. The anthropological record in preliterate societies, for example, gives us a mixed reading.[2] Sometimes infants are fiercely loved and protected precisely because they may not survive without this; sometimes the argument for neglect seems more plausible. We are dealing here with nothing less formidable than our deepest convictions about human nature, maternal instinct, the morality or amorality of social institutions, and the like. Thus when we read about intended or unconscious infanticide practiced by mothers in seventeenth-century Europe, we want more information, in addition to what historians and Western cultural commentators can provide. We want to know, for example, what are the analogues in the animal world? What do nonhuman primate mothers do? How different are human mothers, whose actions are influenced by culture as animals' are

1. See Lawrence Stone, *The Family, Sex and Marriage in England 1500–1800* (New York: Harper & Row, 1977), and John Demos, "All in the Family," *New York Times Book Review*, December 25, 1977, pp. 1, 17.

2. A few of the many studies: Ernestine Friedl, *Women and Men: An Anthropologist's View* (New York: Holt, Rinehart and Winston, 1975); Colin M. Turnbull, *The Mountain People* (New York: Simon and Schuster, 1974); Marvin Harris, *Cows, Pigs, Wars, and Witches: The Riddles of Culture* (New York: Random House, 1974); N. A. Chagnon, *Yanomamö: The Fierce People* (New York: Holt, Rinehart and Winston, 1968); Lorna Marshall, "The !Kung Bushmen of the Kalahari Desert," in *Peoples of Africa*, ed. J. L. Gibbs (New York: Holt, Rinehart and Winston, 1965); and Elizabeth Marshall Thomas, *The Harmless People* (New York: Random House, 1958).

not? And if nonhuman primates are better parents,[3] what does this mean about the corruption of natural impulses by culture? Does the culture warp impulses that may contribute toward survival of the young? Further, what are the homologies on the subject derived from study of the preliterate world, from non-Western societies? What are we to believe? Only this—less and less does it appear that we can expect to find a simple truth if only we search diligently enough. The problems of family and context are no less confusing than questions about the nature of its changes.

Even at the expense of losing the artificial clarity that comes from approaching the family as if it were isolated, we must emphasize the basic interrelatedness of all cultural forms and groupings. At times, the family has been regarded as playing a causal role in relation to other social features. The correspondence between the form of the slim, flexible, mobile, private, supportive, nuclear family and the requisites of urban, capitalistic, secular postindustrial Western societies has been often noted. But which is cause and which consequence has by no means been established. Did the family as we know it make possible other economic, political, and social arrangements, or did it merely respond to forces already in motion?[4] Or were there

3. Again, the evidence is mixed. See, for example: Irenaus Eibl-Eibesfeldt, *Ethology: The Biology of Behavior* (New York: Holt, Rinehart and Winston, 1970); Jane Goodall, "Chimpanzees of Gombe Stream Reserve," in *Primate Behavior: Field Studies of Monkeys and Apes,* ed. Irven De Vore (New York: Holt, Rinehart and Winston, 1965); George B. Schaller, *The Mountain Gorilla: Ecology and Behavior* (Chicago: University of Chicago Press, 1963); H. F. Harlow, "The Nature of Love," *American Psychologist* 13 (1958): 673–85; Konrad Lorenz, *On Aggression,* trans. Marjorie Kerr Wilson (New York: Harcourt Brace Jovanovich, 1963); and Sarah Blaffer Hrdy, *The Langurs of Abu* (Cambridge, Mass.: Harvard University Press, 1977). A reviewer in *Time,* January 9, 1978, comments: "Hrdy's portrait of the langurs [who kill their young] is a far cry from the traditional view of animals as social creatures that act to ensure group survival. But as Lorenz's work was, it is in tune with its times. In stressing chaotic individualism at the expense of the group, *The Langurs of Abu* reads like a jungle version of Tom Wolfe's essay on *The Me Decade.*"

4. See *Max Weber: The Interpretation of Social Reality,* ed. J. E. T. Eldridge (New York: Scribner, 1971), p. 72: "The . . . causes which have influenced any given event are always infinite and there is nothing in the things themselves to set them apart as meriting attention. A chaos of individual judgments about

other factors at work that both family and other social features were reacting to—changes in religious outlook and organization, or technological developments? Should we follow those who concentrate on ideas as historical forces causal in themselves, or others who weight economic factors more heavily as causal influences and argue that ideas follow rather than precede them?

Moreover, there are other contradictions. The modern family has been called a sanctuary, a castle, that succors its beset members from the competitiveness and impersonality of the outside world. And indeed it is a refuge for many. But this kind of family and home has at times been the man's castle, maintained for him by the wife, assisted by children. Often, for all, the family has become less refuge than prison, and the growing numbers of refugees from the family—runaway children, permanently defecting adolescents, wives, and husbands—disturb those who prefer to concentrate on its protectiveness of members from the public domain. The family's very closeness, privacy, and the protracted intimacy among members have been viewed by some as generating violence, mental disorders, and human incapacitation.

What should be done about the family? "Leave it alone. It would manage very well if only we didn't make social policies that disrupt it and undermine its autonomy. It should be a private, self-regulating institution," many policymakers and social critics assert. Christopher Lasch argues that in taking over responsibilities formerly residing in the family, society has "weakened the capacity for self-direction and self-control."[5] Others are shocked at the lack of support government and private agencies offer families. "More policies and programs" are called for. Welfare reform, provision of medical care, child care, assistance for the elderly, payment for housework, are mentioned as essential if the family is to cope with its burdens. But when is support

---

countless individual events would be the only result of a serious attempt to analyze reality 'without presuppositions.' " See also Thomas Burger, *Max Weber's Theory of Concept Formation–History, Laws, and Ideal Types* (Durham, N.C.: Duke University Press, 1976), p. 80.

5. Christopher Lasch, *Haven in a Heartless World: The Family Besieged* (New York: Basic Books, 1977), p. 189.

interference? When is public participation destructive of family integrity, solidarity, and autonomy? The furor aroused by the Moynihan recommendations, which blamed social problems of blacks on the "tangle of pathology" that allegedly characterized black families, engendered protracted scholarly and public debate about critical issues.[6] The debate raised public consciousness about the complexity of the issues involved and the difficulty of being objective and impartial when one studies the family. This applies to fair-minded, scholarly, well-intentioned experts as well as to those who are openly biased.

Given this muddle, how do we dare put out another book on the family, particularly after admitting at the outset that we do not believe definitive answers are to be found, admitting too, that we do not believe it is possible to begin to exhaust the essential components of such a study?[7] It is our hope that this volume will make a contribution by two distinctive features: its multidisciplinary orientation and its emphasis on images. If we cannot find truths or realities or moral imperatives, at least we can strive for a holistic view, one that looks at its subject from many angles at once. No single viewer is as impartial as when his or her vision is joined with its counterparts. We recall Virginia Woolf's description of several persons looking at a vase of flowers in the center of a table.[8] No set of eyes sees the vase in all its fullness; that is humanly impossible. But if we cannot grasp the whole directly,

6. *The Moynihan Report and the Politics of Controversy*, ed. Lee Rainwater and William L. Yancey (Cambridge: M.I.T. Press, 1967).

7. Falling outside the scope of this volume was a systematic consideration of variations in family forms (such as communes, homosexual unions, single-parent families, childless families, upper-class families, serial unions); there is little on ethnic-American families and nothing on rural families. The essays deal most often with particular instances, making no pretense of universality. Attention has deliberately focused on literate, Western, industrialized nations, without attempting to deal with families across very different kinds of cultures or forms of social organization.

8. Virginia Woolf, *The Waves* (London: Hogarth Press, 1931; rpt. 1976), p. 91: "We have come together . . . to make one thing, not enduring—for what endures?—but seen by many eyes simultaneously. There is a red carnation in that vase. A single flower as we sat here waiting, but now a seven-sided flower many petalled, red, puce, purple-shaded, stiff with silver-tinted leaves—a whole flower to which every eye brings its own contribution."

we can gain much by telling each other what we see. Thus our contributions in this volume come from a range of specialists—in the fields of history, art, literature, sociology, anthropology, psychology, social work, political science, law, religion, and social ethics. Here social scientists, humanists, and professionals are speaking together. Since this volume originated in colloquia, two sessions held a year apart, the participant-contributors were able to observe others' reactions to their ideas. There was much that was fresh and new to those viewing the family from other disciplines, notions quite taken for granted within one's own. Talking across disciplinary barriers often has the effect of aerating fixed ideas, shaking up preconceptions, advancing or deepening inquiries not because of new evidence but because of new inflections of taken-for-granted notions. For example, when a historian calls the family "a haven," a feminist calls it "oppressive," and a child psychologist labels it "schizophrenogenic," all are forced to more severe scrutiny of their original interpretations. Such benefits we brought to each other in our meetings and now hope to bring to the reader. In addition to giving freshness of viewpoint, we believe that comparison of the studies of families in other times and in various forms, seen by a range of disciplines, is our only hope for rigor and for establishing some (always provisional) generalizations; this method is the best we have in a subject not amenable to experimentation. In the social sciences, it is a corrective for our biases, a way to minimize our inevitably culture-bound propensities to hold the mirror of our study up to our own minds rather than to the subject under scrutiny.

The second distinctive feature of this volume is that it emphasizes images as both basic and central to its purpose. Actuality and image, fact and fiction—these are distinctions so commonplace that to deny them is a minor heresy, and we do not suggest that they be denied, but we do suggest that their similarities may be attended as fruitfully as their opposition. It is only fair to set this view out immediately as an editorial bias. We did not ask our authors to consider this matter, and no doubt some would uphold these venerable distinctions. The social scientists might define their aim as the examination of social phenomena existing in a relatively uninflected state and having therefore an external existence that is directly discoverable. As scientists they would assert their conviction that a knowable, measurable "reality," however complex, can and must be operationally defined, then examined empirically and with detachment. (Many social scientists these days are less certain about this enterprise; those working within the parameters of ethnomethodological or contemporary phenomenological approaches would modify the above statement, stressing the inevitable participation of the observer in the situation he or she observes, pointing out the socially constructed, culturally provided and maintained definition of "reality" at work.)[9] However humble the social scientists might be about their ability to dissect and fathom truly complex social phenomena like the family, most would still wish and *intend* to approach it as a knowable, external state of affairs, in the world rather than in their own imaginations.

Humanists and artists, on the other hand, reach toward a different knowledge, with different tools, working with indirect evidence; that is, with what creators and commentators have imagined or reflected about their world and themselves. These writers are clearly not looking directly at a first-order reality, but rather are looking at someone else's presentation of his or her perceptions. Historians fall in between: forced to work with second-order data much of the time because often the realities they examine no longer exist, and forced to enter their materials imaginatively, they take responsibility for their reconstruction. Like art, history has concerns with the individual, nonrecurrent features, but shares with the social sciences the attempt to use the materials to generalize about particulars. Yet another group, social planners and activists, examine the knowledge provided from many sources—history, art, and science—and take the additional step of altering what they study by engaging in action themselves or recommending actions to others.

Looked at in one way, this collection of essays merely juxtaposes the views of the family proffered by artists, humanists, social scientists, and professionals, with some of the essays deal-

9. Compare, for example, Hugh Mehan and Houston Wood, *The Reality of Ethnomethodology* (New York: John Wiley, 1975).

ing with "fact" and the others with "fiction." But the editors do not look at the book in such a light. We regard all of this book's verbal and visual materials as conceptualizations; all are images, which both shape and reflect conscious and unconscious attitudes. What we understand an image to be is a critical point. For us, an image is a particular kind of symbol, a symbol that, like all symbols, refers to and makes present something absent. *Like* all symbols, an image is multivocal, ultimately inexhaustible and ambiguous, and it conveys emotional and cognitive meaning at once. But, *unlike* all symbols, images appeal primarily to our senses, and present information through them, reaching us directly, as it were, by arousing in us our own remembered experiences. Images have an immediacy, a natural ability to be convincing because they appeal to us through our senses, circumventing (at least at first) our critical faculties. Images are fundamentally and inevitably rhetorical, then, persuading us of the validity of the information they carry.

Their sensory nature gives images great potential power to convince and manipulate; their messages are often unconsciously delivered and received and, even when received or sent intentionally, not always subjected to critical examination. Governments know this, and so do manufacturers, hucksters, teachers, quacks, charlatans, and performers. In our day, consensus is a rarity rather than the norm. As one sociologist put it (somewhat awkwardly), "Our plausibility structures have collapsed." The breaking of accord on fundamental premises and the contracting of the genuinely sacred domain have conferred upon us greater freedom, to be sure, and also more agony and confusion than we have reason to believe existed in earlier times when differentiation was not so extreme in society and culture. Heterogeneity, complexity, and specialization are the rewards and penalties of evolution, for societies and organisms alike. Without the grounding provided by shared, unquestioned tenets, we are not a single, a genuine culture, but are rather a series of small cultures living side by side, with some overlap and much contradiction. In this state we are manipulable, easy prey for any who appear more certain than the rest of us about their point of view. Mass communication and marketing practices inundate us relentlessly with competing, garbled, urgent images. We had better attempt to identify some of these and learn how they operate if we would expect to wend a judicious and independent course through our contemporary world.

Even when the image makers present images without any clear intentions to persuade but merely to convey information "neutrally," we are influenced and often moved by them. Artists arouse emotions naturally. So do educators, commentators of every kind. Inevitably when images used are positive, they become standards against which we measure ourselves. They become normative (in the sense of obligatory) and operate as models, effecting a great range of action and response—from social legislation to our internal evaluation of our own successes and failures as family members. In "Fun Morality," a classical analysis of this process and its potential dangers, Martha Wolfenstein compares child-care bulletins from 1914 to the 1940s.[10] In these documents, women are shown as naturally enjoying (even exulting in) every moment of their mothering. Every dirty diaper is a little delight. If a mother isn't having fun, something is wrong with her. Feminist literature has done much to correct such shockingly bright images, but in turn it often creates a similar set of pressures by dramatizing women who combine work and family with complete ease and grace, glossing the considerable strains and costs of such a dual career. Some feminist writings, by presenting a hopelessly invincible superwoman, create a standard against which "ordinary" women come up far too short. Similarly, images of successful, adjusted "happy couples," pictured with their clean, energetic (but never obstreperous), unceasingly adorable children, plague us all and by contrast diminish our evaluation of ourselves as family members. Even when we recognize such images as false idols— usually selling us something, playing on our sense of inadequacy—they haunt us in moments of vulnerability.

Now let us enlarge our prior claim that "actuality" and "im-

10. Martha Wolfenstein, "Fun Morality: An Analysis of Recent American Child-Training Literature," in *Childhood in Contemporary Cultures*, ed. Margaret Mead and Martha Wolfenstein (Chicago: University of Chicago Press, 1955), pp. 168–78.

age," "fact" and "fiction," need not be regarded as dichotomous terms but may be bridged by the concept of "image." We have said that an image is a kind of symbol that speaks to us through the senses, making itself known directly by visual appeal and indirectly by providing a word picture that tells us what we can imagine seeing in a particular situation. An image may verbally describe smells, tastes, textures, motions, and sounds, as well as sights. And whether visual or verbal, images are particular and specific, rather than general and abstract. Images may be called virtual symbols; that is, they make their impact without being tested by reason or being present "in fact"; they are a mental representation of something not present to the senses, but brought to us by means of the senses. Despite this particularity and concreteness, images can be built up to make a coherent and abstract comment through accumulation and combination, as in a mosaic, without being explicitly formulated in general terms. Images, like facts, are bits of sense data, located and presented empirically. Thus images are facts *and* symbols. "Facts," too, are symbols, selected bits of evidence, chosen and read to make sense, a sense that the very nature of physiology and the structure of our mental processes insist upon. We hold with the school of philosophy that claims no pure sensation or perception can be apprehended, that all information coming into our awareness is already formulated by our very reception of it. "Everything we conceive, we conceive in some form," as Susanne K. Langer put it. We would apply her comments about "things" to "facts" or "actualities" or "realities":

Our merest sense experience is a process of formulation. The world that actually meets our senses is not a world of "things," about which we are invited to discover facts as soon as we have codified the necessary logical language to do so; the world of pure sensation is so complex, so fluid and full, that sheer sensitivity to stimuli would only encounter what William James has called . . . "a blooming, buzzing confusion." Out of this bedlam our sense-organs must select certain predominant forms, if they are to make sense of *things* and not of mere dissolving sensa.[11]

11. Susanne K. Langer, *Philosophy in a New Key* (Cambridge, Mass.: Harvard University Press, 1951), p. 89.

This unconscious organization of sense data into forms, Langer continues, is the basis of all reasoning. Rudolf Arnheim, too, points out how the reception of specific sense-observations turns out to be the basis for generalization, for all cognition. Arnheim is perhaps extreme in his insistence that visual form is *the* principal medium of productive thinking,[12] but surely we cannot deny that it is a major form of it. On the similarity of the purpose of art and science, Arnheim is also clear: both attempt to understand the forces that shape existence; neither can tolerate capricious subjectivity because both are subject to their criteria of truth. Both require "precision, order, and discipline" to make comprehensible statements. But in the arts the image is the statement, *"containing and displaying* the forces about which it reports."[13] The arts tell us about the significance of direct experience and about our own response, and as such complement science whose purpose is to transcend direct experience and individual outlook. Art, then, generalizes less than science, and focuses upon rather than "transcends" its subject matter. And science intends to present information to us without deliberate value judgments (though some doubt that this is ever possible). Artistic images are never intended to come to us without interpretation; feelings and judgments are built into their form and selection. Artistic images are presented, as Jacques Barzun has said, "in some mood—anger, contempt, derision, indignation, or no less eloquent impassivity."[14]

But as both art and science are based on the same common experiences (whatever we call the "in-here" or "out-there" about which both "speak"), both art and science come out of and flow back into culture. Thus the dichotomies between actuality and image, fact and imagination, science and art, deceive more than they enlighten. We believe (with Robert Nisbet) that the artist's interest in form or style is the scientist's interest in structure or type. But "both are concerned with the illumination of reality,

12. Rudolf Arnheim, *Visual Thinking* (Berkeley and Los Angeles: University of California Press, 1969), p. 294. See especially the preface, chap. 1, and pp. 295–308.

13. Arnheim, pp. 300–01. Emphasis added.

14. Jacques Barzun, *The Use and Abuse of Art* (Princeton, N.J.: Princeton University Press, 1974), p. 126.

with . . . the exploration of the unknown"[15] and, we would add, the unformulated. Then we may say, following Nisbet, that such distinctions as we can preserve do not concur with differences between truth and falsity. Fiction and other arts give us information about values and attitudes essential for our pursuit of understanding. Fiction helps us select the facts we use to judge our lives. Max Weber was one of the most articulate writers on this, reminding us that all facts are only the smallest slice of reality (and this, according to him, makes quantitative demonstration difficult or impossible).[16] Fiction, then, can be seen not so much as falsification of reality but as "a necessary ordering of it," as Joan Rockwell puts it. "Real reality cannot be apprehended as it is: an infinite, equally existent number of discrete and ever-changing entities and events. To see the world in those terms might be accurate but would be impossible to absorb, and meaningless in human terms."[17] Selection and judgment are always necessary.

Fiction and fact, then, image and actuality, we see as aspects of each other, rather than sharply distinct "natural" categories. All originate in culture and whether we emphasize their genuine affinities or contrasts must depend on our purposes. By regarding images as having a bona fide reality we follow the position of the early sociologist Florian Znaniecki that beliefs are real insofar as people believe in them. They become real by virtue of their consequences.[18]

15. Robert Nisbet, *Sociology as an Art Form* (New York: Oxford University Press, 1976), p. 10.

16. Eldridge, *Max Weber*, p. 11.

17. Joan Rockwell, *Fact in Fiction—The Use of Literature in the Systematic Study of Society* (London: Routledge & Kegan Paul, 1974), p. viii.

18. Florian Znaniecki, *Cultural Sciences, Their Origin and Development* (Urbana, Ill.: University of Illinois Press, 1952; rpt. 1963), pp. 135–36: "To a historian who does not function as a philosopher or try to judge the concepts of others as true or false, objective or subjective, but simply reconstructs their content and meaning from written records, an abstract concept is a cultural datum, just as a myth [is] or the characters and plot of a novel." See also Znaniecki's early work, *Cultural Reality* (Chicago: University of Chicago Press, 1919), p. 71: "Objectively, with reference to other objects, the myth is real by all the influence it exercises . . . over individual ideas and emotions, over social organization, and even over the material world."

We are in a social milieu which—beholden though it is to positivism and the materialism of advanced technology— nevertheless because of its very technology (especially television and other mass media) is particularly alive to the importance of images. For all who use the term *image* related to imagination, their very choice of the word suggests "unreality" or "fiction." And often, as a nation and a culture, we accept this connotation patiently, when at other times in history we might have winced. Thus when we speak in ordinary parlance about "projecting images," we acknowledge that we are manipulating appearances to give a particular impression. This in itself is nothing new: our consciousness and acceptance of manipulation are, however. When Erving Goffman's book *The Presentation of Self in Everyday Life* appeared in 1959, it was generally considered a cynical view. His insistence that there was no external reality other than that socially agreed upon and his focus on culture as deception and manipulation of appearances were seen as extreme. But now, a few years later, the president of the United States in discussing a European visit remarked on his efforts abroad as "trying to project an American image." It is significant that he did not say, "I wanted Europeans to see us . . ." or "I wanted them to realize that we are. . . ." The president understood that in political affairs, in public life, "knowledge" is less the issue than interpretation. "They" perceive our "projections"—this statement points to a great shift in consciousness, cynical perhaps, based as it is ultimately on the impossibility of direct knowledge on a face-to-face basis in a mass society, where so much information is highly coded, where labels and clues must be heavily used. Symbolic processes become more significant in brief impersonal interactions among masses of strangers when parts must be equated with the imperceptible, vaster wholes. This is necessary for our social function. But if this state of affairs makes us cynical, it should be said that it is also complex, sophisticated, and immensely interesting. .

It must be noted that this acceptance of the idea that image intervenes between people in communication probably does *not* apply to intimates. For example, it is hard to conceive of someone saying "I tried to give my mother (or my lover) an image of me as . . ." without being considered a violator of trust. The absence of a conscious manipulation of appearances through imagery within the family may indeed be one of its definitive characteristics. Family members build knowledge of each other on more direct, experiential, and unguarded impressions than is the case for other social groups.

Thus in dealing with "images" in this book, while we do not undertake a full, systematic analysis of the nature and function of the relationship of symbols and society, we treat images as forces in themselves, as primary data, bona fide social-cultural statements, as creators of our shared "reality," and as reflectors, but never *simply* reflecting, always coming to us in an inflected form, carrying attitudes. Images are commentaries (indeed all culture is commentary), a narrative tale, a shared interpretation, which we create to tell us who we are, what makes us special, what troubles us and what pleases us, and why we are here. In this volume we see ourselves listening to and watching ourselves.

Van Wyck Brooks's comment with which we opened this essay applies to any study. But the family has its own special peculiarities and special hazards as an object of study. And these hazards contribute to the great diversity of viewpoints, the often sharply different readings and recommendations presented in the essays that follow. Let us name a few of the problems. First, we must be aware that objectivity, elusive and partial in any circumstances, is even less possible in family studies than in most subjects, for everyone has experiences in a family, and there are no control groups. No one is impartial, without powerful positive and negative emotions on the subject, since by definition the experiences in the family, the first and deepest that a human being knows, shape the individual more profoundly than any other set of social-cultural forces. In a sense, everyone is an expert on the family and has an opinion, deriving from ultimately unarguable premises of firsthand knowledge. The family is what the Freudians might call a highly cathected notion, gathering to itself powerful opinions, laden with emotion. In one sense the family is only an idea, itself a construct, nothing more than an image, since we cannot know it impartially, and it is never completely separated from our fantasies, projections, and unconscious responses.

Achieving the proper attitude then to use when studying the family is perhaps the most important single task for all who would do so. The finest thinkers, the most astute critics may go astray here, and lose control of their investigations, as they do not in discussing other issues. No discipline, no methods assure safety from the unconscious; so family studies necessitate the most conscious self-examination we can manage. The other side of the cathected nature of the construct *family* is that in reading, talking, and writing about it, we are writing and thinking about ourselves. It is a litmus, a mirror, an indicator of what we are thinking and feeling. It is more difficult to think directly about the family (if it is possible at all) than to think *with* it, using it as an object in our cultural work of self-definition. Claude Lévi-Strauss brought out this point in his brilliant analysis of how totems function in simple societies.[19] A tribe uses a totem animal with which it identifies to state its relationship to other tribes, to nature, to tribal members. Thus the family, like a tribal totem, is a way of thinking indirectly but practically about metaphysical questions, human interdependence, solidarity and separateness, collectivities and individuals, connections and differences, and the like. Through the family, we are showing ourselves to ourselves; family, like self, cannot be recognized except through symbols and metaphors.

What is the "reality" and what the "construct" then? The clear necessities that the family has customarily attended to in all cultures are sometimes considered its "realities"; it is seen as the collection of people carrying out the irreducible social tasks of creating new members who are then protected and trained to become recognizable "people" as that is understood in a particular sociocultural setting. Any assemblage for any period of time of two or more individuals carrying out these minimum tasks may qualify for the label *family*. This allows for enormous variation, since all that is minimally necessary is a cohabiting couple and, soon after, a protective adult (who may not be one of those involved in cohabitation). Indeed social geneticists promise us that the former requirement may also change and even now

19. Claude Lévi-Strauss, *The Savage Mind* (Chicago: University of Chicago Press, 1966), pp. 109–33.

artificial insemination is not uncommon. For that matter, non-married adults are more and more being permitted to adopt children, so still further shrinkage of definition is imaginable. This minimal definition coexists along with bountiful other definitions, emphasizing different features taken up by "family" at various times in history and social circumstance; uncountable possibilities exist. We can, then, never know what the family "really is," and "really is not." Speaking of it even in the most simplistic behavioristic terms, as a hypothetical external reality, we do not gain clarity. It is as *construct* that "family" interests us, then, and here is where we concentrate in this volume.

As construct, the family is often used as a particular species of idea, what Weber labeled as an "ideal type," a form or model that "ideally" has certain features, seldom reproduced precisely in nature; the use of an ideal type is to identify certain features as "definitive" in order to sharpen our observations.[20] But the problem with "ideal types" is that we soon forget their heuristic purpose and confuse them with some reality that inevitably falls short of the model. How troublesome this becomes is apparent in several of our essays. Disappointed expectations, however sentimental and unattainable they are to begin with, take on the power to poison that which we do have, and which may be serviceable if imperfect.

And as an ideal type, the family is overloaded with significance, conceived of as the necessary opposite of "public life." It is quintessentially the private (and, some feel, the *only* contemporary private) opportunity for vulnerability, trust, intimacy, and commitment, for lasting pleasant and peaceful relations, for fullness of being in the human realm. The family thus is located as the physical site for a vast (and repressed) range of human expression, the valid arena (and again perhaps the only

20. *Max Weber on the Methodology of the Social Sciences*, trans. and ed. E. A. Shils and H. A. Finch (Glencoe, Ill.: Free Press, 1947). See also Thomas Burger (work cited in note 4), part 4, "Ideal Types, Models, and Sociological Theory," pp. 154–79. Burger (p. 159) translates a key paragraph from Weber: "An ideal type is formed by the one-sided exaggeration of one or several points of view and by the synthesis of a great many diffusely and discretely existent component phenomena which are sometimes more and sometimes less present and occasionally absent."

arena) where quality-of-life is a concern. It is in the family that we find the opportunity for psychologically bearable, nonexploitive, personal life. This sharp contrast between public and private, with the family being entirely the latter and the rest of life taking place in the former domain, intensifies family relations inordinately. The family is often referred to as a "crucible" for human development and growth, but might as well be referred to as a cauldron, overheated by its seclusiveness, specialization, and uniqueness.

These factors—cauldronlike intensification, separation from and contrast with other social arrangements and roles, the confusion of ideal type with actuality, and the reification of a construct—have something in common: all of them load down the family impossibly, heaping upon it duties, conscious expectations, sentiments (and the inevitable disappointments and resentments that accrue to them), along with unconscious projections. A powerful and in our view appalling image of this circumstance is offered by the artist Jacques Lipchitz, who has sculpted a massive public monument—an entangled confusion of breasts, hands, humans, and a monster or two—set upon a pedestal whose words are as ponderous as the visual expression:

"GOVERNMENT OF THE PEOPLE."
JACQUES LIPCHITZ
1892–1973

DEDICATION
SYMBOLIZING FAMILY LIFE,
"THE WELLSPRING OF SOCIETY,
THE HOPE OF THE FUTURE"
AND
THE CONCEPT OF GOVERNMENT
BEING OF, BY AND FOR THE PEOPLE,
THIS SCULPTURE IS DEDICATED
TO THE PEOPLE OF PHILADELPHIA.

The dedication calls to mind another unjust burden, vestigial in fact but psychologically of lingering relevance, reminding us that in early America the political commonwealth was an enlargement of the family. To quote historian Bernard Bailyn:

Families [in the seventeenth century] were not merely the basic social institution; they were considered the archetype of all social order, public as well as private. In this micro-community, it was believed, all order germinated, all patterns of inferiority and superiority took shape. The political commonwealth was but an enlargement of the family. Rulers were conceived of as patriarchs whose dominance as heads of commonwealths was justified by God the Father of all.[21]

We might agree that it is still in the family that ideas of order are formed, but the macrocommunity no longer exists. The family is a microcommunity, to be sure, and from it we draw our first and usually deepest ideas about social arrangement, authority, hierarchy, equality, and justice; but so extreme is the distance between family and the rest of society that these ideas are at best irrelevant, at worst disruptive. Emile Durkheim's classical analysis holds up in accounting for the discrepancy;[22] as a society's division of labor grows more complex, and as sufficient numbers of people living together have different ways of life, solidarity is based not on fundamental commonality, sameness, and homogeneity but must arise out of numerous differentiated parts whose specializations make them interdependent (Durkheim thus distinguishes "mechanical" and "organic" solidarity). As societal differentiation continues and diversity expands, the overlap of family and polity shrinks, and an intervening arrangement, community, comes into being.

In the simplest conditions (still found today in some band-level societies, and some tribal ones), the husband-father is the headman or chief; the adult brothers are lineage heads, and elders are in charge of religion as well as government and economy. Kinship is the idiom in terms of which all activities are played out; kinship is the formulation for all relationships. No such thing as an unrelated person exists; to be comprehended, visitors or strangers must be incorporated into the kinship system by adoption or renaming.

The intertwining of family and commonwealth in early

---

21. Bernard Bailyn *et al.*, *The Great Republic: A History of the American People* (Boston: Little, Brown, 1977), in part 1 by Bailyn, p. 105.

22. Emile Durkheim, *The Division of Labor in Society*, trans. George Simpson (Glencoe, Ill.: Free Press, 1933; rpt. 1960).

America was far from the situation found in tribal societies; still it was an expression of a more integrated culture than our present one. In early America, parts replicated a greater whole with more or less exactitude, but always built on the same principles. The same criteria for authority and prestige, for example, were found in church, state, family, economy. Now, in late-twentieth-century America, still some replication of principles governs church, state, and economy,[23] but today the family is a less permeable unit. Paradoxically, some argue that in our time, and culture, the more *impermeable* the boundaries around the family, setting it firmly apart from the public domain, the more satisfying and successful it is in protecting its members. (The other side of protection, its shadow side, is severe isolation, certainly as dangerous as too much permeation.)

Let us conclude by mentioning some additional stresses on the family in our time. A number of scholars have noted the connection between the family as we have become accustomed to it, in its protective-sanctuary manifestation, and the rise of the individual. The "individual," as distinct from the human being, is a peculiarly Western and relatively recent occurrence, so much so that Colin Morris suggests that the concept of "individual . . . be regarded as an eccentricity among cultures."[24] For simplicity's sake we may accept Morris's concept of the individual, marked by concern with "self," self-discovery, and expression; the belief in the uniqueness and value of each human being; the positive valuing of the relations between people; the assessment of people in terms of their inner intentions as well as their external acts. Morris traces the origins of the notion, citing numerous ideological and existential factors, including Christianity, the impact of classical philosophy and learning, the corollary concepts of romantic love and friendship, and social institutional differentiation. Whatever origins of the concept of the individual one wishes to emphasize, there is agreement that the family must

23. See C. Wright Mills, *The Power Elite* (New York: Oxford University Press, 1956).

24. Colin Morris, *The Discovery of the Individual, 1050–1200* (New York: Harper & Row, 1972), p. 2.

preserve and succor this entity. Lawrence Stone has recently made this point most carefully in his discussion of "affective individualism."[25] But here occurs what might be called a built-in stress on the family. In groups where several private selves are strongly developed and regarded as of equal value, and at the same time where collective concerns are placed below individual concerns, conflict is inevitable. And when other, usually highly sentimental, notions about family harmony are superimposed on its emphasis on individual expression, the very failure to achieve harmony itself creates strain.

A second feature of the contemporary family also has a Janus-like appearance. The protective, permissive family allows individuals to flourish, and then must abide the centripetal pulls that flow from such freedom. The family, kept afloat and subsidized by external aids and services, finances and support, has also the greater potentiality for freedom because of this aid, yet must cope with another built-in strain—the withdrawal of the absolute *necessity* of interdependence for survival, a condition that can buttress as well as tax any organization. Emotional need is stronger than ever between family members. Yet instrumental, practical necessities have not deepened or intensified proportionately. We witness many other institutions carrying functions formerly belonging to the family, outside agencies contributing a great range of support—medical care, financial aid, education of children, and the like. This means that a family must *choose* to remain intact, because its members can survive without each other. And remaining intact is an extremely difficult choice. Lasch points this out in *Haven in a Heartless World*: "As the world grows more menacing and insecure and the family fails to offer protection from external dangers, all forms of loyalty become increasingly attenuated" (p. xviii). Thus option is transformed into necessity and brings both advantages and afflictions. Knowledge that divorce exists, that one may cancel the marriage contract, makes it more difficult to put up with the dissatisfying, unfulfilling features of the relationship. If ambivalence is a natural part of every intimate relationship, freedom to

25. See Stone, *Family, Sex and Marriage in England*, esp. pp. 221–69.

leave it often means that ambivalence, instead of being regarded as an inevitable fact of human affairs, is viewed as unnecessary and disagreeable.

The essays in this book show that not only have our images of the family changed over time, but our modes of producing and receiving images have changed in significant ways that bear heavily on the functioning and form of the family and possibly constitute an added strain on it. Today, more than ever before in history, we are at the mercy of images. Susan Sontag remarks that we "consume" images, partly because we are a thoroughly commercial society, as she puts it, a capitalistic society:

A capitalist society requires a culture based on images. It needs to furnish vast amounts of entertainment in order to stimulate buying and anesthetize the injuries of class, race, and sex. And it needs to gather unlimited amounts of information, the better to exploit natural resources, increase productivity, keep order, make war, give jobs to bureaucrats.[26]

But surely other contemporary societies, not capitalistic, are also avaricious where images are concerned; it is urbanized, secular, impersonal, mass societies that need these relatively simple bits of information—fixed, ordered, and agreed-upon—to allow us to proceed. We are what has been called an "information-rich" society, a pleasant way of saying we are inundated with fragmented quantities of data, and we must take shortcuts or go under. In this confusion, simple codes and shibboleths inform and comfort us, forging an often illusory sense of coherence and clarity. Images soothe our worries lest there be no comprehensible "reality," endowing such "reality" with an inevitability and authority that inhere only in that which can be stopped, named in words, or framed in our vision. How commercial formulations fill the hunger for some order and certainty we know too well. But it is not only electronic, patently obvious "mass" entertainments and media that are proffering the images that become our mental and imaginative possibilities; it is also the more tra-

26. Susan Sontag, *On Photography* (New York: Farrar, Straus and Giroux, 1977), p. 178.

ditional, serious, once more independent media, such as print. "Communication" conglomerates include varied and extensive outlets—publishing houses for books, magazines, and newspapers; radio stations and television channels; films, games, and toys—presenting what may well be an overly simple, overly unified, finally exclusive view of possibilities.

The pluralism and diversity of family forms are surely a condition that most thoughtful people would support. The monolithic, pejorative views of variation have at least lost some of their grip on our ideology. But unless the images that surround us reflect that diversity honestly and fully, in effect the diversity is reduced to aberration and insignificance.

Many of the essays in this volume point to the negative or positive impact of certain images of the family on its members and the larger society, to the conflict and contradiction between ideals (or expectations) and our own experiences. None would argue that what we think or show the family to be is unimportant. Surely we must be as diligent and thoughtful about images and our access to them as we are about the family itself. Our image world is a "real" world—the well-being of our imagination deserves no less care than the "fact" of the family.

In these essays, we have tried to suggest some of the rich complexities that cannot, and should not in our view, be eliminated from an examination of the family. At the same time, we have wished always to make the work accessible to a thoughtful lay reader, and as much as possible have minimized technical terms and materials that require extensive background. This subject matter belongs to us all, and as citizens we all benefit when our understandings deepen and spread beyond the encapsulated niches of our own special interests. If there was ever a subject on which expertise should beckon rather than forbid entry, surely it is this one.

The book is arranged in four parts. Part I, *Origins: The Family in Europe and Early America*, is written by four historians; part II, *Reflections: The Family in Literature, Art, and the Mass Media*, by an art historian and specialists in English, French, and American literature and culture; part III, *Observations: The Contemporary*

American Family, by specialists in sociology, anthropology, social work, and social psychology; and part IV, *Responsibilities: Law, Politics, and Ethics*, by professors of law, political science, and social ethics. The Introduction is by the editors, whose fields are anthropology and literature.

BARBARA MYERHOFF
VIRGINIA TUFTE

I. ORIGINS

*The Family in Europe and
Early America*

I

The Family and the City in the Old World and the New

Philippe Ariès

I should like to make some observations in this essay about the relationship between family history and urban history. My central theme will be that when the city (and earlier, the rural community) deteriorated and lost its vitality, the role of the family overexpanded like a hypertrophied cell. In an attempt to fill the gap created by the decline of the city and the urban forms of social intercourse it had once provided, the omnipotent, omnipresent family took upon itself the task of trying to satisfy all the emotional and social needs of its members. Today, it is clear that the family has failed in its attempts to accomplish that feat, either because the increased emphasis on privacy has stifled the need for social intercourse or because the family has been too completely alienated by public powers. People are demanding that the family do everything that the outside world in its indifference or hostility refuses to do. But we should now ask ourselves why people have come to expect the family to satisfy all their needs, as if it had some kind of all-encompassing power.

First, let us take a brief look at Western traditional societies from the Middle Ages to the eighteenth century, that is, before they had been affected by the Enlightenment and the Industrial Revolution. Each individual grew up in a community of relatives,

With the permission of the organizers of the colloquium, an earlier version of this chapter appeared in *Daedalus* (Spring 1977), under the title "The Family and the City."

neighbors, friends, enemies, and others with whom he or she had interdependent relationships. The community was more important in determining the individual's fate than was the family. When a young boy left his mother's apron strings, it was his responsibility to make a place for himself. Like an animal or a bird, he had to establish a domain, and he had to get the community to recognize it. It was up to him to determine the limits of his authority, to decide what he could do and how far he could go before encountering resistance from others—his parents, his wife, his neighbors. Securing his domain in this way depended more on the skillful use of natural talents than on knowledge or savoir-faire. It was a game in which the venturesome boy gifted in eloquence and with a dramatic flair had the advantage. All life was a stage: if a player went too far, he was put in his place; if he hesitated, he was relegated to an inferior role.

Since a man knew that his wife would be his most important and faithful collaborator in maintaining and expanding his role, he chose his bride with care. On her part, the woman accepted the domain she would have to protect, along with the man with whom she would live. Marriage strengthened the husband's position, as a result not only of his wife's work, but also of her personality, her presence of mind, her talents as player, actress, storyteller, her ability to seize opportunities and to assert herself.

The important concept, then, is that of *domain*. But this domain was neither private nor public, as these terms are understood today; rather, it was both simultaneously: private because it had to do with individual behavior, with one's personality, one's manner of being alone or in society, one's self-awareness and inner being; public because it fixed the individual's place within the community and established one's rights and obligations. Individual maneuvering was possible because the social space was not completely filled. The fabric was loose, and it behooved each person to adjust the seams to suit himself or herself within the limits set by the community. The community recognized the existence of the empty space surrounding people and things. It is worth remarking that the word *play* can mean both the act of playing and freedom of movement within a space. Perhaps, by the act of playing, the free space to play in was created and maintained. The state and society intervened in a person's life only infrequently and intermittently, bringing with them either terror and ruin or miraculous good fortune. But for the most part, individuals had to win their domains by coming to terms only with the men and women in their own small community.

The role of the family was to strengthen the authority of the head of the household, without threatening the stability of his relationship with the community. Married women would gather at the wash house, men at the cabaret. Each sex had its special place in church, in processions, in the public square, at celebrations, and even at the dance. But the family as such had no domain of its own; the only real domain was that each male won by his maneuvering, with the help of his wife, friends, and dependents.

In the course of the eighteenth century the situation began to change, influenced by three important trends. The first is the loss of "frontiers," to use American parlance; we might say that in earlier centuries the community had a frontier—or rather several frontiers—that could be pushed back by the audacious. Free areas were allowed to exist, and adventurous individuals were permitted to explore them. But in the eighteenth century, society—or more properly, the state—was loath to accept the fact that there were certain areas beyond its sphere of control and influence. Following upon the Enlightenment and industrialization, the state, with its sophisticated technology and organization, wiped out those frontiers: there was no longer an open area for the venturesome. Today the state's scrutiny and control extend, or are supposed to extend, into every sphere of activity. Today there is no free space for individuals to occupy and claim for themselves. To be sure, liberal societies allow individuals some initiative, but for the most part only in specific areas, such as school and work, where there is a preestablished order of promotion. This is a situation totally different from that in traditional society. In the new society, the concepts of play and free space are no longer accepted; society must be too well regulated.

The second phenomenon that produced this change is directly related to the first: this is the division of space into areas assigned to work and areas assigned to living. The worker is now required to leave what had been the domain in traditional society, the space where *all* activities had taken place, to go to work far away, sometimes very far away, in a very different environment. There the worker becomes subject to a system of rules and to a hierarchy of power. In this new world, the worker may, for all we know, be happier and more secure, involved in association with others, for example, through trade unions.

This specialized place devoted to work was invented by the new society in its abhorrence of uncontrolled space. To run industrial, commercial, and business enterprises successfully requires systems of tight control. Free-enterprise capitalism has demonstrated its ability to adapt, but this flexibility has nothing in common with the old concept of free space; rather it depends on the precise functioning of the unit as a whole. Although enterprises in a free-market economy may not be controlled by the state, they are no less controlled by society at large. One could reasonably argue that this displacement of workers was a form of "surveillance and punishment," as Foucault phrased it, similar to locking up children in school, the insane in asylums, and delinquents in prison. It was certainly, at the very least, a means of maintaining order and control.

The third and last important phenomenon that affected the transformations of the eighteenth and nineteenth centuries is different from the first two; it is psychological. But the chronological correlation with the other two is significant. The era witnessed not only an industrial revolution but an emotional revolution as well. Previously, feelings were diffuse, spread out over numerous natural and supernatural objects, including God, saints, parents, children, friends, horses, dogs, orchards, and gardens. Henceforth, they would be focused within the immediate family. The couple and their children became the objects of a passionate and exclusive love that transcended even death.

From that time on, a working man's life was polarized between job and family. But the people who did not go out to work (women, children, old men) were concerned exclusively with family life. Nor was the division between job and family either equal or symmetrical. Although there was no doubt some room for emotional involvement at work, the family was a more conducive setting; whereas the working world was subject to constant, strict surveillance, the family was a place of refuge, free from outside control. The family thus acquired some similarities to the individual domain in traditional society, but with an important distinction: the family is not a place for individualism. The individual must recede into the background for the sake of the family unit, and especially for the sake of the children. Furthermore, the family had become more removed from the community than in earlier times, and it tended to be rather hostile to the external world, to withdraw into itself. Thus, it became *the* private domain, the only place where a person could legitimately escape the inquisitive stare of industrial society. Even now, industrial society has not given up trying to fill the gaps created by the decline of traditional society; it does, nevertheless, show some respect for the new entity—the family— which has grown up in its midst as a place of refuge. Thus, the separation of space into work areas and living areas corresponds to the division of life into public sector and private sector. The family falls within the private sector.

These, then, were the main features of the new way of life. They evolved slowly in the industrialized West, and were not equally accepted in all places. Two important periods must be distinguished: the nineteenth century before the automobile conquered space, and the first half of the twentieth. The difference between the two lies in the degree of privacy that people enjoyed and in the nature of the public sector.

During the first period, roughly the whole of the nineteenth century, family life among the bourgeoisie and the peasantry was already much as it is today, that is, it was a private domain. But—and this distinction is very important—only women (including those who worked) were affected by the increased privacy; men were able to escape at times, and they no doubt considered it a male prerogative to do so. Women and children had virtually no life outside the family and the school; these comprised their entire universe. Men, on the other hand, had a lively meeting place outside their families and jobs—to wit, the city.

33

In peasant societies, age-old tradition and the innovations of the industrial era are so intertwined that it is difficult for the analyst to distinguish among them. Still, it should be noted that historians today agree that, thanks to the agricultural prosperity in Western Europe during the nineteenth century, a flourishing rural civilization developed there. This was no doubt true of the United States as well. Is it not said that in certain regions of the Midwest immigrants have maintained traditions that have long since disappeared in their original homelands? These flourishing subcultures testify to the enormous vitality of the rural communities at a time when privacy, the family, and the school were making great inroads upon them. The rural exodus had not yet destroyed peasant life; rather, it had made it easier. This was the era of the beautiful costumes and regional furniture we find displayed today in folk museums. It was a time when folk tales were easily collected. It was also, however, a time when, thanks to the schools, many peasants were trying desperately to force open the doors to government careers for their children (who by then had grown fewer in number). The elementary school teacher was an important person in nineteenth-century rural communities; this is not true today. But it is the urban, not the rural, development that I should now like to discuss.

The long nineteenth century marked a high point in the development of the city and its urban civilization. No doubt urban populations had already increased to frightening levels; the poor immigrants who descended en masse upon them from the villages appeared as a threat to the bourgeois property owners, who watched them encamp in their towns and viewed them as an army of criminals and rebels. But this image born of fear need not deceive us today. To be sure, the large city was no longer what it had been in the seventeenth century, that is, a group of separate neighborhoods or streets, each constituting a community with a character of its own. In eighteenth-century Paris, the arrival of a transient population without a fixed place of residence upset this way of life. Traditional patterns of social intercourse based on neighborhoods and streets began to disappear. But new ones that maintained and developed the city's basic functions replaced them.

Central to these new patterns were the café and the restaurant, public meeting places where conversation flowed as abundantly as food and drink. The café was a place for discussion, an invention of the late eighteenth century. Previously there had been eating places, inns, and hostels, places to serve meals in the home or to provide food and lodging for transient guests. There were also taverns and cabarets where people went to drink, and often for the low life to be found there. But they were places of ill-repute, sometimes brothels. Cafés, on the other hand, were something completely new and different. They were strictly an urban phenomenon, unknown in rural areas. The cafés were meeting places in cities, which were growing very rapidly and where people did not know one another as they had before. In England the cafés were enclosed like cabarets, but the name *pub* describes their function well. In continental Europe, cafés opened onto the street and came to dominate them, thanks to their terraces. Cafés with their large terraces were in fact one of the most striking features of nineteenth-century cities. They were all but nonexistent in the medieval and Renaissance sections of the old cities, such as Rome, but they were very much in evidence in those same Italian cities around the large public squares that owe their existence to Cavour's vast urbanization and Italian unity. In Vienna, too, cafés were, and still are, the heart of the city. In Paris the opening of the cafés was probably the reason behind the shift to public life from closed places, like the famous gallery at the Palais Royal, to the linear, open space of the boulevard, the center of the city's night life.

Cafés no doubt originally served the aristocracy rather than the bourgeoisie. But they were quickly popularized and extended to all classes of society and to all neighborhoods. In nineteenth-century cities, there was not a neighborhood without at least one café, and more often several. In working-class neighborhoods, the small café played a vital role; it enabled communication that would otherwise have been impossible among the poorly housed residents who were often away at their jobs: the café served as message center. That is why the telephone became so immediately accessible after its advent. The café became the place where steady customers could make and receive telephone calls, leave and receive messages. It is easy to understand Maurice Aguilhon's surprise at the extraordinary

number of small cafés in a city like Marseilles, each with its little
network of neighbors and friends gathered around the counter
and the telephone. The number and popularity of these cafés
suggest that a new public sector had spontaneously developed in
the nineteenth-century city.

Needless to say, the state's desire for control extended even to
this new public sector. The state immediately understood the
danger represented by the cafés and sought to limit it by establishing and enforcing codes and regulations. But it never completely succeeded. In addition self-righteous people, concerned
with order and morality, were suspicious of the cafés, which
they considered to be hotbeds of alcoholism, anarchy, laziness,
vice, and political wrangling. In France even today urban planners relegate cafés to shopping districts in residential areas and at
a good distance from any elementary or secondary schools. But
the mistrust of the authorities and of the self-righteous has still
failed to diminish the popularity of the cafés. In the nineteenth
century, civilization was based on them.

Now let us compare the role played by the café in that era to
that played by the family. The family was a private place, the
café a public one. But they had one thing in common: they both
managed to escape society's control. The family did so by right,
the café in actual fact. These were the only two exceptions to the
modern system of surveillance and order which came to include
all social behavior. Thus, alongside the growing privacy of the
family during the nineteenth and early twentieth centuries, a
new and lively form of social intercourse developed in even the
largest cities. This explains why the cities of the era were so full
of life, and why the increased amount of privacy did not weaken
the forms of social intercourse, at least among males.

Toward the middle of the twentieth century, these forms of
social intercourse began to break down in Western industrialized
societies. The social and socializing function of the city disappeared. The more the urban population grew, the more the city
declined. I am reminded of the words of the comedian who
suggested moving the cities to the countryside. That, in fact, was
exactly what happened. Immense continuous urban areas developed in all countries, but especially in the United States,

where they have replaced the city. There cities in the old sense have ceased to exist. This phenomenon, one of the most important in the history of our society, must be seen in the light of what we know about the family and the ways it has changed. I should like to show how the decay of the city and the loss of its socializing function have affected contemporary family life.

From the late nineteenth century, even before the advent of the automobile, rich city-dwellers began to regard the crowded cities as unwholesome and dangerous and to flee in search of purer air and more decent surroundings. En masse they began to settle in those neighborhoods on the outskirts of cities that were still sparsely populated, such as the sixteenth and seventeenth *arrondissements* in Paris, near the greenery of the Parc Monceau and the Bois de Boulogne. Later, thanks to the railroad, the streetcar, and, in time, the automobile, they pushed farther and farther out. This trend occurred in all Western industrialized societies, but it was in North America that it developed most fully and reached its most extreme proportions; so we shall examine it there.

Neighborhoods are segregated not only by social class but also by function. Thus, just as there are rich, bourgeois neighborhoods and poor, working-class ones, so, too, there are business districts and residential ones. Offices, businesses, factories, and shops are found in one location, houses and gardens in the other. The means of transportation most often used to get from one place to the other is the private car. In this scheme of things there is no longer room for the forum, the agora, the piazza, the corso. There is no room, either, for the café as meeting place. The only thing there is room for is the drive-in and the fast-food outlet. Eating establishments are to be found in both business and residential districts; depending on their location, they are busy at different times of the day. In business and industrial districts they are humming with activity at lunchtime; in residential neighborhoods they do most of their business at night. During the off-hours, in both places, they are empty and silent.

What is truly remarkable is that the social intercourse which used to be the city's main function has now entirely vanished. The city is either crowded with the traffic of people and cars in a hurry or it is empty. Around noontime, office workers in business districts sometimes take an old-fashioned stroll when the weather is nice, and enjoy a piece of cake or an ice cream cone in the sun. But after five o'clock the streets are deserted. Nor do the streets in residential neighborhoods become correspondingly crowded, except around shopping centers and their parking lots. People return to their homes, as turtles withdraw into their shells. At home they enjoy the warmth of family life and, on occasion, the company of carefully chosen friends. The urban conglomerate has become a mass of small islands—houses, offices, and shopping centers—all separated from one another by a great void. The interstitial space has vanished.

This evolution was precipitated by the automobile and by television, but it was well underway before they had even appeared, thanks to the growth of the cult of privacy in the bourgeois and middle classes during the nineteenth century. To people born between 1890 and 1920 (now between sixty and ninety years old), the green suburb represented the ideal way of life, an escape from the bustle of the city to more rural, more natural surroundings. This shift to the suburbs, far from the noise and crowds of the city streets, was caused by the growing attraction of a warm private family life. In those areas where private family living was less developed, as in the working-class areas along the Mediterranean, societies dominated by obstinate males, community life fared better.

During the nineteenth and early twentieth centuries, the results of the increased privacy and the new family style of living were kept in check by the vitality of community life in both urban and rural areas. A balance was achieved between family life in the home and community life in the café, on the terrace, in the street. But this balance was destroyed and the family carried the day, thanks to the spread of suburbia that came with the new technology: the automobile and television. When that happened, the whole of social life was absorbed by private, family living.

Henceforth, the only function of the streets and cafés was to enable the physical movement between home and work or restaurant. For the most part, these ceased to be places of meeting, conversation, or recreation as the home, the couple, the family came to fulfill most of those functions. Today when a couple or a family leave the house to do something that cannot be done at home, they go in a mobile extension of the house, namely, the car. As the ark permitted Noah to survive the Flood, so the car permits its owners to pass through the hostile and dangerous world outside the front door.

Some of my American friends have suggested that in America the churches for a long time filled a public social function, somewhat as the café had done in Europe. Even today, many churches not only bring the faithful together to worship, but also organize suppers, banquets, and other get-togethers for various age groups, separate from religious services. This function, in my opinion, implies an identity between church and community: certainly it used to be that one went to the church of one's community or parents and did not change. The individual's church was not chosen but given by birth. We might, however, ask whether the socializing function of the church has diminished with the growth of religious mobility. Freedom of choice, the ability to change churches as one changes houses, jobs, or towns, may thus have transformed the church from a public space, or gathering place for the community, into a private club.

I believe I recognize in American society today a tendency to substitute, for public and anonymous socializing, a socializing in private clubs and special groups. The problem then is whether to regard this private socializing as an extension of the family or a substitute for it, and whether it is still providing, in the private sector, a festive function such as was formerly provided by the distractions of the street, the town square, the café, and places of accidental and unexpected meetings. One significant difference in the two sectors is that in the private sector everything is more or less predictable; in the public sector, as I have defined it, all events—even the most banal—have an unexpected and unplanned aspect.

Not long ago I found myself in Rome at midnight in the working-class neighborhood of Trastevere. There were still crowds of people in the streets, but there were no adults, only *ragazzi* of eighteen or twenty. They were mostly boys, because people there have not yet got into the habit, at least in working-class neighborhoods, of letting girls run around at night. Although children and adults are content to sit in front of the television set, adolescents are more interested in the life around them, in personal, spontaneous experiences. The young people of Trastevere were greeted by the marvelous Roman street, still the warm, picturesque setting of their daily life. But what about places where the setting no longer exists? Where do adolescents gather then? In the basements of houses, in underground garages, in the rooms of friends, usually enclosed. They may very well reject their families, but they still retain their tendency to seek seclusion. Today's frontier is this internal wall: it continues to exist even though it no longer has much to protect.

In the so-called postindustrial age of the mid-twentieth century, the public sector of the nineteenth century collapsed and people thought they could fill the void by extending the private, family sector. They thus demanded that the family see to all their needs. They demanded that it provide the passionate love of Tristan and Yseult and the tenderness of Philemon and Baucis; they saw the family as a place for raising children, but, at the same time, as a means of keeping them in a prolonged network of exclusive love. They considered the family a self-sufficient unit, though at times they were willing to enlarge the circle to include a few close friends. In the family, they hoped to recover the nostalgic world of the Jalna novels and to experience the pleasures of family warmth; from the private fortress of the family car they sought to discover the world outside. And they cherished the family as a place for all the childish things that continue even beyond childhood. These trends were intensified by the baby boom. Since then, the family has had a monopoly on emotions, on raising children, and on filling leisure time. This tendency to monopolize its members is the family's way of coping with the decline of the public sector. One can well imagine the uneasiness and intolerance that the situation has created.

Although people today often claim that the family is undergoing a crisis, this is not, properly speaking, an accurate description of what is happening. Rather, we are witnessing the inability of the family to fulfill all the many functions with which it has been invested, no doubt temporarily, during the past half-century. Moreover, if my analysis is correct, this overexpansion of the family role is a result of the decline of the city and of the urban forms of social intercourse that it provided. The twentieth-century postindustrial world has been unable, so far, either to sustain the forms of social intercourse of the nineteenth century or to offer something in its place. The family has had to take over in an impossible situation; the real roots of the present domestic crisis lie not in our families, but in our cities.

2

Images of the American Family,
Then and Now

John Demos

Within the past twenty years professional historians in several countries have directed special attention and considerable energy to the study of family life. "Family history" has become for the first time a legitimate branch of scholarly research. The entering wedge of this research was, and remains, demographic; by now we know more about the history of such circumstances as mean household size and median age of marriage than reasonable people may *want* to know. But investigation has also been moving ahead on other, more "qualitative," tracks: one thinks immediately of recent and challenging studies of the history of women, of sexual mores and behavior, and even of domestic architecture.[1]

Meanwhile, the contemporary experience of families has also come under increasingly intense scrutiny. There is a diffuse sense of "crisis" about our domestic arrangements generally—a feeling that the family as we have traditionally known it is under siege, and may even give way entirely. The manifestations of this concern are many and varied—and by now have high visibility. President Carter spoke often during the 1976 election campaign about the need (as he saw it) for public programs that would strengthen the American family system. And Vice President Mondale came to his present office from a career on the

1. For a short list of leading works in family history, see the Suggested Readings at the end of the book, including those listed for chap. 1.

43

legislative side, where he had earned much unofficial recognition as "the children's senator." There is a new flowering of commissions, task forces, and conferences on one or another aspect of family life—with the current symposium being an obvious case in point.[2]

These two streams of interest have run a similar, but not an intersecting, course. It is arguable, I think, that either one might have developed—just about as it actually *has* developed—had the other never taken life at all. Still, we should perhaps consider the bridges that might usefully be built between them. To put the matter quite simply: what light can a historian throw on the current predicament in family life? For one thing he is tempted right away to strike a soothing note of reassurance. The core structure of the family has evolved and endured over a very long period of Western history, and it is extremely hard to imagine a sudden reversal of so much weighty tradition. Moreover, for at least a century now the American family in particular has been seen as beleaguered, endangered, and possibly on the verge of extinction. The sense of crisis is hardly new; with some allowance for periodic ebb and flow, it seems an inescapable undercurrent of our modern life and consciousness.

Is this, in fact, reassuring? And does such reassurance *help*, in any substantial way? Somehow I feel that historians must try to do better.

These considerations will serve to frame (and perhaps to excuse) some features of the present essay. The *scale* of my discussion will be very large indeed—nothing less than the entire sweep of American history. The *substance* will be somewhat more modest, in that I shall concentrate for the most part on "images" of the family (not behavior); but even this encompasses a broad, and highly variable, territory. The *tone* will be, at least occasionally, judgmental and partisan; I shall not wholly suppress my

2. Two recent publications exemplify the trend: Kenneth Keniston and the Carnegie Council on Children, *All Our Children: The American Family under Pressure* (New York: Harcourt Brace Jovanovich, 1977), and Assembly of Behavioral and Social Sciences, National Research Council, *Toward a National Policy for Children and Families* (Washington, D.C.: National Academy of Sciences, 1976).

sense of the gains derived, and the prices paid, as I discuss various perceptions of domestic life in the past.

More specifically, I shall propose a three-part model of family history as a way of periodizing the field. In doing so I will necessarily lump together many diverse, and often intricate, bits of research—and it goes without saying that other historians might fashion quite a different set of lumps. In choosing to deal with images of family life I am giving my argument an implicit social and economic bias, for such images have been created largely by people of Anglo-Saxon origin in the more comfortable layers of our social system—in short, by middle-class WASPs. Nonetheless this same middle class has, in our country, tra- ditionally played a style-setting role—even for those who might seem to espouse alternative ways and traditions. Immigrants, blacks, workers of all sorts, are thus profoundly implicated here. The nature of these connections is highly complex—one might well say, ambivalent. But the larger point is that Americans of every color, every creed, and every economic position have been drawn toward the cultural middle. And embedded just there are the very images we must now try to examine.

THE FAMILY AS COMMUNITY

Let us begin with the settlement phase of American history, carving out—as the first part of our sequential model—a period of time lasting into the nineteenth century. It should be recog- nized, incidentally, that this inquiry does not lend itself to precise chronological markings; the end of one stage and the start of the next are so fully merged that we might well think in terms of a transitional process. And if, for the first stage, we assign a terminal date of 1820, we mean to indicate only a midpoint in that transition. The precursors of change were visible in some quarters as early as the Revolutionary era, and the process was still working itself out during the time of the Civil War.

Now I must introduce a rather perverse twist. When we seek to approach the colonial American family, one thing we notice immediately is that the "image" itself is rather thinly sketched. In short, people of that rather distant time and culture did not have a particularly self-conscious orientation to family life; their ideas, their attitudes in this connection, were far simpler than would ever be the case for later generations of Americans. Family life was something they took largely for granted. It was no doubt a central part of their experience, but not in such a way as to require special attention. This does not mean that they lacked ideas of what a "good family" should be and do—or, for that matter, a "bad" one—just that such notions carried a rather low charge in comparison with other areas of social concern.[3]

In any event, there are some points that we can deduce about their orientation to family life, and a few that we can pull directly out of the documentary record they have left to us. Here is a particularly resonant statement, taken from an essay by a "Puritan" preacher in the early seventeenth century:

A family is a little church, and a little commonwealth, at least a lively representation thereof, whereby trial may be made of such as are fit for any place of authority, or of subjection, in church or commonwealth. Or rather, it is as a school wherein the first principles and grounds of government are learned; whereby men are fitted to greater matters in church and commonwealth.[4]

Two aspects of this description seem especially important. First, the family and the wider community are joined in a relation of profound reciprocity; one might almost say they are continuous with one another. (This is, incidentally, a general premodern pattern—in no sense specific to American life and conditions—which was analyzed first and most incisively by Philippe Ariès, in his path-breaking study of twenty years ago published in English under the title *Centuries of Childhood*.[5]) To put the matter in another way: individual families are the building blocks out of which the larger units of social organization are fashioned. Families and churches, families and governments, belong to the

3. On the colonial family, see John Demos, *A Little Commonwealth: Family Life in Plymouth Colony* (New York: Oxford University Press, 1970), and Edmund S. Morgan, *The Puritan Family*, rev. ed. (New York: Harper & Row, 1966).

4. William Gouge, *Of Domesticall Duties* (London, 1622).

5. See Philippe Ariès, *Centuries of Childhood: A Social History of Family Life*, trans. Robert Baldick (New York: Alfred A. Knopf, 1962).

same world of experience. Individual people move back and forth between these settings with little effort or sense of difficulty.

The membership of these families was not fundamentally different from the pattern of our own day: a man and a woman joined in marriage, and their natural-born children. The basic unit was therefore a "nuclear" one, contrary to a good deal of sociological theory about premodern times. However, non-kin could, and did, join this unit—orphans, apprentices, hired laborers, and a variety of children "bound out" for a time in conditions of fosterage. Usually designated by the general term "servants," such persons lived as regular members of many colonial households; and if they were young, the "master" and "mistress" served *in loco parentis*. Occasionally, convicts and indigent people were directed by local authorities to reside in particular families. Here the master's role was to provide care, restraint, and even a measure of rehabilitation for those involved; they, in turn, gave him their service. Thus did the needs of the individual householders intersect the requirements of the larger community.[6]

But it was not simply that the family and the community ran together at so many points; the one was, in the words of the preacher, "a lively representation" of the other. Their structure, their guiding values, their inner purposes, were essentially the same. Indeed the family was a community in its own right, a unit of shared experience for all its individual members. It was, first and foremost, a community of work—in ways hard for us even to imagine today. Young and old, male and female, labored together to produce the subsistence on which the whole group depended. For long periods they worked literally in each other's presence—if not necessarily at the same tasks. In other ways as well the family lived and functioned as a unit. Most leisure-time activities (which consisted largely of visiting with friends, relatives, and neighbors) were framed in a family context, as were education, health care, and some elements of religious worship.

In broaching the subject of religion, however, we raise new considerations; in effect, we encounter another, quite different

6. See Morgan, *Puritan Family*, chap. 4.

community. To see this point as clearly as possible, we must make a brief detour into some esoteric particulars of church organization. Consider the typical seating plan of colonial churches (at least in New England).[7] (1) Men and women were separated on opposite sides of a central aisle. (2) Within these sex-typed enclaves individual communicants were assigned places in accordance with certain "status" criteria. (In general, the oldest, wealthiest, and most prominent citizens sat at the front.) (3) Children were relegated to still another section of the church (usually in the back, sometimes in an upstairs gallery). Now these arrangements have an important bearing on our present inquiry. Presumably, the typical family started out for church together, but upon reaching their destination they broke apart and went off in different directions. The church had its own mode of organization, vividly reflected in its spatial aspect: preacher in the pulpit, elders sitting just below, regular parishioners carefully distributed on the basis of sex, age, and social position. Family relationships were effectively discounted, or at least submerged, in this particular context. In sum, the family community and the religious community were fundamentally distinct—though formed from the same pool of individuals. Much later (in most cases, the early nineteenth century), Protestant congregations went over to the pattern that still prevails today, with seating inside the church arranged on a family basis. And the change had a profound symbolic significance. No longer was the family simply one form of community among others; from thenceforth it constituted a special group, whose boundaries would be firmly declared in all imaginable circumstances.

There is one more vital aspect of colonial family life which deserves at least to be mentioned. Since the functions of the household and the wider society were so substantially interconnected, the latter might reasonably intervene when the former experienced difficulty. Magistrates and local officials would thus compel a married couple "to live more peaceably together" or to

7. On the practice of seating in the meetinghouse, see Robert J. Dinkin, "Provincial Massachusetts: A Deferential or a Democratic Society" (Ph.D. diss., Columbia University, 1968), and Ola Winslow, *Meetinghouse Hill, 1630–1783* (New York: Macmillan, 1952).

alter and upgrade the "governance" of their children. This, too, is the context of the famous "stubborn child" laws of early New England, which prescribed the death penalty for persistent disobedience to parents. Such extreme sanctions were never actually invoked, but the statutes remained on the books as a mark of society's interest in orderly domestic relations.[8]

We need not dwell further on specific aspects of colonial family life, but it may be useful to have a summary term or concept in order to facilitate comparisons with subsequent parts of the story. And, in view of all we have said, perhaps the most appropriate choice would be: "the family as community."

THE FAMILY AS REFUGE

As noted earlier, it is hard to say just how and when this colonial pattern began to break down; but by the early decades of the nineteenth century at least some American families were launched on a new course, within a very different framework of experience. For the most part these were urban families, and distinctly middle-class; and while they did not yet constitute anything like a majority position in the country at large, they pointed the way to the future.[9]

Here, for the first time, American family life acquired an extremely sharp "image"—in the sense of becoming something *thought* about in highly self-conscious ways, *written* about at great length and by many hands, and *worried* about in relation to a host of internal and external problems. Among other things, there was a new sense that the family had a history of its own—that it was not fixed and unchanging for all time. And when some observers, especially "conservative" ones, pondered the direction of this history, they reached an unsettling conclusion: the family, they believed, was set on a course of decline and decay. From a stable and virtuous condition in former times, it

8. See Edwin Powers, *Crime and Punishment in Early Massachusetts, 1620–1692: A Documentary History* (Boston: Beacon Press, 1966), pp. 268, 283ff.

9. See Kirk Jeffrey, "The Family as Utopian Retreat from the City," *Soundings* 55 (1972): 21–41, and Barbara Laslett, "The Family as a Public and Private Institution: An Historical Perspective," *Journal of Marriage and the Family* 35 (1973): 480–92.

had gradually passed into a "crisis" phase. After mid-century, popular literature on domestic life poured out a long litany of complaints: divorce and desertion were increasing; child-rearing had become too casual and permissive; authority was generally disrupted; the family no longer did things together; women were more and more restless in their role as homemakers.[10] Do these complaints have a somewhat familiar ring even now? In fact, it is from this period, more than one hundred years ago, that one of our most enduring images of the family derives—what might be called the image, or the myth, of the family's golden past. It seems to me that too many around us continue to believe that there is some ideal state of domestic life which we have tragically lost. The consequences of this belief are profound—since it implies that our individual efforts and our public policies in regard to family life should have a "restorative" character. But this is another topic, best left to a different setting.

To resume the discussion of nineteenth-century family life: how shall we characterize the main line of ideas and attitudes which were increasingly coming to the fore in this period? One point is immediately striking. The nineteenth-century family—far from joining and complementing other social networks, as in the earlier period—seemed to stand wholly apart. Indeed its relation to society at large had been very nearly reversed, so as to become a kind of adversary relation.

The brave new world of nineteenth-century America was, in some respects, a dangerous world—or so many people felt. The new egalitarian spirit, the sense of openness, the opportunities for material gain, the cult of the "self-made man": all this was new, invigorating, and liberating at *one* level—but it also conveyed a deep threat to traditional values and precepts. In order to seize the main chance and get ahead in the ongoing struggle for success, a man had to summon energies and take initiatives that would at the very least exhaust him and might involve him in terrible compromises. At the same time he would need to retain

10. Examples of this viewpoint may be found in William A. Alcott, *The Young Wife* (Boston, 1837), William Thayer, *Hints for the Household* (Boston, 1853), and Artemas B. Muzzey, *The Fireside* (Boston, 1854).

some place of rest, of harmony—some emblem of the personal and moral regime that he was otherwise leaving behind.[11]

Within this matrix of ideas the family was sharply redefined. Henceforth the life of the individual home, on the one hand, and the wider society, on the other, represented for many Americans entirely different spheres ("spheres" was indeed the customary term they used in conceptualizing their varied experiences). The two were separated by a sharply delineated frontier; different strategies and values were looked for on either side.

We have already noted some of the new "home" values, but it is necessary to investigate them more fully. Home—and the word itself became highly sentimentalized—was pictured as a bastion of peace, of repose, of orderliness, of unwavering devotion to people and principles beyond the self. Here the woman of the family, and the children, would pass most of their hours and days—safe from the grinding pressures and dark temptations of the world at large; here, too, the man of the family would retreat periodically for refreshment, renewal, and inner fortification against the dangers he encountered elsewhere.[12]

Pulling these various themes together, we can reasonably conclude that the crucial function of the family had now become a *protective* one. And two kinds of protection were implied here: protection of the ways and values of an older America that was fast disappearing and protection also for the individual people who were caught up in the middle of all this change. We have already accepted, as a way of summarizing the colonial part of our material, the notion of "the family as community." Perhaps we may now adopt, for the nineteenth century, the image of "the family as refuge." Two short passages, chosen from the voluminous domestic literature of the period, will serve to exemplify this notion:

From the corroding cares of business, from the hard toil and frequent disappointments of the day, men retreat to the bosoms of their families, and there, in the midst of that sweet society of wife and children and

11. See Jeffrey, "Family as Utopian Retreat." Also Barbara Welter, "The Cult of True Womanhood: 1820–1860," *American Quarterly* 18 (1966): 151–74.
12. An immensely popular expression of this viewpoint was the novel by Catherine Maria Sedgewick, *Home* (Boston, 1854).

friends, receive a rich reward for their industry. . . . The feeling that here, in one little spot, his best enjoyments are concentrated . . . gives a wholesome tendency to [a man's] thoughts, and is like the healing oil poured upon the wounds and bruises of the spirit.

We go forth into the world, amidst the scenes of business and of pleasure; we mix with the gay and the thoughtless, we join the busy crowd, and the heart is sensible to a desolation of feeling; we behold every principle of justice and of honor, disregarded, and the delicacy of our moral sense is wounded; we see the general good sacrificed to the advancement of personal interest; and we turn from such scenes with a painful sensation, almost believing that virtue has deserted the abodes of men; again, we look to the *sanctuary* of *home;* there sympathy, honor, virtue are assembled; there the eye may kindle with intelligence, and receive an answering glance; there disinterested love is ready to sacrifice everything at the altar of affection.[13]

This imagery had, in fact, particular features which deserve careful notice. For one thing, it embraced the idea of highly differentiated roles and statuses *within* the family—for the various individual family members. The husband-father undertook an exclusive responsibility for productive labor. He did this in one of a variety of settings well removed from the home-hearth, in offices, factories, shops, or wherever. So it was that family life was wrenched apart from the world of work—a veritable sea-change in social history. Meanwhile, the wife-mother was expected to confine herself to domestic activities; increasingly idealized in the figure of the "True Woman," she became the centerpiece in a developing cult of Home. Intrinsically superior (from a moral standpoint) to her male partner, the True Woman preserved Home as a safe, secure, and "pure" environment.[14] The children of this marital pair were set off as distinctive creatures in their own right. Home life, from their point of view, was a sequence of preparation in which they armored themselves for the challenges and difficulties of the years ahead.[15] The children, after all, carried the hopes of the family into the future;

13. Quoted in Jeffrey, "Family as Utopian Retreat."
14. See Welter, "Cult of True Womanhood."
15. See Bernard Wishy, *The Child and the Republic: The Dawn of Modern American Child Nurture* (Philadelphia: University of Pennsylvania Press, 1972).

their lives later on would reward, or betray, the sacrifices of their parents. Taken altogether, and compared with the earlier period, these notions conveyed the sense of a family carefully differentiated as to individual task and function, but unalterably *united* as to overall goals and morale. Like other institutions in the "Machine Age," the family was now seen as a system of highly calibrated, interlocking parts.

It is clear enough that such a system conformed to various *practical* needs and circumstances in the lives of many Americans—the adaptation to urban life, the changing requirements of the workplace, the gathering momentum of technology. But it must have answered to certain *emotional* needs as well. In particular, I believe, the cult of Home helped people to release the full range of aggressive and assertive energies so essential to the growth and development of the country—helped them, that is, to still anxiety and to ward off guilt about their own contributions to change. At the same time there were costs and difficulties that we cannot fail to see. The demands inherent in each of the freshly articulated family roles were sometimes literally overwhelming.

The husband-father, for example, was not just the breadwinner for the entire family; he was also its sole representative in the world at large. His "success" or "failure"—terms which had now obtained a highly personal significance—would reflect directly on the other members of the household. And this was a grievously heavy burden to carry. For anyone who found it *too* heavy, for anyone who stumbled and fell while striving to scale the heights of success, there was a bitter legacy of self-reproach—not to mention the implicit or explicit reproaches of other family members whose fate was tied to his own.

Meanwhile, the lady of the house experienced another set of pressures—different, but no less taxing. The conventions of domestic life had thrown up a model of the "perfect home"—so tranquil, so cheerful, so pure, as to constitute an almost impossible standard. And it was the exclusive responsibility of the wife to try to meet this standard. Moreover, her behavior must in all circumstances exemplify the selflessness of the True Woman. Her function was effectively defined as one of service and giving to others; she could not express needs or interests of her own.

This suppression of self exacted a crushing toll from many nineteenth-century women. Few complained outright—though modern feminism dates directly from this era. But there were other, less direct forms of complaint—the neurasthenias, the hysterias, indeed a legion of "women's diseases," which allowed their victims to opt out of the prescribed system.[16]

The system also imposed new difficulties on the younger members of the household. In the traditional culture of colonial America the process of growth from child to adult had been relatively smooth and seamless. The young were gradually raised, by a sequence of short steps, from subordinate positions within their families of origin to independent status in the community at large.[17] In the nineteenth century, by contrast, maturation became disjunctive and problematic. As the condition of childhood was ever more sharply articulated, so the transition to adulthood became longer, lonelier, more painful.[18] And there was also another kind of transition to negotiate. For those who absorbed the imagery of Home the moment of *leaving* was charged with extraordinary tension. To cross the sacred threshold from inside to outside was to risk unspeakable dangers. The nostalgia, the worries, the guilt which attended such crossings are threaded through an enormous mass of domestic fiction from the period. Marriage itself was experienced as the sudden exchange of one family for another—with a little of the flavor of a blind leap.[19]

In sum, the "ideal family" of the nineteenth century comprised a tightly closed circle of reciprocal obligations. And the entire system was infused with a strain of dire urgency. If the family did not function in the expected ways, there were no

16. See Ann Douglas Wood, " 'The Fashionable Diseases': Women's Complaints and Their Treatment in Nineteenth-Century America," *Journal of Interdisciplinary History* 4 (1973): 25–52.

17. Demos, *A Little Commonwealth*, chap. 10.

18. Joseph Kett, *Rites of Passage: Adolescence in America, 1790 to the Present* (New York: Basic Books, 1977).

19. See, for example, the marriages described in Sedgewick, *Home*. This theme is explored by Ellen K. Rothman in "A Most Interesting Event: Marriage-Making in Nineteenth-Century America," unpublished paper (Brandeis University, 1975).

other institutions to back it up. If one family member fell short of prescribed ways and standards, all the others were placed in jeopardy. There is a short story by T. S. Arthur—an immensely popular author during the middle of the century—which makes this point very clearly.[20] A young couple marry and set up housekeeping. The husband is an aspiring businessman, with every prospect of "success." His wife shares his ambitions and means to become an effective "helpmeet"; however, her management of the household is marred by a certain inefficiency. The husband regularly returns from his office for lunch (an interesting vestige of premodern work rhythms), but soon a problem develops. The wife cannot hold to a firm schedule in preparing these meals, and often her husband is kept waiting. Earnest conversations and repeated vows of improvement bring no real change. Finally, one particular delay causes the husband to miss a crucial appointment—and the consequences for his business are devastating.

Domestic fiction played out similar themes in the relation of parents and children. Only the most careful and moral "rearing" would bring the young out safe in later life; anything less might imperil their destiny irrevocably. Conversely, the well-being of parents depended in large measure on their offspring. If the latter, having grown to adulthood, were to stray from the paths of virtue, the old folks might feel so "heartbroken" that they would sicken and die.[21] Here the stakes of domestic bonding attained an aspect of life-threatening finality.

THE FAMILY AS ENCOUNTER GROUP

To some degree the image of "the family as refuge" remains with us today. Many people still look to home life for buffering, or at least for relief, against the demands and pressures of society at large. There is a continuing sense of inside-outside, and an idea of domestic inviolacy well expressed by the cliché that "each man's home is his castle."

20. T. S. Arthur, "Sweethearts and Wives," in *The Root of Bitterness*, ed. Nancy F. Cott (New York: Dutton, 1972).
21. The plot line in Sedgewick's novel is a case in point.

And yet for some time the tide has been running in another direction. It seems reasonable, therefore, to posit a third stage in family history, while acknowledging that the second has not yet exhausted itself. To identify the new trend precisely is no easy task, and my suggestions in the following pages must be regarded as provisional at best. I am speaking here less as a scholar and more as an everyday observer—indeed a participant-observer (!)—of contemporary family life.

Domestic imagery can be expected to reflect changes in the social context of experience, and for millions of Americans that context is now a different one. The twentieth century has gathered up a host of "modernizing" forces; one overused but still helpful phrase for describing the process is "the rise of mass society." Truly, we do take significant parts of life in the mass—as workers (mostly for large organizations), as consumers (mostly of highly standardized services and products), as citizens (mostly under a "big government"). For many Americans this situation has brought a measure of security and comfort unprecedented in previous generations. Jobs are less liable to disruption, income is steadier, health care is somewhat more regular, and so on. And yet these gains have been purchased at a cost. Comfortable as many of us are, we have a sense of flatness, even of emptiness, about large sectors of our experience. Increasingly we feel that we are not masters of our own fate, that our individual goals and deeds count for nothing when weighed in such a large aggregate. We cannot, in short, make much of a difference in our own lives. Thus ever larger numbers of us do not bother to vote (what difference is made by one ballot more or less), and we are disinclined to protest inferior products, inefficient services, or even blatant injustice when such things directly touch our lives. "Apathy" is the currently fashionable word to describe our social climate—and it does seem to hit the mark.

For a shorthand contrast between this situation and the social climate of a century ago we need only consult the favorite period metaphors. We have moved, it seems, from the "jungle" of the nineteenth century to the "rat race" (or the "grind") of our own day. This progression expresses clearly a lessened sense of *threat*—and also a growing feeling of monotony and meaninglessness.

56

The implications for family life—specifically, for images and expectations of family life—are profound. As the threat is tempered, the wish for *protection*, for armoring, wanes. Or rather it shades gradually into something else. Home is less a bunker amidst the battle than a place of "rest and recuperation" (pursuing the military analogy). According to this standard, families should provide the interest, the excitement, the stimulation missing from other sectors of our experience. If we feel that "we aren't going anywhere" in our work, we may load our personal lives—especially our family lives—with powerful compensatory needs. We wish to "grow" in special ways through our relations with family partners; a familiar complaint in counseling centers nowadays is the sense of blocked opportunities for growth. We want our spouses, our lovers, even our children, to help us feel alive and invigorated—to brighten a social landscape that otherwise seems unrelievedly gray. Again, some contrasts with the earlier setting may be helpful. *Then* Home was to be a place of quiet, of repose. *Now* it must generate some excitement. *Then* the True Woman served as the appointed guardian of domestic values; as such she was "pure," steady, in all ways self-effacing. *Now* there is the figure of the "Total Woman"—who, to be sure, keeps an orderly house and seeks consistently to help her man, but who is also sensual and assertive within limits.[22]

Indeed an entire spectrum of roles and responsibilities within the family is increasingly in question. No longer can we automatically accept that principle of differentiation which, in the nineteenth century, assigned to each household member a "sphere" deemed appropriate to his or her age and gender. Some families now advocate an *opposite* principle, which exalts the diffusion and mixing of roles. Mother must do her share of the "breadwinning," Father must do his share of the household chores, and so forth and so on. Much of this, of course, comes directly from the Women's Movement, and involves a long-overdue effort to right the balance of opportunity between the sexes. However, that is not the whole story. If Father is urged nowadays to help with the children or wash the dishes or take care of the laundry, this is not just in order to lighten the burdens

22. Marabel Morgan, *The Total Woman* (Old Tappan, N.J.: Revell, 1975).

that have traditionally fallen on Mother. There is also a feeling that such activities are *good for him*. Somehow his sensibilities will be expanded and his personal growth advanced—just as Mother expands and grows through her work outside the home. As a further benefit of these rearrangements the couple discovers new highways and byways of marital communication. Since they share so much more, they understand each other better; and their relation to one another is "deepened" accordingly. Even children are invited to join in this celebration of openness and reciprocity. The parents believe that they must listen carefully and at all times to their children, even that they can *learn* from their children—ideas which would, I think, have seemed quite preposterous just a few generations ago.

If all goes well—if reality meets expectation and conforms to image—Home becomes a bubbling kettle of lively, and mutually enhancing, activity. But, alas, all does *not* invariably go well; so we also have, for the first time in American history, a negative image—an "anti-image"—of the family. Seen from this viewpoint, domestic relationships look dangerously like an encumbrance, if not a form of bondage, inhibiting the quest for a full experience of self. Monogamous marriage is liable to become boring and stultifying; in other things, after all, variety is "the spice of life." Moreover, responsibility for children only compounds the problem. The needs and requirements of the young are so pressing, so constant, as to leave little space for adults who must attend to them. "Spice" and "space": these are, in fact, the qualities for which we yearn most especially. And the family severely limits our access to either one.

I shall resist the temptation to evaluate these different images of family life—though actually I have doubts about both of them. More pertinent in the present context is the point at which they converge. Obviously, they are opposite faces of the same coin. Each affirms the primacy of family experience in relation to larger goals of personal growth and self-fulfillment. The difference lies in the *effects* imputed to such experience—in the first case, a beneficial effect, in the second an adverse one. Both images assume a deep threat of inward stagnation, implicit in the "rat race" which surrounds us all.

There are, of course, other ways to fight the rat race.

58

Encounter-groups, T-groups, consciousness-raising of all kinds should certainly be mentioned here—as well as the vicarious excitements that come, for example, from celebrity-watching. Presumably these activities are not antithetical to good, *growing* family life; on the contrary, their effects should be complementary and enhancing. Indeed the term which I would like to propose as a caption for this third (current) stage of family history is: "the family as encounter group." For the central values attaching to domestic experience nowadays—at least as I read them—are those which underscore significant personal encounters.

CONCLUSIONS

I wish to reemphasize, in closing, the distortion introduced by any discrete model of family history. The problem is not simply one of arbitrary chronological boundaries; there is also a risk of failing to see the cumulative element in all historical process. "Stage three," we have noted, retains a good part of "stage two"—and even some traces of "stage one." (We continue, after all, to see individual families as the "building blocks" of the nation as a whole.) Thus our present arrangements are best construed as a complex and heavily layered precipitate of our entire social history.

Two points about this history deserve some final underscoring. In both the second and the third of our major stages the family has been loaded with the most urgent of human needs and responsibilities. Indeed I would say *over*loaded. In each case the prevalent imagery conjures up a *compensatory* function: the family must supply what is vitally needed, but missing, in social arrangements generally. It must protect its individual constituents against imminent and mortal danger, or it must fill a void of meaninglessness. To put the matter in another way: the family is not experienced in its own right but essentially in its relation to other circumstances and other pressures. It is for this reason, I believe, that we have become so extraordinarily self-conscious about family life—and, more, have broached it for so long from an attitude of crisis.

There is a concomitant of this attitude which also has deep

59

historical roots. Briefly, we have isolated family life as the primary setting—if not, in fact, the only one—for *caring* relations between people. The nineteenth-century images made an especially powerful contribution here: each family would look after its own—and, for the rest, may the best man win. Relationships formed within the world of work—which meant, for a long time, relationships between men—would not have an emotional dimension. Nineteenth-century women seem, on the evidence of very recent scholarship, to have maintained "networks" of affection which did cross family boundaries, but even this pattern recedes as we follow the trail toward the present.

Much of the same viewpoint has survived into our own time, and it underlies certain continuing tensions in our national experience. The United States stands almost alone among Western industrialized countries in having no coherent "family policy." More particularly, our inherited habits and values—our constricted capacity for extrafamilial caring—partly explain public indifference to the blighted conditions in which many families even now are obliged to live. The results are especially tragic as they affect children, and they leave us with a terrible paradox. In this allegedly most child-centered of nations, we find it hard to care very much or very consistently about *other people's children*. The historian may think that he understands such a predicament; he does not, however, know how to change it.

3

Family Types, Social Structure, and Mobility in Early America: Charlestown, Massachusetts, A Case Study

RALPH J. CRANDALL

In the Great Migration of the 1630s, New England's first settlers brought with them family institutions that English men and women had revered for centuries. In America they would continue to honor, as their ancestors had done, these same family institutions. Into a total concept of family they would integrate in the new circumstances of frontier life their ideas on sexuality, marriage, parents, children, grandparents, relatives, a dwelling place, household furnishings, and a tradition of godly living. Formal marriage for them was a holy and convenient institution, the center of life and the shelter of children, serving the dual function of satisfying sexual impulses and, more importantly, creating new families through the birth and rearing of children. Sons and daughters joined their parents in praise of God; they carried on the family tradition in the community and helped in the home, shop, and field.

Every two years, in a rhythm as dependable as the seasons, another infant arrived in the home; the fertility cycle of two decades or more frequently resulted in ten or more children. For William and Anna Frothingham of Charlestown, there was no relief from fussing infants: Anna bore their first child in 1631, only a few months after their arrival in New England, and delivered their tenth and last child seventeen years later in 1648, only three years before William's death.[1] Fortunate parents lived to see the children of their sons and daughters in the home as the generations met, but many mothers died in childbirth and infant mortality was high. Fathers usually remarried, often choosing widows with children, and the new union provided a home for the youngsters.

Not only was marriage a pivotal institution of New England life, but children had an important and well-defined place in the union. In the portraiture of the seventeenth century, however, depiction of boys and girls as prim and proper miniature adults tends to obscure their roles and status as children. Until children reached majority, many families tried to shield them as much as possible from the ravages and corruption of the adult world. Parental supervision was exercised, often with severity when children disobeyed, but usually with regard to biblical instruction and good example. Parents attended to the welfare of their offspring in countless ways but especially in making plans for the distribution of property at death. Often their wills are couched in affectionate language conveying the parents' love and distributing clothing, personal trinkets, and the tangibles of life to children, grandchildren, and, in some instances, adopted children. Orphans were given guardians and placed in new homes, and the towns were expected to provide schools to offer moral, religious, and secular education.

These attributes of the family are usually assumed to apply to society in general, and historians of early New England have relied upon them heavily to form a composite view of the Puritan family. Such a picture, however, applies most specifically to one stratum of the society, the rich and high placed, because the evidence comes mainly from literary sources, which were created by the wealthy articulate. But if other materials are used, such as probate, town, and land records, other strata emerge which suggest great diversity in family patterns and community relationships.[2]

1. Thomas Bellows Wyman, *The Genealogies and Estates of Charlestown, in the County of Middlesex and Commonwealth of Massachusetts, 1629–1818*, 2 vols. (Boston, 1879), 1:381.

2. For discussions of the Puritan family in seventeenth-century New Eng-

Here I shall examine several levels of family life in Charlestown, Massachusetts, a New England seaboard community that ranked with Boston and Salem in the importance of its trade and settlement. Like Boston it was a mixed community of merchants, ship captains, farmers, laborers, sailors, and drifters, a more complex and diversified society than the farming villages of the interior or the new towns founded by the second generation, the children of the Great Migration. Perhaps, as nearly as any New England settlement, it contained the varieties of families that inhabited English seaboard communities. More than 250 householders and their dependents, nearly one-twentieth of the Great Migration to New England, settled in Charlestown in the 1630s.[3] Its population in the second and third generations retained the character of the first immigrants, even though people were leaving to found towns elsewhere in New England. Charlestown families fall into at least three categories: (1) merchant-planters; (2) artisan-yeomen; (3) laborer-indigents. Although members of these three groups shared many aspects of life and held many attitudes in common, their experiences of family and community were quite diverse.

THE MERCHANT-PLANTERS

Charlestown's merchant-planters were the most visible and well-defined group in its emerging society. Accounting for approximately one-quarter of the town's population during the seventeenth century, they created in this port a society characterized by wealth, education, religiosity, institutional services, and continuing associations with England.[4] They were middlemen, investors, and land speculators. Seldom found toiling in the shop and field, they were employed in building mercantile

---

land, see Edmund S. Morgan, *The Puritan Family: Religion and Domestic Relations in Seventeenth-Century New England*, rev. ed. (New York: Harper & Row, 1966); John Demos, *A Little Commonwealth: Family Life in Plymouth Colony* (New York: Oxford University Press, 1970).

3. See Ralph J. Crandall and Ralph J. Coffman, "From Emigrants to Rulers: The Charlestown Oligarchy in the Great Migration," *The New England Historical and Genealogical Register*, 131 (1977): 3–27 (hereafter cited as *Register*).

4. Crandall and Coffman, p. 9.

empires: acquiring ships, wharves, and warehouses, and whole-saling English goods in the colonies. They bought large tracts of land in the wilderness, which they converted into farms with hired help or held for speculation. Nicholas Davison typifies Charlestown's merchant-planters. This young shipmaster and merchant served as Thomas Cradock's agent in New England and handled the affairs of his Medford farm. But he also cap-tained ships to Barbados and England, acquired docks and warehouses in Charlestown, and invested heavily in New Eng-land real estate. Not only did he hold mortgages on property in Cambridge, Lynn, Salem, and Boston, but he also owned fifteen hundred acres in Windsor, Connecticut.[5]

The wealth of the merchant-planters distinguished them from the rest of the population. Despite their practice of giving sig-nificant gifts of land and money to their offspring before making their wills, many at death possessed property of more than a thousand pounds.[6] Their property was diversified and often located outside Charlestown. Francis Willoughby's wealth is representative. Arriving in town in 1638 from Portsmouth, Hampshire, he quickly secured permission from his friends among the selectmen to erect a wharf and warehouse and to build a shipyard. For the next thirty years he improved upon his excellent beginning in New England, and at his death in 1671 left an estate valued at more than four thousand pounds to be divided among his nine children. His inventory listed four warehouses, a brewhouse, shares in four ships, stocks of English wares, a large farm at Cape Ann, 1,450 acres of undeveloped land lying between Woburn and Andover, Massachusetts, as well as a gift from the Massachusetts General Court of 1,000 acres not yet laid out.[7]

5. *Suffolk Deeds* (Boston, 1880–1902), 1:12, 29, 80, 81, 94, 96, 98, 109, 151, 205, 209.

6. For example, three fairly representative Charlestown merchants of this period, Richard Russell, Richard Sprague, and Francis Willoughby, left estates valued at £3,505, £2,357, and £4,040 respectively. See Middlesex County Probate Records, Middlesex County Courthouse, Cambridge, Massachusetts, Case numbers 19688, 21088, 25103.

7. Isaac J. Greenwood, "The Willoughby Family of New England," *Register*, 30 (1876): 72.

In addition to their impressive wealth, men like Willoughby enjoyed some formal as well as practical education. Although in the community as a whole perhaps half the adult male population were literate, almost all the merchant-planters could read and write, many having acquired an education in preparatory schools or having served as mercantile apprentices.[8] At least one merchant of the immigrant generation, Thomas Coytmore, was an English university graduate. Others would later attend Harvard College.

Their religiosity may have also distinguished the merchant-planters from the remainder of the Charlestown community. Most were church members who actively supported Puritanism. The immigrant generation frequently had a connection with Puritanism that extended a decade or more into their English experience. In England they had belonged to reforming organizations, such as the Massachusetts Bay Company or the London Feoffees for Lay Impropriations, a group dedicated to promoting Puritan preachers and lecturers throughout England and Wales. At least eight of the merchant-planters settling in Charlestown had invested in the Massachusetts Bay Company, and some had connections with other London groups.[9] In Charlestown they were the first to be seated in the meetinghouse, and they were given pews that put them near the ministers. Pews nearest the ministers were assigned to the wealthy, the back seats and the balcony to the less privileged. In the governing of the church the merchant-planters influenced, if not determined, the choice of church officers, usually gaining appointees sympathetic to their wishes. Their spiritual concern is expressed in eloquent statements of faith included in their wills, and in their regard for the family Bible, which was deemed a treasure to be passed from generation to generation.[10]

As leaders of the movement to America, the merchant-planters felt seriously their responsibilities to the community and

8. Crandall and Coffman, "From Emigrants to Rulers," p. 9.

9. Crandall and Coffman, pp. 9–10.

10. See Robert J. Dinkin, "Seating the Meeting House in Early Massachusetts," *New England Quarterly* 43 (September 1970): 450–64; Crandall and Coffman, "From Emigrants to Rulers," pp. 9–10.

could be counted as members of committees, officers of the church, and officials of the local government. By virtue of their station and freedom from the routine of shop and field, they filled the important governmental positions in the town, monopolizing the most powerful offices. The artisan-yeomen and laborer-indigents customarily deferred to them. Even when it became apparent that the merchant-planters were using government for their own economic ends, the community chose them as leaders. Thus in 1637 the selectmen (composed largely of this group) decided to limit proprietorship in the town's land to "freemen and constant members of the church." This policy permitted the merchant-planters to amass vast areas of land. In the first decade they controlled over 70 percent of the land, a concentration that was reminiscent of some English towns.[11]

The political and economic interests of the merchant-planters permitted them to keep in contact with the homeland, and they retained their Englishness to a degree that set them apart from members of the other two groups who were obliged to concentrate their energies in America. Charlestown merchants like Abraham Palmer and Richard Russell acted as attorneys for English acquaintances and participated in commercial ventures that took them to London and the West Indies. In the 1640s a few Charlestownians even returned to their old homes to fight beside other family members for the cause of the Commonwealth and Protectorate.[12]

This society created by the merchant-planters in Charlestown determined that their family patterns would evolve separately from the other two groups. Their growing wealth affected the

11. Charlestown Town Records, 17 vols., Charlestown, 1873 (microfilm ed.), 2:48; see also *Third Report of the Record Commissioners Containing Charlestown Land Records*, 1638–1802 (Boston, 1883), and Crandall and Coffman, "From Emigrants to Rulers," p. 13.

12. One such person was William Rainborough, Jr., a wealthy Charlestown merchant-mariner from Wapping hamlet, who was the brother of Thomas Rainborough, a career soldier who led the republican section of the English Army officers in 1647. See Henry F. Waters, *Genealogical Gleanings in England* (Boston, 1901), pp. 161–71; Henry N. Brailsford, *The Levellers and the English Revolution*, ed. Christopher Hill (Stanford: Stanford University Press, 1961), p. 277.

manner of living of the family in various ways, most particularly in the form of comfortable furnishings, wide personal and kinship associations, and extensive travel. The merchant-planters lived in comparative elegance. Even the immigrant generation who had been most dedicated to plain living treasured the few costly, imported furnishings that they brought from England. Katherine Coytmore, the widowed matriarch of an extended merchant-planter family, reveals in her will the elegant features of a typical merchant-planter's home. To her granddaughters Elizabeth, Anna, and Bethia Tyng she willed her domestic treasures: "two Persian carpets," two boxes of "East India dishes," a "Turkey carpet," "two faire window cushions," and "my great looking glass." Undoubtedly these granddaughters, like other youths of their group, regarded these furnishings as a customary inheritance, to be cherished and handed on later to their own children.[13]

The grandchildren of Katherine Coytmore were socialized in an extensive network of family and personal associations. Mother Coytmore, like a well-set diamond, sparkled in the center of a cluster of wealthy merchant-planter families in Charlestown. Her daughter Parnell married Increase Nowell, owner of a three-hundred-acre farm on the north side of the Mystic River in Charlestown and a leader of the Winthrop fleet of 1630. Another daughter married Thomas Graves, a prominent Charlestown mariner, who was later appointed rear admiral by Oliver Cromwell. A third daughter became the wife of William Tyng, a merchant and ship captain who settled in Boston. Finally, her son Thomas, who had matriculated at Christ's College in 1628, settled in Charlestown with his wife, Martha Rainborough, in 1637, and became a mariner-merchant. Following Thomas's untimely death in 1643, his widow married Governor John Winthrop.[14]

The Coytmore clan left no extensive literary record that details the impact of this family cluster upon the rearing of their

---

13. Middlesex County Probate Records, Case no. 4769.

14. See John Insley Coddington, "A Royal Descent from King Edward III of England to Thomas Coytmore of Charlestown, Massachusetts, Elizabeth wife of William Tyng of Boston . . .," *The American Genealogist* 32 (1956): 9–23.

children. The diary of Samuel Sewall of Boston, however, who had almost weekly contact with the Coytmore clan in Charlestown, reveals in much detail the socialization of children in merchant-planter families. Although the Sewalls were scattered throughout the Massachusetts Bay Colony, residing in Boston, Salem, Newbury, Dedham, Brookline, and Rowley, they continued to function as a family unit in spite of this wide separation. It was common for the diarist to leave his children with other members of the family. At least three times Sewall placed them for long periods with their grandparents. In his commonplace book under 21 May 1680, he recorded: "I carry Sam. to Newbury, where his Grandmother nurses him till May 18, to see if change of air would help him against convulsions."[15] Daughter Judith was placed in the household of Ezekiel Northend, Sewall's sister's husband, where she was instructed by her father to have "her advice with her Uncle . . . as her father" (p. 166). This advice indicates that other heads of households exercised parental authority over the Sewall children. Samuel Sewall, Jr., lived for three years with a relative in Newton, the Reverend Nehemiah Hobart, while he attended Harvard College. His younger brother, Joseph, entered the Hobart household in 1693 and remained there for a stay that may have lasted a year or two. His daughter Elizabeth often resided with her paternal uncle Stephen of Salem and lived there continuously from August to November 1696. In May 1693 she spent a month with her relatives in Newbury. Her sister Mary lived in the home of Michael Wigglesworth for a full year between August 1703 and July 1704 (pp. 165–66).

In the Sewalls' household there were also the children of relatives. Nathaniel Dummer, who was related to the Sewalls through Sewall's mother, Jane Dummer, lived in the household from July 1685 until the following fall. A niece lived with the family from November 1689 until the next July. Samuel Hirst, Sewall's grandson, entered the household sometime before 1717 and remained there until 1719 when he enrolled at Harvard College. For the next six years he lived from time to time with

15. Quoted in Charles G. Steffen, "The Sewall Children in Colonial New England," *Register*, 131 (1977): 164.

the Sewalls. Another of Sewall's relatives, Jane Toppan, lived in the household for fifteen years (p. 166).

The many relatives living in Sewall's household, and in the households of Charlestown families of similar rank, illustrates the role of the extended family in the rearing of merchant-planter children. The youngsters were also affected by the sociability of their parents, who moved in a wide circle of friends and business acquaintances and entertained frequently in their homes. Children had opportunities to listen as their parents spoke with ship captains from England and the West Indies about British affairs and about exotic peoples in faraway places. They also overheard their fathers discuss with other merchant-planters in the Boston Bay problems of town government, colonial politics, and imperial relations. Often merchants came to dinner, perhaps after the weekly lecture in the meetinghouse, when their conversation touched on the sermon and then moved to problems of market and state. With the children present, even some observations about their future were likely. In Samuel Sewall's diary for Wednesday, October 13, 1686, a typical evening dinner was thus reported:

Carried Mistress Bridget Hoar behind me to Cambridge-lecture, where Mr. Lee preached. After Lecture [I] was invited to Dinner by the late Deputy Governor[.] At his table sat down [with] Deputy Governor and his Lady, Mr. Lee, Morton, Bayly, Hubbard of the Village, Russell, Sewall, Wyllie, Ballard, Leverett, Brattle, Williams [of] Derefield.[16]

A few days later Sewall "dined about 3. or 4. aclock at Mr. (Richard) Russell's," after attending the installation of the new Charlestown minister.[17] Such a round of ceremonies in the homes was not unusual for members of this class. Their weeks and months were filled with numerous gatherings with friends. Their children were introduced naturally and consciously into this social set and were prepared to assume in time their places in society.

The merchant-planter families were unique also in the degree

16. "Diary of Samuel Sewall, 1674–1729," *Massachusetts Historical Society Collections*, 5th ser. 5 (1878): 153–54.

17. Sewall, p. 155.

of travel they enjoyed. Most of them could escape the everyday routine of the farmer and tradesman and visit friends and acquaintances in other parts of New England. Lawrence Hammond, the prominent Charlestown merchant, reveals in his diary the comparative flexibility and mobility of a merchant-planter. He and his family, like the Sewalls and others of their group, traveled frequently and sometimes for long distances. On Friday, May 11, 1688, Hammond and his wife "rode to Wenham" to call on friends. They remained there until the following Wednesday, then spent a day in Salem before returning to Charlestown. The next month Lawrence went alone to Concord to spend four days comforting the recently widowed Mrs. Peter Bulkeley. Later, in 1691, Mr. and Mrs. Hammond sailed from Charlestown to Barnstable to visit members of their family. They arrived at Barnstable March 7th and stayed there until the 19th, and then spent four days returning home, stopping at Sandwich, Plymouth, and Braintree.[18]

The Artisan-Yeomen

Representing a great majority of Charlestown's population in the seventeenth century were the artisan-yeomen, who lived in a world different in many respects from that of the merchant-planters. Because the colonial economy generally did not support a trade year-round, the artisan-yeomen combined the skills of craftsman and farmer to earn a living. Many of the immigrant generation abandoned their crafts permanently to become full-time farmers. Their goods and crops contributed to the New England economy and were sold to many parts of America. Although these workers toiled in shop and field, and operated routinely in a narrow community, many of them moved frequently and thus resided in several towns during their lifetimes.

An inescapable pattern of work, town service, and religious activity dominated the lives of the artisan-yeomen. Governed by the rhythm of seasons, they and their families prepared the soil for spring planting. Seeding the ground and weeding it followed

18. "Diary of Lawrence Hammond," *Proceedings of the Massachusetts Historical Society*, 2d ser. 7 (1892): 146, 153–54, 160.

in due course, as they divided their time between driving off wild animals and gathering in wild hay from the marshes. In the fall all members of the families worked together to harvest the wheat, corn, and oats in advance of the killing frosts. In winter the men returned to their trades, which they had put aside during the growing season, to turn out shoes, staves, bricks, and other products that could be exchanged for essentials.

When the artisan-yeomen were not engaged in these chores, they gave their time to the community, serving year after year as surveyors of highways, as fence-viewers, and wardens. These tasks entailed many hours of labor—constructing town buildings, roads, fences, dams, and mills, in short, performing the service tasks of the town. Seldom did they rise (as the merchant-planters did) to the high office of selectman or deputy to the legislature. Their obligations also extended to the church, which expected of them a tithe and attendance. Although some never sought church membership, and others were denied it, they were required to attend services. Seated behind the merchant-planters in the meetinghouse, in keeping with their inferior status in the community, they often listened to an over-scrupulous minister chastise them for their ambition, pride, and vanity, and warn them to repent or suffer the wrath of God. Sincerely Puritan, most artisan-yeomen searched their hearts for evidences of saving grace and sought to convince the visible saints in the congregation that they had experienced salvation. Bearing a heavy responsibility for both their own salvation and that of their children, they catechized their sons and daughters at home, read the Bible to them, and taught them the truths of scripture, while they pondered at the same time whether they were among God's elect.

These artisan-yeomen, tied to the community by routines of work, service, and worship, found their horizons limited by the boundaries of the town, as were their economic resources. Since they lacked capital to invest in outlying farms and ventures, they were constrained to consolidate the property holdings that had been given them by the town. To achieve this end, they frequently bought lands adjacent to their homesteads and sold unwanted acreage in remote areas.

Despite their confining routines and land practices, the

artisan-yeomen were highly mobile. Although they seldom traveled to distant places to visit friends or relatives, they often migrated to other towns in search of better opportunities. The immigrant generation in this seaboard community was especially restless, unlike the first settlers in Andover, Massachusetts, an inland community; eventually more than 50 percent of their group left Charlestown to settle elsewhere.[19] Some families moved two or more times. Their restlessness was noted by Charlestown's minister Thomas Allen, who confided to his clerical colleague, John Cotton, that many of his congregation delayed baptizing their children because they were unsure how long they would remain in the community.[20] Undoubtedly, these migrations reflected a desire of artisan-yeomen to escape the burdens of life in Charlestown. For example, Thomas Goble, wife Alice, and infant son Thomas had a promising beginning in Charlestown. Granted a small piece of land by the selectmen, Goble took immediate steps to qualify as a fully enfranchised member of the community when he sought church membership and applied for the freeman's oath. Despite his encouraging start, Goble experienced little success, and by 1638 he possessed only sixty-nine acres in the community, not sufficient land to provide security for his family. Having spent over one hundred pounds on the cost of immigrating and five years of hard labor on his small farm, he moved in 1639 to Concord where fortune rewarded effort and he and his family gained position in the community.[21]

For Goble and his group, movement from one community to another was sometimes precipitated by litigation. The time that they spent in court suing one another is astonishing—they

19. See Philip J. Greven, Jr., *Four Generations: Population, Land, and Family in Colonial Andover, Massachusetts* (Ithaca: Cornell University Press, 1970), pp. 39–40 for immobility in seventeenth-century Andover. For the internal migrations of Charlestown's emigrant generation, see Crandall and Coffman, "Appendix," in "From Emigrants to Rulers," pp. 21–27, 121–32, 207–13.

20. Allen to Cotton, October 1642, Massachusetts Archives, 240: 44 ff.

21. In 1666 the two sons of Thomas, Sr.—Thomas, Jr., and Daniel—were listed in the Concord Book of Possessions as owning six hundred acres. Lemuel Shattuck, *A History of the Town of Concord: Middlesex County, Massachusetts, From Its Earliest Settlement to 1832* . . . (Boston, 1835), p. 39.

appear to have been as litigious-minded as the merchant-planters, a remarkably combative group—and the court records suggest much strife in seventeenth-century Charlestown. Even family members among the artisan-yeomen turned against each other. For example, in 1670 Daniel Whittemore of Charlestown took his brother Samuel to court demanding recompense for Samuel's lodging that winter in addition to the services Samuel had rendered cutting and hauling wood. Two other brothers, Nathaniel and Abraham, submitted depositions against Samuel which influenced the court to award 3.5 pounds to Daniel. After Samuel lost in court, he left the Charlestown area for a while, settling in Dover, New Hampshire.[22]

Despite their litigious conduct, the artisan-yeomen showed great concern for their families and regarded the family as a unit, emphasizing its fortunes above any individual member's. They may have been more inclined than the merchant-planters to use their children as units of labor in the family enterprise. As their children matured, fathers could expect their wealth to increase through the assistance of strong, healthy sons who could clear new arable land, plant and harvest crops, and work in the shop. Regarding their children as sources of additional labor, they were less inclined than the merchant-planters to treat children as individuals or to place their specific needs above the needs of the family.[23]

Seldom did the parents alienate property before their deaths to establish a son in his own household. Often an independent-minded son would have to find his own means or be patient until his father's death. Sometimes the son moved to a frontier area where land was inexpensive and where a little capital would suffice. The artisan-yeomen were also less likely to leave wills than merchant-planters, perhaps reflecting less concern for the fate of the children other than the eldest. For those who left wills, their decisions about the distribution of property suggest

22. Bradford Adams Whittemore and Edgar Whittemore, "The Whittemore Family in America," *Register*, 106 (1952): 36–38.
23. Ralph J. Crandall, "New England's Haven Port: Charlestown and Her Restless People: A Study of Colonial Migration from 1629–1775" (Ph.D. diss., University of Southern California, 1975), pp. 106–07.

strong interest in the collective family and the perpetuation of the family in the community—which usually meant the well-being of the eldest male child. Although primogeniture was not established by law in New England, the artisan-yeoman tended to give the bulk of his landed estate to the eldest son, thereby insuring the continuance of the family position in the next generation. The regard for the eldest son was less personal than familial, based on desire to assure the family's survival.[24] For Stephen Fosdick of Charlestown the survival of the family name dominated his thinking as he prepared his will. The will instructed his heirs: "Sixthly, I give to my Grandchild Samuel Fosdick the sonne of John Fosdicke, after my sonne John Fosdick's decease, the house and barn, and the yard and garden belonging to it within Charlestown, . . . to him and his heirs . . . *and so to rune in the generation of the Fosdicks forever.*" Giving a similar piece of property to grandson John Fosdick, he instructed him too that it was "never to go out of the generation of the Fosdicks forever."[25]

To show the contrast, let us look again at the merchant-planters and their high degree of concern for each of their children. Their sons were usually given a start in life before the parents' deaths. In his will, Charlestown's Robert Long indicated that he had already given "a competent estate" to his son Zechariah and prayed that "the Lord [would] give him grace to improve it to his Honor and glory."[26] Francis Willoughby, whom we have met before, indicated the dashed hopes and aspirations of a merchant-planter for his son. In addressing Jonathan in his will, Francis reminded Jonathan and other members of the family of his bitter disappointment in his son's behavior:

Whereas my son Jonathan being my eldest child hath cost me much money, both in breeding up and several other ways to the value of near a treble portion already, and for other serious and deliberate considera-

24. See John J. Waters, "The Traditional World of the New England Peasants: A View from Seventeenth-Century Barnstable," *Register*, 130 (1976): 3–22.

25. Middlesex County Probate Records, Case no. 8130.

26. Middlesex County Probate Records, Case no. 14299.

tions which I am not willing here to mention, I will and bequeath to him the sum of ten pounds, with such of my wearing apparell as my dear wife shall see fit: it being a grief to me, that he should run out an Estate so unprofitably as he hath done to his present suffering.[27]

With better fortune than Willoughby's, some merchant-planters, probably to a greater degree than the artisan-yeomen, made provisions for their sons, but retained ownership of their property until their death. Robert Long in conveying property to his son John stated that he "freely gave my sonne . . . the house he now lives in." He had also provided a home for his daughter, Hempthorne, but was less generous to her in his will: "I give her leave to live in my house she now lives in so long as she continues a widow."[28]

In sum, the artisan-yeomen's regard for their children appears to have been less specific, less personal, and less future-oriented than that of the merchant-planters. Nonetheless, wills and other documents indicate the artisan-yeomen's concern for their wives and children and for preservation of the family unit. Certainly in both groups, circumstances fostered a greater attachment to family than was possible for the indigent-laborer.

INDIGENT-LABORERS

The least stable group of Charlestown inhabitants was the indigent-laborers. These people are elusive and difficult to describe because they seldom appear on the records of the community. Often without property, they rarely joined the church, became freemen, or held town office. Usually the evidence of their existence is negative: arrest and punishment for the petty crimes of rowdiness, drunkenness, and profanity, or being "warned out" of the town. Although the evidence is scant, we can assume that many indigent-laborers probably lived and worked in Charlestown in the seventeenth century. Several types composed the indigent-laborer population: the most numerous were young single men who came to Charlestown seeking temporary employment. Some of these would later enjoy considerable suc-

27. Middlesex County Probate Records, Case no. 25103.
28. Middlesex County Probate Records, Case no. 14299.

cess. A few were artisan-yeomen who had been stripped of their means by calamity or misfortune. In this group also were to be found single women, widows, and partial families, usually dependent widows with children. Almost from the beginning, destitutes were numbered among Charlestown's population. The town's poor increased dramatically after 1675, mainly because of Indian hostilities on the frontier that drove refugees by scores into Charlestown and Boston, but also because of shipwrecks, epidemic disease, and other disasters that left helpless dependents. In 1675 Boston, Charlestown's sister city, petitioned the General Court for some general relief from the refugees of King Philip's War, asking it "to settle some generall way where by those persons or families who by the outrage of the Enemy were bereaved of all means of their subsistence or forced from their habitations, many whereof are come into this town, may find . . . relief and redress."[29] Charlestown received thirty new families as a result of the Indian depredations, and the congestion in this and other seaboard communities unsettled the social equilibrium.

Because of the growing number of its native poor, Charlestown became increasingly reluctant to accept responsibility for the poor of other communities who sought work on the docks or in the warehouses. And starting around 1670 it began to "warn out" indigent-laborers who appeared there. Usually these warnings out were merely a legal device signifying that the town's acceptance of a stranger would not extend to paying for his welfare in case he should become impoverished and a burden. In some cases, however, the constable escorted unwelcome transients beyond the town's borders.

In striking contrast to the rest of Charlestown's population, the indigent-laborers led a wandering and rootless existence. While the artisan-yeomen sometimes moved as many as four times about New England during a lifetime, they sought permanence wherever they lived. The indigent-laborers were less stable, going wherever work was available. In Charlestown they hired out as dock hands and warehousemen, living a few weeks

29. *A Report of the Record Commissioners of the City of Boston, Containing the Boston Records from 1660–1701* (Boston, 1881), p. 97.

or months in the port, or they gained employment with the merchant-planters who operated large farms in the interior. Some of Charlestown's poor lived part of the year in the town and spent the rest of the time working as fishermen or cattle drivers on the farms and in the fishing villages of Maine and New Hampshire's eastern frontier. A typical indigent-laborer of the seventeenth century was Richard Smith who provided in his will, a rare document for this group, an account of his unstable life in the wilderness:

I Richard Smith of Burghfield in Berkshire . . . being aged about 55 years . . . having lived in . . . New England . . . in the County of Middlesex was at Watertown 14 years where I served Jeremy Norcross and from thence came to John Nap in Watertown and from thence came to Sudbury and from thence I . . . went to Boston and there was married and buried my . . . wife and one child and then went and lived in the eastern part of America from one place to another and at the last came from Mrs. Dummer at Yorke where I . . . lived one year and a half and came to the aforesaid Thomas Reed his house and there was taken sick and laid in a low condition and now like to die having nothing to relieve me . . . and being in expectation of death do . . . then cause this . . . my last will to be made.[30]

The peripatetic existence of men like Richard Smith prevented the family as an institution from evolving as fully among this group as it had among the merchant-planters and artisan-yeomen. For the indigent-laborers, the living arrangements and opportunities for socialization fell far short of those enjoyed by their Charlestown neighbors. Single men and women as well as some families often lived under crowded conditions, probably finding room and board in the homes of their employers. Others were forced to rent space wherever they could find it. For example, a carpenter in Charlestown, John Greenland, petitioned the General Court in 1640 that he had "been an inhabitant in Charlestown by the space of two years last past and all that while sojourned in other mens houses because he had none of his own."[31] Those indigent-laborers with wives and

30. Middlesex County Probate Records, Case no. 20747.
31. Edward Everett Hale, Jr., "Note-book kept by Thomas Lechford, Lawyer, in Boston, Massachusetts Bay, from June 27, 1638, to July 29, 1641," American Antiquarian Society, *Transactions and Collections*, 7 (1885): 320–21.

children were sometimes fortunate enough to rent vacant dwelling houses in the community, sometimes called tenements, perhaps maintained by the merchant-planters for this group. But separate housing for indigent-laborers in the seventeenth century was most likely the exception rather than the rule.

Regardless of whether indigent-laborers resided with other families or separately, the quality of their family life was low. Probably few of this group were married. Those who were married often were lodged separately, with wives, husbands, and children scattered. In addition, the possessions of this group were minimal, usually a few items of clothing and perhaps some tools and a bedstead. Children, especially, suffered in this environment. Rarely treated as individuals with unique needs, they could not, for the most part, learn from their parents the habits and customs of the most stable groups in the community. And, what was more important, they could not expect to inherit real or personal property that would give them a stake in the community.

As the number of indigent-laborers increased, town and provincial leaders became concerned about the negative impact of this group upon community life. Frequently outside the pale of family authority or the rule of other local institutions, the indigent-laborers posed a serious threat to the good order of the town. The selectmen of Cambridge, a community bordering Charlestown with a similar population mix, recognized this problem when it ordered in 1665 that "Jacob Coale, Arthur Henbury, and John Jackson, single men and inmates" appear before them to "give an account of their abode, and orderly cariage and to give satisfaction of their orderly submission to family government, or otherwise they must expect that the selectmen will order their abode as the law enjoynes."[32] Some towns were greatly distressed that their young sons were inclined to leave and become transients. Writing to John Winthrop in 1644, John Brown of Taunton lamented that "we have diverse young men that use to wander."[33]

32. *The Records of the Town of Cambridge, Massachusetts, 1630 to 1703* . . . (Cambridge, Mass., 1901), p. 160.
33. *Winthrop Papers* (Boston, 1927–1947), 4: 464.

Once an indigent-laborer had left his or her community of origin, it was difficult to return. Relieved of the burden of periodically supporting the indigent-laborer, the town was reluctant to assume it again, and it resisted the effort of neighboring communities to send back transients. Frequently a legal struggle ensued as to which town should be responsible, and the indigent-laborer was apparently a loser. To avoid this problem, a single woman in Cambridge, Jane Bourne, sought some guarantees before she left her home in search of employment. She asked the selectmen to grant her "liberty to provide for herself in some other town," with the understanding that if her new life did not work out, she could return to Cambridge without opposition and still be "accepted as one of the poor of this place."[34]

Bourne's statement that she wished to be accepted as one of the "poor" of Cambridge suggests perhaps the most difficult problem facing indigent-laborer families in Charlestown. As individuals and as a group, they were starkly visible and categorized as New World failures. Their dress, housing, and transiency, as well as their frequent inability to provide even the basics of life, prompted the remainder of the community to perceive them and to label them as "indigents" or "town poor" or "laborers." Such damning classifications, moreover, were accepted and perpetuated by the group itself, probably in order to assure the aid necessary to survival. As Bourne referred to herself as one of the "poor" of Cambridge, so undoubtedly had others of this group resigned themselves to this status.

DIVERSITY IN SOCIAL STRUCTURE AND FAMILY LIFE

The three categories of families that made up the social structure of Charlestown in the seventeenth century retained their distinctiveness throughout the provincial period, but the dynamics of the three classes varied. Among the merchant-planters, almost no slippage in social rank or economic strength occurred. Families that had appeared on New England's shores in the 1630s with wealth, education, and leadership abilities passed their heritage on to their children, and a family tradition of

34. *Records of the Town of Cambridge, pp.* 63–64.

wealth and service was begun. Thus, Richard Russell, who arrived in Charlestown in 1640, became a wealthy merchant and served his town and colony as selectman, delegate to the General Court, Speaker of the House of Deputies, and treasurer of the colony. His son, James, as well as his grandson, Daniel, and great-grandson, Chambers Russell, each in turn filled similar offices of responsibility and increased the family wealth through mercantile activity. Judge James Russell, who died in 1798, revealed in a letter to his son, the Honorable Thomas Russell, the extraordinary sensitivity of this group to family tradition and achievement:

Our family has great reason to bless God that the reputation of it has been preserved. You are the fifth generation. In the year 1646, Richard Russell entered public life. From that time to the present, I may say, the family have had every office of profit and honor which the people could give them, in the town of Charlestown, in the county of Middlesex and the State of Massachusetts; and I do not find that there was any one left out of office for misbehaviour. Let our hearts be filled with gratitude to Him who has thus distinguished us,—never to be obliterated from any branch of the family; and let us evidence this gratitude to our Maker by making good improvement of our talents.[35]

The middle group, the artisan-yeomen, was undoubtedly the most mobile group in Charlestown. Great opportunity existed for its intelligent and aggressive members, and many artisan-yeomen experienced rising fortunes in the seventeenth and eighteenth centuries. The Whittemores of Charlestown, for example, began with Thomas, who arrived in the Boston Bay in 1639. He was a plain yeoman farmer and left only a modest estate of 286 pounds at his death. But his sons and grandsons improved on that record. By the third generation, ship captains, merchants, and "gentlemen" could be counted among the Whittemores, and several of this family had been elected to the prestigious town offices. Despite their success, some of this group slipped into the ranks of the "laborers" or "town poor" in each generation.

Certainly the indigent-laborers experienced the least success.

35. Richard Frothingham, Jr., *History of Charlestown, Massachusetts* (Boston, 1845), p. 146.

Initially, some indentured servants may have received property from the town and achieved some stability in the New World. Also some single men overcame their propensity to wander and became responsible citizens. But it is likely that most "indigents" and "laborers" found themselves trapped in a vicious cycle of poverty, transiency, and dependency. They remained, for the most part, as marginal folk in the settled areas, serving as examples to the remainder of the community of what was in store for those who failed to practice the Puritan virtues of sobriety, thrift, and industry.

The social structure of seventeenth-century Charlestown suggests varieties of family experience in early New England. Probably the diversity of Charlestown's family life typified New England's seaport communities, especially Boston and Salem, where New England society was the most complex. A simpler existence may have prevailed in the wilderness communities founded by the second generation and by the youths of the succeeding generations. Without doubt, a rough equality in social structure and family life was a fact, at least for a time, in the remote interior villages. But for Charlestown and other mercantile communities in New England, a diversity in social structure and family life appeared very early and persisted throughout the provincial period.

4
Changes in the American Family: Fiction and Reality

David E. Stannard

A good deal of attention is being paid today to what is commonly called the "crisis" of the modern American family. The volume in which this essay appears, and the colloquia from which it emerged, are among many efforts to come to terms with the problems inherent in this so-called crisis. It is not difficult to list symptoms:

1. Today one in every three marriages ends in divorce, and it is now estimated that almost half the children born in the 1970s will spend part of their childhood in one-parent households.
2. Throughout the twentieth century there has been a steady decline in mean household size and a corresponding, though much more dramatic, increase in the percentage of single-person households.
3. During the past generation or so, the percentage of working women with school-age children has more than doubled, to the point where today the majority of women with school-age children are employed outside the home.[1]

Such a litany could (and often does) go on for pages. But a summary is possible. More and more Americans are choosing not to get married; those who do marry are having fewer children

1. Unless otherwise indicated, all statistics in this essay are based on government reports summarized in *Vital Statistics of the United States* published by the Bureau of the Census and National Office of Vital Statistics.

and more are experiencing divorce. This is the simple and fundamental empirical basis for the claim that the family is today in a state of crisis and decline. But, both quantitatively and qualitatively, such evidence is much too thin. If we are to begin to understand the state of the family today and come to grips with the genuine problems that beset it, we must open up the evidence and place the statistics in long-range historical context. Even on the most superficial level, the three examples cited above can be more instructive if examined with greater care.

1. While it is true that today one of every three marriages ends in divorce, compared with one in five twenty years ago, it is also true that the figure of twenty years ago marked a similar increase over that of fifty years ago—when about one in eight marriages ended in divorce. In fact, the divorce rate has not stopped increasing since the first accurate statistics were compiled in 1860.

2. As for the matter of mean household size and percentage of single-person households, again the trend is much more historically continuous than is commonly suspected; while the percentage of single-person households, for instance, has doubled during the past three decades, during the previous six decades it had tripled.

3. A similar pattern can be perceived in the figures concerning married women in the labor force. It is true that the situation today represents a dramatic change since 1950—but the change from 1940 to 1950 was also dramatic, and between 1900 and 1940 the percentage of married women in the labor force more than quadrupled.

In short, our current "crisis" has deep historical roots that tangle and entwine with other matters of social import. To evaluate properly where we stand today, we need, in addition to numerical assessments, the sort of historical social analysis that precedes this essay. The writings in this volume by Crandall, Ariès, and Demos vary strikingly in scope and method, to say nothing of the wide array of sources they draw upon, from genealogical registers to religious ritual to ladies' magazines and city planning. And each of them adds new or corrective information to our current stock of knowledge in family history.

The essay immediately preceding this one, by Ralph J. Crandall, is both new *and* corrective; further, it displays a welcome sensitivity to the problem of excessive generalization. Not content with accepting the truism that there was great variety in the world of family life in early America, Crandall shows the complexity of these matters within a single town at a very early period of development. By using source materials far too often ignored by historians of early America, he joins a growing community of writers who have resisted the impulse to construct monolithic models of social life at various points in American history.

Philippe Ariès and John Demos raise some troubling questions. Well known as historians with great demographic and psychological skills, they are scrupulous about detail and bold in conjecture almost in the same breath. Although their subject matter differs vastly in both geographic and historiographic terms, they move toward conclusions that are remarkably similar. Ariès and Demos share a sense of the deep trouble within the modern family, and both of them attribute this trouble to what they see as an excess of responsibility that the modern family has been forced to bear. Ariès claims, for example, that the modern family is simply unable "to fulfill all the many functions with which it has been invested"; to repeat Demos's key word (and one that reappears with some frequency in other essays in this volume), the modern family has become "overburdened" and is being unfairly asked to "supply what is vitally needed, but missing, in social arrangements generally."

I have great admiration and respect for the work of these two historians. In their previous writings, and in these two essays, each has displayed remarkable insight and imagination, and in particular an ability to perceive and analyze the relevance of facts seemingly distant from the immediate topic (Ariès's concern with the café, for example, or Demos's use of church seating arrangements). I can think of no more than two or three other historians who have even come close to their revolutionizing influence in the writing of family history. But in the present case I think they are wrong. Or to be more precise, I think they have missed a step, the most recent step, in the development of family history; and, in addition, they have come perilously close to

85

romanticizing the past. To demonstrate the quality of these reservations I must return to parts of their chronology.

Traditionally, the early years of the nineteenth century have appeared to historians as a "watershed" era in the history of most Western societies. In recent times this supposition has been given a good deal of factual support. Whether it is Michel Foucault's series of works on the dramatic turn toward the institutionalization of European social life at this time or David Hackett Fischer's ongoing work on the early nineteenth-century transition toward modernity in America, historians have recently been inundated with material suggesting that this was a period that witnessed—to borrow Foucault's language—a "mutation in discourse."[2] Fischer's term for this same phenomenon in the United States is "deep change," probably suggested by some of the recent work of Clifford Geertz. In any case, it has recently been recognized that during this time of "romanticism and reform" (to use the traditional term), there emerged in Western thought a new way of viewing the world. It was not, however, a clear and settled and holistic picture. Indeed, as the label *romanticism and reform* itself suggests, this was a time of great ambivalence and tense cultural contradiction within the American scene.

It was a time when Americans were building cities at an astonishing rate—and celebrating the virtues of rural life. They were waxing sentimental about the American Indian as a noble savage, as the "child of nature"—while simultaneously they were acting to exterminate Indians en masse. Americans then were exhilarated by the contemplation of the new nation's future—and deeply fascinated by ancient Egyptian religion, lore, and architecture. They organized communes—and idealized privacy. They congratulated themselves on their egalitarian and philan-

2. See Michel Foucault, *Madness and Civilization* (New York: Random House, 1965); *The Birth of the Clinic* (New York: Pantheon, 1973); and *Discipline and Punish: The Birth of the Prison* (New York: Pantheon, 1978); and David Hackett Fischer, *Growing Old in America* (New York: Oxford University Press, 1977). I have also drawn on Fischer's unpublished manuscript "America: A Social History, the Main Lines of the Subject, 1650–1975."

thropic enterprises—and built an economic system based on acquisitiveness and competition.

Amid this social tumult, the family could not remain untouched. Ariès and Demos correctly point out that with the growing schism between the public and private realms during this period—when, as Ariès puts it, a "man's life was polarized between job and family," and when that polarization developed, in Demos's words, into "a kind of adversary relation"—the family withdrew from the social world to become an idealized retreat. It was within the comforts and confinement of this retreat that women perfected the so-called cult of domesticity and that children became subjects of unprecedentedly prolonged and sentimentalized nurturing.[3]

But within this retreat, as well, there soon emerged new tensions that gave rise to something truly unprecedented and truly portentous. Women and children became individuals. They developed new powers and newly independent wills. In a world that was witnessing the steady loss of family control of the means of production, in which men were becoming more and more solely responsible for family income but also more and more alienated from the work process itself, the family emerged as the one institution in which the highly touted ideal of individualism could find true expression. Children were seen as the proud progeny of the new nation, and what Philip Greven has recently termed the "genteel" mode of child-rearing became dominant. And women, temporarily tied *down* in the domestic sphere, found strength in the fact that they were also tied *together*, thus establishing a necessary precondition for the eventual emergence of the powerful feminist movements of the late nineteenth and twentieth centuries.[4] In short, although in terms

3. Among the many recent discussions of this topic are: Bernard Wishy, *The Child and the Republic: The Dawn of Modern American Child Nurture* (Philadelphia: University of Pennsylvania Press, 1968); Nancy F. Cott, *The Bonds of Womanhood: "Woman's Sphere" in New England, 1780–1835* (New Haven and London: Yale University Press, 1977), esp. pp. 84–92; and Philip Greven, *The Protestant Temperament: Patterns of Child-Rearing, Religious Experience, and the Self in Early America* (New York: Alfred A. Knopf, 1977), esp. pp. 265–95.

4. See Greven, *Protestant Temperament*, and Cott, *Bonds of Womanhood*.

of ideally prescribed function the family had become Christopher Lasch's "haven in a heartless world," in terms of emerging social reality it was in fact an institution that was already beginning to come apart at the seams.[5]

It may well be, as Lawrence Stone has recently argued regarding the English scene, that many of the changes evident in this period were already coming into being in the eighteenth century. During this era of what Stone calls "affective individualism," husband-wife companionship intensified, as did parent-child intimacy; at the same time individuals were increasingly being regarded as unique, echoing Rousseau's famous and revolutionary opening to *The Confessions* that "I am like no one in the whole world"; finally, in connecting with the edges of the public sphere, these changes translated into a greater concern for privacy and a greater freedom to choose one's own occupation and spouse.[6] But although these changes were certainly evident in eighteenth-century New England, as well as in the mother country, the fact is that it took the rise in the nineteenth century of both romanticism and proletarianism to give the American family its definitive shove toward the modern.

Romanticism—with its concern for sensuality, imagination, emotion, eroticism, introspection—was focused on a glorification of the self; but, in addition, what Baudelaire once said of the great romantic paintings of Delacroix might well be said of the whole romantic temper: "It was a volcanic crater artistically concealed behind bouquets of flowers." As for the family in this period, it was—as Demos points out—romantically "pictured as a bastion of peace, of repose, of orderliness, of unwavering devotion to people and principles beyond the self"; but behind these bouquets of rhetorical imagery, the crater was slowly heating up for an eventual eruption of self-assertion and self-concern. Industrialization brought proletarianism and a social structure that objectified labor and alienated it from other pursuits, separating life into antagonistic realms of work and home and segregating

5. Christopher Lasch, *Haven in a Heartless World: The Family Besieged* (New York: Basic Books, 1977).

6. Lawrence Stone, *The Family, Sex and Marriage in England 1500–1800* (New York: Harper & Row, 1977).

the individuals who composed the family. The family of romantic literary and artistic *pre*scription was as Demos depicts it, but it was the withdrawn, estranged, proletarianized family of social and economic *de*scription that existed at the very eye of the American postindustrial storm.

In the world of art, in both painting and literature, the flourishing of the twin romantic and proletarian tendencies was seen in the emergence of the artist as loner, as alienated but sentimentalized bohemian. In the world of commerce, this movement was reflected in the development and celebration of the individual entrepreneur, the self-made man, the singular captain of industry. And in the world of the family—for each of its constituent units of father, mother, and child—home life was becoming the only space that could still be controlled and owned: as in the outside world, each of these newly self-conscious family members soon began carving out a glorified piece of that environment for himself or herself to dominate.[7] During this process, as David Fischer has recently said, one member of the traditional family unit became relegated to a drastically reduced status: the aged grandparent, with little to contribute any longer to the vitality of family life, lost virtually all of his or her former power.[8]

In short, what was happening in society at large was, with a bit of lag time, being mirrored in the family: the movement *from* what for many years sociologists and anthropologists have described as "moral order" and *to* what they characterize as "technical order." Moral order is a term used to describe social units organized around principles of what is "right" and, as Robert Redfield says, it is based on "sentiments, morality, conscience—and in the first place arises in groups where people

7. On the rise of artistic alienation in the nineteenth century, see César Graña, *Modernity and Its Discontents: French Society and the French Man of Letters in the Nineteenth Century* (New York: Harper & Row, 1967); on the world of commerce and the world of the family, and for an insightful discussion of romanticism and proletarianism, see Eli Zaretsky, *Capitalism, the Family and Personal Life* (New York: Harper & Row, 1976).

8. Fischer, *Growing Old in America*; cf. David E. Stannard, "Growing Up and Growing Old: Dilemmas of Aging in Bureaucratic America," *Aging and the Elderly*, ed. Stuart Spicker (New York: Humanities Press, 1978).

89

are intimately associated with one another." In contrast, technical order describes social units organized around principles of
"mutual usefulness" and is based on "necessity or expediency."[9]

To describe the shift in family life as one from the moral to the
technical is not to make a pejorative judgment; it is simply to
recognize what had to be. With the rise of institutions to take on
many of the family's and the local community's functions—the
hospital, the prison, the school, the asylum, the almshouse, and
so on—the family was left with more subjective responsibilities,
responsibilities that it then parceled out to its individual members. The roles of father, mother, and child became specialized.
But then, with the rise of professional social science and the
so-called helping professions in the twentieth century, even these
"subjective" roles drained away into the hands of others.

In all of this, it is essential to remember that great benefits
were intended to derive from the implementation of these role-
usurping institutions and professions, and that many great benefits *did indeed* derive from them. We must not romanticize the
past; we must not forget the wretched conditions of health,
education, poverty, and the treatment of social deviance that
were greatly mitigated by the creation of these outside-the-
family agencies. Nor should we blame our historical predecessors
for lacking what we only possess as a benefit of hindsight—the
recognition that, in the midst of this massive social experiment,
some social glue was loosened. That social glue was what Peter
Berger now calls the "mediating institutions," those loosely
organized, relatively nonbureaucratic cushioning units (the local
church, the social club, the volunteer societies, indeed the world
of the café, as Ariès reminds us) that served to integrate the
public and private realms.[10] When this happened—and it happened earlier than either Demos or Ariès suggests, as Max
Weber, Émile Durkheim, and others well knew—the result was
a sense of society/family and family/individual isolation. Without
that "glue" holding public and private in some sort of mutually

9. Robert Redfield, *The Primitive World and Its Transformations* (Ithaca: Cornell University Press, 1953), pp. 20–21.

10. Peter Berger, *To Empower People: The Role of Mediating Structures in Public
Policy* (Washington: American Enterprise Institute, 1977).

supportive relationship, individuals began to break free from the restraints of traditional social order. But, as Durkheim pointed out before the turn of the twentieth century, "to free the individual from all social pressure is to abandon him to himself and demoralize him," with the result that individuals then "tumble over one another like so many liquid molecules, encountering no central energy to retain, fix and organize them."[11]

Durkheim, of course, was not the only one with prescience. More than three generations earlier Alexis de Tocqueville had envisioned a future America "made up of an innumerable multitude of men, alike and equal, constantly circling around in pursuit of the petty and banal pleasures with which they glut their souls. Each of them, withdrawn into himself, is almost unaware of the fate of the rest."[12]

Was Tocqueville right? Was Durkheim? The statistics cited at the beginning of this essay may give us some clue as to the answer. But here are some more. (1) The average American child spends from two to four hours a day watching television; by the time he or she is midway through adolescence this amounts to the equivalent of fifteen to twenty months of continuous, nonstop viewing.[13] (2) In two modern studies of middle-class father/child contact, the following results were reported: in the first study, fathers estimated the amount of time spent with their preschool children to be fifteen to twenty minutes per day; in the second study, an observational study of fathers of infants, "the mean number of interactions per day was 2.7, and the average number of *seconds* per day was 37.1."[14]

And this is the family situation that Ariès, Demos, and others describe as "overburdened," as having "a monopoly on emotions,

11. Émile Durkheim, *Suicide* (1897; rpt. New York: Free Press, 1951), p. 389.

12. Alexis de Tocqueville, *Democracy in America* (1848 ed.; rpt. New York: Anchor-Doubleday, 1969), pp. 691–92.

13. Urie Bronfenbrenner, *Two Worlds of Childhood: U.S. and U.S.S.R.* (New York: Simon and Schuster, 1973), p. 106.

14. P. Ban and M. Lewis, "Mothers and Fathers, Girls and Boys: Attachment Behaviors in the Year-Old," paper read at meeting of Eastern Psychological Association, New York, April 1971; F. Rebelsky and C. Hanks, "Fathers' Verbal Interactions with Infants in the First Three Months of Life," *Child Development* 42 (1971): 63–68. Emphasis added.

on raising children, and on filling time." It seems clear, I think, that these writers have made the mistake of extending and expanding the early nineteenth-century *ideal* of the family into the present, assuming a basic and underlying continuity of form though one that has undergone much cosmetic surgery. On the contrary, I would contend, far from being *over*burdened, the legacy of the nineteenth century in this regard has been the *under*burdened family; and far from monopolizing emotions, child-rearing, and leisure time, the modern family has turned away from these responsibilities and has delegated them to others—to professionals, to institutions, and to the mass media.

The logical extension of social and family life in the nineteenth century (which itself, as I have said, grew out of a kind of fusion of the romantic and proletarian tempers) has been realized as a frantic search for individual *self*-fulfillment in a domestic milieu in which parents now "manage" the family unit, as Kenneth Keniston has observed, "like the executives in a large firm—responsible for the smooth coordination of the many people and processes that must work together to produce the final product."[15] Thus, shorn of responsibility and of intrafamily power, individual family members have come to rely on outside sources of support, outside sources well beyond the level of Berger's "mediating institutions," large bureaucratic sources that, by definition, virtually defy efforts at individual family influence.

Again, I do not wish to assail these developments, nor do I wish to regard the past sentimentally. But if the modern family wishes to live comfortably and well in the present, it must live *fully* in the present. And it does not.

For some years now, several of our better sociologists and anthropologists have exerted care, in the description and analysis of change, to sort out *cultural* change from *social* change. This distinction is essential to an understanding of the stresses now being felt within the American family, and by the agencies that have been delegated the responsibility of easing those stresses.

15. Kenneth Keniston and the Carnegie Council on Children, *All Our Children: The American Family under Pressure* (New York: Harcourt Brace Jovanovich, 1977), p. 17.

Culture, to cite one recent writer on this theme, can be described as "the framework of beliefs, expressive symbols, and values in terms of which individuals define their world, express their feelings, and make their judgments." Society (or more properly, social structure) is thus seen, on the other hand, as "the ongoing process of interactive behavior."[16] For the purposes of shorthand, it is not too distorting to describe culture as "fiction"—not to suggest that it is false, but to draw on its more basic meaning as that which is "fashioned or formed," and to regard social structure as "reality"—as having an "objective existence," as being that which "is."

Within all human organizations there is almost perpetual change. Both the world of fiction and the world of reality change. But if a reasonable degree of total organizational balance is to be expected, the world of fiction and the world of reality— that is, culture and social structure—must maintain a certain mutuality of social perception and purpose. If they do not, a condition of social schizothymia (for want of a better term) is virtually inevitable: a confusion of identity and an ideationally inappropriate state of self-definition. What we are witnessing today, I believe, is what I referred to earlier as "the most recent step," one not considered by Ariès and Demos—a virtual polarization of the social and cultural spheres, of reality and fiction, as they impinge upon and involve the family. This polarization results from an ongoing modernization of the actual family role as part of the evolving social structure without, at the same time, an appropriate relinquishing of the defined cultural fiction of the family that dominated nineteenth-century family mythology.

Let me be a bit more specific. In terms of the family today, the "fiction" we have inherited is one that imposes an enormous burden (one that Ariès and Demos vividly portray) on the family's two traditional pillars: wife/mother and husband/father. But this *apparent* burden by itself does not sufficiently describe the crisis about which so much is said today. For at the same time that we as a people continue to cling to this cultural fiction of the family as the psychological axis of our lives, we are rapidly

16. Clifford Geertz, "Ritual and Social Change: A Javanese Example," *American Anthropologist* 59 (1957): 33.

becoming impelled in our actual social relationships to do everything in our power to make this fiction a fiction in that other,
more common and colloquial sense—a falsehood.

On the one hand we have come to believe it the unassailable
right of each adult to strive for independent meaning in his or her
life, while on the other hand we are restrained from developing
the expensive and complex social policies this state of affairs
would dictate, because we are haunted by the idea that the small,
tightly knit nuclear family is the only proper bearer of family
responsibility. For a culture to "work" in the best interests of
those who compose it, the dominant fictions and realities of a
given time and place must mesh. In the present, for the American family, fiction and reality are at odds.

Recently this clash of perceptions was made very evident with
the publication, within weeks of each other, of perhaps the two
most sophisticated and important books in years on the plight of
the modern family. *All Our Children: The American Family under
Pressure*, prepared by Kenneth Keniston and the Carnegie Council on Children, is in part a vast compendium of criticism regarding the present state of the American family: everything from
malnutrition to suicide rates, from income distribution to legal
services, from schools to television, is examined and found to be
embedded one way or another in the problem that is contemporary family life. In the end, the study proposes a major governmental commitment to these matters in the form of a "national family policy." It is a classic and impressive effort on the
part of what we might call the liberal-realist community.

But, in a long critique in the *New York Review of Books*,
Christopher Lasch assailed *All Our Children* for failing to recognize that what is really required is a "thoroughgoing critique of
professionalism and the welfare state." Keniston, Lasch writes,
"takes for granted the family's dependence on experts and seeks
merely to regularize and regulate this relationship." Lasch's criticism is telling. He argues that Keniston "and other social demo-
crats" refuse to recognize that what they are calling for is "more
bureaucracy"—which, by definition, would still further remove
the family from control of its own destiny. The ideal of "parent
participation" in such programs is a will-o'-the-wisp to Lasch,
who concludes by asserting that "the well-meaning attempt to

strengthen the family by improving the professional services that minister to it will merely strengthen the professions instead."[17] Lasch is, of course, correct. That *is* what will happen; though in the process a new *form* of family life will certainly emerge, one that is consistent with what I have called the reality of modern social life.

Lasch has other ideas. His own book, *Haven in a Heartless World: The Family Besieged*, is an all-out assault on bureaucracy and the "helping professions." Lasch would return to the family the sense of authority and competence which he feels institutionalized contemporary life has stripped away from it. But Lasch, as David Brion Davis pointed out in a review of the book (again, in the *New York Review of Books*), repeatedly "falls into an uncritical nostalgia for a golden age when the functions of the family formed 'an integrated system' insulated from the intrusions of a heartless world."[18] Such a golden age, of course, never existed except as an ideal in the minds of nineteenth-century romantics. Indeed, as we have seen, during the same era in which that romantic ideal was being fabricated, it was also being undermined as a social reality.

Perhaps we should remind ourselves of one elementary fact. The family, like all persistent social institutions, is simply a construct designed for social purposes. Not the least of its traditional purposes is to care for and nurture the weak, in particular the very young and the very old. For over a century the American family has been gradually unburdening itself of this responsibility; as it has turned its nurturing functions over to other more recently created institutions, family members have been freed to pursue independently an unprecedented range of self-gratifying endeavors. We may applaud this development or we may lament it, but on the whole we have simply ignored it and have clung to a romantic fiction that long ago outlived its usefulness—a fiction that has now become an excuse for social inaction as we fail to scrutinize or control, or to provide with

17. Christopher Lasch, "The Siege of the Family," *New York Review of Books* 24 (November 24, 1977): 15–18.

18. David Brion Davis, "The Invasion of the Family," *New York Review of Books* 25 (February 23, 1978): 37–39.

adequate support, those expanding institutions that have become the family's surrogate care-givers. Just as we now shunt our aged off into poorly run, underfinanced, nonfamilial institutional settings at the first sign of creeping dependency, so too have we now begun to treat our children, marching them off in hordes to day-care "franchises" (regarded by investors as a "hot growth industry"), where they become what education writer Joseph Featherstone calls Southern Fried Children.

It is here, then, in our abdication of responsibility for those whose care traditionally belonged to the family, that we can locate the real crisis in the modern American family, a crisis founded on our inability or unwillingness to allow our fictions to catch up with our realities or our realities to accord with our fictions.

II. REFLECTIONS

*The Family in Literature, Art,
and the Mass Media*

5

William Hogarth: The Ravaged Child in the Corrupt City

DAVID KUNZLE

The rich iconography of the child and family in Western painting since the Renaissance remains a great source of untapped
information for the social historian. Philippe Ariès has looked at
many pictures and considered them within broad lines of development, but specialized studies which take into account the
problems peculiar to the study of imagery, as opposed to other
sources of documentation, are generally lacking. The iconography of any given period and place may both confirm and seem
to contradict conclusions drawn on the basis of literary or archi-
val materials. The image of the child developed in Italian Renaissance art, for instance, belies the impression we have of that era
as one largely indifferent to the special characteristics of children
and their various stages of development. The splendid figures of
adolescents ranging from early puberty to near manhood, familiar from the masterworks of Italian Renaissance and Mannerist
art, have no discernible points of reference in the literature. The
sense developed by Leonardo da Vinci of the uniqueness of each
stage of the infant's or child's growth, or the ability manifest in
many painters to see ideal and heroic proportions in the infant
male without his appearing one whit less of a child—these were
obviously foreign to Montaigne, no observer of the visual arts,
who saw in children "neither mental activities nor bodily
shape."[1] It is almost the rule that in Italian art children have a

1. We may therefore pause to doubt the generalization of Philippe Ariès in

great deal of bodily shape, and show much mental as well as physical activity. In the earth-based putti of Raphael's Sistine Madonna, the gaze eloquent at once of adult wonder and childish curiosity, the pose which bespeaks the mature intellect while the form remains so infantile, contributed essentially to the canonization of the painting by the popular taste of the nineteenth and twentieth centuries.

Another iconographic area which should reward extensive investigation is that of Dutch seventeenth-century art. The privileged status of the child, the relatively liberated condition of women, and the humane treatment of servants in that precociously bourgeois republic are attested in memoirs and other literary documents.[2] Painting, notably that of Pieter de Hooch, reveals as no other medium can the particular triangle of relationships which existed between three traditionally inferior elements in society: child, woman, and servant. They, rather than the men, are the natural denizens, makers, and emanations of the Dutch home. The rendition of space and atmosphere in Dutch middle-class houses, their hushed penetration by exterior light (Vermeer) should be studied in conjunction with what social historians can tell us of Dutch family structures and domestic habits.

The relatively idyllic view of child, mother, and family life generally, which is transmitted by the Dutch painters, stands in sharp contrast to the embittered and contentious view of women, marriage, and family responsibilities which comes to us from German Protestant broadsheets of the same period. In the brutal power struggles between husband and wife the children do not, however, appear as primary victims.[3] But there is a rich and untapped source of information about family habits and family morality in the German sixteenth- and seventeenth-century

---

Centuries of Childhood, trans. Robert Baldick (New York: Alfred A. Knopf, 1962), p. 38. "*Most people probably felt,* like Montaigne, that children had 'neither mental activities nor bodily shape.'" Emphasis added.

2. See Paul Zumthor, *Daily Life in Rembrandt's Holland* (London: Weidenfeld and Nicolson, 1962). Ariès does not seem to regard Holland as unique or as a vanguard society in the development of European domesticity.

3. See David Kunzle, *The Early Comic Strip* (Berkeley and Los Angeles: University of California Press, 1973), chap. 8.

broadsheets, which are satirical, moralistic, and also pedagogic
in the sense that some served to instruct the young. They illuminate the cult of domesticity, certainly part-inspired by the teach-
ings and example of Martin Luther, in an early bourgeois Protestant society.

William Hogarth drew on both the tradition of the satiric
broadsheet, politically acclimatized in England by the eighteenth
century, and that of Dutch domestic genre painting, which was
eagerly collected in that country. Hogarth has not lacked interpreters; his work has always been acclaimed in general and
quarried piecemeal, as the most significant single body of hard
facts about English manners of his age. What follows is an
attempt to show that Hogarth's perception of the child was as an
essentially parentless creature in a society which reneged upon
parental responsibility within both the private nuclear family,
and the public family formed by social institutions. The public
responsibilities Hogarth took upon himself, establishing himself
as moralist, educator, and social activist—as father-figure to
middle- and lower-class society, and gadfly to the upper
classes—in a way unprecedented for any artist in any country,
and comparable only to Dickens in the nineteenth century.

The term "Hogarthian London" popularly conjures up a teem-
ing, steaming city of ramshackle slums, filthy garrets, gloomy
gambling dens, and taverns rank with prostitutes, drunkards, and
thieves. It is the view of a particular artist at a particular moment
of the eighteenth century, which appears to us as a projection
into a later age, paralleled in literature by the social criticism of
Dickens and Mayhew rather than the still rural vision of
Hogarth's friend and literary counterpart Henry Fielding.

Dickens accepted Hogarth's view of London as morally and to
a great extent physically his own, despite the fact that the
novelist would hardly have recognized the geography of London
in 1730, still a collection of villages compared with what it had
become a century later. Hogarth touched many of what Dickens
considered, and we today still consider, the characteristic evils of
industrial life, long before the Industrial Revolution had even
started. Dickens was very familiar with Hogarth's work, displayed it in his Gad's Hill home, and referred admiringly to it on
several occasions. He saw in the artist a sensitivity like his own,

singularly well tuned to the derelictions, corruptions, and cruelties engendered by city life. Like Hogarth, he saw the city as the destroyer of family, a vulture battening upon childhood. But there are major differences, of course, in their definition of the concepts of childhood and family, and in the remedies they offer for the destructive process.

Like most writers of the post-romantic era, Dickens sought in the countryside escape from urban corruption. Hogarth did not. He is unique among major British painters in having shown only a very minimal pictorial response to landscape, then a popular artistic category in itself. It is true that later in his life he acquired a small house in Chiswick, then well outside London, but he does not appear to have needed the countryside as a refuge from the town, nor did he conceive it as possessing particular aesthetic merits lacking in the interior and street scenes which were his constant subject matter. This is not merely because Rousseau was not available to him; well before that apostle of nature, ever since the beginning of capitalism and urbanization, and carried in part by the revival of the pastoral tradition in the Renaissance, the feeling had been growing that the countryside and only the countryside, only the simpler, rustic life, could regenerate the corrupt, commercialized character of urban social relations.

It seems as if Hogarth was so obsessed with this corruption, and yet at the same time so imbued with a faith that it might still be reformed or cured, that the question of an alternative environment never arose. Since the mid-eighteenth-century city did not stand as the universal, ever-expanding, and overwhelming phenomenon which it was to become a century later, reform rather than outright escape may have yet presented itself as a viable way of dealing with it. But if Hogarth worked with a vision of reform through private philanthropy, he saw very clearly that it was not individual and separate abuses that had to be reformed, but a whole structure which was the basis and vehicle of corruption—social custom, law, church, constituted authority in its various forms—a structure which, having usurped the systems of rural or feudal community, was unable to offer any protection or security whatsoever.

The humanitarian movement which spread under the reigns of

William III and Anne decayed rapidly under the first two Georges. The Poor Laws were modified toward a greater rigidity; provision for orphans, whose numbers increased with the wars of Marlborough and the general growth in population, diminished. The cost of Poor Law Relief actually fell from £819,000 in 1698 to £689,000 in 1750.[4] No parliamentary assistance was given to charity schools. Crime, pauperism, and drunkenness increased. Hogarth grew up and matured as an artist during this period of humanitarian decay. Nowhere is his satire sharper than when he considers the fate of children, and the forces which determine that fate. Children, the embellishment of so much family portraiture and genre painting of the baroque era, are in Hogarth like festering sores on a rotting body politic: children unwanted and rejected, the fruit of loveless marriages, capricious lecheries, or depraved professions; the offspring of parents who pass on to them only their physical diseases and moral vices.

They are not however—unlike in Dickens—deliberately and ritually beaten, despite the fact that we assume the beating of children to have been normal and widespread at this period. In Hogarth, children get morally, not physically, beaten. Hogarth's are the children of all social classes, but especially those of the lower orders who appear to have been born parentless and thrown in infancy upon the cruel world, where they live as prematurely aged and vitiated adults. They are incarnations of the social principle that the fruit of rotten trees ripens rotten, and is either crushed underfoot when it falls, or else survives to add to the surrounding rottenness.

Hogarth's first really important and independent enterprise, *A Harlot's Progress*, was planned and executed in 1730, at the time he married and was under particular pressure to establish himself as an artist and provider. Hogarth's marriage, as far as we can tell, was happy, but he was to have no children of his own. He developed, however, a fierce instinct which we may legitimately term "paternal," an aggressive sense of propriety, toward a kind of artistic offspring which would be to his credit socially and

4. R. H. Nichols and F. A. Wray, *The History of the Foundling Hospital* (London: Oxford University Press, 1935), pp. 2–5.

aesthetically, and profit him economically. He had hitherto, in the 1720s, engaged in artistically "illegitimate" or socially and economically marginal activities which had yielded only poor results—book-illustration and broadsheet satires, all badly paid, constricting in subject matter, and open to plagiarization and exploitation by middlemen. Henceforth, with the *Harlot's Progress*, he would initiate and control all aspects of the genesis, evolution, and distribution—the begetting and rearing—of his productions. As a particularly crucial measure of protection, he got Parliament to pass England's first artistic copyright act (known ever since as "Hogarth's Act," 1735).

We are presented at the outset with what is now discernible as a centuries-long historical evolution, which Hogarth compresses into the few years of the harlot's career, an evolution which had begun long before Hogarth was born, and was to reach its maturity only deep into the nineteenth century: the movement from the countryside to the town, from innocence to corruption, from the "natural family" life to lonely competition for survival, from work with a materially productive community to domestic and sexual service productive only of distress and disease. Hogarth's harlot progresses rapidly from virginal girlhood to premature old age and death—making along the way a child which, born into the city itself, and formed by the same circumstances which ruined its parent, is doomed from the start. Sociologists have tracked this movement over the nineteenth-century period, with reference to the transformation of country girls, become superfluous and a burden at home, into the domestic servants of the urban rich, into factory workers, beggars, and prostitutes, beyond the reach, care, or control of parents, thrown upon their own devices and treacherous or coldhearted parent-substitutes.[5]

Hogarth's buxom country wench, who is called Mary or Kate Hackabout, falls into temptation at the very outset (fig. 1). She has been sent to London in the York waggon (the cheap way— her family must be poor) in care of her cousin Tom, for whom

5. See Joan Scott and Louise Tilly, "Women's Work and the Family in 19th-Century Europe," in *The Family in History*, ed. Charles Rosenberg (Philadelphia: University of Pennsylvania Press, 1975), p. 145.

she has brought a present of a goose; but poor goose that she is, she is left unprotected, at her point of disembarkation, against the lusts of wolves and wolverines. Two other young girls arriving, with the same purpose, in the same York waggon, have what would appear to be the proper protection, a clergyman engaged in reading the direction of the place to which he is bringing the girls to safety.[6] Prudently, the girls stay inside the waggon, although one wonders whether they, too, will not be exposed to temptation, and are not doomed to fall, like the pots nearby, disturbed by the munching horses of the careless rider. The clergyman, the church, standing within a yard or two, chooses to ignore the vicious seduction initiated in the foreground—it is none of his business, and he is impotent anyway before those who usurp parental authority and offer these debased parodies of parental attention. The bawd was identified as the notorious Mother Needham; the man behind, hand in pocket masturbating at his prospects, was recognized as the wicked "Colonel" Charteris who, we read in a biography published at the time when he was on trial for rape, employed "some noted Procuress to furnish him from time to time with a variety of fresh Country Girls, which were to be hired (to prevent Suspicion) to live with him as Servants."[7] Charteris was a friend of the prime minister, so he escaped punishment.

6. Many writers have assumed the clergyman is Kate's father. Among them are Rouquet, *Lettre de Monsieur xx à un de ses amis à Paris*, 1746, p. 4; John Nichols, *Biographical Anecdotes of William Hogarth*, 1781; G. C. Lichtenberg, *The World of Hogarth, Lichtenberg's Commentaries on Hogarth's Engravings*, translated from the German and with an Introduction by Innes and Gustav Herdan (Boston: Houghton Mifflin, 1966), p. 4ff.; and Ronald Paulson in *Hogarth's Graphic Works* (New Haven and London: Yale University Press, 1965), 1:144, cautiously countenances the possibility. It seems to me extremely unlikely that Hogarth intended such an identification, first because of the inherent implausibility of a daughter being seduced within yards of a father come expressly to protect her from this very eventuality, and second because, as this essay will show, Hogarth is throughout his life concerned with the concept of the father-substitute in a world where real fathers are absent or delinquent. The eighteenth-century writers evidently assumed the father was present because they knew he *should* be present.

7. The whole scene is more or less duplicated by Steele in *The Spectator* 1711/12. Steele "projects the same mixture of pity, tenderness and prurience,"

Country girls arrived in London with social ambitions. By the second plate, Kate has become an accomplished courtesan, provided with an exotic child-servant from a "child-race"—the Negro—and an exotic pet which apes her antics and dress. Expelled for infidelity by her wealthy Jewish keeper, she rapidly declines, is arrested in a garret for receiving stolen goods, or else simply as a common harlot (scene III), and is sent to Bridewell women's prison, in the company of children too young and idiotic looking to be considered responsible for whatever crime they are charged with (scene IV). Hogarth is clear on this, and this is what differentiates him from the long tradition in popular moralization: the girls have sinned, but they are victims of evil social forces and cruel laws which punish them and leave their seducers to prosper.[8] The authorities which conspire against her are: the ruthless harlot-hunting Justice Sir John Gonson (a notorious figure in real life), entering in the third scene and himself hanged in effigy by an inmate graffitist, in the next; the villainous and sadistic jailer and his thieving wife (scene IV); and the doctors who engage in a trivial and despicable quarrel about the relative merits of their cures, at the very moment the harlot is dying, thus mocking the misery of their patient, and ignoring that of her child, who scratches his verminous head as he tries to smoke a piece of bread (scene V).

The child, moving rapidly into the center of the European social stage, is the centerpiece of Hogarth's final plate (fig. 2). While the sisterhood, the harlot's colleagues, pay their last respects with hypocritical and drunken wailing and sniveling, and with lecherous gestures, the chief mourner, the pathetic remnant and fruit of the harlot's career, is left to play with a top—a symbol, perhaps, of the emptiness of his existence. No one takes the slightest notice of him. Officialdom—clergyman, undertaker—is occupied in pursuit of its own amorous designs.

Hogarth followed up his tremendously successful *Harlot's*

---

in the view of Ronald Paulson, *Hogarth, His Life, Art, and Times* (New Haven and London: Yale University Press, 1971), 1:239.

8. Cf. Kunzle, *Early Comic Strip*, pp. 272–81, with seventeenth-century Italian examples of the careers of harlots and courtesans where the girls are presented as individually to blame for their fate.

FIGURE 1. Unprotected by family, a country girl arrives in London to find a job as a servant. In this first scene from William Hogarth's *A Harlot's Progress*, her path from innocence to corruption begins as she falls victim to a procuress amid the evils of the city.

FIGURE 2. Ending her downward path through the temptations and degradations of city life, the harlot is mourned by the only "family" she has: her drunken and hypocritical colleagues. Her child, pathetic fruit of her career, is ignored by all as he plays in front of the casket.

FIGURE 3. This scene from *A Rake's Progress* shows the plight of the urban, lower-class child in two lights. The illegitimate little girl tries to revive her mother, who faints on seeing her debauched lover (the girl's father) half-mad in a debtor's prison. The hard-faced and prematurely aged little boy, demanding money for the beer he has brought, is already part of the soured, corrupt work force of the prison.

FIGURE 4. Hogarth's painting of Moses brought before the Pharaoh's daughter shows a child afraid and alone, nervously clinging to his mother as he is transferred across class boundaries in order to salve the conscience of the rich. This painting was one of Hogarth's major gifts to the Foundling Hospital, which became an important public art gallery in London. (Courtesy: The Thomas Coram Foundation for Children.)

FIGURE 5. In a brief respite from portraying the child as victim, Hogarth depicts the spontaneity and freshness of the Graham children, who enjoy the protection of a real family. Their father was the apothecary at the Royal Hospital for War Veterans in Chelsea. (Courtesy: The Tate Gallery, London.)

FIGURE 6. This scene from *Marriage à la Mode* shows parents exploiting their children. The bored young couple at right are being forced into a loveless marriage as the middle-class nouveau-riche father buys a titled husband for his daughter, and the diseased aristocrat of ancient lineage sells his son in order to pay off the debts incurred by his artistic extravagance.

FIGURE 7. In the final scene of *Marriage à la Mode*, the deformed child of the loveless marriage kisses his dying mother. She has taken an overdose of laudanum after her husband has been slain by her lover in a duel, and the lover has been executed for murder. The real pain of the servant holding the child is opposed to the hypocritical pain of the grandfather "stealing" his daughter's ring.

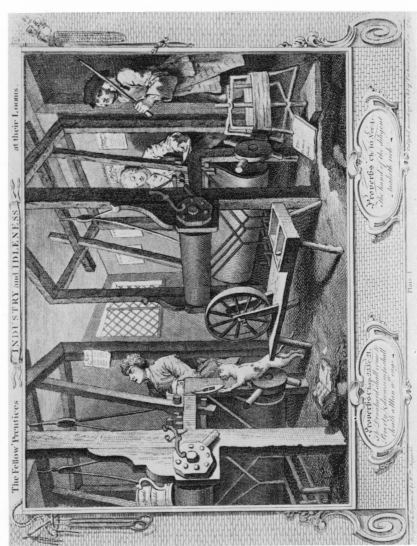

FIGURE 8. *Industry and Idleness* portrays the careers of two orphans, Goodchild and Idle, who begin as apprentices to a weaver. Their parent-substitute, the master weaver (actually, a textile magnate in this proto-industrial society), threatens punishment for idleness. The real educational force, however, seems to be literary: ballad sheets chosen by the wicked, religious tracts chosen by the good.

FIGURE 9. The pastime of the rich is the vice of the poor. This boisterous gang of already hardened child-gamblers was added by Hogarth to the scene in *A Rake's Progress* where the social gambling of the nouveau riche (attendance at court) is rudely disrupted by an arrest for debt.

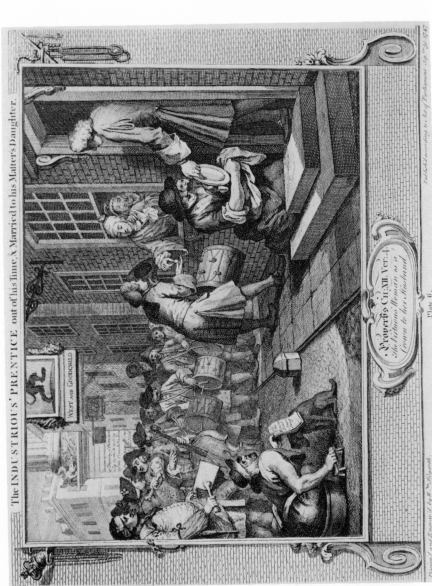

FIGURE 10. Goodchild marries the daughter of his master and adoptive father and becomes a partner in the firm. He is pictured here, at the wedding breakfast, as he gives the ritual tip to the guildsmen who come to congratulate him. Except for the glimpse of the wife through the window, Hogarth ignores Goodchild's private family to focus upon the wider social family for which Goodchild, rising in the scale of civic office, is supposed to assume responsibility.

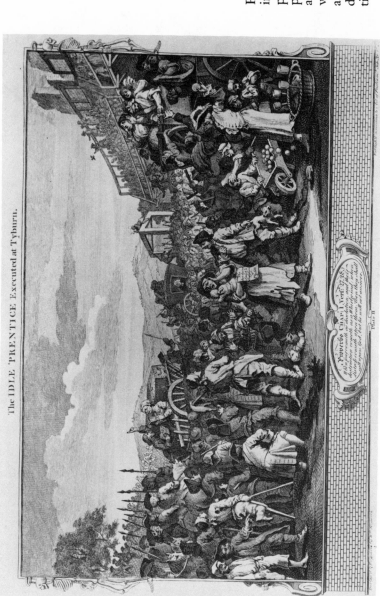

FIGURE 11. Idle's career ends in his execution for theft. The public execution becomes a pretext for drunken revelry and brawling, in the course of which a baby is thrown down and various unattached children are caught up in temptations and violence.

FIRST STAGE OF CRUELTY.

FIGURE 12. Here in the sequence titled *Cruelty*, Tom Nero, a parentless charity boy, begins his career. Twenty-one children are depicted in this plate, torturing small animals—dogs, cats, and birds. Protests against cruelty to animals, as also toward children, is more a nineteenth- than an eighteenth-century phenomenon.

The generous Steed in hoary Age
Subdu'd by Labour lies,
And mourns a cruel Master's rage,
While Nature Strength denies.

The tender Lamb o'er drove and faint,
Amidst expiring Throws,
Bleats forth its innocent complaint
And dies beneath the Blows.

Inhuman Wretch! say whence proceeds
This coward Cruelty?
What Int'rest springs from barbrous deeds
What Joy from Misery?

FIGURE 13. Fully grown, the ex–charity boy, now a cabdriver, vents his fury on a larger animal. In the background, a small child is accidentally run over by a cart. The coupling of animal and child as primary social victims shows a sensibility very unusual at this time.

FIGURE 14. In the final scene of *Cruelty*, the authorities punish individual cruelty with institutionalized cruelty. Doctors, with judicial and scientific sanction, dissect and disembowel the corpse of a hanged man. The only innocent in the macabre scene is the dog who eats his former tormentor's heart.

FIGURE 15. In Hogarth's perhaps most famous plate, *Gin Lane*, the London street is a madhouse where gin is fed to babies, little charity girls, the crippled, and the insane. A drunken and diseased mother lets a child fall to its death, and an insanely dancing man has skewered a baby. The campaign to reduce dependence on gin, drunk by the poor to assuage hunger and despair, resulted in a dramatic decline in infant mortality.

FIGURE 16. Associated with his feeling for the child is Hogarth's compassion for the weaker, lower, and oppressed classes. A novel social attitude is evident in this portrait of his servants, which is a unique document in the history of art. (Courtesy: The Tate Gallery, London.)

Progress with the progress of her male equivalent, the rake, in eight scenes. Tom Rakewell, like Kate Hackabout, is thrown as a mere adolescent upon the temptations of the town, made available to him through the fortune left by a miserly and neglectful father (scene I). The Harlot had been of low, rustic origin, and rose socially, only to fall into the deepest degradation; her male successor is of middle-class, nouveau-riche origin, and is also ruined by social ambition. At the outset, however, he is put in the position of being not only the exploited—the willing victim of tailors, thieving lawyers, and the sundry artists and sportsmen he patronizes (scene II)—but also the exploiter: of the simple country girl whom he, as a student, had seduced on the promise of marriage, and who now honorably spurns his attempt to buy her off with money. She remains faithful to him in the most heroic and improbable fashion: after his debaucheries (scene III) she rescues him with her meager savings from arrest for debt at the hands of the villainous-looking minions of the law (scene IV); she attempts to interrupt his marriage to a rich old hag (scene V); and finally, when, having lost his all gambling (scene VI), Tom is reduced to debtor's prison and madhouse, she assumes the role of mourner—the role, ironically, of Mary Magdalene, the reformed prostitute of the Bible, mourning the dead Christ, whose position in an unmistakable iconographic parallel Rakewell near-duplicates (scene VIII). She has, quite properly, left their child at home for this truly frightening scene; but in the previous one the child adds her strident voice and efforts to comfort and revive her mother (fig. 3), who has fainted on encountering her beloved, already half-mad in his debtor's jail.

The girl's counterpart, on the other side of this plate, is the boy demanding money for the beer he has brought; he might be the harlot's son, whom we last saw, three years earlier, when he was about five, and now, at age eight, is imbued with an air of hardened cruelty. Once again the social parent-substitutes, the representatives of authority, the law (I and V), the military (III), and the aristocracy (V and VI) are the active instruments of corruption. Hogarth shows that authority has broken down in various symbolic ways also: the Tablet of the Ten Commandments is cracked (V); the law, as represented by the portraits of Roman emperors (III), has been desecrated: the good emperors have had their heads torn out, only Nero is intact. Here the world itself (or a map of it) is set on fire. And in the madhouse (VII) it is the same: the upper classes, represented by two elegant young tourists peering in hypocritical dismay and curiosity at the naked, urinating man who, thinking he is a king, unconsciously mocks the very concept of royalty—these fine young ladies incarnate the ultimate corruption of a society which, having driven people mad, mocks them in their madness.

It was not only in paintings and prints that Hogarth gave voice to his distress at the plight of unwanted children. He became a social activist on their behalf. In the first half of the eighteenth century, to counter the governmental and official torpor we noted above, there was much practical response to the new concern for children, in the creation of numerous philanthropic institutions, notably charity schools and hospitals of various kinds, including for maternity. These were not municipal or ecclesiastical foundations, but the result of individual humanitarian efforts. Hogarth was involved in many of them, such as the prison reform committee of 1729, St. Bartholomew's Hospital, the Bethlehem or Bedlam Hospital (the same where his Rake had died), and in particular the Foundling Hospital, which has been called "the most imposing single monument erected by eighteenth-century benevolence."[9] Hogarth was no mere figurehead director; he contributed not only money but also labor and time in committee work, and his art. His *Progresses* pleaded, indirectly, for just such a charitable institution as the Foundling; but he also donated to the hospital building large, impressive paintings in a serious style and of a more traditional subject matter: *Christ Healing the Sick at the Pool of Bethesda*, which includes a mother with a crippled child being brutally pushed away, and the *Parable of the Good Samaritan*, two canvasses for St. Bartholomew's Hospital, still *in situ;* and among the paintings he presented to the Foundling were *Moses Brought before the Pharaoh's Daughter*, and a portrait of Thomas Coram, chief in-

9. David Owen, *English Philanthropy 1660–1960* (Cambridge, Mass.: Harvard University Press, Belknap Press, 1964), quoted by Paulson, *Hogarth, His Life, Art, and Times*, 2:35.

stigator of the hospital, also happily still *in situ*. The portrait of Coram, the kindly old sea captain, like Hogarth childless after many years of happy marriage, is regarded as a major monument in the history of art, and in the development of the heroic bourgeois portrait. A new type of man, the middle-class philanthropist, brought forth a new category of art.

Hogarth was personally present at the opening of the hospital on 25 March 1741. He must have noted the great crowd, the manner in which the mothers were received, and the condition of the children. The women who brought the children were dismissed with no questions asked. As an eyewitness saw it:

On this occasion the expressions of grief of the women whose children could *not* be admitted were scarcely more observable than those of some of the women who parted with their children. So that a more moving scene can't well be imagined. All the children who were received (except three) were dressed very clean, from whence and other circumstances they appeared not to have been under the care of the parish officers, nevertheless many of them appeared as if stupefied with some opiate, and some of them almost starved, one as in the agonies of death through want of food, too weak to suck, or to receive nourishment, and notwithstanding the greatest care appeared as dying when the governors left the hospital, which was not until they had given proper orders and seen all necessary care taken of the children.[10]

In that first year, 136 infants were admitted, more than twice the number originally planned for; but of those who lived to be sent into the country, and to be apprenticed, the survival ratio appears to have been good.

Moses Brought before the Pharaoh's Daughter, the subject which old Coram had put on the seal of the corporation, as well as that of Hogarth's presentation painting (fig. 4), reproduces the hierarchy of social classes which constituted the hospital. The numerous artistocrats elected as governors in the original charter, who included twenty-three dukes, thirty-four earls, and twenty-two members of the Privy Council, could identify with the Egyptian princess in her palace. The middle-class governors

10. Nichols and Wray, *Foundling Hospital*, p. 39, with spelling and punctuation modernized.

and managerial staff could identify with the steward or treasurer (described as imbued with "austere dignity"):[11] the lower servants with Moses' mother and the princess's servants whispering to the right; and the children of course with the foundling Moses himself, confronting the ruling class itself, as they must frequently have done in the hospital buildings and grounds which became a kind of cultural club and rendezvous for the rich. (Some of the foundlings, incidentally, grew up to become, if not leaders of a nation, relatively successful citizens, who later visited the hospital in fancy carriages.)

But Hogarth has also, I believe, inserted into the painting certain criticisms which have hitherto passed unnoticed. The major one is of the attitude taken toward the children by the foster-parents with whom they were boarded out for the first few years. Moses' foster-mother (hired and treated as such, although she is also the real mother) gazes with evident pleasure at the money the grumpy old steward pours into her hand.[12] Since the recent cleaning of the painting, the coins (again) glisten with particular brilliance, and it is evident that the artist meant to emphasize this money transaction, and the two parties' involvement in it: he the parsimonious treasurer displeased at having to disburse so much for a mere single child, of an inferior and subject people; she the foster-mother so pleased at getting paid off as to raise the suspicion that money was her primary motivation in accepting the child; neither showing any concern for the child who is thus bought and sold, and who is so obviously—and naturally—afraid at this moment, overawed by the magnificent princess, and clinging nervously to his mother's sash.

11. Nichols, *Biographical Anecdotes*, p. 31. My own interpretation of his expression is different (cf. below).

12. In the painting the smile on her face is unmistakable. Even if we accept that her eyes are directed at the child rather than the money, why should she show pleasure at the prospect of having to surrender her son? In the engraving after the painting, however, which was done some years later (1752), her expression has been radically altered to one of distress. Perhaps someone influential pointed out to Hogarth the impropriety of his meddling with the biblical story where nothing suggests that Moses' mother is anything but virtuous and maternal. It is not even stated that she receives the foster-parent's fee on handing over the child, only that it is promised to her when she is given the baby to nurse.

Hogarth's critical excursion here is all the more remarkable in that it is not justified by the biblical text, which is inscribed on the frame "Exodus II Chap 10th Verse: And the child grew; and she brought him unto Pharaoh's Daughter; and he became her Son; and She called his name Moses." The payment is mentioned not in this verse but in the preceding one, given to another painter, Francis Hayman, to illustrate. The inscription below Hayman's painting, whose position right next to Hogarth's on the hospital wall facilitates comparison,[13] runs "Exodus II Chap. 9th Verse: And Pharaoh's Daughter said to her, take this Child, and nurse it for me and I will give thee thy Wages." Hayman's picture, presented at the same time as Hogarth's, to a degree in rivalry, and so unlike it, is all sweet sentiment and maternal tenderness. The (foster) mother reaches eagerly for the infant, which is lovingly cradled by the princess's maid. The gesture of the pharaoh's daughter toward Moses, that of directing the child to be given away to the nurse, is more or less repeated by Hogarth in the reverse situation. The gesture of Hogarth's princess, as well as her aristocratically languid reclining pose, seems to us, and was perhaps even intended by Hogarth, as that of a lady whose adoption of a child of the lower classes is an act of public policy rather than a movement of the heart. The bourgeoisie tended to see the aristocracy as deficient in maternal feeling. Artists later in the century, under the influence of Jean-Jacques Rousseau, moralize the theme "Return from the Nurse" by showing the child fearful at being thrust suddenly into an alien and luxurious environment, clinging to the nurse, as in Hogarth, and the unnatural, aristocratic parents annoyed at having to take their child back. (The princess's pose in Hogarth's painting is actually rather similar to that of the unmaternal and flighty Countess Squanderfield at her levee in *Marriage A-la-Mode*, which Hogarth had recently published and which we shall describe shortly.) Her lack of apparent enthusiasm may be taken in conjunction with the whispering of the servants behind her: the "Ethiopian" was judged by a contemporary critic[14] to be passing on to her companion the rumor that Moses was in fact

13. It is reproduced by Paulson in *Hogarth, His Life, Art, and Times*, vol. 1, fig. 203.
14. Nichols, *Biographical Anecdotes*, p. 31.

the illegitimate child of the princess; she could not, therefore, afford to show too much affection toward him. Whatever Hogarth may have intended in this respect, he has conceived of Moses, despite his two mothers, despite the biblical story, despite the ostensible purpose of the picture which was to show the philanthropic exemplar sanctified and in action, as a child afraid and alone.

The Foundling Hospital became a fashionable enterprise, and was certainly of good publicity value for Hogarth, as recent writers on the artist have not failed to stress. By the 1740s he was fairly well known as a printmaker and satirist, and also as a portrait painter, although he never became a fashionable face-painter as Reynolds was shortly to become. His most ambitious portrait after the Coram was, logically enough, a painting of children—the children, significantly, of the apothecary at the Royal Hospital for war veterans at Chelsea. Hogarth already had considerable experience with family portraiture, which became very popular among the English aristocrats who wished to demonstrate their commitment to the new (bourgeois) concept of the family. But these "conversation pieces," as they were called, tended to be very small in scale, and cramped and crowded in their arrangement. One feels that the children do not really have enough room to run around in, despite the grandeur of the spaces they inhabit; that their childish antics are self-conscious performances, or that they are inhibited by the grown-ups.[15] In *The Graham Children* (fig. 5) and *The MacKinnon Children*,[16] parents are altogether absent, which is still unusual in family portraiture, although there are scattered examples from earlier periods, especially seventeenth-century Holland. One wonders whether the choice was more Hogarth's than that of the parents, at this time when the painter was intensively occupied with the foundlings. *The Graham Children*, unlike the usual family portrait, is not about a family hierarchy but about spontaneity and freshness, feminine and gracious in the girl, of an animal vivacity in the

15. For instance, *The Cholmondeley Family*, repr. Paulson, *Hogarth, His Life, Art, and Times*, vol. 1, fig. 109.
16. Repr. Paulson, vol. 1, fig. 179.

boy, over whose shoulder the cat watches the bird with fearsome intensity.

Such pictures represent a brief and private respite from Hogarth's abiding public preoccupation with the child as victim, a theme to which he returned in his most exquisite narrative painting, and in his most carefully elaborated and engraved satirical story, *Marriage A-la-Mode*. The child appears only at the very end, but once again he starts with a demonstration of parental irresponsibility and selfishness, within a convention still largely accepted in practice by all classes at this time: the marriage arranged for economic and social advantages. It is now a matter not only of implicit or explicit neglect, although moral neglect is certainly one of the issues. It is a matter also and primarily of the active exploitation of children in order to promote corrupt socioeconomic ambitions: the middle-class, nouveau-riche father who buys his daughter a titled husband, and the aristocrat of ancient lineage, physically and financially crippled by his sexual and artistic-architectural extravagance, who sells his son to the highest bidder (fig. 6).

In their forced, loveless marriage, the children are seduced into aristocratic vices. The young low-born countess compensates for the boredom of marriage, and expresses her new status by the acquisition of bad art on various levels, and later, bad artists of various kinds; the young Earl Squanderfield reveals his moral turpitude through his liaisons with pathetic child prostitutes and, when venereal disease threatens, through his recourse to the lowest class of quack physician (III). The countess repays his infidelity with one of her own (IV); and even as she makes the assignation, she shows her contempt for the sacred duties of maternity. A mother she is, as we know by the coral bauble over her chair; but the family to which she commits herself is an entourage of more or less suspect artistic performers and groupies. Here is the child she and her friends dote upon: a gross, enameled, effeminate Italian castrato singer, who warbles in an unnatural treble voice for the pleasure of those with infantile musical tastes. The countess's taste in fine art embraces both the senile and the infantile: she has bought old, smoky, violent paintings of mythological seduction and rape, appropriate to the senile sensibility of an aristocracy looking backward to exhausted continental and Catholic models; and, on the floor, the latest acquisition at the latest auction, absurdly childish, primitive or Oriental knickknacks. The only object which makes any sense at all does so in a satirical fashion. The Actaeon figure symbolizes the earl's impending cuckoldry, and mocks the depravity at once of aristocratic artistic taste and aristocratic morals. The mockery here is incarnated in another child representative of the child-race: the Negro servant boy. Out of the mouths of babes and sucklings—and primitive people—shall come forth satiric truth. There are other occasions when Hogarth uses the child to mock adult foolishness.[17]

Sinner as she is, the countess is capable of a kind of heroism, pleading for forgiveness before her husband, who dies in a duel of honor with her paramour in a masquerade bagnio, the place of the illicit rendezvous; and, finally, committing suicide by an overdose of laudanum, because she has lost both her husband, killed by the lover, and the lover, executed by the law. In these circumstances the child, hitherto present only in the form of the coral amulet, makes a belated, but tragic appearance (fig. 7). Crippled and deformed as he is, he attempts to deliver a departing kiss, his unhealthily flushed face contrasting with the deathly pallor of his mother's cheek. Her father, the alderman, meanwhile, with an expression of pained concern, withdraws from his dying daughter's finger the wedding ring which he had led her into defiling (her feelings about the marriage in the first place were eloquently expressed in the opening scene, where she idly draws this same ring through a handkerchief). Avarice dictates the father's last ritual gesture, which actually defrauds the crown, in English law at this time the sole legal heir to a suicide's estate.[18]

The child is surely a male.[19] Most art historians and commen-

17. For instance, in *Chairing the Member* from the *Election* series (1753), the children—again Negroes—are perched on the gatepost upper right.

18. Martin Davies, *The British School*, 2d ed., rev. (London: National Gallery Catalogues, 1959), p. 65, n. 81.

19. Davies, p. 65, n. 85, deduced this from the costume. With characteristic caution he adds: "A girl is not excluded; but it was usual that even very young girls should wear a cap." The earliest commentary, published the year after Hogarth's prints and therefore representative of contemporary opinion (*Mar-*

tators, misled by the female dress customary for infant boys, have taken him to be a girl, who would normally wear a cap (as we remember from the Rake's daughter, and the three Graham daughters). The fact that it is a boy is of some moment: chance has favored the degenerate artistocratic line by producing in the nick of time the necessary male heir, and guaranteeing the perpetuation of the name; but nature, punishing the family by transmitting the physical taints of the father onto the child, has already rendered further propagation unlikely. The child has a leg brace for his rickets, and a black patch over his (perhaps) hemophiliac taint, in almost exactly the same place as that of the father, in the first scene.[20]

In his later work Hogarth gives no indication that, despite his efforts with the Foundling Hospital and other charitable endeavors, he saw any sign of improvement in the social situation, especially vis-à-vis children. While his personal financial situation continued to improve, his reputation polarized, and he became himself the butt of much personal abuse and satire. More combative than ever, in his late middle and last period, he conjures up the most desperate vision of the plight of the urban child.

Hogarth attempted to follow up *Marriage A-la-Mode* with the complementary story of a happy marriage, which was to have a rural setting in contrast to the urban one of the first. But, having executed a few sketches of wedding ceremonial—dance and banquet—and finding himself confronted with the inevitable scenes of connubial and family bliss, he gave up, in the realization that happiness and virtue and the rustic life did not lend themselves to moral exegesis, to comic or interesting effects. There is another parallel with Dickens here, of which I am reminded by Sylvia Manning's essay on Dickens, who concludes

riage A-la-Mode: An Humorous Tale in Six Canto's in Hudibrastick verse; being an Explanation of the Six Prints Lately Published by the Ingenious Mr. Hogarth. London, 1746, p. 58), recognizes the child as a male: "Nurse with a rueful aged face, / Brings Master for a last Embrace."

20. Even to the watchful eye, this taint has seemed so unnatural as to be simply unthinkable. The designer at the University of California Press, which published my *Early Comic Strip*, carefully whited it out on the detail photograph I supplied, mistaking it for a technical blemish of the photograph.

his epic narratives of unhappy families with rapidly sketched epilogues of happy families. Like Hogarth's, Dickens's remain mere sketches, a few perfunctory and quite unconvincing paragraphs, showing how in the next generation, somehow, miraculously, in a kind of never-never land, the happy family shall arise.

But Hogarth was already or soon to be at work on another subject which was to provide for a demonstration of virtue of a kind, and to be ingeniously interwoven with a life of vice. He called it *Industry and Idleness* (1747). He starts with two fatherless youths, first shown as apprentice weavers (fig. 8). The master-weaver is reinforced in his traditional role of parent-substitute, but it is significant, I think, that he is not shown as physically present in the room, supervising the work, watching over his charges. They are left basically to their own devices, to work or fall asleep, to read good Christian or bad popular literature. The essentially absent master merely looks in to threaten the physical punishment of Tom Idle. Such punishment looms nearer, in a much less well-intentioned way, in the third plate, where the parish beadle is about to smite Idle, and roll him, perhaps, right into the open grave gaping beside him, as he gambles his life away. The group of children around him are already hardened criminals in the making, as much gripped by the game as adult professionals. Gambling vagrant children must have been a very common sight in London; and Hogarth later added a boisterous little knot of seven boys to his much earlier depiction of the Rake's arrest, in the second state of the engraving (fig. 9).

We have to assume that Idle and Goodchild, despite their names, start with equal chances, both apprenticed, perhaps, out of the Foundling Hospital. They are old enough to be responsible, and it is by choice that Idle casts off both his apprenticeship and the church he profanes—that institution Hogarth does not believe in anyway, and which serves Goodchild only for purposes of courtship and professional advancement, as he shares his hymnal with his master's daughter and wife-to-be (II). While Idle is sent to sea (V), spurning at once his mother's tears and the warning of the gallows, Goodchild, now a partner in the business, celebrates his wedding (fig. 10). His hard work and virtue qualify him to become a good father, but, characteristically, we never see his biological family, his private family, not even his wife, except in a glimpse through the window here, for they are of no interest to Hogarth. We see only the wider social family for which Goodchild, rising in the scale of civic office, assumes responsibility. And here things go wrong from the start, through factors beyond Goodchild's control. At the wedding breakfast customary compliments are exchanged: the groom gives a money gratuity to the well-dressed guildsmen who come to congratulate, but nothing to the pathetic crippled ballad-singer, whose dog knows better than even to beg for payment for *their* music. At the banquet celebrating Goodchild's election as Sheriff of London (VIII), it is only the fat and gluttonous and undeserving officials who get to eat, while the poor and hungry are rudely turned away. When he administers justice (X), Alderman Goodchild tearfully condemns his former fellow apprentice who is certainly guilty of some crime, but not necessarily that for which he is to be hanged: he is a thief, but not necessarily a murderer, and the oath sworn against him by his treacherous accomplice is sworn on the *left* hand by an usher who accepts a bribe behind his back. The poor mother of the accused, meanwhile, is rudely pushed away and prevented from seeing her son.

In the last two plates the procession celebrating Goodchild's election as Lord Mayor of London is almost as chaotic and drunken as that following Tom Idle to the gallows. In the former, a child is injured (significantly, center foreground) while oblivious royalty beams down upon the riotous crowd. In the latter, ecclesiastical paternal authority is derelict in its duty: the fat Anglican prison chaplain rides comfortably in his coach, neglecting Idle who is exhorted to repent by a lower-class non-Conformist, a Wesleyan minister. And the public execution, instead of serving as a moral warning, becomes a pretext for drunken rioting and quarreling, in the course of which a baby is trampled underfoot, and an unattached older child is subjected to the kind of temptation that started Idle off on his evil career. He stands with folded arms, undecided as yet whether to steal the gingerbread which a vendor cries to the crowd (fig. 11).

Hogarth did not make any paintings of *Industry and Idleness* as he had of his previous three stories. He was aiming, increasingly, at a cheaper and more popular market, at the master craftsmen and tradesmen responsible for the moral welfare of the young apprentices, and at the city fathers themselves. He was working with the Fielding brothers, Henry the novelist and the blind magistrate Sir John, who were enquiring into the causes of poverty, crime, drunkenness, and infant mortality, seeking out not individual and moralistic, but structural, that is legal and administrative explanations for social abuses.

The city fathers of London, so proud of the city's independence of crown and parliament, its democratic government, its system of elected officials, its legal autonomy, and—not least—the flourishing of its trade and manufactures, had not provided a humane framework for society. For all the private philanthropic energy, little was legally, or substantially, or visibly changed. The charitable institutions were insufficient. It is a charity boy from St. Giles Parish, called Tom Nero, who begins his career in *Cruelty*, in the four-part progress of that title, by torturing small animals—dogs, cats, and birds. This scene groups twenty-one children in a street (fig. 12). Childish vice is prophetically punished in effigy by child art—the graffito, which was a matter of more than casual interest to Hogarth.[21] In the next plate (fig. 13), although gainfully employed, Tom enlarges upon his cruel instincts. Fully grown now, he vents his fury upon larger animals. His savage beating is provoked, be it noticed, by the starved horse collapsing and the coach overturning because it had been overloaded with lawyers too mean to pay separate fares, and too cowardly and callous to protest the coachman's cruelty. Meanwhile, in the background, a small child is run over and killed by another accident, this one caused by simple negligence and slothfulness. In the third plate, called *Cruelty in Perfection*, Nero slaughters his mistress, his unwilling accomplice in theft, committing a sadistic murder, which leaves gaping slashes at wrist and throat, a double murder too, for she was pregnant.

The authorities take a revenge which punishes cruelty with more cruelty, butchery with butchery (fig. 14). The doctors who with full moral and scientific sanction dissect and disembowel the corpse of a hanged man (disemboweling had been in

21. See Hogarth's *Analysis of Beauty*, 1753, fig. 105, pl. 1 (Joseph Burke edition, Oxford, 1955), p. 136. For Hogarth's theories on the facial character and posture of the child, cf. pp. 136–37, 140–44, 154–55.

Elizabethan times the final and most degrading stage in the execution itself—now it was used to further scientific progress)—the doctors, barbarian-surgeons, are clearly as morally corrupt, in their own way, as the criminal himself. The only justified revenge is that taken casually by the dog who eats his former tormentor's heart—the pre-child here and the only innocent in this macabre judicial atrocity.

Hogarth was very proud of his *Cruelty* sequence, which he believed had actually reduced the incidence of cruelty to animals in the streets of London. Certain animal sports became prohibited by law. Hogarth sold these plates together with a pair called *Beer Street* and *Gin Lane* (fig. 15); he called the group of six "Hard Prints for Stony Hearts," advertised them heavily in the popular press, produced and priced them as cheap as possible. *Beer Street* and *Gin Lane* were made as part of a campaign aimed at raising the price of gin, the lethal drink of the poor, and lowering that of beer, the healthy beverage of the productive laborer. Henry Fielding believed gin to be at the root of all the most prevalent crimes, the "principal substance (if it may be so called) of more than a hundred thousand people in this metropolis." Fielding continues, "What must become of the infant who is conceived in gin? With the poisonous distillations of which it is nourished both in the womb and at the breast."[22] The Gin Act of 1751 (the date these prints were published) is regarded as a turning point in the social history of London; it certainly helped check the marked decline in population which demographers have noted during the years 1730–60.

Gin Lane is perhaps Hogarth's most famous single plate. It is, with the *Reward of Cruelty,* the most horrible scene Hogarth ever devised. It imprinted itself indelibly on my memory when I first saw it in an old album of Hogarth's collected prints, reengraved from the original copper plates.[23] I discovered this album, which I could barely lift, and which is still the largest volume I have

22. Paulson, *Hogarth, His Life, Art, and Times,* 2:99.
23. *The Works of William Hogarth from the original plates restored by James Heath, Esq., R. A.* . . . [with] Explanations . . . by John Nichols, London, printed for Baldwin, Cradock and Joy, 1822. The volume measures 25 ½ by 20 inches.

ever held in my hands, as an eight- or nine-year-old, in a huge
ornate cupboard in my grandfather's house, a cupboard which
was a building in itself, a magical house full of real and false
drawers, twisted pillars and ornate locks and hinges, containing a
fairyland of objects, strange old games and foolish old puzzles.
The books in the house of my grandfather (a wealthy but rather
uncultured man), which included apart from the Hogarth album
many Dickens first editions, had been acquired by a less uncultured uncle. He had died young, as I believed, of tuberculosis, a
disease surrounded by much deadly mystery for me as a child,
the same which I was led to suppose had also deprived me of my
father, in unexplained circumstances, when I was two. So the
Hogarth album offered me, at the outset, a link with the mys-
tified immediate family past. I perused it with fascination and
fear. Hogarth has never left me since. It was, I am convinced,
that first impression, the emotion of that particular childhood
encounter, which much later decided me, after many necessary
detours, to enter the history of art as a profession. My family
context was one in which death, disease, cruelty, hatred, and
anger were all carefully suppressed. My family was not only
culturally but also emotionally innocent. A cultural sensibiliza-
tion and a profound, if vicarious, emotional experience first came
together for me in Hogarth. Disease, cruelty, and terror first
spoke to me directly in Hogarth's *Reward of Cruelty* and *Gin Lane*.
What my family suppressed, Hogarth revealed. Hogarth knew
how to talk to children. The particular horror I have to this day
of physical political torture or medical mutilations has had the
curious effect of turning me toward those pictorial distortions,
dismemberments, and assaults which we call cartoon and caricature, and toward that threshold which caricature and satiric art
often occupies, between the tragic and comic. The threshold is
also that between the world of the child, where fantasy and
distortion is natural, and that of the adult, where distortion
is—or used to be—considered inappropriate. Hogarth felt himself precariously poised between the primitive, caricatural, anar-
chic, spontaneous, magical world of the child, which was also
that of the people, and the sophisticated, aesthetically controlled
world of the adult, which was that of the elite—the wealthy art
connoisseur who prized neoclassical decorum. Hogarth had the

instincts of the childish graffitist, whom he loved to show in action, and the ambition of an academic painter, whom he sought to rival.

The academic or "grand manner" painter looked to the art of the past for his themes and stylistic models; the graffitist or comic artist to the present reality. The work of the satirist in art tended to be regarded as childish or low, and it is a curious paradox in the history of our culture, which some Marxist theory of art might explain, that interaction with the present (that is, the attempt to determine the future) was viewed as a sign of immaturity, while obedience to the past (Renaissance, classical antiquity) alone could generate truly "great," that is epic or tragic art. Hogarth raised the infant comedy to the level of "maturity" and respect traditionally commanded by tragedy. He integrated the comic with the tragic by creating a profoundly tragic world out of what are essentially comically degraded (or regressive) forms.

There are, perhaps, a few farcical or tragi-farcical elements in *Gin Lane*—the man, perhaps, chewing on the bone in rivalry with his dog. But there is no doubt as to the seriousness of Hogarth's purpose, and his own horror at what he depicts. Goya, in scenes of comparable physical brutality, at least could assume, in the captions, postures of detachment.

The gin is force-fed to starving babies, to silence them. It is also fed to the crippled and insane. Little charity girls drink it, in the shadow of those literally blinded and rendered murderous by it. Previously, Hogarth had depicted mad people only in the hospitals; now they fill the streets. The London street is a madhouse, and a charnel house. Passivity and activity are equally lethal. Next to an impromptu burial of the dead, an insanely dancing man has skewered a baby. In the foreground, a mother, in her diseased and drunken stupor, lets a child fall to its death from the gin-soaked breast he has been sucking. The distinction between life and death is elided; the man in the corner foreground is both alive and dead, with his hand still clutching glass and bottle. And London, that is the world, collapses all about.

These late prints were specifically directed at the lower

classes, or (as the buying public) those immediately above and in contact with them. As a representative of the upwardly mobile middle class, Hogarth wished to expose the vices he saw particularly threatening to the lower classes, although these same vices were practiced, with much impunity, by the upper classes, whom the lower, by a natural social law, tended to imitate. The lower classes stood in relation to the upper as children do to parents. Focus upon the lower classes is another manifestation of Hogarth's concern for children, and vice versa. From the mid-eighteenth century and particularly from the 1760s with the advent of conservative Tory administrations, the reforming impetus of the first half of the century on the one hand dwindled into sentimental idealization of the lower classes, particularly the peasant, and his equivalent in the family hierarchy, the child; on the other hand, this same impetus hardened into an outright hostility toward the poor and their children, which sharpened, of course, immeasurably after the French Revolution.

Hogarth, whose late work overlaps chronologically with the early work of Jean-Jacques Rousseau, was never for a moment tempted by the sentimental view of either the lower classes, or the child. He sought no escape from reason into emotion, from the adult into the childish or rustic world, from the larger social into the private, nuclear family. He did not segregate them. He saw few situations from which children would normally be excluded, whether it be a cockfight, a gambling den, or a debtor's prison; he never depicted a scene from which adults would be categorically excluded—such as a schoolroom. The adult made the child what it was, society made the family what it was. *Society* was the family and the real dereliction was not that of the biological parent, but that of the authority structure. This may be regarded as an archaic, premodern, preindustrial conception. But within it, children are already primary victims, and this is decidedly modern.[24]

24. It may be useful to complete the panorama by listing other examples in Hogarth's satiric oeuvre of oppressed and/or vitiated children, apart from those already mentioned (there are virtually no examples of happy or cherished children). The numbers refer to plates in Paulson, *Hogarth's Graphic Works*, vol. 2. *Rake's Marriage* (145)—small boy in tattered clothes, serving mercenary wedding in church. *Morning* (164)—small footboy numb with cold. *Noon*

Associated with his feeling for the child, and inseparable from it, is Hogarth's real sympathy, such as no artist before him had evinced so consciously, for the weaker and lower and oppressed classes, especially women, prisoners, and servants. (The servant is often also a child, thus doubly subject.) As Hogarth himself grew out of and superseded what he consciously saw as his own state of childish or youthful economic servitude and exploitation, as he rose from hack engraver to become the father of the first native British school of art, as he rose from the lower-middle class, the son of a petty schoolmaster who had been imprisoned for debt when William was a child (there is another parallel with Dickens here), to enjoy the status of prominent citizen of moderate wealth and a household of five servants—Hogarth never lost sight of what he had been. He painted his servants (fig. 16) with all the human sympathy he felt for his friends and equals— perhaps more, for there is some suffering in these simple faces. This document, which one may take together with the portrait of

---

(165)—little girl ravenously picking spilled food from gutter. *Evening* (166)— boy in tattered clothes, sleeping in street. *Strolling Actresses* (168)—screaming baby being spoon-fed by older child (?); drunken children. *Enraged Musician* (170)—small boy exhibitionist urinating before shocked little girl; bawling baby. *Mayor Goodchild* (191)—little girl in foreground hurt by falling furniture; small boy selling (no doubt gruesome) ballad of Tom Idle. *Election Entertainment* (215)—small boy center foreground pouring more wine for already drunken revelers; small girl extreme left stealing ring from political candidate; child extreme right loudly complaining at neglect by father, a pious hypocrite about to be bribed and, ironically, also a tailor who leaves his son with shoes and stockings completely out-at-toe. *Cockpit* (228)—children joining in the betting and in certain instances indistinguishable from stunted and wizened men. *Times I* (233)—allegorical print attacking desperate state of nation reduced to poverty by Pitt government, with family groups foreground right victimized by minister's aggressive military policy: woman huddled and dying in street, with naked baby prostrate (dead?) beside her; another mother bringing collapsed (dead?) baby to crazily fiddling soldier; despairing mother with wailing children. *March to Finchley* (277)—terrified child foreground left clings to father, an enlisted soldier, who callously ignores both him and his weeping mother; another guardsman, centerpiece of whole composition, gloomily indifferent to or morally paralyzed by strident accusations of pregnant woman that he is abandoning her and their imminent child; far right, alarmed and hollow-eyed baby, precariously perched on shoulder of mother serving liquor to already drunken soldier.

the Shrimp Girl, is unique in the history of art. It reminds us that already in Hogarth, embryonically, we may detect that essential nexus of feeling which sees the child not merely as the center of the private family in the nineteenth-century sense, with the strength of innocence and natural virtue, but as the biological quintessence of the socially childish—that is, the weak, vulnerable, presently inferior strata in society as a whole.

Dickens is to wrestle mightily with this feeling, and all too often suppress its proper development. Stephen Blackpool, in *Hard Times*, his only working-class hero, whose social oppression the novelist dramatizes with crystalline clarity, is ultimately infantilized by the author, and left to die in total and childish confusion and ignorance. Like Stephen Blackpool about his social condition, Victorian writers were "all in a muddle" about childhood. Hogarth was much clearer, and his clarity may serve as a beacon when we seek to clarify all the muddles about family and childhood that have developed since then.

6
Families in Dickens

Sylvia Manning

When we think about the image of the family presented to his Victorian audience by the immensely popular novelist Charles Dickens, what comes to mind? Something, I imagine, like this:

They were in another scene and place; a room, not very large or handsome, but full of comfort. Near to the winter fire sat a beautiful young girl . . . and a comely matron. . . . The noise in this room was perfectly tumultuous, for there were more children there, than . . . in his agitated state of mind [he] could count; and, unlike the celebrated herd in the poem, they were not forty children conducting themselves like one, but every child was conducting itself like forty. The consequences were uproarious beyond belief; but no one seemed to care; on the contrary, the mother and daughter laughed heartily, and enjoyed it very much. . . .

But now a knocking at the door was heard, and such a rush immediately ensued that she with laughing face . . . was borne towards it the centre of a flushed and boisterous group, just in time to greet the father, who came home attended by a man laden with Christmas toys and presents. . . . The joy, and gratitude, and ecstasy! They are all indescribable alike. It is enough that by degrees the children and their emotions got out of the parlour and by one stair at a time, up to the top of the house; where they went to bed, and so subsided.

And now . . . the master of the house, having his daughter leaning fondly on him, sat down with her and her mother at his own fireside.

But a search through tomes of Dickens for descriptions of this sort will not yield much satisfaction. In Dickens's stories there are virtually no happy, natural families. There are some happy, constructed families—families created by various substitutes in the natural roles—but they function successfully (when they do) for only a limited time. Happy families, natural or constructed, are found only under exceptional circumstances or at the boundaries of the novels. The most typical exceptional circumstance is geographic: the norm of Dickens's world is the city, or London; the successful families are found for the most part outside the city, and they generally break down when their extra-urban retreats are invaded by urban forces. The "boundaries of the novels" are either the past or future time before or after the story we read—a time that is referred to at the beginning or at the end of the novel but never depicted dramatically—and more commonly the future; or a special realm of existence defined by the story, as in the description above. That passage comes from *A Christmas Carol,* and it is a scene that the Ghost of Christmas Past shows Scrooge of the later life of the woman Scrooge didn't marry because his heart was already wedded to gold. The story, with its Christmas moral, its ghosts, and its open didacticism, is far from the quasi-realism of Dickens's novels. This scene is a scene in a romance, shown by a ghost, of something that *might have been*: how many more removes from "reality" can we get?

Despite its atypicality, we can learn more from looking further at *A Christmas Carol.* Everyone remembers Scrooge, the ghost of his dead partner Marley, the three Christmas ghosts, and Tiny Tim. Tiny Tim is the crippled child of the Cratchit family; Cratchit is Scrooge's clerk. As Scrooge observes them under the tutelage of the Ghost of Christmas Present, the family positively reeks love and Christmas joy. But Cratchit is miserably underpaid, and the family exists on the verge of poverty: Dickens emphasizes several times the specialness of their having a joyous meal, and even this one is a bit skimpy. Furthermore, when we see them again, with the Ghost of Christmas Yet to Come, the family is in mourning, for Tiny Tim has died. At the very end of the novel—in the penultimate paragraph, in fact—Dickens tells us in a subclause that of course Tiny Tim did *not* die: a sweep of the romancer's hand brings us the requisite happy ending. Yet the scene about Tiny Tim's death is enormously effective, in a lachrymose way, and that kind of reader's experience is not simply erased by the narrator's reassurance. The Cratchits, insofar as they are real, are hedged about with suffering.

Here is another Dickensian family in which the father is a clerk. It is much more typical:

R. Wilfer was a poor clerk. So poor a clerk, through having a limited salary and an unlimited family, that he had never yet attained the modest object of his ambition: which was, to wear a complete new suit of clothes, hat and boots included, at one time. . . .

If the conventional Cherub could ever grow up and be clothed, he might be photographed as a portrait of Wilfer. His chubby, smooth, innocent appearance was a reason for his being always treated with condescension when he was not put down. . . . [He] was the conventional cherub, after the supposititious shoot just mentioned, rather grey, with signs of care on his expression, and in decidedly insolvent circumstances.

. . . Mrs. Wilfer was, of course, a tall woman and an angular. Her lord being cherubic, she was necessarily majestic, according to the principle which matrimonially unites contrasts. She was much given to tying up her head in a pocket-handkerchief, knotted under the chin. This head-gear, in conjunction with a pair of gloves worn within doors, she seemed to consider as at once a kind of armour against misfortune (invariably assuming it when in low spirits or difficulties), and as a species of full dress. It was therefore with some sinking of the spirit that her husband beheld her thus heroically attired. [*Our Mutual Friend*, chapter 4]

The comic life of Dickens's manner shouldn't mask entirely its miserable subject. Marital incompatibility has not prevented the growth of a large family:

Not to encumber this page by telling off the Wilfers in detail and casting them up in the gross, it is enough for the present that the rest were what is called "out in the world," in various ways, and that they were Many. So many, that when one of his dutiful children called in to see him, R. Wilfer generally seemed to say to himself, after a little mental arithmetic, "Oh, here's another of 'em!" before adding aloud, "How de do, John," or Susan, as the case might be. [Chapter 4]

How different this is from the glorious uproar of the excerpt from *A Christmas Carol*. The family here seems a unit defined by social convention and perhaps economic necessity, and in consequence its increase is not a cause of joy, but of exhaustion. Its life is a contest of selfhoods, waged through psychic battery.

Other families are much worse off: wives and children are physically battered, or husbands are shrunk to impotence. The Wilfers eat skimpily, but other families go hungry. One is hard-pressed to think of any family in Dickens where one finds a man and a woman, married, with children born to them, living in relative happiness together. Usually one parent is missing (dead or mysteriously absent), and the best known heroes are, appear to be, or soon become, orphans. Oliver Twist, of unknown paternity, grows up in a workhouse, his mother having died there in childbirth. David Copperfield is posthumous, and when after a few idyllic (but also unfathered) years his mother remarries, the man turns out to be a child-beater. His mother dies and David runs away from his stepfather. Pip is an orphan at the beginning of *Great Expectations*, brought up by his much older sister and her husband Joe. Joe is one of Dickens's finest human beings, but Mrs. Joe, Pip's blood relative, is a termagant. Pip describes her:

My sister Mrs. Joe Gargery, was more than twenty years older than I, and had established a great reputation with herself and the neighbors because she had brought me up "by hand." Having at that time to find out for myself what the expression meant, and knowing her to have a hard and heavy hand, and to be much in the habit of laying it upon her husband as well as upon me, I supposed that Joe Gargery and I were both brought up by hand. . . .

My sister, Mrs. Joe, with black hair and eyes, had such a prevailing redness of skin, that I sometimes used to wonder whether it was possible she washed herself with a nutmeg-grater instead of soap. She was tall and bony, and almost always wore a coarse apron, fastened over her figure with two loops, and having a square impregnable bib in front, that was stuck full of pins and needles. She made it a powerful merit in herself, and a strong reproach against Joe, that she wore this apron so much. [Chapter 2]

Not only is housewifery somehow a reproach to the husband, but mothers (or substitute-mothers) like Mrs. Joe are responsible for an oppressive sense of guilt suffered by children. Dickens's fine consciousness of this parental molding in fact makes it impossible for him to hold any real sense of original sin. If Pip is to grow up ridden by his childhood association with a convict on the moors, his inward sense of criminality is first cultivated at home:

As for me, I think my sister must have had some general idea that I was a young offender whom an Accoucheur Policeman had taken up (on my birthday) and delivered to her, to be dealt with according to the outraged majesty of the law. I was always treated as if I had insisted on being born in opposition to the dictates of reason, religion, and moral-ity, and against the dissuading argument of my best friends. Even when I was taken to have a new suit of clothes, the tailor had orders to make them like a kind of Reformatory, and on no account to let me have the free use of my limbs.

. . . she pounced on me, like an eagle on a lamb, and my face was squeezed into wooden bowls in sinks, and my head was put under taps of water-butts, and I was soaped, and kneaded, and towelled, and thumped, and harrowed, and rasped, until I really was quite beside myself. (I may here remark that I suppose myself to be better ac-quainted than any living authority with the ridgy effect of a wedding-ring, passing unsympathetically over the human countenance.) [Chap-ter 2]

Notice how the objects and emblems of familial relationship have become weapons: the maternal bosom is an apron bib stuck full of pins; washing and dressing are acts of violence; the wedding ring is a skin-scraper; birth itself is an act of aggression. Mrs. Joe feeding her family is similarly dreadful:

My sister had a trenchant way of cutting our bread-and-butter for us, that never varied. First, with her left hand she jammed the loaf hard and fast against her bib—where it sometimes got a pin into it, and sometimes a needle, which we afterwards got into our mouths. Then she took some butter (not too much) on a knife and spread it on the loaf, in an apothecary kind of way, as if she were making a plaister—using both sides of the knife with a slapping dexterity, and trimming and moulding the butter off round the crust. Then, she gave the knife a final smart wipe on the edge of the plaister, and then sawed a very thick round off the loaf: which she finally, before separating from the loaf, hewed into two halves, of which Joe got one, and I the other. [Chapter 2]

The language surrounding the staff of life moves from the un-palatable and indigestible plaster, associated with the apothecary whose work is at least delicate and medicinal, to the wood-chopping implicit in "sawed" and "hewed" at the end.

Dickens also took care to observe the more passive but equally pernicious forms of familial dereliction. A comic version of such neglect occurs in *Great Expectations,* alongside the miserable Gargerys. Pip makes the acquaintance of the Pockets:

Lifting the latch of a gate, we passed direct into a little garden overlooking the river, where Mr. Pocket's children were playing about. And, unless I deceive myself on a point where my interests or prepossessions are certainly not concerned, I saw that Mr. and Mrs. Pocket's children were not growing up or being brought up, but were tumbling up.

Mrs. Pocket was sitting on a garden chair under a tree, reading, with her legs upon another garden chair; and Mrs. Pocket's two nursemaids were looking about them while the children played. "Mamma," said Herbert, "this is young Mr. Pip." Upon which Mrs. Pocket received me with an appearance of amiable dignity.

"Master Alick and Miss Jane," cried one of the nurses to two of the children, "if you go a-bouncing up against them bushes you'll fall over into the river and be drownded, and what'll your pa say then?"

At the same time this nurse picked up Mrs. Pocket's handkerchief, and said, "If that don't make six times you've dropped it, Mum!" Upon which Mrs. Pocket laughed and said, "Thank you, Flopson," and settling herself in one chair only, resumed her book. Her countenance immediately assumed a knitted and intent expression as if she had been reading a week, but before she could have read half-a-dozen lines, she fixed her eyes upon me, and said, "I hope your mamma is quite well?" This unexpected inquiry put me into such a difficulty that I began saying in the absurdest way that if there had been any such person I had no doubt she would have been quite well, and would have been very much obliged and would have sent her compliments, when the nurse came to my rescue. [Chapter 22]

The irony of Mrs. Pocket's absurd question reaches through the whole of the novel, touching its central themes. Mrs. Pocket, the nonmothering mother, asks about a mother of someone who doesn't have a mother and never knew even an adequate substitute-mother. It is of course perfectly suited to Mrs. Pocket that whether or not the mother really exists is indifferent. Pip is rescued by the nurse only in the sense that attention is turned away from him and back to the handkerchief:

"Well!" she cried, picking up the pocket handkerchief, "if that don't make seven times! What ARE you a-doing of this afternoon, Mum!" Mrs. Pocket received her property, at first with a look of unutterable surprise as if she had never seen it before, and then with a laugh of recognition, and said, "Thank you, Flopson," and forgot me, and went on reading.

I found, now I had leisure to count them, that there were no fewer than six little Pockets present, in various stages of tumbling up. I had scarcely arrived at the total when a seventh was heard, as in the region of air, wailing dolefully.

"If there ain't Baby!" said Flopson, appearing to think it most surprising. "Make haste up, Millers!"

Millers, who was the other nurse, retired into the house, and by degrees the child's wailing was hushed and stopped, as if it were a young ventriloquist with something in its mouth. Mrs. Pocket read all the time, and I was curious to know what the book could be. [Chapter 22]

The book, we will learn later, is a book of the peerage, a book that traces the lineage of the titled families of England. It represents primarily Mrs. Pocket's foolish snobbery, her conviction that she ought to have married a title and therefore merits endless compensation for having taken Matthew Pocket instead. It also represents the empty notion of family that we encounter most often in the phrase "of good family." The confusion that surrounds the notion of "good" in relation to "family" is of major concern to this novel in which true family ties are neglected, derogated, or broken in favor of snobbish social notions of "family."

Pip next observes that whenever any of the children come near Mrs. Pocket, they trip themselves and fall. The physical explanation for this tumbling turns out to be a footstool concealed under her skirts. Advised by Flopson, she attempts to replace it with a maternal lap, and then Pip meets the adult male victim of this family:

Mrs. Pocket . . . inexpertly danced the infant a little in her lap, while the other children played about it. This had lasted but a very short time, when Mrs. Pocket issued summary orders that they were all to be taken into the house for a nap. Thus I made the second discovery on that first occasion, that the nurture of the little Pockets consisted of alternately tumbling up and lying down.

Under these circumstances, when Flopson and Millers had got the children into the house, like a little flock of sheep, and Mr. Pocket came out of it to make my acquaintance, I was not much surprised to find that Mr. Pocket was a gentleman with a rather perplexed expression of face, and with his very grey hair disordered on his head, as if he didn't quite see his way to putting anything straight. [Chapter 22]

The matter of families in *Great Expectations* is worth pursuing through another variation, the partial family represented by the characters Miss Havisham and her adopted daughter, Estella. Miss Havisham pretends to be Pip's benefactress when she isn't: she is a false fairy godmother, as his sister is a false mother. She adopted Estella, she later claims, initially out of a desire to have a child to love, but as the child grew beautiful that original impulse was diverted into an ambition—unfortunately successful—to make that child into an instrument of revenge upon men. In consequence, Estella grows up beautiful but unable to love.

The ills of the complete but unhappy families are perpetuated by one of the parents. Repeatedly the unhappy families, natural or constructed, are seen from the point of view of the child: they are circumstances to escape from. Dickens embellishes these images with cruel parodies of the traditional family ceremonies: in *Great Expectations* Pip finds that Christmas dinner is an occasion for belaboring the wickedness of small boys; in *Dombey and Son* little Paul Dombey's christening, a frozen affair from which his frail constitution appears never to recover, is attended in the mourning garb for his mother. For a large number of Dickens's children, and especially his heroes, the workplace offers the first opportunity to escape from familial oppression. The boy's first work may be arduous or otherwise unpleasant, but it also provides respite from tribulations at home. This relation between home and workplace is curiously opposed to the generally accepted notion that the nineteenth century conceived the ideal of hearth and family as haven from the economic jungle of the workplace.

Let us look further at some of the exceptions to the apparent rule of unhappy families. First, the exceptions of physical place. In *Little Dorrit*, a later novel, Dickens offers a group of secondary characters who are the Meagles family. The parents speak of themselves as Father and Mother Meagles. They have an adorable daughter, named Pet. They live in an adorable cottage, but in Twickenham, well outside the London city limits. And the family isn't entirely sunny: the fourth member is another girl Pet's age whom the parents adopted when Pet's twin sister died and to whom they gave the unfortunate nickname Tattycoram. Tatty is unhappy, and although the question of blame in the situation is complex, the fact is that the novel opens with her resolves, soon acted upon, to run away. Furthermore, Mr. Meagles suffers an unworthy strain of the virus that infects the world of this novel: a hankering after money and title, and the admiration of those who have them. And as this element of his character links him to the entire social frame of the novel, so the river Thames links Twickenham to London, and down the river comes Henry Gowan to lure Pet into a marriage that disrupts her filial relationship. The Meagles aren't happy for long.

In *David Copperfield* there is a family in Yarmouth put together by Mr. Peggotty through his adoptions of the cousins Ham and Emily and the widow Mrs. Gummidge. The family works well, until David brings from London his friend Steerforth, who seduces Emily and thus breaks the long understood engagement of Emily and Ham. In the events that follow, the family is dispersed.

In *Bleak House*, John Jarndyce puts together a family of sorts by adopting three cousins, one illegitimate. The last, Esther, assumes the role of housewife, although she is no older than the other two. But the family's happy beginnings are not fulfilled: they are poisoned by the interminable legal suit that has ruined the Jarndyces for generations. At the end of the novel Esther marries, and her wedding gift from cousin John is a new Bleak House in which to start again. The last chapter tells us that indeed she did start again; the second Bleak House, however, is in faraway Yorkshire, and its family arrives only in the closing pages of the story.

I am not suggesting that Dickens is making any statement about the viability of the city or about its influence in the demise of the happy family. Dickens was a London man and could not have lived anywhere else. The point is that the world of his novels is so very much the city world that the extra-urban settings constitute a sort of never-never land. They create a partial unreality akin to that of the romance in *A Christmas Carol.* And even in those settings, the happiness of families is limited.

The second Bleak House with its happy, natural family brings us to the major group of exceptions: the happy families-to-be at the ends of Dickens novels. Sketched roughly in the last chapter or two, with husband and wife and perhaps children, they are almost invariable. Now first we should note that they constitute a vision which Dickens can promise but not render dramatically. But furthermore, they constitute a context for the incessantly miserable families that is paradoxical. The paradox is indicated in the curious circumstance that despite the content of his novels Dickens is widely imagined as the portrayer of the stereotypical happy family. Within the stories the paradox lies in the fact that the state to which all of Dickens's sympathetic characters (except some lovable eccentrics) aspire is that of being embosomed in the stereotypical happy family.

The paradox may be explained best through a comparison. Between 1872 (two years after Dickens's death) and 1885, an oddly Victorian anti-Victorian writer named Samuel Butler wrote *The Way of All Flesh.* He didn't allow the novel to be published in his lifetime, and it appeared only in 1903, a year after his death. In that novel the hero, Ernest Pontifex, lives a truly Dickensian childhood, and Butler shows how cruelly Ernest's maltreatment by his parents reenacts their maltreatment at the hands of their parents. Ernest nonetheless gets caught in a terrible marriage, and produces children. But eventually he learns the lesson of the story: that family life is to be avoided. A lucky accident leads to the annulment of the marriage, Ernest puts his children out to foster parents, and he sets forth at the conclusion upon a determinedly bachelor ever-after. In Dickens's novels, on the other hand, the happily-ever-after is the happy family. Typically, the heroes and heroines progress from the unhappy families in which they are children to the happy families that the wedding in the final chapter promises them. In other words, after 750 pages or so of miserable families, the heroes and heroines are rewarded for their struggles with the promise of a family. It doesn't make much rational sense.

One can point out that there is a difference: in the state of deprivation, the heroes and heroines are the powerless children of the miserable families; in the state of promise, they are the adults, whose confidence that they will do better springs eternal. But that doesn't quite resolve the paradox. The paradox continues for the same reason that contemporary readers, and Dickens himself, don't seem to have noticed it was there in the first place: because in the novels the complete and happy family is an ideal strong enough to withstand the most effective portrayals of its anti-image.

The happy family represents a number of desiderata: protection, nurture, emotional security, physical warmth and food, children's laughter, and above all the endless flow of love to satisfy an endless thirst. It can bear this freight for an audience of tens of thousands on both sides of the Atlantic. This function is illustrated with remarkable clarity in *Dombey and Son*. Florence Dombey is the archetype of Dickens's deprived children, since her deprivation of family is not merely accidental or the result of natural ills (like sickness and death) but the willful cruelty of a father who has no use for girls. Across the street from the magnificent Dombey house there lives another family that Florence watches by the hour from her window. She sees happy children, bright lights, loving greetings between children and father at the end of a workday. The family, like Florence's, is motherless, but unlike hers is blissful nonetheless. Here is most of what we are told about them:

It was the house that had been empty, years ago. It had remained so for a long time. At last, and while Florence had been away from home, this family had taken it; and it was repaired and newly painted; and there were birds and flowers about it; and it looked very different from its old self. But she never thought of the house. The children and their father were all in all.

When he had dined, she could see them, through the open windows, go down with their governess or nurse, and cluster round the table; and in the still summer weather, the sound of their childish voices and clear laughter would come ringing across the street, into the drooping air of the room in which she sat. Then they would climb and clamber upstairs with him, and romp about him on the sofa, or group themselves at his knee, a very nosegay of little faces, while he seemed to tell them some story. Or they would come running out into the balcony; and then Florence would hide herself quickly, lest it should check them in their joy, to see her in her black dress, sitting there alone.

The elder child remained with her father when the rest had gone away, and made his tea for him—happy little housekeeper she was then!—and sat conversing with him, sometimes at the window, sometimes in the room, until the candles came. He made her his companion, though she was some years younger than Florence; and she could be as staid and pleasantly demure with her little book or work-box, as a woman. When they had candles, Florence from her own dark room was not afraid to look again. But when the time came for the child to say "Good night, papa," and go to bed, Florence would sob and tremble as she raised her face to him, and could look no more. [Chapter 18]

The family's arrival, mysteriously, after the house has been vacant a long time and while Florence is away, suggests their emblematic function in Florence's agony of loneliness and desire. She knows nothing more about them, and neither do we. They are the ideal family: always there, passingly glimpsed, beckoning, hardly describable.

Does this complex set of images of the family in Dickens tell us anything? The motion toward conclusions tempts us back to origins, to explanations of origin that might "explain away." Is the vision in these novels eccentric? That is, is it peculiar to Dickens, the reflection of his personal history, explicable through biography, or of his perception of life, explicable through psychoanalysis? Or contrarily, is the vision a realistic reflection of contemporary social reality? Or is it merely the product of aesthetic necessity, governed by the satiric mode of the novels or the simple but imperative need to be interesting? (Remember at the opening of *Anna Karenina* Tolstoy's announcement that "all happy families resemble one another; every unhappy family is unhappy in its own way.") Taken singly, these lines of inquiry lead to useful studies, but not to "explanations." Even taken together, they are somewhat to the side of what concerns us in this volume. Dickens's vision came out of his culture and was in turn widely reabsorbed by it; what, then, do the novels tell us?

They tell us, for Dickens and for the tens of thousands who read his stories and attended his readings from them and the plays based upon them, of preoccupation and paradox. We find the same, if less intensely, in other novelists of the nineteenth century: that is, the extensive portrayal of less-than-wholly-pleasant families combined with the persistence of the happy family as ideal and reward. I mention Jane Austen and Thackeray as two, though I will refrain from illustrating these instances. In literature both before and after, however, we do not find this phenomenon in nearly the same degree. At the turn of the century we find a series of heroes who learn Ernest Pontifex's lesson. Heroes like D. H. Lawrence's Paul Morel and James Joyce's Stephen Dedalus (in *Portrait of the Artist*) achieve self-conception through the escape from family. In eighteenth-century literature, for the most part, the family is simply not of concern: Augustan literature looked to man (and sometimes woman) in society, in relationships between men and women, but to the family only occasionally or in the bourgeois novels that anticipated the dominant nineteenth-century mode.

I am not saying that the family is of concern only in the Victorian period. That would be absurd. But the centrality, intensity, and complexity of the vision of the family in this literature is special to it. And we are its legatees: our continuing idea, despite all experience, of a loving group about the Christmas tree—Mommy, Daddy, girl, boy, baby, dog, cat, and station wagon—descends in considerable part from the imagined world of the Victorians; so do all jokes that work on the assumption that you hate your mother-in-law.

7

The Shark Who Swallowed His Epoch: Family, Nature, and Society in the Novels of Emile Zola

Demetra Palamari

"A great producer, a creator, has no other function than to eat his century in order to create life from it"—thus Emile Zola thought of himself as "a shark who swallows his epoch."[1] His particular focus in "creating life" was the family, and his fame rests on the series of twenty novels subtitled *The Natural and Social History of a Family of the Second Empire*, in which he traced the fortunes of the Rougon-Macquart family through all levels of French society in the second half of the nineteenth century. In this great work, Zola examined the family closely and realistically, considering its relation to the social and cultural context; moreover he used the family as a metaphor for social evolution, as a vehicle for an explication of natural laws, to set forth the actual unfolding of the principles of Darwin and Comte in their specific, historical, and human manifestations. These ideas, powerful in his time, were selectively interpreted and presented, sometimes deliberately and accurately, at other times unconsciously—reflecting his own peculiarities, as we shall see. His description of himself as a consuming shark illuminates a major theme that is woven in and out of many of the novels: social forms are secondary elaborations, often corrupted and corrupting, in conflict with the amoral repetitiveness of life itself, blind nature living by tooth and claw

1. *Nouvelle Campagne* (Paris: Bibliothèque-Charpentier, 1923), p. 259.

but ultimately ever renewing itself, hence indestructible. Human institutions, societies, nations, individual personalities, whole historical epochs arise and decay (often brought down by their own blindness, selfishness, and artifice). Humanity continues; the animal world continues; new epochs are born out of the old ones, and they too will decay and die. Zola is fascinated with the interplay of nature and culture, the absorption of the latter by the former, the corruption of the former by the latter; over and over his imagery reconsiders their relatedness, their antagonism and their common basis in the unquenchable amoral rhythms rooted in the imperishability of life itself.

In the center of this set of concerns is the family: an anomalous institution, neither fully cultural nor yet a part of nature. It is the absolutely essential organization without which there is no humanity, yet it becomes the agent for repressive and antinatural forces, thus life-threatening as well as life-sustaining in this capacity. The family is used by Zola to demonstrate the paradoxical nature of the human beast, neither wholly angel nor brute, stranded between nature and culture, subject to the laws of both, which, often contradictory, inevitably generate destructive choices and consequences. Zola illuminates his time, to be sure, but he goes considerably beyond this and draws to our attention some of the genuinely paradoxical features of the family, features that we do well to attend in our studies of any century of society.

Zola makes the family the principal actor in his artistic creation. In the preface to the Rougon-Macquart novels, he states his aims:

I want to explain how a family, a small group of beings, acts in a society. . . . I will show how this group behaves as an actor in a historical epoch. I will create its action in all of its complexity, I will analyze both the sum of the will of each of its members and the general direction of the group.[2]

In this passage Zola reveals conceptions basically inspired by

2. *Les Rougon-Macquart* (Paris: Bibliothèque de la Pléiade, 1960), 1:3. All quotations from the Rougon-Macquart novels are from this edition and are my translation unless otherwise indicated.

Comte: that social groups, including families, are, like a single organism, made up of interdependent parts whose full mutual functioning is necessary to the survival of the whole. Sickness or malfunction of one part jeopardizes the totality. Elsewhere he remarks, "In society as in the human body, a solidarity exists which connects the different members, the different organs, in such a way that if one organ decays many others are affected and a very complex sickness declares itself."[3] And in one of his most powerful images, he gives us the fullness of this view. At the conclusion of *Nana*, we are shown a woman who has been corrupted by society, literally sickened by contact with it, and who has in turn fed that sickness back into society, spreading it among those parts with which she has contact. Solidarity of social classes is a fact of life for Zola. None survives if one part is overlooked. Justice is thus part of a natural reciprocity. Insofar as society is a human invention, humanity poisons itself. Indeed it is one of Zola's express purposes to show how the social milieu that mankind has produced makes itself felt.[4] Humanity's invention, culture, has forever set mankind apart from animal nature and so has changed the course of evolution. This is a point which Zola perceives and shows, while he consciously denies it, asserting over and over that the same laws apply to all of life, mankind and nature. He recognizes the differences made by culture, denies them, is ambivalent about them, and this ambivalence is reflected in his views of the family and individuals. "Metaphysical man is dead, our whole terrain is now physiological man" (p. 50), he believes, but it is just as clear that his view of family definitely implies a metaphysic. Physiology, whether he wishes it or not, has not exhausted his inquiry. Ultimately Zola is too great an artist and observer to obey his own conscious principles in as simple and deterministic a fashion as he would like.

And what is this ambivalence about the family? It seems strikingly similar to some of the views still with us among contem-

3. Quoted by Armand Lanoux, *Les Rougon-Macquart* (Paris: Bibliothèque de la Pléiade), 1:xx.

4. *Le Roman Expérimental* (Paris: François Bernouard, 1928), p. 25. Zola says that he wishes to "show man living in the social milieu which he has produced himself."

porary European and American commentators. The family in the course of social evolution has inherited an impossible burden, that of standing between a harsh and brutalizing external reality and the individual. With the disappearance of the intermediate units—the community and the extended kin group—the family becomes the only situation in which the human being can hope to find love, trust, and intimacy, in which one can dare to be vulnerable. As urbanization and industrialization develop, the family is increasingly exposed to impersonal exploitive forces and less and less able to offer its members succor. As the agency expected to enforce society's hopelessly rigid, unjust standards, the family itself generates pressures that make it a danger to its own members. In the lower classes the family is oriented to mere survival, economical and physical, and this it does inadequately and sporadically in Zola's novels. Nothing is left over beyond the survival struggle; socialization of children, the other major task of the family, is out of the question. And those families mercifully freed from the desperate requirements of mere existence— to be found among the bourgeoisie—are no more viable, for there, socialization takes place but is as deadly as the traditional enemies of the poor. The family, imperiled from within and without, is more necessary than ever, and, paradoxically, pressed beyond its capacities by this inordinate necessity.

Is Zola indeed without hope for the family? As a social institution, yes—for families, like societies and individuals, perish, eliminated in the course of life itself, which proceeds by the cycles of cleansing and regeneration built into nature; nature in its innate tendency toward health and survival continually sheds impurities, eliminates harmful elements.[5] Families evolve from biological factors and are founded on genealogical ties; they establish relationships grounded in sexuality, the helplessness of infants, and maternal protectiveness. The family is part of nature, self-renewing, perpetual, still amoral but viable; as such it

---

5. *Le Docteur Pascal*, 4:999. Pascal states: "But you don't understand at all if you imagine that I believe in ultimate destruction because I show the wounds and the cracks. I believe in life which unceasingly eliminates harmful bodies, which furnishes flesh to heal wounds, which is, despite all, directed towards health, towards a continual renewal within the impurities and death."

may falter and become corrupt, but as a form it will never disappear. The family is an expression of life itself. Even when children are degenerate, when generation after generation has produced monsters, cripples, casualties, and predators, "we must not despair," says Zola, speaking of the Rougon-Macquart family, for "families are an eternal becoming" (4:1017). As part of society, a cultural institution, the family may be doomed, but it has inherent within it the capacity for renewal. A member of the Rougon-Macquart family, Doctor Pascal, expresses Zola's belief in "the courageous challenge of eternity" when, in spite of "so many terrible Rougons, after so many abominable Macquarts, another one was born. Life was not afraid of creating another" (4:1219). Life can afford to make mistakes. It cannot stop itself from creating because "despite the sick and crazy it creates, it is never tired of creating" (4:1219). "The final triumph of life" (4:953), in which Pascal (and Zola) believe, is put forward repeatedly. Even when the end of the epoch is upon him and his characters, when Paris is defeated, brought down from internal decay as well as external threats, imagery of renewal prevails as much as imagery of defeat:

The end of all and yet, beyond this furnace, howling still, lively hope was being reborn under the great calm sky with its sovereign clarity. It was the certain return of youth, of eternal nature, of eternal humanity, the promised renewal for which we work and hope, the tree which throws out a new and powerful branch when one has cut off an old rotten one. [*La Débâcle,* 4:911–12]

The family as the agency for perpetuating life also contains seeds of renewal, despite its polluting participation in cultural and social agencies.

Zola's point of view, as I have said, was profoundly influenced by ideological currents originating with Darwin and Comte. He conceived of his project in 1869 on the eve of the fall of the Second Empire. The twenty-year rule of Napoleon III, a period of relative economic prosperity and accelerated growth, was at an end. The Industrial Revolution was in full development, Paris was being rebuilt according to the innovative plans of Baron Haussmann, and the scientific discoveries that were taking place at an increasing rate fostered a growing belief in the unlimited possibilities of science. It was a time when great fortunes were made and easily lost, when life styles and institutions were in flux, while the poor remained characteristically exploited, ignored, and vulnerable. Such was the society that produced Zola's Rougon-Macquart family and the pressures they faced.

Social inequities were always before Zola, and his deep sensitivity to injustice was no doubt exacerbated by society's optimism, complacency, and remaining faith in the reasonable nature of mankind and science's power to control nature. Zola was deeply affected by the impact of science, less by its ability to master nature than by its capacity to allow us to comprehend the most general and inexorable laws of life and nature. And he was strongly attracted to scientific methods. Indeed he aspired to be a scientist in his objective and experimental studies of the family. Paradoxically, he was far from objective. While he was intent upon being "nothing but a reporter, who is careful not to judge or conclude,"[6] and at the same time a naturalist desirous of "describing his society and its ills accurately so that they *may be cured*" (italics mine),[7] he was avowedly biased from the outset. The requirement that the scientist be open-minded, willing to accept whatever the data demonstrate, was apparently not one Zola felt he needed to obey. He was always both an activist and an artist, and this, combined with his other aspirations, created inevitable contradictions in his attitudes and purposes.

Although Zola has been much criticized for his "scientific" literary pretensions, we should note that these aspirations caused him to use documentation in a methodical and thorough fashion new to the novel. He thus became a valuable informant on his society. Zola tried to bring his directly observed material to fictional life by seeing it through what he terms "the realistic screen." The novelist cannot actually present us with "real life"; his material passes through the screen of his perception; but Zola

6. *Le Roman Expérimental*, p. 103.

7. *Le Roman Expérimental*, p. 73. Zola states here: "We have understood that it is not sufficient to remain an inactive spectator in the face of good and evil while enjoying one and defending oneself against the other. Modern morality aspires to a greater role; it looks for causes and wants to explain and act on them; it wants, in a word, to dominate good and evil, to create and develop the one while fighting with the other to eliminate and destroy it."

maintains that the screen of the realist is the one that causes the least distortion to the material being transformed. Although contemporary criticism has tended to emphasize the allegorical and symbolic elements of his creation, this does not negate his "realism."[8] And indeed, to be a sensitive and intelligent novelist, one must be attuned to one's milieu and understand the underlying feelings and motivations of individuals, as well as the functioning of social units. Zola believed that the novelist combines this particular awareness with an artistic vision in constructing a fictional world designed to give the reader a special understanding of the society described.[9]

This concept of Zola is important to us here, for novels are a unique resource in the study of social phenomena. In any analysis of the family, human emotions must be included if we are to understand from *within* what we have never been, known, or experienced. But emotions are elusive, unrecorded in census data, legal documents, or parish registers, unavailable for tabulation or analysis by the demographer or the social historian. If we seek to understand the human emotions of another era, we must go to literary productions—to autobiographies, biographies, family histories, journals, diaries, and letters; to poetry and the drama; but especially to the novel, which has an advantage over other forms because of its length and its use of a variety of discursive methods. Only an artist can imaginatively construct

8. Zola was perhaps better equipped to create a "realistic," comprehensive, and living picture of the family than any other writer of his period for he lived in close contact with several levels of his society. He began his career as a journalist and later became a newsworthy subject himself. The Rougon-Macquart novels themselves were a popular event rather than a purely literary one, since many of them appeared serialized in newspapers before their publication in book form. From 1878, the date of the publication of the seventh novel of the series, *L'Assommoir*, his popularity has not waned. Zola became at that time, and remains today, one of the most widely read French novelists. *Nana*, translated into a multitude of languages, is one of the best-selling novels of all time in both Europe and America. And Zola influenced other writers on both continents, De Maupassant, George Moore, Frank Norris, Theodore Dreiser, James T. Farrell, to name only a few.

9. Zola writes, "A great novelist is, in our time, he who has a sense of the real and expresses nature with originality by making it live with its own life." *Le Roman Expérimental*, p. 178.

an image in which we *participate*, through our senses, nearly directly. We *experience* French family life of this period mainly through Zola's powerful imagination.

Let us turn now to Zola's novels to examine more fully the statements, implied and direct, that they make about the family in his society.

FAMILIES DESTROYED BY OUTSIDE PRESSURES

Germinal (1885) takes place in a northern coal-mining province and deals with a family of miners, perhaps the most socially and economically oppressed people that Zola presents. In this environment, families exist for two reasons, economic survival and sexual satisfaction. Sex is almost the only relief from misery, cold, and hunger; in the few hours of leisure their lives permit, the couples mate relentlessly. Salaries in the mine are so low that only those who are attached to a group with combined salaries can survive, and they can barely do so. Economic necessity forces people to remain in the family group. Despite the hardships, the members of the central family of the book, the Maheus, show affection for one another and a certain solidarity against the world. But they are a helpless little group struggling against a crushing machine that has no specific human leader and therefore no one to receive their grievances, no one with whom they can negotiate. The owners of the mine are repeatedly referred to by the characters in the novel as *les gens là-bas* (the people way over there). Thus even though the members of the Maheu family make some attempt to support each other emotionally and materially they have no chance against the odds of their environment. Eventually they are destroyed through catastrophes external to the family. The father and one son are shot by soldiers during a strike, the eldest daughter is killed when a mine caves in, and a small daughter dies of starvation. By the end of the novel, the family of seven is obliterated.

The seventh novel in the series, *L'Assommoir*, published a few years earlier, had dealt with people almost as oppressed economically as the Maheu family but in a city environment. The heroine, Gervaise, has two children by Lantier, with whom she had lived in Plassans, her home town. When they come to Paris, he leaves her for another woman, and eventually she marries a worker named Coupeau, with whom she has a third child, Nana. Gervaise more or less drifts into both of these relationships, for her environment has not instilled in her the idea that she is capable of making choices that might ameliorate her condition. She expresses very modest desires for her life:

Mon Dieu! I'm not ambitious, I don't ask for much. My ideal would be to have a steady job, always enough to eat, some fairly clean corner to sleep in—you know, bed, table, two chairs, nothing more. Oh, also I'd like to bring up my children, make good citizens out of them, if I can. I've one more dream, not to get beaten up, if ever I live with a man again. No sir, getting knocked about isn't my idea of fun. And that's all you see, that's all I want. . . . Oh yes, the time will come when I'll want to die in my own bed. After a life-time of hard work, I'd like to die in my own bed, in my own home.[10]

When Coupeau persuades her to marry him, she gives in because of a "cowardice of the heart." After the marriage, the couple prospers and for a time Gervaise and Coupeau, with her children, seem to have formed a protective group against the poverty and filth around them. But the pressures are too great. Coupeau has a bad fall at work and, while convalescing, begins to drink heavily. To alleviate some of the growing frustrations of her life, Gervaise turns to gourmandism. The disintegration of her family is heralded by a magnificent feast that she gives in a confused attempt to satisfy her vague, unfulfilled longings. She pawns her wedding ring for wine, a symbolic act that forecasts the ultimate collapse of her marriage and life.

Her former lover, Lantier, comes to live with the couple, and Gervaise eventually begins sleeping with either man indiscriminately. She works to support her children and the two men, one an alcoholic and the other a rogue. Not only does she lack the energy to protest, she has never believed that life would treat her other than miserably. In the end, Gervaise dies of alcoholism and starvation in a little hole under the stairs of the apartment house where she and her family were once prosperous. For Gervaise, marriage and family are a heavy burden, but they are the only

10. *L'Assommoir*, trans. Atwood H. Townsend, (New York: New American Library, 1962), p. 47.

accepted destiny for a woman in her society. They cannot save her from the pressures of poverty and filth or provide sustenance or sanctuary for her; actually they hasten her emotional and physical deterioration.

FAMILIES DESTROYED BY PRESSURES FROM WITHIN

In *Germinal* and *L'Assommoir* the family is destroyed by external pressures. It must struggle for mere survival but the negative social forces—poverty, crime, filth, physical and moral degradation—are so strong that it loses even this desperate fight. The family, Zola shows us, is not sufficiently strong to withstand the external catastrophes that assail it.

But even when the survival of the family itself is assured—when there are adequate food, shelter, respectability, and even some luxury—it does not follow that an atmosphere of peace and harmony is attainable. In the novel *Pot-Bouille* (1882, translated as *Piping Hot*), the negative forces are of a different but no less severe kind, still generated by society but now enforced and administered by the family itself. Here in the bourgeois family we see its members victimized by social standards instead of natural afflictions, a parallel Zola drew in his notes to this novel when he called it "another *Assommoir*—this time with a respectable exterior."[11]

The setting of *Pot-Bouille* is an apartment house in Paris, characterized by Zola as "a bourgeois chapel." It reeks of respectability. But in the center of the house is the servants' staircase and inner court. Here, in this place that Zola calls "the sewer of the house,"[12] all is dank and redolent of stale odors, coming from the kitchens of all the apartments. The servants shout malevolent gossip and vulgarities from window to window. The facade of respectability that conceals the vulgarity of the servants' court is an analogy for the strict moral facade and inner corruption that characterize every family in the house. Perhaps the Josserand family is the most representative, with four children, including

11. *Pot-Bouille* (Paris: François Bernouard, 1928), Notes, p. 430.
12. *Piping Hot*, trans. Percy Pinkerton (New York: Boni and Liveright, 1924).

two daughters of marriageable age. The daughters must be married, and the search for husbands is the mother's obsession, for marriage is the basis of their moral system and world view. In truth, marriage is a mask of morality, for it is usually a facade for adulterous intrigues.

The Josserands are prepared to do anything to marry off their daughters, and the girls care little about the choice of husbands, for their paramount concern is to be married. Berthe's mother lies about her daughter's dowry and steals a small inheritance from her retarded son in order to enlarge the sum. She says she would do anything so that the girl's marriage will take place:

"Very well, monsieur, since that is so, that marriage shall take place. It is my daughter's last chance. I would rather cut off my right hand than let it slip. . . . When you're driven to it, why you're capable of anything at last."
"Then, madame, I presume you would commit murder in order to get your daughter married."
She drew herself up to her full height.
"So I would," she retorted angrily. [p. 143]

Pushed into this extreme position, the mother shows herself as a victim crippled by society, who in turn victimizes and oppresses her daughter. And of course we may expect the daughter, in her turn, to practice these tyrannies on her young.

The plot is a maze of illicit liaisons for which marriage and family are a thinly respectable facade. It ends with a final description of the servants' court: "When it thawed, the walls dripped with damp, and a stench arose from the little dark quadrangle. All the secret rottenness of each floor seemed fused in this stinking drain" (p. 452). A servant remarks: "Dear me, mademoiselle, if it's this hole or that hole it don't matter. All are pretty much alike. If you've been in one of 'em you've been in all. They're all pig-sties" (p. 454).

The novel condemns bourgeois morality and hypocrisy. The family, which is supposed to uphold the highest moral standards, does not serve this function at all. Though the family is a central element of their lives, its members have virtually no affection for one another and are continually trying to escape its oppressive bonds, at the same time that they cling to its emotionally lifeless form, for it is the societal justification of their moral code.

It is a code so rigid and hostile to all that is natural—all that is spontaneous in humanity—that it is completely unenforceable. In creating such rigid moral standards society becomes not a protector but an enemy of life, love, and honesty. Ideally, it is the family that provides order against external chaos, but to do so it must be allowed a degree of flexibility and naturalness. Too great rigidity in this, and indeed in all social institutions, itself engenders chaos. In Zola's novels this rigidity is shown as oppressing bourgeois and lower classes alike. Love and spontaneity reappear because these aspects of life cannot be eliminated, but they are garbed in their dark manifestations—as exploitive sexuality, brutal confrontations, violent outbursts—more disruptive, disorderly, and threatening to the social order than they would have been if allowed a proper place to begin with.

It seems that Zola, despite his claims of impartiality, has violated his own principle; success, harmony, and satisfaction have been eliminated as possibilities, if not because of external, then because of internal threats. If a family survives the brutalization of poverty and urban decay (and has had the luck to have escaped the ineluctable operation of bad heredity), it is still not assured escape, for then its very success may contribute to its downfall.

ZOLA'S THEMES

Of the Rougon-Macquart novels, *Germinal*, *Pot-Bouille*, and *L'Assommoir* contain the most explicit and fully expressed examples of the breakdown of family life, but there are many additional instances in the other novels of the series, covering all levels of society.[13] In almost every treatment of the family, Zola underscores two principal themes: the family is a central and necessary part of the social structure; at the same time it is corrupt and dissolute.

13. For example, the peasant family is treated in *The Earth*, the provincial bourgeois in *The Conquest of Plassans* and *The Joy of Living*, and the aristocratic family in *The Rush for the Spoils*.

The novel *Nana* (1880) suggests, perhaps, one reason why Zola assaults the family so brutally. The daughter of Gervaise and Coupeau, Nana comes from society's lower ranks; she disappears from their broken home at an early age and eventually becomes the most famous courtesan-prostitute of the Parisian demi-monde. Nana represents the powerful, creative, yet destructive force of sex. Men become obsessed by her because she incarnates a sexual desire and satisfaction that are not available to them in their marriages and families. She ruins men financially and morally, but she is not vicious; rather she is simply an unconscious force: "the actual woman remained as unconscious as a splendid animal, and in her ignorance of her mission was the good-natured courtesan to the last."[14]

Nana's function in her society and the symbolic importance given her in the novel offer an intriguing insight into the difficulties in which the institution of the family found itself. The society that Zola recreates is based on deception and inhumanity, its poor mercilessly exploited, hidden, and ignored. Indeed, Zola states that one of his main purposes for writing is to reveal the situation of the lower classes as objectively as possible.[15] But it is not only poverty that is hidden and disavowed in Zola's society; the restrictive bourgeois morality conceals and crushes all passion and spontaneous emotion. Zola seeks to reveal the hypocrisy of this code.

What is Nana? Who is this paradoxical, bewitching, dangerous, alluring woman? Nana represents two complex but related ideas: the dark unseen side of the social fabric and, at the same time, the spontaneous sexual nature in every human being. Zola calls her the "Golden Fly," for she comes from physical and moral filth, feeding upon it and carrying it to the polished world of the prosperous, where mere contact with her brings corruption and decay. Zola sees Nana as an ominous force that permeates the whole of society: "This was the epoch in her existence

---

14. *Nana*, trans. Victor Plarr (New York: Boni and Liveright, 1924), p. 32.

15. In the notes for *L'Assommoir*, Zola speaks of his intentions in writing the book: "To show the milieu of people and to explain their actions by this milieu. Without, however, drawing conclusions. Not to praise the worker or condemn him. An absolutely exact reality. A frightful picture which will contain its own moral."

when Nana flared upon Paris with redoubled splendour. She loomed larger than heretofore on the horizon of vice, and swayed the town with her impudently flaunted splendour" (p. 437). The ambivalence of this image of Nana, her simultaneous incarnation of darkness and glorious light—an image that we shall again encounter—is most explicit here.

A METAPHOR FOR THE DESTRUCTION OF A SOCIETY

Why, we must ask, do Nana and the dark forces she represents have such power over the family and society? It is perhaps that these forces gain uncontrollable power precisely because they are denied. In depth psychology, Jungian interpretation in particular, it is agreed that whenever an organism, individual, or institution attempts to repress or disown an integral part of its being, it is precisely this element that will grow disproportionately, eventually overcoming and destroying the more positive elements surrounding it. Nana comes from the abject poverty that is ignored or denied by the bourgeois and aristocrats. Her life energy stems from a full and spontaneous sexuality, also denied (yet at the same time desired) by these groups. Thus Nana's death represents the destruction of an entire epoch; the society is dying because it has refused to attend to its own ills, hypocritically denying the decadence and corruption represented by Nana and her kind. It has denied the brutalization of her humanity through physical misery and has, at the same time, denied itself the vitality of her looser moral code, overdone to be sure, but still less exclusive of life than their own. Nana dies in a Paris hotel, disfigured by a hideous disease, an obvious metaphor for the fall of Paris to the Germans:

Venus was rotting. It seemed as though the poison she had assimilated in the gutters, and on the carrion tolerated by the roadside, the leaven with which she had poisoned a whole people, had but now remounted to her face and turned it to corruption.

The room was empty. A great despairing breath came up from the boulevard, and swelled the curtain.

"To Berlin! To Berlin! To Berlin!" [p. 504]

But just before this conclusion, Zola dwells on the deteriorated vision of Nana's corpse, using her body not as metaphor for a social epoch, but for nature itself. Subtly, the image carries a different message and mood, shading from battlefield, through mud, to earth itself. It is earth and the natural in its most chaotic, vegetative, formless manifestation. Life is represented here in its conventionally repulsive side. Yet it is natural processes being mentioned: mucous, scabs, boils, processes by which the body cleanses and cures itself. Societies, it seems, do not have similar mechanisms for renewal:

Nana was left alone, with upturned face in the light cast by the candle. She was fruit of the charnel-house, a heap of matter and blood, a shovel-ful of corrupted flesh thrown down on the pillow. The pustules had invaded the whole of the face, so that each touched its neighbor. Fading and sunken, they had assumed the greyish hue of mud, and on that formless pulp, where the features had ceased to be traceable, they already resembled some decaying damp from the grave. One eye, the left eye, had completely foundered among bubbling purulence, and the other, which remained half open, looked like a deep black ruinous hole. The nose was still suppurating. Quite a reddish crust was peeling from one of the cheeks, and invading the mouth, which it distorted into a horrible grin. [p. 504]

The extended passage is composed of imagery that is ugly, befouled, seemingly utterly dead, diseased, and hopeless, but then Zola inserts one glimpse of redemption: "And over this loathsome and grotesque mask of death, the hair, the beautiful hair, still blazed like sunlight and flowed downwards in rippling gold" (p. 505).

Here he shows us Nana's light, significantly retained in her hair, that indestructible part of the body which cannot die, for it retains its luster even when the rest of the organism is decayed. Hair is a complex symbol used for many meanings, fertility, sexuality, animality, and Zola has used it this way before, to suggest not only nature but the regenerative properties of nature. It is in cemeteries, enriched by corpses, that grass grows in abundance:

This rich soil where grave-diggers could no longer dig without over-turning scraps of human bodies, was incredibly fertile. From the road, after the May rains and the June sunshine, you could see the top of the grass which grew up over the walls; inside it was a sea of dark green, deep, enlivened by large flowers of singular brightness. [*La Fortune des Rougon*, p. 5]

So it is we come full circle. Life continues and social institutions rot and die; nature renews itself. Love precedes death but in turn is followed by rebirth. Nana, like a part of any organism that is sickened, poisons the entire system, although, ironically enough, to begin with she was a natural creature and was poisoned by her contact with society. Zola has used Nana to make one of his strongest statements about social evolution and natural laws working themselves out in society. The family, in this context, is essential but flawed, even a danger to its own members.

ATTEMPTS AT PORTRAYING IDEAL LOVE AND HAPPY FAMILY LIFE

Did Zola create any optimistic pictures of family life or love? He tried to do so a few times. In *The Dream* (1888) he sets out to weave a tale of delicate ideal love but creates instead a fantasy so heavy and cloying that it is difficult to believe it could have been written by an author of his talent and stature.[16] In *Doctor Pascal* (1893), the last novel in the series, Zola presents a happy couple. Their financial situation is not a threat to their marriage and they have genuine love for each other. Alas, the book is one of the least artistically successful novels of the series. Zola seems unable to bring the characters and their love to life.[17]

Zola may have failed to create successful pictures of happy family life and marital love because such situations did not seem real to him. Apparently he could not create what did not emerge naturally from the social scene he knew. In his novels he seems to have reflected society, and one is tempted to suggest that his

16. Reviewing the novel, Anatole France said: "Furthermore, I admit that Zola's purity seemed meritorious. It cost him dear—he paid for it with all of his talent." Quoted in Zola, *Oeuvres Complètes*, Cercle du livre précieux (Paris, 1966), 5:1324.

17. Claude Roy says of *Le Docteur Pascal:* "The writing becomes banal and flat, the style stiffens with clichés, the characters become mannequins. . . ." "Le Génie de l'amour sublime," *Zola*, Collections Génies et Réalités (Paris: Hachette, 1969), p. 168.

immense popularity attests to the accuracy of the world he created. Directly and indirectly his novels state that in his society the family with integrity was something of a rarity. Zola indicts, as both cause and consequence, the entire social and moral mentality of his epoch. He seems to be saying that it is impossible for families at the lower end of the social structure to withstand the burdens in a society that ignores social justice. Families disintegrate under the pressures of hunger, cold, dirt, alcoholism, violence, and lethargy, and the disintegration itself adds to society's problems. We are led to believe that in previous centuries, when the family was embedded in the community, it received important material and moral support from the social structure, and in return, bolstered the structure. In Zola's world, such support has been lost.

The families of the lower classes are not the only casualties of the social attitudes Zola depicts. Bourgeois and aristocratic families are also menaced morally, if not physically. Just as Zola's society refuses to acknowledge any physical conditions not in harmony with the bourgeois adage of *enrichissez-vous* (get rich), so it condemns any human urge that endangers the facade of rigid morality designed to hold the family together. It is an oppressive morality that condemns the spontaneous and natural, and the family is its vehicle. Ironically, then, the family brings about its own breakdown. In upholding a morality that is false and applied only superficially, the family becomes corrupt. To remain a viable institution morally, the family must avoid extremes, neither encouraging too much restraint nor allowing too much laxity. The nineteenth-century family that Zola portrays fosters both of these extremes by professing a morality that allows for almost no natural urges and tacitly condoning the violation of its own rules.

In chapter one of this book Philippe Ariès remarks that "the real roots of the present domestic crisis lie not in our families but in our cities." He refers to the stress on the twentieth-century family as it tries to satisfy many of the needs that in the nineteenth century were fulfilled by social intercourse in a more public domain. Undoubtedly he has focused on a major underlying cause for the difficulties of the contemporary family, and he may be accurate in placing the origin outside the family structure itself. My reading of Zola's works, however, suggests that the problems of the family pointed out by Ariès were already acute, in Zola's view, during the last half of the nineteenth century and that they seem to stem from both the family itself and the social order. The picture of the family given by Zola in the Rougon-Macquart novels indicates that, in the case of the poor, whether rural or urban, the family gives no protection to the individual against the ills of the social order, while the bourgeois or aristocratic family is so morally repressive in its very nature that it causes its own breakdown. Ideally, the family should serve both the individual and society, for it socializes the individual and at the same time upholds the social moral order. In Zola's view, the French family of the mid-nineteenth century, beset by economic and moral problems, was no longer capable of performing these necessary functions.

8

The Changing Image of the American Jewish Mother

Beverly Gray Bienstock

The Jewish Mother—gossipy, plump, overprotective of her children, obsessed with the healing powers of chicken soup—is an American cultural stereotype of wide currency, a familiar figure in novels, movies, advertisements, comic strips, and comedians' monologues. Although many non-Jews can find in the Jewish Mother points of resemblance to their own mothers and grandmothers, the implication in literature and the popular media is that Jewish Mothers belong to a separate and unique species, a view that appears to be shared by a number of social scientists. The sociologist Zena Smith Blau, for one, suggests that the child-rearing methods of immigrant Jewish mothers in this country have significantly contributed to their children's remarkable educational and occupational achievements.[1] Matthew Besdine, a clinical psychologist, attributes the high mean IQ and low mortality rate of children born to Jewish immigrants to the positive effects of Jewish mothering.[2] Sociologist Pauline Bart, who has studied the neuroses suffered by middle-aged women once their children no longer need them, takes a less optimistic view of Jewish child-rearing practices, asserting that, when various ethnic groups are compared statisti-

1. Zena Smith Blau, "In Defense of the Jewish Mother," *Midstream* 13 (February 1967): 42–49.
2. Matthew Besdine, "Jewish Mothering," *Jewish Spectator* 35 (February 1970): 7–10.

cally, Jewish women are found to be the most intensely traumatized by the loss of the maternal role. Bart thinks that this is due to their widespread tendency to overprotect their children and that women belonging to other ethnic groups suffer an equal degree of role-loss only when their child-rearing patterns approach those of the Jewish mothers. Bart's conclusion neatly coincides with the old saw, "You don't have to be Jewish to be a Jewish mother, but it helps."[3] The importance of Bart's study lies in its focus on the long-range effects of different types of mothering, a subject of fundamental consequence to Jews and non-Jews alike.

My concern, however, is not with the sociological facts of Jewish motherhood, but with the *image* of the Jewish Mother as shaped by writers from the turn of the century to the present. While the current notoriety of the Jewish Mother stems from her featured comic role in best sellers and popular media, in the not-too-distant past she was simply an immigrant wife and parent, of interest to no one but her immediate family and the ethnic community in which she made her home. Clearly her wider reputation was molded by the daughters and particularly the sons who grew up to write books and plays about her, disseminating an image that has left its imprint on American culture as a whole. Remarkably, in the course of a few generations, that image has totally reversed itself: the heroic Jewish Mother of the early immigrant literature has in later works become a maternal vampire.

To explain this astonishing metamorphosis, one may look, of course, to the Jewish immigrant family's painful adaptation to American life.[4] The move from Eastern Europe to the ethnic ghettos of New York and other large cities produced major changes in the traditional Jewish domestic roles: the mother assumed new prominence in the family but also came to repre-

3. Pauline B. Bart, "Depression in Middle-aged Women," in *Woman in Sexist Society: Studies in Power and Powerlessness*, ed. Vivian Gornick and Barbara K. Moran (New York: Basic Books, 1971), p. 109. Bart has published similar findings under the title, "Mrs. Portnoy's Complaint."

4. A similar approach is taken by Charlotte Baum, Paula Hyman, and Sonya Michel in *The Jewish Woman in America* (New York: Dial Press, 1976); their conclusions differ somewhat from mine.

sent the status quo against which her sons must later revolt. Psychologists might argue that the son's rejection of his mother is a classic behavioral pattern common to most cultures. My interest here is in the rather concentrated literary manifestations of such rebellion as they appear in Jewish works of the 1930s through the 1960s. If the Jewish Mother as she appears in literature is less a mirroring of reality than a selective interpretation of that reality, the writer becomes as important as the subject matter; thus in studying the changing image of the Jewish Mother I am most concerned with the changing attitudes of those who write about her. There are some dangers in this, to be sure. An author is not identical with a protagonist: Alexander Portnoy, in his deeply felt complaint against his upbringing, should never be confused with Philip Roth. And yet it seems fair to note that virtually all works containing Jewish Mothers view these women from the perspective of the growing (or grown) child, generally the son. In terms of generation, gender, and basic life style, the writers all appear to identify with the child rather than with the parent.

THE IMMIGRANT PERIOD (1880–1929)

Although some Jews had lived in the United States since colonial times, it was not until the huge influx of Eastern European Jews after 1880 that American Jewish literature really began.[5] The tightening of immigration laws in the mid-1920s drastically reduced the number of new arrivals, but for literary purposes the immigrant period can be seen as extending to the last year of that decade. Most Jewish authors between 1880 and 1929 wrote works reflecting their personal experiences as immigrants, and many revealed the upheaval in Jewish family life. In the old country, the roles of husband and wife had been clearly defined, based largely on their religious obligations: the husband's chief duty was to serve God through prayer and ritual, while his wife

5. We should remember that the Jews who immigrated at the turn of the century were generally poor people from the villages and towns of Russia and Eastern Europe. They had little contact with the much smaller group of German Jews who had arrived some fifty years earlier and were by now firmly entrenched in the American middle class.

ran the household in accordance with Jewish law. In the Jewish *shtetel*, male piety and religious scholarship were so highly honored that a wife sometimes undertook to support the family by running a small business. This left her husband free to read the holy books, more than making up for his lack of earning power by the prestige that he brought to his family and himself. In America there was little room for the Old World Talmudist. Forced to find work as a peddler or sweatshop laborer, he suffered a tremendous loss of dignity and self-esteem. In the meantime his wife, long trained in the practical art of making ends meet, effectively ran the household, always maintaining a humble acceptance of the male prerogative.

Anzia Yezierska's semi-autobiographical *Bread Givers* (1925) reveals a common pattern: the first-generation housewife constitutes her family's emotional and even economic backbone, but she remains in awe of her husband's learning and supports his waning authority. Sholem Asch's *The Mother*, first published in 1925, chronicles the expansion of the female's sphere of responsibility along with the orthodox male's fall in prestige. As in so many novels of this period, the father of the family is a devout man unfit for the labor market. He takes a sweatshop job, but only over his wife's heartfelt objections. This wife and mother is the true center of Asch's novel: in her total dedication to the needs of others, in her self-denial and her practical ability to coax forth meals from her "magic pots," she gives her family the strength it needs to survive. When her own life ebbs, she will transmit to her daughter her own loving and all-protective spirit so that the family circle can be preserved intact.

Asch's immigrant mother figure, in her staunch support of traditional family values, conforms closely to the sentimental Old World image of the Yiddishe Momma.[6] In another enormously popular work of the period, Samson Raphaelson's

---

6. The *shtetel* image of the self-sacrificing "Yiddishe Momma" is discussed by Mark Zborowski and Elizabeth Herzog in *Life Is with People: The Jewish Little-Town of Eastern Europe* (New York: International Universities Press, 1952), pp. 293–94. In America this image was furthered through Jacob Gordin's immensely popular Yiddish drama, *Mirele Efros*, sometimes called the *Jewish Queen Lear*. The sentimental hit song "My Yiddishe Momma" (by Yellen and Pollack) was introduced by Sophie Tucker in 1925.

Broadway play *The Jazz Singer* (1925), this sentimentalizing continues, but here the mother is less a preserver of the old ways than a mediator between two conflicting systems of values. *The Jazz Singer* pits a son with show business aspirations against a pious father who expects his Jakie to follow in his own footsteps as a cantor. The mother fills a key intermediary role: her intense loyalty to her husband forbids her to condone her son's behavior but, as the practical member of the household, she can appreciate Jack's newfound material success. A fundamental difference between father and mother is underscored by the gifts Jack brings them: "For a mama diamonds, and for a papa a praying shawl."[7] Ultimately it is the mother who pleads with Jack to take the place of his dying father at Yom Kippur services. In the play, Jack's deeply buried religious feelings emerge at last, and he sacrifices his Broadway debut for the world of his fathers. But the Al Jolson film (1927) ends differently, with Jack fulfilling his commitment to his father by simply postponing the Broadway opening. The final sequence shows Mama beaming proudly from a stage box as her son performs his Mammy routines to loud acclaim. Here, in applauding Jack's secular performance, the mother has tacitly chosen her son's way of life over that of her husband. By implication, the father's Old World values are seen as self-defeating. It is the mother, with her common sense and her greater willingness to adapt to American standards, who serves her children best.

THE 1930S

The Depression era confirmed the direction in which the Jewish family was tending. In the face of economic disaster, the simple daily need to put food on the table necessarily took precedence over spiritual obligations, and traditional piety was increasingly displaced by the practical virtues associated with the Jewish Mother. While the values within the home were shifting, so were the roles of its occupants, with America affecting all of them differently. American-born, American-bred children of immigrants, now grown to young adulthood in large numbers, began

7. Samson Raphaelson, *The Jazz Singer* (New York: Brentano's, 1925), p. 55.

to feel caught between two worlds. Job discrimination, college quotas, and other types of de facto anti-Semitism kept them from entering fully into the mainstream of American society, and yet the ways of their ancestors appeared to them unattractively foreign. For some of these young people the left-wing movements of the 1930s provided a chance to participate in American life along with a means of protesting the abuses of the American system. Their alliance with members of the political and artistic avant-garde also served as an effective form of rebellion against their parents' circumscribed life style.[8] Carrying their personal rebellion into their literary works, vigorously attacking the status quo, many young Jewish writers of this second generation condemned the Jewish family of their own day for its bourgeois aspirations. Since the mother was so consistently regarded as the true head of the household and since she was identified so completely with material as opposed to spiritual interests, it was she who was singled out by her writer-sons as an agent of American capitalism. Ironically, a woman who might well have been active in the early days of the American labor movement came to be seen through her children's eyes as a reactionary figure because of her primary concern with her family's physical well-being.

Michael Gold's *Jews Without Money* is a rare product of the thirties in that it exalts its mother figure without reservation. This thinly fictionalized autobiography, published in 1930, turns back the clock to Gold's Lower East Side childhood and casts his mother in the role of proletarian martyr. *Jews Without Money* abounds with tributes to her vitality and her devotion: "She would have stolen or killed for us. She would have let a railroad train run over her body if it could have helped us. She loved us with all the fierce painful love of a mother-wolf, and scolded us

8. This is not to imply that first-generation Jews were politically conservative. A number of them were dedicated socialists and played leadership roles in the struggle for trade unionism. It can be said, however, that their activities had a heavily ethnic flavor: they were not comfortable outside the circle of their fellow Yiddish-speaking Jews. By contrast the activists of the second generation rejected narrow distinctions based on ethnic origin and prided themselves on their international outlook.

continually like a magpie."[9] In his mother's example, Gold feels he has found his life's work: "Mother! Momma! I am still bound to you by the cords of birth. I cannot forget you. I must remain faithful to the poor because I cannot be faithless to you!" (p. 158). Gold sees his own intense Marxism as a direct outgrowth of his mother's spirit. But in a sense *Jews Without Money* chronicles his movement away from her values, for his belief in the rise of the masses has supplanted her faith in the Jewish messiah; he cannot continue to worship her gods. Despite Gold's genuine love and respect for his mother, he is not bound by her outlook. His own commitments serve instead to estrange him from her values and her world.

Like Gold, Clifford Odets, whose *Awake and Sing!* was first staged in 1935, is writing under the influence of the Communist party. And like Gold he deals with a young man who moves beyond his family circle and takes a stand against the bourgeoisie. But Odets's play differs from Gold's book in that Gold, looking back to his ghetto childhood, saw his own pragmatic mother as a working-class heroine, while Odets, depicting a contemporary family in the Bronx, creates a mother made grotesque by her material concerns. Now *she* has come to represent the bourgeois status quo against which her son must rebel. *Awake and Sing!* crystallizes the pattern that much American Jewish literature will follow. In the Berger household, the father seems almost not to exist. Thirty years a haberdashery clerk, he has long relinquished to his wife the role of family head. Bessie Berger's strengths include shrewdness, common sense, and a great love of life, but her fear of poverty and her commitment to the values of the middle class make her intolerant and sometimes cruel. Thus she coolly marries off her pregnant daughter to a meek young man with good prospects. From her son Ralph she expects not learning or piety but dazzling financial success. Her reaction to Ralph's fiancée is typical:

Bessie: A girl like that he wants to marry. A skinny consumptive-looking . . . six months already she's not working—taking charity from an aunt. You should see her. In a year she's dead on his hands.

9. Michael Gold, *Jews Without Money* (New York: International Publishers, 1930), p. 158.

Ralph: You'd cut her throat if you could.

Bessie: That's right! Before she'd ruin a nice boy's life I would first go to prison. Miss Nobody should step in the picture and I'll stand by with my mouth shut.

Ralph: Miss Nobody! Who Am I? Al Jolson?

Bessie: Fix your tie![10]

Michael Gold had spoken of his mother as ready to kill to uphold the family welfare. Bessie expresses much the same sentiment, but so tied is she to purely mercenary values that her courage seems less noble than monstrous. She is not a thoroughgoing monster; we see her in moments of tenderness and regret. Nevertheless, because of a wrongheaded commitment to the capitalist system, she is destroying the dreams of others.

Odets's play depicts a mother who verges on caricature. In her strength and her materialistic drive she represents all that is wrong with America; Ralph, by rejecting her values, creates hope for America's future. Other works treating the contemporary scene, however, have less hopeful conclusions. Typically they retain the Jewish Mother as a symbol of bourgeois materialism, but show the son as coming to surpass her in his headlong race toward success. Such a work is Jerome Weidman's popular novel, *I Can Get It for You Wholesale* (1937), featuring a young man on the make in the New York garment industry. Much of Harry Bogen's ambition derives from his memories of a lower-class upbringing. In contrast to his father, who remained a flunky all his life, he will dedicate himself to "the best and quickest way to make money."[11] Harry's mother speaks reverently of her late husband, and yet we see her tacitly endorsing Harry's chosen path. When he brings home large rolls of cash, she rewards him with blintzes and calls him a good boy. "You're making it in a nice way?" she asks, but she accepts his evasive explanation by saying, "Maybe it's better I shouldn't worry. I'm sure if it's your business, Heshie, it must be nice" (p. 89). Mama's basic appreciation of the things that money can buy seems clearly to have helped in molding Harry's own values.

10. Clifford Odets, *Awake and Sing!* in *Masters of Modern Drama*, ed. Haskell M. Block and Robert G. Shedd (New York: Random House, 1962), p. 656.

11. Jerome Weidman, *I Can Get It for You Wholesale* (New York: Simon and Schuster, 1937), p. 97.

But Mama Bogen is not solely a materialist, nor will she condone her son's every act. Initially she had delighted in Harry's expensive presents, but she comes to question his unscrupulous methods. What we see here is a son who accepts and then moves beyond his mother's expectations. She believes in both money and morality; he is only concerned with the former. In the novel's last pages, we are prepared for the belated severing of the umbilical cord. Although he has always been remarkably dependent upon his mother's love and approval, Harry now takes steps to establish a life of his own. Henceforth Mama's weekly allowance will be cut back so that he can dangle diamonds in front of a svelte *shikse*. Here a mother who has infused her son with her own materialism discovers that he has left her far behind.

Relationships of this sort within second-generation immigrant families have been studied by Franz Alexander, head of the Institute for Psychoanalysis at the University of Chicago. He concludes that the father's household role indeed diminishes in the course of the immigrant experience, and that the father's inability to cope with his new environment causes the family to transfer to the American-born son its hopes for its future welfare. These findings point to an intimate tie between familial affections and economic goals, with the mother in particular bestowing the full force of her approval on the person most likely to succeed. So it happens that "the son usurps the father's place in the mother's affections as well as in economic importance and acquires an inordinate ambition. He wants to justify all his mother's hopes and sacrifices and thus appease his guilty conscience about his father. He can only do this by becoming successful at whatever cost."[12] Alexander is hinting here that the source of the son's aspirations is a nascent proto-erotic link between his mother and himself. Such a link has been suggested by Henry Roth's brilliant *Call It Sleep* (1934), in which the

12. Franz Alexander, *Our Age of Unreason: A Study of the Irrational Forces in Social Life*, rev. ed. (New York: J. B. Lippincott, 1951), p. 198. Pages 197–201 also contain pertinent insights into the immigrant family. Alexander specifically praises the accuracy of Budd Schulberg's *What Makes Sammy Run?* (1941), a novel much like *I Can Get It for You Wholesale* in its portrayal of a ruthlessly ambitious second-generation Jewish son.

relationship between father, mother, and son is classically Oedi-pal.[13] The question of mother-son eroticism also looks ahead to the notorious novels of the 1960s.

The Jewish writers of the Depression era are, in general, less concerned with the erotic bond between mother and son than with the purely economic one. As a common-sense matriarch, the Jewish Mother inspires her son to become a model of success-ful assimilation by pursuing monetary goals. Increasingly the writers of this period, caught up in left-wing movements and the need to cast off their own family ties, protest against what they see as her bourgeois values. They do this by showing the son either in a state of rebellion or bent on surpassing his mother in terms of material greed. No writer of the thirties paints the Jewish Mother as wholly monstrous. Her intentions certainly are always good. But in leading her sons to worship at the altar of Mammon, she is guilty of a sin that these writers cannot forgive.

THE POSTWAR YEARS

By the end of World War II, the Jewish writer was coming to be accepted as a full-fledged member of the American literary estab-lishment. The defeat of Hitler (and, later, the founding of the state of Israel) made the American public receptive to Jewish authors and Jewish subject matter as never before: Norman Mailer, Irwin Shaw, and other writers returned from the United States Army with wartime novels that received nationwide acclaim. Meanwhile members of an earlier generation continued to write about the Jewish family. No longer young rebels, these writers now commonly approached their Jewish heritage with

13. Henry Roth, *Call It Sleep* (New York: Cooper Square, 1934). This novel, set in the year 1907, is too special a work to fit neatly into any paradigm. Its father figure is distinctive in that he is not at all weak in the usual sense. Instead Albert Schearl is an aggressive, even violent man who inspires fear and loathing in his only son. Still, it is possible to see Albert as acting out of a sense of disorientation common to immigrant males. His gentle wife Genya, mean-while, makes the home an oasis of love and security for young David. Thus in David's mind, at least, she has replaced her husband as the effective head of the household. The relationship between mother and son is a rich one, but seems to hold psychological dangers for the growing boy. If the book is seen in this light, the pattern I have been tracing is preserved.

more detachment and less emotional fervor. Their treatment of the Jewish Mother would seem to follow one of three paths: comic condescension, nostalgic exaltation, or Freudian alarm.

The first of these tendencies can be illustrated by the ethnic sketches of Arthur Kober in the *New Yorker*. Kober's writing career began in the 1930s. While other, more serious writers were engaged in social protest, he entertained his readers with comic tales of the Gross family and its frantic assault upon the middle class. The distance between Kober and his characters is self-evident: he feels nothing but tolerant amusement for the status-conscious daughter, her accountant boyfriend, and her parents with their fractured English. But again, the mother is automatically linked to material concerns. In her eagerness to see her daughter well mated, she pooh-poohs a cheap engagement ring, rejects the accountant as not prosperous enough, and tries to lure a reluctant suitor with visions of "a beyoodyful home with a beyoodyful cabnet radio and victrolleh."[14]

Kober's *Parm Me* (1945), a collection of *New Yorker* pieces, opens with a revealing dedication entitled "And to You, Dear Mother" in which he reminisces about his childhood in East Harlem, and about a mother who cared for a chronically sick husband and five children while running a dry goods store. Unlike Michael Gold, Kober does not sentimentalize his mother, but instead pokes fun at the pretensions she has acquired in the wake of his own public triumphs. Mrs. Kober now serves tea in fragile cups rather than heavy glasses, and her well-worn shawl "has been replaced by a mink coat (fency-schmency!) that she proudly wears because it represents, to her, the most tangible evidence of the success of her son's play" (p. vi). Whatever gratitude Kober may feel toward his mother is concealed beneath a flippant tone. In terms of education and prestige he has so far surpassed her that she now exists for him as an object for comic exploitation. Out of this attitude comes the Jewish Mother as a source of humor, as the familiar butt of the Jewish joke.

The journalist and historian Charles Angoff views the Jewish immigrant past with nostalgic exaltation. In his novel *Journey to the Dawn* (1951) he uses memories of his own childhood to paint a

14. Arthur Kober, *Parm Me* (London: Constable, 1945), p. 53.

glowing picture of the Jewish mother and grandmother. Alte Bobbe, the benevolent matriarch of a large extended family, nurses the sick, solves personal problems, and makes ends meet in times of financial strain. When her sons find themselves caught between their religious duties and their need to provide for a growing family, it is she they turn to for common-sense advice. In writing of the heroic Alte Bobbe, Angoff is looking back to a somewhat romanticized version of his past. His feelings toward the maternal figure resemble those of Michael Gold, but he has considerably prettified his picture of ghetto life. This tendency toward nostalgia can be seen in the memoirs of other successful men, such as Alfred Kazin's *A Walker in the City* (1951). Kazin too, peering back through the rosy mists of memory, pays tribute to the mother's saving dignity and strength.

A third trend involves a more skeptical view of the mother's influence on her sons. Samuel Ornitz, a novelist versed in psychology and sociology, published *Bride of the Sabbath* in this same year, 1951. Ornitz's novel, set in the immigrant period, depicts a young boy so overwhelmed by the devotion of his mother and grandmother that he is later unprepared for adult love. The mature Saul Kramer is loved and mothered by three very different young women, but cannot fully respond to any of them. When he marries a pregnant dancer, his dreams fuse her with his mother's memory: "My mother was in labor, but you were my mother."[15] None of Saul's three lovers, however, seems capable of a happy maternal experience. For Saul, only orthodox Jewish women like the one who bore him can come to know the joyous side of motherhood. This story of a son who is unable to move beyond his mother, unable to sever the umbilical cord, points forward to the equally neurotic heroes of Bruce Jay Friedman and Philip Roth in the next decade. These authors too will be less concerned with the Jewish Mother's materialism than with her stunting of her son's emotional life.

THE 1960s

It was during the 1960s that the Jewish Mother became an integral part of the American scene. So ubiquitous was she in

15. Samuel Ornitz, *Bride of the Sabbath* (New York: Rinehart, 1951), p. 383.

literature and popular media that social scientists began to study her habits. Meanwhile Jewish community leaders felt required to plead eloquently in her defense, and real-life Jewish Mothers deplored the ways in which her notoriety reflected on them. But the general public, oblivious to all of this debate, continued to enjoy the Jewish Mother's contribution to latter-day American folk humor.

The motivations of the writers of the 1960s are complex. Well-educated and well-entrenched in American life, they found a wide range of subject matter open to them. Yet many returned to the Jewish Mother, revealing in their treatment of her a continuing effort to detach themselves from her values and her expectations. This implies a special sort of identity crisis at work. The sixties, like the thirties, was a period of revolt against the bourgeois status quo; it was also a period in which ethnicity was rediscovered and reaffirmed. Among the younger intellectuals, it was now deemed chic to be a member of an oppressed minority group. By this time, however, Jews were no longer visibly oppressed—and in literary circles, at least, they were no longer a strict minority. In point of fact, they themselves were now the status quo, and none too happy about it. In the face of this, the Jewish writer of the third literary generation evolved a new strategy. It entailed blaming the mother for fostering the traits of which he himself feels ashamed. By turning the Jewish Mother into a comic monster he assuages his guilt feelings about his own material success as well as his own chosen estrangement from his ethnic and familial roots. At the same time, the Jewish Mother's comic aspects allow the Jewish writer to fulfill the public's sense of him as an entertainer. Following in the old tradition of the Jewish vaudeville comics and of such popular humorists as Arthur Kober, he amuses the world at large while exorcising his private ghosts.

A prime example of the Jewish Mother's new comic visibility is Dan Greenburg's *How to Be a Jewish Mother* (1964). This little book, which went through six printings in one year, gives tongue-in-cheek instructions in such techniques as Making Guilt Work and How to Act When He Finally Becomes Engaged. A Last Word by the Author's Mother predictably combines pride, indignation, concern with upward mobility, and the slightly mangled syntax we have come to expect of her: "So you've read his book and, God willing, enjoyed it. Do I have to tell you how proud a mother would be of a son like that? I don't. Now maybe he'll give up all this foolishness and go into a worthwhile profession."[16] Greenburg's book capitalizes on the public's amused familiarity with the Jewish Mother stereotype. Although he tells us at the outset that "you don't have to be either Jewish or a mother to be a Jewish mother,"[17] his comedy would be lost if his readers were approaching his subject without preconceptions. As Greenburg depicts the Jewish Mother, she is fairly benign, not potentially harmful; she may embarrass her children by clinging too close, but they are not permanently stunted by her mothering. Neither, however, does Greenburg suggest that there is any advantage in being the offspring of a Jewish Mother. It is simply something one endures, like influenza. Greenburg's book, it appears, is written less out of hostility than affectionate good humor. Still, as in the case of Arthur Kober, there is the sense of the grown-up child condescending toward his mother and his upbringing for the sake of a few belly laughs.

Among the recognized novelists who have lately dealt with the Jewish Mother, Bruce Jay Friedman and Philip Roth stand preeminent. In their writings, the son's ambivalent need to assert his independence of his mother is explored with comic gusto. Much of the controversy surrounding these works stems from the fact that the erotic bond between mother and son, hinted at by Franz Alexander and distinguishable between the lines of *Bride of the Sabbath* and *Call It Sleep*, is now for the first time brought into the open. The Jewish Mother of Roth and Friedman is not merely materialistic and overprotective: in withdrawing her affections from her husband and lavishing them on her son, she effectively curbs the son's movement toward manhood. The sixties had made a virtue of candor in all aspects of life. Taking full advantage of their new verbal freedom, Roth and

16. Dan Greenburg, *How to Be a Jewish Mother: A Very Lovely Training Manual* (Los Angeles: Price, Stern, Sloan, 1964), p. 99.

17. Greenburg, p. 11. See also Mell Lazarus's syndicated comic strip "Momma," in which the leading character is given an Anglo-Saxon name although her manner is recognizably that of a Jewish Mother.

Friedman detail the son's thwarted sexuality in order to probe, to shock, and to amuse.

Bruce Jay Friedman, best known as a magazine humorist and comic playwright, has treated the Jewish Mother in *A Mother's Kisses* (1964), a novel marked by a hip crossbreeding of psychological observation and outrageous black humor. When Joseph, a hapless fellow from Brooklyn, sets out for the college his mother has chosen for him, she leaves behind her meek husband and drab daughter in order to help him adjust. Although Joseph still requires mothering, he is obsessed with sex, and his mother compounds his anxieties by dwelling on her own voluptuous charms. Her favorite tactic involves picturing herself in sexual jeopardy, thus arousing in Joseph the need for heroic action to protect her virtue. But she can also alienate him by making advances that border on the sexual, suggesting they hold hands in movies and rewarding his heroics with special kisses: "They were wide, and gurgling, and had some suck to them. As he received each one, he felt as though a large, freshly exposed, open-meloned internal organ had washed against his face."[18] At long last, Joseph's virulent outburst sends his mother packing. But his ambivalence continues: only when the noise of the departing train covers his words does he shout after her, "I never enjoyed one second with you" (p. 286). Joseph seems to take no pleasure in his impending liberation from his mother's kisses. Is he recalling perhaps that he has never enjoyed one second *without* her?

Friedman's funny but appalling tale of motherly love is far too exaggerated to ring wholly true. Nor, surely, was it meant to. On an intellectual level we can regard Friedman as using comic hyperbole to convey the ambiguous bond between mother and son. Though the work is narrated in the third person, we can even view the mother's behavior as colored by her son's frenzied imagination. Still, the outrageous extension of the by-now-familiar caricature, compounded by the grossness of this mother's sexuality, remains somewhat distasteful. It is tempting

18. Bruce Jay Friedman, *A Mother's Kisses* (New York: Simon and Schuster, 1964), p. 181.

to speak of *A Mother's Kisses* as a supremely bitter example of the writer-son looking back in anger and responding with venom.

Similar charges, of course, have long been leveled against Philip Roth. Roth is so often seen as having maligned Jewish motherhood that his name is now anathema in some segments of the Jewish community. Roth, however, steadily maintains that *Portnoy's Complaint* is not autobiographical and not a condemnation of the Jewish Mother as such. He admits, certainly, to having scrutinized his own family ties.[19] But *Portnoy's Complaint* (1969) evolved from a decision to flesh out the existing folklore that now surrounds the nice Jewish boy and his mother.[20]

Alexander Portnoy, although outwardly a mature and successful public figure, is in fact a first cousin to Friedman's self-doubting, self-obsessed Joseph. And Sophie Portnoy, like Joseph's mother, is a domineering, castrating, enticing, meddling, and thoroughly maddening monster who refuses her son a life of his own. In *A Mother's Kisses*, we as readers can presumably verify the facts of the mother's behavior as they occur. But, and this is a key distinction, we see the world of Portnoy's adolescence only as he himself now sees it: in retrospect. Thus all the hideous details concerning his mother have been filtered through his own neurotic mind. It is significant that Portnoy sometimes catches himself recalling that he enjoyed his childhood. Only now on the psychoanalyst's couch does this young man who has dabbled in Freud and pop sociology come to seek in his parents the blame for his own lack of self-respect. Roth himself puts it this way: "Portnoy is less oppressed by these people—who have little real say in his life anyway—than he is imprisoned by the rage that persists against them."[21] Thus it is Portnoy, not Roth, who looks back in anger. It is Portnoy who is in revolt against his

19. Philip Roth, "Writing and the Powers That Be," in *Reading Myself and Others* (New York: Farrar, Straus and Giroux, 1975), p. 9. Roth goes on to say here, "I have never really tried, through my work or directly in my life, to sever all that binds me to the world I came out of. I am probably right now as devoted to my origins as I ever was."

20. Roth, " 'How Did You Come to Write That Book, Anyway?' " in *Reading Myself and Others*, pp. 37–40.

21. Roth, "Writing and the Powers That Be," in *Reading Myself and Others*, p. 9.

heritage, a revolt complicated by his own guilty attachment to it.

The underlying cause of Portnoy's rebellion is lucidly sketched out by Alan Warren Friedman. He sees it as rooted in Portnoy's awareness that, despite his parents' total involvement in his life, he has not achieved the perfection he feels they expect of him. "The resulting guilt—the sense of having achieved nothing of substance (though thriving as the world measures these things) and the need to maintain the facade of success—leads, naturally enough, to his taking the offensive, to his evading introspection by accusing his parents of unforgivable acts."[22] In so doing, Portnoy automatically follows in the footsteps of other Jewish sons. True to the folklore that has existed since the mid-1930s, he casts the bulk of the blame on the Jewish Mother. What he dislikes in himself—his need to succeed, his paranoia, his longing for the Other in the form of the *shikse*—he accuses his mother of putting there.

Portnoy's Complaint, then, is not still another portrait of the Jewish Mother, but rather a brilliant study of the male mentality that has made the Jewish Mother an archetype of awesome proportions. Yet Roth has managed to have it both ways: while probing in all seriousness the Jewish Mother image, he has used its comic aspects to amuse those readers who want to be amused. In the folklore of modern America, the Jewish Mother is intrinsically funny. Portnoy on his couch exploits this source of humor, turning a plea for help into a nightclub comic's monologue. And Roth, too, is exploiting our sense of the mother as a comic monster: he plays her for laughs, though writing a serious book about her son's desperate manipulation of her image.

Looking backward we realize that the Jewish immigrants moved into the American mainstream with surprising speed. Their traditional stress on education and on social prestige helped them to adapt themselves remarkably well to the values of a new culture. Inevitably, children proved to be far more flexible than

22. Alan Warren Friedman, "The Jew's Complaint in Recent American Fiction: Beyond Exodus and Still in the Wilderness," *The Southern Review* 8 (Winter 1972): 57.

their parents; seeking success in American terms, these children learned to shrug off a whole network of traditions, beliefs, and relationships.[23] Yet an inheritance of this size cannot be cast away without guilt, and it may be guilt we see surfacing in much of the literature written by American Jews. Toward the mother the child feels most grateful, and consequently most guilty. Recalling the ruthless way in which he left her behind to pursue the American dream, he defends himself by converting her into a monster of motherhood. The modern Jewish writer perpetuates the Jewish Mother image in response to several complementary urges. In portraying her, he can draw upon his emotional ambivalence while intellectually exploring a current social phenomenon. Moreover, he can appeal both to those readers (Jews and non-Jews alike) whose guilt feelings mirror his own and to those who find in the Jewish Mother an unambiguous source of fun.

The development of the Jewish Mother as a negative stereotype brings to mind those other areas of twentieth-century life in which the mother has been singled out as the primary villain. Katharine M. Rogers, studying the history of misogyny in literature, notes that the excessively idealized nineteenth-century mother was bound to give way in our own more cynical age to her opposite. Granted that misogyny is, to some extent at least, a basic element in a male-dominated literary environment, it is no surprise that "the menace which earlier centuries attached to the devouring whore, ours attaches to the devouring mother."[24] Christopher Lasch's recent book on the family unit points to the common post–World War II assumption that schizophrenia is fostered by "Momism": "the psychological dominance of the mother in the modern middle-class family."[25] In *Of Woman Born*, Adrienne Rich poignantly explores the dilemma of the child-

23. Will Herberg makes some useful points along these lines in *Protestant-Catholic-Jew: An Essay in American Religious Sociology* (Garden City, N.Y.: Doubleday, 1955), pp. 7–58, 186–226.

24. Katharine M. Rogers, *The Troublesome Helpmate: A History of Misogyny in Literature* (Seattle: University of Washington Press, 1966), p. 264.

25. Christopher Lasch, *Haven in a Heartless World: The Family Besieged* (New York: Basic Books, 1977), p. 156.

bearing woman who is made to feel guilty for the whole act of procreation.[26] The common denominator in these works is an awareness that the mother-figure, once held in such high sentimental esteem, is increasingly being looked upon as flawed, and even downright dangerous. The scrutiny of the Jewish Mother, then, has value not only in terms of the impact of Americanization on one ethnic group, but also as a prime example of our current tendency to derogate the necessary—and profoundly meaningful—institution of motherhood.

26. Adrienne Rich, *Of Woman Born: Motherhood as Experience and Institution* (New York: W. W. Norton, 1976). This work covers much useful territory in delineating the mother's role in society past and present.

9

Images of the Family in the Mass Media: An American Iconography?

BILLIE JOYCE WAHLSTROM

Although we know how many television murders the average American child has seen by the time of graduation from high school (18,000) and how many commercials (350,000), we know really very little about images of the family in the mass media. We can count the viewers of a television series or commercial and identify them by sex, age, location, and buying habits, but we have not yet developed satisfactory methods for studying particular images in the popular media or assessing their impact. The problems in such a study are complex, not the least being the diversity of forms of the media. Mass-produced print media range from newspapers, magazines, and books to comics, greeting cards, t-shirts, advertising brochures, mail-order catalogs, labels, pinball-machines, billboards, paper napkins, and matchbooks. Non-print media include television, radio, records, tapes, and films of many kinds. Surrounding us in almost unlimited numbers and variety, with new ones by the hundreds added each day, mass-produced images assail us in our homes, streets, supermarkets, and at our recreation. Surely we should regard them as important subjects to be studied.[1]

1. The various ways that television, film, radio, and printed words affect people are being studied by a number of responsible media researchers and groups, for example, the President's Commission on Violence. This interest arises from figures such as the following: the average American reads a newspaper 52 minutes per day; ingests between 10,000 and 20,000 edited words per

It is not simply the sheer volume that gives these images their importance. Increasingly, scholars are turning their attention to what these images tell us about the culture that produces them and the people who consume them. Although we may have difficulty thinking of images in these secular settings as equivalent in American culture and mythic life to saints' images for Byzantine Christians or totemic representations for tribal peoples, a number of scholars today are suggesting these parallels. Spencer C. Bennett in an essay, "Christ, Icons, and Mass Media," sees a "new age of iconography":

In our new age of iconography we are strangely akin to the formality of Byzantine Christianity and the conceptions that go with it. The icons of those early days of faith were universal in implication, strong in outline but vague in the portrait of any one personality. . . . Both ages are the same in that they provide us with images and roles but not with individuality. The icons of the saints left much to be desired in terms of character portrayal but they leave no doubt as to the role the saint played in the life of the church.[2]

Values and roles are taught in many ways, of course, but some recent research testifies to the lasting impact of what Freud spoke of as "optical memory-residues" upon our consciousness.[3]

Modern critics are looking to art historian Erwin Panofsky, author of classic studies on Renaissance iconology, for ways of assessing twentieth-century images in mass culture. By insisting that iconography begin with identification of form and object, then concern itself with subject matter ("motif" and "concept"), and finally concentrate on the "deep meaning," the "symbolical value," of an image within the cultural context, Panofsky established a method for explaining an image in such a way that its

---

day; listens to radio about 1 1/4 hours per day (more if the person owns an FM radio); hears about 11,000 pre-processed words in the six hours the television set is on each day; and absorbs about 10,000 other words from billboards, bumper stickers, cereal boxes, and magazines. Alvin Toffler, *Future Shock* (New York: Bantam, 1971), p. 166.

2. Spencer C. Bennett, "Christ, Icons, and the Mass Media," in *Icons of Popular Culture*, ed. Marshall Fishwick and Ray B. Browne (Bowling Green, Ohio: Bowling Green University Press, 1970), p. 91.

3. Cited in Marshall Fishwick's essay, "Entrance," in Fishwick and Browne, p. 2.

meaning could be checked against meanings derived from historically related documents.[4] Recent theories of structuralism have helped legitimate the application of Panofsky's methodology to images in mass media. Structuralism's radically antihierarchical approach to history and society emphasizes the importance of the media, if as structuralist Hayden White asserts, "All cultural data have precisely the same value as evidence of a culture's fundamental form."[5] No one, certainly, can look at all the images put out by the mass media in a given year, let alone at all the images in the history of American mass media, but we can look for broad outlines and recurring patterns. Even if we look only in selected media for images that interest us, Panofsky's standards and structuralist principles suggest that such a limited study of frequent images would yield some evidence of the culture's fundamental form.

Several assumptions, then, underlie the current iconographical approach. First, the mass media are indexes of popular belief. For a long time, the media were criticized for their supposedly deleterious effect on American morality, sensibility, and way of life. Frederic Wertham's *Seduction of the Innocent* represents the criticism that blames popular media for bringing "chronic stimulation, temptation and seduction" into the American home.[6] But, as critical as we may be of some images the media give us, those images may come from and go directly to the heart of our culture. As Marshall McLuhan says in *The Mechanical Bride*, "Ours is the first age in which many thousands of the best-trained individual minds have made it a full-time business to get inside the collective public mind."[7] Mary Noel, a critic of popular literature, explains that, because a medium's survival depends on its ability to please its buyers, the medium reflects their concerns: "Because popular literature is a deliberate and success-

4. Erwin Panofsky, *Studies in Iconology: Humanistic Themes in the Art of the Renaissance* (New York: Oxford University Press, 1939), pp. 3–16.

5. Hayden White, "Structuralism in Popular Culture," *Journal of Popular Culture* 7, no. 4 (Spring 1974): 760.

6. Frederic Wertham, *Seduction of the Innocent* (New York: Rinehart, 1954), p. 10.

7. Marshall McLuhan, *The Mechanical Bride: Folklore of Industrial Man* (Boston: Beacon Press, 1967), p. v.

ful effort to please the people, it is perhaps as good an index to that elusive subject of popular opinion, tastes, and impressions as the historians can find. The very artificiality of its aims and methods makes it objective."[8]

Secondly, each culture has a unique configuration of what Erwin Panofsky and Ernst Cassirer call "symbolical values,"[9] articulated in a variety of cultural products, ranging from painting and literature to mass media. A culture develops this configuration through its internal processes; each culture engages in a continuous dialectic that traces the dimensions of its fears and desires. When this dialectic is acted out, it becomes ritual, a ceremony with an established form or method of performance. When the dialectic is expressed in a narrative format, it becomes myth, a written or oral presentation using established patterns and conventions. When the dialectic is expressed pictorially, it becomes icon, a graphic representation with established compositional elements and motifs. The configuration of values articulated symbolically in icon, ritual, and myth lends elements of similarity to the three, making comparisons between images and text (that is, icon and myth), for example, valid.

A third assumption that underlies the current approach is that certain images from the mass media are equivalent to other cultures' sacred images partly because the mass media are taking on religious functions. Theologian Harvey Cox argues that the historical process of secularization (what Marshall McLuhan calls "desacralization") has given media the power—once held exclusively by religion—to inform values. In *The Secular City*, Cox ties the historical process of secularization to the development of technology, which finally provides media with means of rapid production and dissemination of materials for mass audiences.[10] In this context, the ability of CBS to reach millions of us at the same instant with the same message lends that message transcendence. Elsewhere, Cox says the media are essentially in the religion business because:

8. Mary Noel, *Villains Galore . . . The Heyday of the Popular Story Weekly* (New York: Macmillan, 1954), pp. 1–2.

9. Panofsky, *Iconology*, p. 8.

10. Harvey Cox, *The Secular City: Secularization and Urbanization in Theological Perspective*, rev. ed. (New York: Macmillan, 1966).

They provide the heroes, myths, sacraments, and beatific visions for more and more people every day. The fact that mass media piety is not recognized as such and therefore not criticized and called to account does not make it any less influential. In fact, religion is probably more influential in those cultures where the values it supports are not seen as "religious" but are simply a part of the culture at large. Fish seldom take special note of the water they are swimming in.[11]

Giving the label *iconography* to the study of images in the media does indeed suggest religious dimensions. I agree with media analysts Robert Jewett and John Lawrence in their belief that "religion may have merely changed its theatre and neglected to place its name on the marquee. The move from cathedral to the tube, screen or stereo offers the faithful many of the values sought in traditional religion."[12]

That the mass media show us what is culturally and personally important is attested by the frequent use to which many scholars—among them the historian John Demos and the psychologist Arlene Skolnick—put them in substantiating findings from other disciplines. For although images from the popular media may carry heavy emotional baggage, they likewise exist as multidimensional realities, what the American iconographer Marshall Fishwick calls "visible and incontrovertible facts."[13] Fishwick remarks on the value of icons generally: "Icons have a way of funding us, and sustaining whatever sense and form our lives assume. When we can no longer draw from an icon bank we quickly go bankrupt."[14] It is this power to sustain the sense and form of our lives that makes the study of icons so revealing of the culture in which they occur.

Through the centuries, one of the biggest depositors to our icon bank has been the family. Scanning the mass media for images of the family, I have chosen to focus on four kinds: (1) men and women *before* marriage; (2) men and women *after* marriage; (3) children; (4) various family forms. I shall draw on a

11. Harvey Cox, "The Consciousness Industry: A Theological View of the Media," *Public Telecommunications Review* (October 1973), p. 8.

12. Robert Jewett and John Lawrence, "The American Monomyth: From Star Trek to Bunnyland" (manuscript copy, p. 41).

13. Fishwick, "Entrance," p. 2.

14. Fishwick, p. 4.

number of recent studies by scholars of popular culture as well as on my own observations and will look mainly at images in three narrative forms from television—situation comedies, soap operas, and series—and one from the printed media—comic strips. And I hope I shall be forgiven if I refer now and then to a few of the approximately 700,000 (or the exactly 887,680 if we believe Alvin Toffler) advertising messages I have actively received.

When we look for images of the family in the mass media, we find that they occur less frequently than we might expect. George Gerbner, dean of the Annenberg School of Communications at the University of Pennsylvania, recently reported that on television over a ten-year period there has been a "striking underrepresentation of the family—except in comedies."[15] The underrepresentation extends to other media as well. The family is a mainstay, however, of several mass genres besides comedy, among them television's soap operas, the nineteenth-century domestic novel, and its twentieth-century counterpart, the supermarket-distributed romance. All these reach a mass audience and have as their focus what Edith Efron calls "the mating-marital-reproductive cycle set against a domestic background."[16]

The media as a whole, however, have assigned the family to a secondary position. In doing so, they are following a more general cultural consensus about the family's relative importance or, at least, reflecting a traditional view common to much of American history and literature, the idea that the *individual* is our primary concern. Unlike the family-centered European novel, the canonical works of American fiction tend to focus on a "loner," a male, to varying degrees separated from or at odds with community and family. Leslie Fiedler, discussing the American novel, comments that while other cultures have recourse to "seduction and marriage" as their "subject par excellence," the great American novel is "the womanless *Moby Dick*."[17]

15. "The Family on TV Is Underrepresented," *Los Angeles Times*, 23 June 1977, part 4, p. 22.

16. Edith Efron, "The Soaps—Anything But 99-44/100 Percent Pure," *Television*, ed. Barry G. Cole (New York: Free Press, 1970), p. 156.

17. Leslie Fiedler, *Love and Death in the American Novel*, rev. ed. (New York: Dell, 1969), p. 5.

Family life in American fiction appears almost exclusively in regional or ethnic novels and in domestic novels by women, beginning with Susan Warner's *The Wide, Wide World* in 1850 and including Kate Chopin, E. D. E. N. Southworth, Ellen Glasgow, Sarah Orne Jewett, Willa Cather, Edith Wharton, and other authors who were widely read by the public but seldom taught in the schools until the recent feminist movement brought about their reevaluation.

In today's popular media generally, as in traditional American literature, the most common narrative is that of a lone male in a heroic situation rather than a domestic one. As the United States Commission on Civil Rights reported in *Window Dressing on the Set,* "the television male is not family bound."[18] This is not surprising when we consider that in television male characters outnumber females three to one, according to Gerbner.[19] Boyle and Wahlstrom found the same ratio in their recent study of educational films and comic books, and noted also that the few adult women in these media suffered a disproportionate number of instances of violence.[20] The Commission on Civil Rights found the same to be true of women in television.[21] With women appearing so infrequently in the media, and playing the roles of victims when they do appear, and with men in the media busily engaged in confronting danger, images of the family are certain to be scarce.

18. *Window Dressing on the Set: Women and Minorities in Television,* A Report of the United States Commission on Civil Rights, Washington, D.C., August 1977, p. 33.

19. *Los Angeles Times,* 23 June 1977, p. 22.

20. Caren Boyle (Deming) and Billie Joyce Wahlstrom, "Cultural Analysis: Unmasking the Makings of Oppression," *University of Michigan Papers in Women's Studies* 1, no. 1 (February 1974): 18.

21. *Window Dressing on the Set,* pp. 36–38. The United States Commission on Civil Rights reported: "To determine whether any of the groups [of characters] suffered more violence than they committed, it was necessary to control for the proportionately greater number of male characters involved in violence. This was done by creating a victimization ratio. . . . Thus, nonwhite females who were rarely portrayed in violent scenes were, nevertheless, more likely than any other group to be portrayed as victims rather than as perpetrators of violence. . . . White female characters emerged as the next group more likely to suffer the consequences of violent action than to commit it" (p. 37).

MEN AND WOMEN BEFORE MARRIAGE:
THE HERO AND THE VIRGIN

If we begin the examination of images of family life in the mass media with a brief look at how people are pictured before marriage, we will have a standard by which to judge the effect of marriage and family life upon them. The male before marriage is essentially the hero. In his simplest form, he appears in comics as Superman, Batman, Aquaman, Captain America; in his more sophisticated guise, he is Kojak, Baretta, Perry Mason, Matt Dillon, and Captain Kirk. In any case, he is recognizable as a solitary figure, skilled in physical activities, violent, above the law, highly mobile, independent, and somewhat anti-intellectual.[22] Women find him attractive, and he saves, befriends, and occasionally dates them; but he assiduously avoids what Leslie Fiedler calls "civilization . . . the confrontation of a man and a woman which leads to the fall to sex, marriage, and responsibility."[23] Superman never marries Lois Lane; Perry Mason never marries Della Street; Matt Dillon never marries Kitty. American culture (at least as shown by the media) indulges its preference for womenless narratives and reflects an antifemale bias that carries over into a disvaluing of those things traditionally associated with women, and thus with home and family. The hero avoids family life, for it is considered incompatible with those confrontations that provide him with the chance to be heroic.

Because women represent at best only 25 percent of the total number of figures in the media, we do not have so full a picture of them as we do of men. The potential wife is what Marshall McLuhan calls the "frisky coke-ad girl."[24] We recognize her also

22. The following studies all define the hero more extensively: Ray Allen Billington, *America's Frontier Heritage* (New York: Holt, Rinehart and Winston, 1966); John Cawelti, *The Six-Gun Mystique* (Bowling Green, Ohio: Bowling Green State University Popular Press, 1970); Henry Nash Smith, *Virgin Land: The American West as Symbol and Myth* (New York: Random House, 1950), and Dixon Wecter, *The Hero in America: A Chronicle of Hero-Worship* (New York: Scribner's, 1972). See also Boyle and Wahlstrom, "Cultural Analysis."

23. Fiedler, *Love and Death in the American Novel*, p. 6.

24. McLuhan, *Mechanical Bride*, p. 68.

on the covers of old copies of the *Saturday Evening Post,* and in Breck ads—attractive, virginal, "fun to be with." For the would-be wife, virginity is as essential as toughness is for the would-be husband. Potential wives are not active sexually, for women are seen as responsible for the social regulation of sex, that is the preservation of the family.[25] Unacceptable women leer, ogle, and hint, as did Valerie Shaw in *The Doctors* when she said to her dinner companion, "A smart woman judges a man by his mouth. . . . Yours is strong and sensual."[26] Good women never hint; they limit their activities to dating, dancing, and chaste kissing. A woman is entitled (and encouraged) to do a little comparison shopping when it comes to rating young men's kisses but she can make no major purchases. The desirable woman is epitomized by Blondie, according to Marshall McLuhan, because she is "twice bathed, powdered, patted, deodorized, and depilatorized."[27] It is true that in some of the series, situation comedies, and soap operas one can find other varieties of the desirable woman: strong ones as in *Bionic Woman, Wonder Woman, Charlie's Angels, Police Woman;* humorous ones in situation comedies—Laverne and Shirley, Brenda in *Rhoda;* serious ones in soap operas. While some of these are as unlikely to marry as the heroic males, what all have in common is their sexuality. Women in all these shows constantly worry about their attractiveness, their femininity. Often even the superwoman will defer to non-supermen when it comes to the capture of criminals they have tracked down.

MEN AND WOMEN AFTER MARRIAGE: AN AMBIGUOUS VISION

With such potentially perfect marriage partners as the chaste and feminine female and the super-masculine male, one might expect images of married males and females to be idyllic. Occasionally they are, but more frequently they are not. The negative images

25. Kay J. Mussell, "Beautiful and Damned: The Sexual Woman in Gothic Fiction," *Journal of Popular Culture* 9, no. 1 (Summer 1975): 84–85.
26. Efron, "The Soaps," p. 157.
27. McLuhan, *Mechanical Bride,* p. 68.

MEN BEFORE MARRIAGE

Marvel Comics' Captain America and Falcon. In today's popular media, the most common narratives are those of males in heroic situations rather than domestic ones.

Marlboro Cowboy. The potential husband in popular media is physically strong, highly mobile, and independent. (Courtesy of Philip Morris, Inc.)

Boots of Destiny. Until tamed by his wife, a man is shown as having a violent, physically demanding life and absolute control over his destiny.

Come to
Marlboro
Country.

You get a lot to like
with a Marlboro.

Marlboro

18 mg. "tar", 1.2 mg. nicotine
av. per cigarette, FTC Report

Warning: The Surgeon General Has Dete...

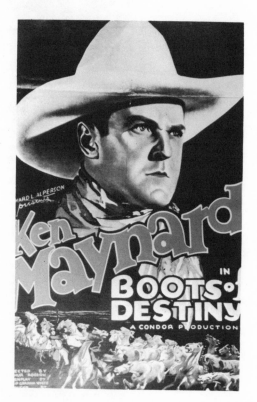

WOMEN BEFORE MARRIAGE

A Chest of Dreams and Silver. The popular media promote the belief that the goal of a good girl is marriage and family.
"Love that Coke." The potential wife is what Marshall McLuhan calls the "frisky coke-ad girl." (Courtesy of the Archives. The Coca-Cola Company.)
THE SATURDAY EVENING POST *Cover.* Attractive, virginal women have been seen as responsible for the social regulation of sex. (Courtesy of *The Saturday Evening Post.* © 1923 Curtis Publishing Co.)

A Chest of Dreams and Silver

MEN AFTER MARRIAGE

Cartoon, Los Angeles Magazine. Married men are fatter, older, balder, and lazier than their unmarried counterparts. (Courtesy of Punch/Rothco.)
Cartoon, The New Yorker. With his "I do," a man surrenders to passivity, and his attempts to regain masculine identity are pathetic.
The Better Half. The father and husband is constantly belittled and portrayed as stupid, infantile, and emasculated. (*The Better Half* by Barnes. Courtesy of the Register and Tribune Syndicate, Inc.)

"Remember when you were going to be a legend in your own lifetime?"

"I got the first three for only twenty-seven fifty. My sole obligation is to purchase six additional species from the dozens to be offered over the coming twelve months."

Drawing by O'Brian; © 1974 The New Yorker Magazine, Inc.

"Stanley's one of the IN crowd, all right — inept, insecure, and intolerable."

WOMEN AFTER MARRIAGE

Fat Woman: Negative Image of Domesticity. Married women are often shown as usurpers of power, retaining their vitality at the expense of their husbands. (Courtesy of Deborah Rogers, Ltd.)

THE NEIGHBORS: *Woman Buying a Hat.* Once women have achieved the dominant position in the family, there is a kind of domestic harmony—everyone knows who is boss. (Courtesy of the Chicago Tribune–New York News Syndicate, Inc.)

THE NEIGHBORS: *Woman Serving Dinner.* The good wife does not work after marriage. In the formula of the love comic, one works *until* one meets the right man. (Courtesy of the Chicago Tribune–New York News Syndicate, Inc.)

The Neighbors

By George Clark

"I don't want anything so feminine my husband will try to be boss again."

The Neighbors

By George Clark

"Now take my Gracie. If I hadn't married her she would still be waiting on tables."

CHILDREN

Shout Advertisement. The ideal child is the "good bad" one who is naughty enough to avoid being called a "mama's boy." (Courtesy of Johnson Wax.)
PEANUTS: *Charlie Brown.* The good child must not be perfect. Our good boys—from Huck Finn to Beaver Cleaver—are not too domesticated. (Courtesy of United Feature Syndicate, Inc.)
Little House on the Prairie. Although more pronounced in boys, spunkiness is part of the ideal for girls as well. (Jacket from *Little House on the Prairie* by Laura Ingalls Wilder, illustrated by Garth Williams. Courtesy of Harper & Row, Publishers, Inc.)

WOMEN AFTER MARRIAGE:
A POSITIVE EXAMPLE

Hermine Finkenzeller, Audi 5000 Structural Engineer: "In My Family I Pick the Car." Recognizing that women who work after marriage make up a large part of the consumer market, advertisers are beginning to show a few images of strong, intelligent married women functioning successfully outside the home. (Courtesy of Volkswagen of America, Inc.)

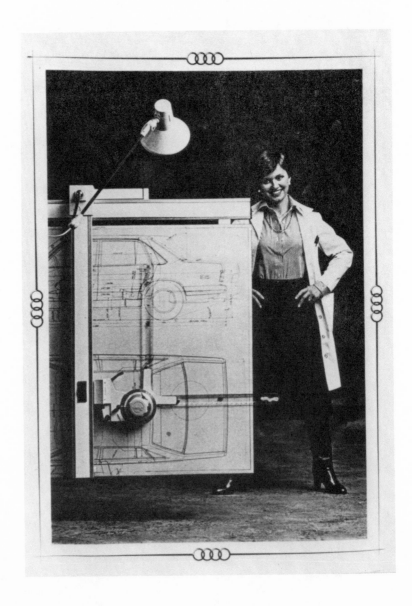

"IN MY FAMILY, I PICK THE CAR AND LET MY HUSBAND PICK THE COLOR."

HERMINE FINKENZELLER, AUDI 5000 STRUCTURAL ENGINEER

Isn't it usually the other way round? Finkenzeller: Well, I suppose it's a bit unusual for a woman to be a structural engineer. But I am and it happens that my husband is not. Actually, he's very good at his job, but he's in an entirely different field. I've been designing automotive components for 15 years. These drawings of the Audi 5000 are the ones I did as a member of the engineering team that designed the car.

Was it hard getting started as an automotive engineer? Finkenzeller: In the very beginning, yes. But that was years ago. Today, it's easier for a woman to be accepted as an engineer. Consider how many women chemists and physicists there are now. Things have opened up. I'm respected by the people I work with for what I can contribute as a structural engineer.

But don't men usually know more about cars than women? Finkenzeller: Why do you assume that? Because they played with a little red car, as children, and girls played with dolls? That hardly qualifies a man as an automotive authority. In Europe, some men seem to know technical terms about cars. But a lot of men think in romantic terms about cars. Behind the wheel they see themselves as something they're not, perhaps race drivers. Women don't seem to have this problem. Their attitude toward cars is more rational. A car satisfies their needs, not their fantasies.

How will a woman feel about the Audi 5000? Finkenzeller: Good. They will like its layout. It's probably the most intelligent 15½ feet of engineering on the road today. Women will appreciate that we didn't devote half the car to the power plant. You can't sit people under a hood. My colleagues developed a 5-cylinder gasoline engine that has plenty of power, yet doesn't take up unnecessary space. So the car seats five people very comfortably. It is a big car. As a matter of fact, I believe in your country it's the largest German luxury car for the money, less than $9,000.

Will men like the Audi 5000? Finkenzeller: Men? Yes. I think they will love its power and handling – and a lot of women will, too. The Audi 5000 may be a rather elegantly conservative car but it's not sedate. It's very fast. With front-wheel drive, it takes corners beautifully, especially for such a big, luxurious car. It's really a lot of fun to drive. People are surprised to find out how responsive the car is. That amuses us. And, of course, delights us, too.

Do you own an Audi 5000? Finkenzeller: No. Not that I wouldn't like to. It's just that my family has no need for a car with all that room. There's only my husband and our one child. What would we do with all the room there is in the Audi 5000? So, instead, we own the Audi Fox. I think that's what you call it in America. It's smaller. But it's also a very nice car. Do you know, I worked on the design of that car, too.

Are you always this sensible? Finkenzeller: Sensible? If you mean logical and precise, I would say yes when it comes to doing my work. In my job, I have to be very precise. But, if what you really want to know is whether I'm ever emotional or even romantic, perhaps you should ask my husband about that.

OPTIONS

DUN'S REVIEW *Cover*, below; at right, REDBOOK *Advertisement*, LOS ANGELES TIMES. The opportunity to engage in rewarding professional and business activities influences many of today's young people in the decisions they make about home and family life. The mass media reflect new as well as traditional family patterns. (Cover reprinted with permission of *Dun's Review*, from the April 1979 issue. Advertisement courtesy of Redbook Publishing Company.)

Tell her babies can be a burden and a go-getter sees Red.

Today, more young women want to shape their own lives. Both before and after they bring a new life into the world. They're not your ordinary young mothers. They're the movers and doers. The go-getters.
They think children and career. Diapers and degree. Family and self-fulfillment.
And Redbook is their magazine.
Because Redbook helps them fulfill their children's needs without neglecting their own.
        Consider the April issue:
        How wanting a baby affects desire. Reading a child's
        distress signals. What it means to adopt.
Besides helpful articles, there's the new Redbook look. A compelling flow-through format that makes for cover-to-cover reading.
It's no wonder Redbook attracts the highest percentage of go-getting women, 18-to-34. (And the highest percentage of go-getters whose get-up-and-go hasn't gone, no matter *what* their age.)
Working...college-educated...affluent women. Physically and mentally active. Women on the go both at home and abroad. The go-getters who've got it.
When you want to get go-getters, see Redbook.
More than any other magazine,
Redbook is the one go-getters go for.

Redbook and young go-getters go together.

The Redbook Publishing Company A Member of The Charter Inc. Communications Group

FAMILIES ON TELEVISION

"Bonanza." The abridged family, which has at least one member absent, is common in the media because its asymmetrical nature gives rise to a variety of situations denied the traditional family. (Courtesy of NBC.)

"I Remember Mama." The large and complete family in the media shows no signs of disappearing. Such a family articulates the desire for warmth, belonging, and security. (Courtesy of CBS, Inc.)

Cartoon, Best Cartoons of the Year, 1970. Television families do not necessarily duplicate the actual activities of real families who, for example, have their television sets turned on an average of six hours a day. (Courtesy of Dave Gerard.)

Gerard

"You notice the families on these TV shows never waste their time watching TV?"

of men and women after marriage owe their existence to many facts, some of which are cultural and others media considerations. It is the nature of stereotypes in the mass media to be attached to specific settings. Thus, the characteristics assigned to unmarried persons—heroism and toughness in males, attractiveness and virginity in females—are qualities that cannot be transferred to married characters in a domestic setting. In addition, the very format of series, situation comedies, soap operas, and comics requires one conflict after another. Turmoil is more interesting than a steady diet of marital bliss.

Positive images of family life are not, of course, entirely absent from the mass media. They are found, for instance, in comics, although married people in this medium are quite rare. In love comics, "The ideal teen-age girl is . . . fully dedicated to being a good wife to the man she loves. Marriage is her dream and making that dream a reality is her constant goal."[28] To facilitate her marriage, she is willing to make important concessions to the man she loves. That means she does not work after marriage: giving up a career as a fashion model or secretary is not really a major sacrifice because in the formula of the love comic one works *until* one meets the right man.[29] In fact, a job may even be used as a means of finding Mr. Right. So, too, the college education culminating in the M.R.S. degree. But even in love comics, marriage and family serve as the resolution of plot rather than as the central theme, a pattern long familiar in European comedy.

Neither sitcoms nor soap operas thrive on positive images of men and women after marriage, although the potential for happy life keeps sitcoms funny and prevents soap operas from becoming unbearably dreary. In television series, however, we see many positive images of the family: *Family, I Remember Mama,* and *The Waltons* all come to mind. In some of these we see a sentimentalized vision of the American home, like that described by John Demos: "[a] bastion of peace, of repose, of orderliness,

28. Philippe Perebinossoff, "What Does a Kiss Mean? The Love Comic Formula and the Creation of the Ideal Teen-Age Girl," *Journal of Popular Culture* 8, no. 4 (Spring 1975): 827.

29. Perebinossoff, p. 827.

of unwavering devotion to people and principles beyond the self. Here the woman of the family, and the children, would pass most of their hours and days—safe from the grinding pressures and dark temptations of the world at large; here, too, the man of the family would retreat periodically for refreshment, renewal, and inward fortification . . . ."[30] As wonderful as this vision sounds, it is increasingly being called Victorian, paternalistic, or fictional by scholars, including feminists and others studying the family.

It is in advertising that we find most of the positive images of males and females after marriage. Domestic happiness is good business. Advertisers dangle happiness before prospective buyers: if women achieve security from the home, then men achieve self-respect through providing that security. Capitalizing upon this idea, advertisers offer a wide range of products that have as their subtext message, "Be a good provider (and thus a good father and husband) by buying this product for your family." In exchange, the male provider receives extra attention: he and his children are served specially prepared meals by the wife. After all, "Nothin' says lovin' like somethin' from the oven, and Pillsbury says it best!" Advertising of this sort plugs right into the world of the soap opera where, as Efron says, marriage "consists of two ingredients: 'love' and homemaking."[31]

In a world increasingly filled with depersonalized encounters and depersonalizing experiences, it is no wonder that we find images of domestic peace attractive. But the world is also becoming more accessible, and in its complexity, more interesting, so that by contrast the daily routines of home and family may seem dull or oppressive. Recent assumptions about the rights of each person to have a life with fulfillments inside or outside the home have brought widespread discontent with traditional roles, especially among women. Economic necessity, which has forced people out of the home and given many women feelings of productivity and independence, has also made audiences more alert to the excitement of the outside world and the ordinariness of the family. Current economic and social conditions may have

30. See chapter 2.
31. Efron, "The Soaps," p. 158.

increased the number of negative images of the family but they did not create them: such images are part of a strong American tradition of the male hero, male worth being connected with life outside the domestic sphere.

In comic strips, married men show remarkable consistency: they are fatter, older, balder, and lazier than their unmarried counterparts.[32] With his "I do," a man is pictured as surrendering to passivity. The pitiful existence of the married man in soap operas is typical. As Efron remarks, "love in the soaps tends to be a kind of hospitalization insurance, usually provided by females to male emotional cripples. A female rarely pledges herself to honor and obey her husband. She pledges to cure him of his alcoholism, to forgive his criminal record, paranoia, pathological lying, premarital affairs—and, generally to give him a shoulder to cry on."[33] His efforts to retain a masculine identity are rather pathetic. The husband's obesity is a vain symbolic attempt to build up his sense of self. In McLuhan's words, "[Dagwood's] swashbuckling, midnight forays to the icebox, when he returns covered with mayonnaise and the gore of catsup, is a wordless charade of self-pity and Mitty-mouse rebellion. Promiscuous gormandizing as a basic dramatic symbol of the abused and the insecure has long been understood."[34] The relation of craving for food to lack of meaning in one's life applies not only to men but to middle-aged women who, like Edith Bunker, quickly develop bulges once the children have grown up.

Psychologists Judith M. Bardwick and Suzanne J. Schumann, looking at the image of men in advertising, discovered a curious duality:

The image of the American man in TV commercials as muscular, knowledgeable, dominating, independent, sexy, cosmopolitan, athletic, authoritative, and aggressive exists only when he is seen away from his family. In embarrassing contrast the American father and

32. Pierre Couperie, Maurice C. Horn, Proto Destefanis, Edouard Francois, Claude Moliterni, and Gerald Gassiot-Talabot, *A History of the Comic Strip*, trans. Eileen B. Hennessy (New York: Crown, 1968).

33. Efron, "The Soaps," p. 158.

34. McLuhan, *Mechanical Bride*, p. 68.

husband is portrayed as passive, stupid, infantile, and emasculated. . . . But, outside the house trouble is what he's looking for. Swift as a panther, stealthy as a cougar, free as a mustang, he speeds to his rendezvous with status, independence and violence.[35]

This duality is not so marked in advertising's treatment of the married woman. The National Advertising Review Board in its 1975 report found advertising about women to be almost uniformly offensive: "It is especially true that in the advertising of household products, women too often are portrayed as stupid— too dumb to cope with familiar everyday chores, unless instructed by children, or by a man, or assisted by a man, or assisted by a supernatural male symbol."[36] In advertisements, the married woman is often depicted as totally concerned with cooking, cleaning, and laundering and unable to cope with them. As the National Advertising Review Board sums her up, she is "obsessed with cleanliness . . . embarrassed or feeling inadequate or guilty because of various forms of household dirt."[37] Recently a few advertisers, recognizing as a potential market the increasing number of women in the work force, show positive images of married women employed outside the home.

Two television formats—soap operas and situation comedies—focus on negative aspects of the family. Soap operas derive their plots from the things that can go wrong in marriage. Directed primarily at women who stay at home and might be suffering from the actual problems of isolation, they work to engage their viewers' sympathies, convincing them that their lives (as boring, sedate, or uneventful as they might be) are better than those on television, although perhaps less interesting. In an average week, thirteen nationally televised soap operas yielded multiple examples of the following: (1) filing of divorce papers, (2) dropping of divorce actions, (3) marriage in name only, (4) drugs, (5) unwanted pregnancies, (6) propositions, (7) auto accidents, (8) trips to the hospital, (9) battered wives, (10) assorted lies and other deceptions, (11) attempted suicide, (12) adultery,

35. Judith M. Bardwick and Suzanne J. Schumann, "Portrait of American Men and Women in TV Commercials," *Psychology* 4 (April 1967): 15.

36. Cited in *Window Dressing on the Set*, p. 13.

37. Cited in *Window Dressing on the Set*, p. 13.

(13) poisoning, (14) nervous breakdowns, (15) various illnesses, (16) drunkenness, and (17) imprisonment.[38] Our continued fascination with these dark portraits of family life may grow out of a cultural desire to see the family survive: after witnessing such extremes, we may find life in our own families more tolerable. Thus soap operas may in fact work to alleviate real-life family problems.

Situation comedies are quite different, for although they deal with the same sorts of family issues, they do so less positively. The laughter sitcoms engender is not a result of good clean fun. While soap operas seem to defuse our fears of the family, sitcoms feed upon them, lumping these fears with our fears of "evil foreigners." One look at the number of nonwhite family sitcoms shows us that American cultural minorities are more "acceptable" when we can laugh at them.[39] In fact, just as we have begun to see a lessening of racial distrust, evidenced by more third-world people in noncomedic roles, sitcoms have increasingly taken on topics—rape, abortion, male sterilization, alcoholism, and death—that are not generally thought funny; thus they can continue to resonate with our fears. The predominance of families and third-world peoples in sitcoms seems to me a negative fact, indicating our cultural unwillingness to give up either racism or our adolescent preferences for rebellious heroes in favor of mature interests in family life.

THE CHILD AS ANGEL AND THE CHILD AS DEMON

Images of children in the mass media raise special problems. First, they are scarce. For example, since 1972 when media analysts began collecting data on parental status, only 6.8 percent of the adult characters on television were found to have

38. Based on summaries printed weekly in Monday's *Los Angeles Times*, "View" section.

39. The report of the United States Commission on Civil Rights cited above devotes several sections to the way blacks are portrayed in situation comedies and on television in general. Their contention about minority figures in comedy is that "the humor is still that black people are 'dumb nigger' types" (p. 20).

children.[40] Secondly, children are consistently used in a symbolic way. Fiedler, speaking about the child in literature, points out that the child seldom means just itself: "So ubiquitous and symbolic a figure is, of course, no mere reproduction of a fact of existence; he is a cultural invention."[41]

The child as innocent is familiar through its representation in the traditional symbol of the Christ child, who bridges the gap between humankind and God. This child, without the deification, is widely distributed throughout the media. Little Orphan Annie, Charlie Brown, the Wilder girls in *Little House on the Prairie* are all good children, but, importantly, they are not perfect. Throughout the popular media, if children are too good they become evil. Little boys must have an element of Dennis the Menace in them, or they become Little Lord Fauntleroy. They must be naughty enough to escape being called a "mama's boy." Our good boys—from Huck Finn to Beaver Cleaver—are not too domesticated. This need for spunkiness, although more pronounced in boys, is also found in girls. Without it, girls tend to end up like Little Eva, nice, but not around for the end of the story. The Wilder girls, Nancy Drew, radio's Baby Snooks, and even Buddy on the television show *Family*, all disobey occasionally and evidence a general impishness. Fiedler indicates the mixed nature of these children by calling them "Good Bad" children as opposed to "Good Good" ones.

Although the "Good Good" children are unpleasant, there is as well the truly evil child, the enfant terrible who is Rosemary's Baby. Although it might appear that this child is a recent creation of the media, it exists in the same religious tradition that provides the innocent child. As Fiedler explains, it was "Augustine's observation that the innocence of childhood is more a matter of weakness of limbs than of purity of heart."[42] Whereas it is the "Good Bad" child who appears in advertisements graphically demonstrating the need and use of good cleansers and laundry detergents, the truly evil child turns up in film,

40. *Window Dressing on the Set*, p. 33.

41. Leslie Fiedler, *No! In Thunder: Essays in Myth and Literature* (Boston: Beacon Press, 1960), p. 253.

42. Fiedler, *No!*, p. 255.

television, black humor cartoons, popular literature, and underground comics. A number of films, exploiting the recent interest in the book of Revelations with its prediction of the coming of the Antichrist, have utilized the shock value inherent in an evil infant. *Rosemary's Baby* and its successors, *The Omen*, *The Exorcist*, and *Carrie*, show the penalty for having given birth to the wrong child or having been an inadequate parent. Aside from their biblical connotations, images of the demonic child seem to dramatize our fears that we might not be good parents or that, despite our good parenting, our children might turn out badly.

Images of children in the mass media are thus difficult to categorize, for they may represent fears, yearnings, or philosophies beyond themselves in ways that images of the mother-in-law or aging husband do not. As an example, William H. Young has suggested that Little Orphan Annie "represents the social conservatism of the middle classes, symbolizing faith, hope, and charity—'but not too much charity.' "[43] Some of the images of children may represent general fears about life, its unpredictability, its ability to trick us by appearances. Others may symbolize our desire to start over again, this time with correct values. We need closer study of the images of children in the popular media.

FAMILY FORMS:
THE ABRIDGED FAMILY AND THE ALTERNATE FAMILY

Besides traditional families—those with two parents, two children, two pets—American mass media often picture nontraditional families, responding perhaps to changes in the real world and, at the same time, trying to make the family more interesting. Although there are several kinds, I shall mention only two, the abridged family and the alternate family (as opposed to the nuclear family and the extended family). The abridged family has at least one of its traditional members absent. This may be a

43. William H. Young, "Little Orphan Annie," *Journal of Popular Culture* 8, no. 2 (Fall 1974): 312.

reflection of the growing number of single-parent homes, but it is not really new in the popular media, the motif of the absent father or missing child having been around for many years. What may be surprising is that these abridged households, although they have troubles not found in traditional homes, are not unhappy places; life goes on quite well. Use of the abridged family does not seem to depend upon the demographic makeup of the medium's audience. Children's comic books, for example, where one might expect to find traditional families, are filled with these abridged households. Spider-Man, an orphan, lives with an aged aunt; Superboy lives with foster parents. Among television series and sitcoms, *The Courtship of Eddie's Father, My Three Sons, Bonanza,* and *Nanny and the Professor* all picture families from which the mother is missing but in which there is happiness, contentment, achievement, support, and affection. In another television series, *Family Affair,* the family consists of three orphaned children, their uncle, and his butler. (As an aside, families without mothers and wives tend to employ cooks, housekeepers, butlers, and nannies, while families without husbands and fathers such as television's *One Day at a Time* and *Alice* never seem to have enough money to hire help.)

Like the abridged family, the alternate family is usually presented as a successful one. Alternate families are composed of unmarried persons of different sexes, or of unrelated persons of the same sex, living together and showing concern for one another. The number of people living in one of these families can vary from two upward. *The Odd Couple, Laverne and Shirley* on television, the Justice Society and the Avengers in comics; Uncle Wiggily and his muskrat housekeeper in children's literature are all obvious examples. Here the ideal seems to be freedom with companionship, love without permanent commitment. George H. Douglas explains Uncle Wiggily's living arrangement in his hollow stump bungalow and touches on the real meaning underlying these alternative family arrangements: "Nurse Jane apparently exercised a certain amount of civilizing influence over Uncle Wiggily, and took a kind of maternal interest in him, making sure he wore his rubbers on rainy days, and so on, but never quite assuming the wifely powers to put the damper on his comings and goings."[44] In all alternate families, *freedom* is the watchword, but it is freedom without loneliness. Uncle Wiggily has Nurse Jane but no one with "wifely powers." Laverne has Shirley; Felix has Oscar; the Lone Ranger has Tonto. And the members of the Justice Society—Power Girl, Dr. Fate, Green Lantern, Flash, Wild-Cat, and Hawkman—all have each other but no one to interfere with their comings and goings.

What all of these images of the family in American mass media add up to is hard to say. It is clear that the emergence of certain patterns and groups of images tells us something about the culture in which they originate. The mass media project and reflect cultural desires and repugnances but, because they serve the general public, they offer as much variety and as little offense as possible. Although the media do not reflect all American subcultures, they try to offer a cross section of beliefs found in middle America, including the contradictions. As a result, it is easy for an individual to repudiate the iconicity of a given image, to say that any given picture means nothing special. Not all mediated images function as icons for every person even in an age in which the mass media are the primary sources of images. But that does not stop certain images from having iconic—that is, essentially transcendent, symbolic, or, broadly speaking, religious—significance for others, both adults and children.

In the past, as Philippe Ariès and others have pointed out, the socialization of children depended on parents and other relatives, along with members of the individual's immediate community. Today the mass media, the schools, and the peer group share in the process. Many of the images the media offer are formulaic, oversimplified, and interchangeable from one medium to another, but we cannot deny their impact both on our ideas of family life and on family life itself. Most American children today spend more time at the television set than with their parents or in the classroom, and a recent study shows that many children prefer television to their own fathers.[45]

44. George H. Douglas, "Howard R. Garis and the World of Uncle Wiggily," *Journal of Popular Culture* 8, no. 3 (Winter 1974): 509.

45. Robert M. Liebert, John M. Neale, and Emily S. Davidson, *The Early*

Like the family itself, mass-produced images of the family are probably "here to stay."[46] We can regard these images intelligently, cherish their diversity, encourage educational and public service agencies to take greater responsibility in their creation, and exploit them for our own good purposes. We can take care that we do not permit them to crowd out of our lives icons from art, history, and literature. Above all, we must be wary lest we allow cold commercializations to substitute for personal experience with real human beings, and for the manifold richness of our own family lives.

Window: Effects of Television on Children and Youth (New York: Pergamon Press, 1973). See especially the study done by Brenda Dervan.

46. Mary Jo Bane, *Here to Stay: American Families in the Twentieth Century* (New York: Basic Books, 1976).

III. OBSERVATIONS

The Contemporary American Family

10

The Significance of Family Membership

Barbara Laslett

Recent sociological discussions of the family are curiously incon-
sistent. The growth of a counter-culture in the 1960s and early
1970s which both rejected and posed alternatives to traditional forms of the family, and interpretations of student and
antiwar activism as the results of a breakdown in the socialization
functions of the family, led to a questioning of the adequacy and
viability of the norms that governed traditional family life. To
use Arlene Skolnick's phrase, the nuclear family was thought to
be "alive, but not well." In contrast to this view, other discussions of the contemporary family have emphasized its robust-
ness. Mary Jo Bane, for instance, concluded that the demographic
data she analyzed show "surprising evidence of the persistence of commitments to family life" and that the family is "here
to stay."[1]

Marriage and divorce statistics mirror the apparent contradictions that these two views of the family exemplify. In the United
States, marriage continues to be an exceedingly popular institution. A comparison of marriage rates in twenty-two selected
countries shows that, in 1965, only Egypt had a higher marriage

With the permission of the organizers of the colloquium, an earlier version of
this chapter appeared in *Social Problems* 25 (June 1978), under the title "Family
Membership, Past and Present."

1. See Arlene Skolnick, *The Intimate Environment: Exploring Marriage and the
Family* (Boston: Little, Brown, 1973), pp. 356–58; and Mary Jo Bane, *Here to
Stay: American Families in the Twentieth Century* (New York: Basic Books, 1976),
p. xiv.

rate than the United States, while in every year between 1970 and 1974, the United States rate was higher than that of any other country included in the comparison. Of course, the high rate of marriage in the United States may well be affected by the fact that Americans have the highest divorce rate in comparison with seventeen of these same countries. Although there has been a slight decline in the American remarriage rate since 1974, the divorce rate has been increasing steadily since 1965.[2] Nevertheless, Bane suggests that "it is not marriage itself but the specific marital partner that is rejected."[3]

In addition to marriage and divorce statistics, other aspects of family life have been attracting public and professional interest. Whether or not the increasing attention to family violence indicates higher incidence or simply more public discussion of this issue is difficult to know; in either case, child and wife battering are clear indications of family "troubles." Even the rise in the profession of marriage and family therapy can be interpreted in two ways—as indicating increasing problems within the family or greater efforts on the part of family members to resolve the problems they face.[4] The question may therefore be asked, why is the contemporary family "not well—but here to stay?"

Several answers have been given to why the family is not well. Skolnick suggests that past conceptualizations of the family tended to sentimentalize it, to view it in utopian terms and to ignore the strains and conflicts that daily family living involves. Other writers have suggested that large-scale political and economic changes have contributed to the difficulties the modern family now faces.[5]

2. Hugh Carter and Paul C. Glick, *Marriage and Divorce: A Social and Economic Study*, rev. ed. (Cambridge, Mass.: Harvard University Press, 1976), pp. 387, 391. The marriage rate has declined somewhat since 1972 but has not changed the status of the United States as compared to other countries.

3. Bane, *Here to Stay*, p. 34.

4. On increasing attention to family violence, see Suzanne K. Steinmetz, *The Cycle of Violence: Assertive, Aggressive and Abusive Family Interaction* (New York: Praeger, 1977). In 1960, the membership of the American Association of Marriage and Family Counselors was 237; by 1976 it had risen to 4,230.

5. For comments on political and economic changes and their effect on the family, see Richard Flacks, *Youth and Social Change* (Chicago: Markham, 1971);

Functional theory, particularly as expressed by Parsons, has provided one answer to why the family is "here to stay." This view emphasizes the increasing division of labor within and between social institutions—structural differentiation—which has characterized the process of historical change. Under these conditions, the family has assumed a more specialized set of functions for the larger society, that of primary socialization agent for children and the stabilization of adult personalities. Thus, "the family . . . [is] not in any general sense less important, because the society is dependent *more* exclusively on it for the performance of *certain* of its vital functions."[6]

Other authors have recently elaborated upon some of the consequences of the family's "socio-emotional specialization" in contemporary society. Berger and Kellner state that "marriage occupies a privileged status among the significant validating relationships for adults," and suggest that "the character of marriage has its roots in . . . the crystallization of a so-called private sphere of existence . . . defined and utilized as the main social area for the individual's self-realization." Weigert and Hastings see "the basic relationships of the nuclear family—conjugal love, parental support or filial piety, and sibling ties—as central to the processes of identity formation." They see the family as a little "world" in which "selves emerge, act, and acquire a stable sense of identity and reality." And Zaretsky introduces a class dimension to understanding the family's specialized role: "Under capitalism an ethic of personal fulfillment has become the property of the masses of people. . . . Much of this search for personal meaning takes place within the family and is one reason for the persistence of the family in spite of the decline of many of its earlier functions."[7]

---

and Eli Zaretsky, *Capitalism, the Family and Personal Life* (New York: Harper & Row, 1976).

6. Talcott Parsons and Robert F. Bales, *Family, Socialization and Interaction Process* (Glencoe, Ill.: Free Press, 1955), pp. 9–10.

7. Peter Berger and Hansfried Kellner, "Marriage and the Construction of Reality," in *Life as Theatre: A Dramaturgical Sourcebook*, ed. Dennis Brisset and Charles Edgley (Chicago: Aldine, 1975), p. 221; Andrew J. Weigert and Ross Hastings, "Identity Loss, Family and Social Change," *American Journal of*

233

Noting that in modern society the development of personal identity and the satisfaction of socio-emotional needs have become specialized functions of the family leaves two important questions unanswered. What are some of the social processes and structural changes by which this theoretically identified "functional necessity" has been transformed into social reality? And does the family, in practice rather than in theory, have the resources—both material and emotional—to satisfy the increased demands that its specialized role now assigns to it? Drawing upon recent research in demographic and family history, I shall try to answer the first of these questions. My thesis is that changes in household composition, in the demography of kinship, and in the relationship between the family and other institutions have contributed to the increased emotional significance of the family. These structural changes, increasing in number in the United States since the end of the nineteenth century, have influenced the process of socialization and thus have made family membership more significant in achieving personal growth, self-definition, and emotional satisfaction.[8] Comparable changes may also be found in other Western nations that have shared similar historical experiences. Changes in ideology have been a factor in this development as well.

To assert that family membership is a more salient feature of individual identity in contemporary society than in the past is not necessarily to support a sentimental view that would focus solely on the positive outcomes such as increased warmth, understanding, and mutual concern. The intense feelings that intimate relationships may generate can be both positive and negative. In fact, when strong feelings are involved, conflict, abuse, and family dissolution may be more frequent than when

---

Sociology 82 (May 1977): 1172; and Zaretsky, *Capitalism, the Family and Personal Life*, p. 30.

8. For purposes of this paper, the twentieth-century family will be contrasted with the family in earlier historical periods, although such a gross dichotomy, of course, obscures variations in the rates and timing of the developments affecting the family; see Barbara Laslett, "The Family as a Public and Private Institution: An Historical Perspective," *Journal of Marriage and the Family* 35 (August 1973): 480–92, for an argument that legitimizes distinguishing the twentieth-century family from the family in earlier historical periods.

they are not. Thus, to suggest how the family has become more important as a source of personal identity and fulfillment is not to say that it succeeds in satisfying the demands that its increasing importance imposes. Several social scientists have indeed suggested that contradictions within the modern American family make it unlikely that it will be successful in this respect.[9] It is precisely this disparity—between demands which are both structurally and ideologically encouraged and the ability to satisfy them—that is central to understanding contemporary family life in both its traditional and nontraditional forms.

FAMILY STRUCTURE AND SOCIALIZATION

Research on the history of the family in Western Europe and North America shows kin membership in most households, both past and present, to be composed primarily of nuclear family members. It is important, however, to distinguish the family, defined in terms of the co-resident domestic group, from the kinship group that extends beyond the household. The most frequently used data for investigating the structure of family life in past times are parish and census records and other types of nominal listings, which usually report information on the co-resident domestic group. Empirical research findings on kinship ties beyond the household are more difficult to obtain and fewer of them are available. Conclusions based on household-level data provide only partial information about the history of the family since the residential unit is but one way in which the family can be defined.[10]

9. See, for example, Christopher Lasch, *Haven in a Heartless World: The Family Besieged* (New York: Basic Books, 1977), and Philip Slater, *Footholds: Understanding the Shifting Sexual and Family Tensions in Our Culture* (New York: E. P. Dutton, 1977).

10. For discussions which indicate that historically kin membership of most Western European and North American households has been composed primarily of nuclear family members, see Peter Laslett, ed., *Household and Family in Past Time* (Cambridge: Cambridge University Press, 1972). See Michael Anderson, *Family Structure in Nineteenth-Century Lancashire* (Cambridge: Cambridge University Press, 1971), for a study that investigates kinship ties beyond the household. For arguments on whether findings about the organization of the co-resident domestic group can be used to describe family structure in past times,

Dispute over the proper unit of analysis in historical family research may have contributed to the contradictory interpretations of the changes that have taken place in the family over time. While, as I have already mentioned, several social scientists have argued that the family has become increasingly important, others have taken the opposite view. It is unclear, however, whether these assessments refer to the nuclear family or the extended family or how the relationship between these two family forms can best be understood. The discussion that follows pertains to this issue and will bring together the results of several approaches not usually considered in relation to each other. I shall look first at findings on the household unit and then at the demographic changes that have affected the size and structure of the kinship group. I shall explore also the impact of migration and urbanization on the availability of family members, and the relationship between the family and other social institutions. How important are these various factors in the composition of the family and for the socialization of its members?

HOUSEHOLD COMPOSITION

As already indicated, in past times the nuclear family was the predominant type of co-residential domestic group. This finding does not imply that all people lived in nuclear families for all of their lives; life-cycle variation in the kin composition of the residential family has been found in several historical studies. Despite these sources of variation, however, there continues to be support for the view that the nuclear family household was, and is, the modal category of the co-resident domestic group in most Western societies in both the preindustrial past and under contemporary forms of social and economic organization.[11]

---

see P. Laslett, ed., *Household and Family;* and Lutz K. Berkner, "The Use and Misuse of Census Data for the Historical Analysis of Family Structure," *Journal of Interdisciplinary History* 6 (Spring 1975): 721–38.

11. Among historical studies that show life cycle variation in the kin composition of the residential family, see Lutz K. Berkner, "The Stem Family and the Developmental Cycle of the Peasant Household: An Eighteenth-Century Austrian Example," *American Historical Review* 77 (April 1972): 398–418; Tamara K. Hareven, "Family Time and Industrial Time: Family and Work in a Planned

While predominantly nuclear in its kinship structure, the preindustrial and early industrial household was likely to include others who were unrelated to the conjugal family members. Among such persons were servants, boarders and lodgers, apprentices, employees, and other people's children. Modell and Hareven show that "the proportion of urban households *which at any particular time* had boarders or lodgers was between 15 and 20 percent." Thus in nineteenth-century America many persons interacted with non-kin as part of the daily environment of their own homes. Today, on the contrary, non-kin are unlikely to be included in the household. In 1970, only 3.5 percent of all households covered by the federal census had one or more non-relatives of the head as resident members. [12]

Under contemporary conditions, socialization within the household primarily involves interactions between parents and children. The objects of identification, role modeling, and other psychodynamic processes in personality development are therefore limited by the characteristics of nuclear family members, and the socialization process will reflect the personalities and personal histories of individuals linked together by family ties only. Under these conditions, individuals are more likely to become identified with membership in a specific family unit. This feature of contemporary household composition has relevance for the creation of themes that become identified with a particular family. According to Hess and Handel:

A family theme is a pattern of feelings, motives, fantasies, and conven-

---

Corporation Town, 1900–1924," *Journal of Urban History* 1 (May 1975): 365–89; and B. Laslett, "Household Structure on an American Frontier: Los Angeles, California, in 1850," *American Journal of Sociology* 81 (July 1975): 109–28.

12. See John Modell and Tamara K. Hareven, "Urbanization and the Malleable Household: An Examination of Boarding and Lodging in American Families," *Journal of Marriage and the Family* 35 (August 1973): 467–79; and B. Laslett, "The Family as a Public and Private Institution: An Historical Perspective." Since taking in boarders was related to the family life cycle, overall figures may underestimate the proportion of persons affected by including "strangers" in the co-resident domestic group. For data on households in 1970 with one or more non-relatives of the head as resident members, see U.S. Bureau of the Census, *Census of Population: 1970, Subject Reports, Final Report PC(2)-4A, Family Composition* (Washington, D.C.: Government Printing Office, 1973), p. 246.

tionalized understanding grouped about some locus of concern which has a particular form in the personalities of the individual members. The pattern comprises some fundamental view of reality and some way or ways of dealing with it. In the family themes are to be found the family's implicit direction, its notion of "who we are" . . .[13]

The development and reiteration of such themes are likely to provide the basis for a more heightened sense of differentiation between family and non-family members in the present than in the past, when households included both kin and non-kin.

In earlier times, the influence of non-kin was likely to continue through adolescence, since many young adults lived in homes other than their parents'. They left home to find work, to become servants and apprentices, and, some have argued, for education and character-building. This pattern occurred in various parts of Western Europe and North America. In the late nineteenth century, at least in the industrializing economies of the New World, adolescents seem to have experienced a lengthening period of dependence upon their parents. Prior to that time, however, many spent their adolescence outside the parental home, and contact with kin was more likely to be a special occasion than a daily or weekly occurrence.[14]

Although these aspects of household composition influence the socialization of both adults and children throughout the life cycle, we can perhaps see the significance of these changes most clearly in relation to adolescence, a period that contemporary

13. Robert D. Hess and Gerald Handel, "The Family as a Psychosocial Organization," in *The Psychosocial Interior of the Family: A Sourcebook for the Study of Whole Families*, ed. Gerald Handel (Chicago: Aldine, 1967), p. 18.

14. See Demos, *A Little Commonwealth*; Edmund S. Morgan, *The Puritan Family* (New York: Harper & Row, 1966); Edward Shorter, *The Making of the Modern Family* (New York: Basic Books, 1975); Susan Bloomberg, "The Household and the Family: The Effects of Industrialization on Skilled Workers in Newark, 1840–1860" (Paper delivered at the meetings of the Organization of American Historians, Denver, April 1974); Michael B. Katz, *The People of Hamilton, Canada West* (Cambridge, Mass.: Harvard University Press, 1975); and Margaret Little and Barbara Laslett, "Adolescence in Historical Perspective: The Decline of Boarding in 19th Century Los Angeles" (Paper delivered at the annual meetings of the American Sociological Association, Chicago, September 1977).

psychologists characterize as a search for a separate identity on the part of young people. The increased identification of the self with a particular family unit, and the greater clarity of boundaries between family and non-family members, may have increased the need to differentiate one's self from the family group as part of the transition to adulthood, thereby sharpening parent-child conflict during adolescence. Furthermore, the wish to establish one's own identity is more likely to be experienced by both parents and children as a rejection of and rebellion against the more clearly formulated identity of a particular family.[15]

Under the conditions of contemporary family living, parents are more likely than in past times to develop strong identification with their children. Each stage of the child's development poses developmental tasks for the parents as well, reawakening themes and conflicts from their own youth and posing psychological tasks associated with aging. It is, therefore, not surprising that two contemporary concerns of psychodynamic thought center simultaneously on problems of adolescence and "the mid-life crisis." These "crises of growth" reflect in part the increased intensity of family relationships and the increased importance of family membership for personal identity to which historical changes in household composition have contributed.

DEMOGRAPHY AND KINSHIP

Three demographic factors are of particular importance in comparing the size and structure of the kinship group in past and present Western societies; mortality, age at marriage, and fertility. Although several types of kin will be considered, ascendant kin are most relevant for discussing the availability of persons

15. For a discussion of adolescence as a period of search for a separate identity, see Erik H. Erikson, "Identity and the Life Cycle," *Psychological Issues* 1 (1959). A discussion of other factors which may contribute to conflict in adolescence and early adulthood in the present more than in past times may be found in John Modell, Frank Furstenberg, and Theodore Hershberg, "Social Change and Transitions to Adulthood in Historical Perspective," *Journal of Family History* 1, no. 1 (Autumn 1976): 7–32.

likely to intentionally assume roles in the socialization process, particularly for children.[16]

Mortality

In the past, people generally did not live long enough for there to be a sizable pool of older relatives with whom contact was possible. In 1900, the expectation of life at birth (for the white population) in the United States was 48.2 years for males and 51.1 years for females. In 1970, these figures had risen to 68.0 years for males and 75.6 years for females. Although some nineteenth-century American mortality data is available, questions have been raised about its adequacy; the decline in mortality in the twentieth century, however, when vital registration data have become increasingly available, is clearer.

Infant mortality made a major contribution to death rates in earlier times; nevertheless, higher mortality in the past affected adults as well as infants. At age 20, the life-expectancy of white males was 42.2 additional years in 1900 and 50.3 additional years in 1970; the comparable figures for white women were 43.8 and 57.8, respectively. One consequence of these changing mortality rates is that "the chances that today's typical bride and groom will both survive the next 50 years (to their golden wedding anniversary) are more than twice as great as were the chances of such survival for their counterparts in 1900–02."[17]

16. Demos has discussed the potential significance of older siblings in the socialization process of children in large families in Plymouth Colony; see his "Demography and Psychology in the Historical Study of Family Life: A Personal Report," in *Household and Family in Past Time*, ed. P. Laslett, pp. 561–70. Shorter, however, says that in Europe only two or three children were in residence simultaneously and, given the tendency for employment to begin at relatively young ages, it is the older siblings who were most likely to have left their parents' homes; see Shorter, *Making of the Modern Family*, p. 26.

17. For data on life expectancy in 1900 and 1970, see U.S. Bureau of the Census, *The Statistical History of the United States: From Colonial Times to the Present* (Washington, D.C.: Government Printing Office, 1976); and for a discussion of the decline in mortality in the twentieth century based on vital registration data, see Conrad Taeuber and Irene B. Taeuber, *The Changing Population of the United States* (New York: John Wiley, 1958). For anniversary estimates, see

Thus, fewer parents and grandparents were available in the past to participate in the socialization of their children and grandchildren.

Differential mortality by sex is also relevant to kin contacts. In twentieth-century America, there has been an increasing sex difference in life expectancy. While the length of life (at birth and older ages) of both sexes has increased between 1900 and 1970, the increase for women has been greater than the increase for men. Contemporary research shows the importance of parents for continued kin contact among their adult children, and the mother's survival may be particularly important in this respect since women are more active than men in maintaining family ties. Thus women's longevity may help to sustain contacts among related adults.[18]

Age at Marriage

The median age at first marriage in the United States in 1890 was 26.1 years for men and 22.0 years for women; in 1950 it was 22.8 and 20.3 years; and in 1974 it was 23.1 and 21.1 years, respectively. The late nineteenth-century figures may well represent the high point of an upward trend, since available data indicate that people married at younger ages in the colonial period. In the twentieth century, however, compared to the late nineteenth, children are born (and are more likely to survive) earlier in their parents' life span. Under such circumstances, family members will be available both for more of the individual's life, because of increases in the life expectancy of the older

---

Metropolitan Life, "Likelihood of a Golden Wedding Anniversary," *Statistical Bulletin* 57 (February 1976): 4. For statistics on the change in age of adult mortality, see U.S. Bureau of the Census, *Statistical History*, p. 56.

18. Bert N. Adams shows the mother's importance for adult kin contact in *Kinship in an Urban Setting* (Chicago: Markham, 1968), pp. 27–28, 167. Linkages along the male line may be stronger when there are economic ties between fathers and their children. The decline in family business and self-employment in the twentieth century, discussed by Peter M. Blau and O. D. Duncan in *The American Occupational Structure* (New York: John Wiley, 1967), p. 41, would lessen the economic basis for contacts between fathers and their grown children.

generation, and for greater periods of the family life cycle, because new families begin at earlier ages.[19]

Fertility

While the pool of potential kin may be affected by declining mortality and age at first marriage, changing fertility rates are also relevant for estimating the size and structure of the kinship group in the present compared to the past. Fertility in the United States has declined.[20] The question, then, is whether lowered fertility offsets the effects of decreased mortality so that the number of living relatives per family in the present is no different than in the past.

Historical data that could illustrate this question directly are not available. However, Goodman, Keyfitz, and Pullum provide helpful material in their estimates of the number of living female relatives available to women of various ages. These researchers used the fertility and mortality data of the United States in 1967 and Madagascar in 1966, that is, a country with low fertility and low mortality which illustrates the modern demographic profile was compared to a society with high fertility and high mortality, the preindustrial pattern. In general, the results show that in societies with low fertility and low mortality, older relatives are more available and younger relatives are less available. The advantage in terms of the size of the kinship pool does not appear to be marked for one type of society compared to another. Gray's application of the Goodman, Keyfitz, and Pullum model to 1920, 1930, and 1970 United States demographic rates shows, however, that to the extent that there is a difference more living kin

19. See U.S. Bureau of the Census, *Current Population Reports, Series P-20, no. 271, Marital Status and Living Arrangements: March 1974* (Washington, D.C.: Government Printing Office, 1974), p. 1; and *Statistical History of the United States*, p. 19. Age at marriage also has an impact on the size of the kinship group; this is most clearly seen where marriage occurs early, and high fertility has been encouraged; see Herbert G. Gutman, *The Black Family in Slavery and Freedom, 1750–1925* (New York: Random House, Pantheon Books, 1976) for a discussion of the way these factors have affected the black family.

20. See Ansley J. Coale and Melvin Zelnik, *New Estimates of Fertility and Population in the United States* (Princeton: Princeton University Press, 1963); and Taeuber and Taeuber, *Changing Population*.

are available to contemporary Americans than in earlier periods. Furthermore, it should be remembered that migration, a significant feature of American life throughout its history, is higher among younger than among older adults. Thus, although more young adults may have been alive in preindustrial times, they were less available to interact with other family members than their numbers alone would suggest.[21]

The demographic factors reviewed here have implications for our understanding of patterns of family interaction and processes of socialization both within the household and within the extended kin group. Glick says that "the larger the family the larger the proportion of time that children are likely to spend interacting with each other, whereas the smaller the family the greater the proportion of time the children are likely to spend interacting with their parents."[22] Thus, changes in mortality, fertility, and age at marriage, as well as changes in household composition, are likely to affect the processes of role modeling and identification that occur within the contemporary family by increasing the impact of parents in the socialization process. Furthermore, demographic changes have also meant that more ascendant kin are available, particularly grandparents, uncles, and aunts, who may elaborate life-cycle models within the kinship group. Given the increased importance of family member-

21. It could be argued that contemporary Madagascar and preindustrial America are so different that the estimates by Goodman, Keyfitz, and Pullum cannot be used even suggestively. There are several reasons to reject this position: (1) the model is purely mathematical and takes account of no other characteristics of Madagascar society except its gross reproduction rate and expectation of life at birth; (2) the demographic rates used to generate the model's estimates for Madagascar are sufficiently close to the preindustrial American figures to validate their usefulness as suggestive (although certainly not conclusive) indicators. For details of this study see, Leo A. Goodman, Nathan Keyfitz and Thomas W. Pullum, "Family Formation and the Frequency of Various Kinship Relationships," *Theoretical Population Biology* 5 (February 1974): 1–27. For Gray's application of the Goodman, Keyfitz and Pullum model see Anke VanHilst Gray, "An Analysis of the Availability of Kin to Older Americans," unpublished paper, Dept. of Sociology, University of Southern California.

22. Paul C. Glick, "Updating the Life Cycle of the Family," *Journal of Marriage and the Family* 39 (February 1977): 11.

ship established in the early years of the socialization process, for both children and adults, and the improved means of contact and communication that technological advances have made available, kin contact may be more frequent than in earlier historical periods despite the lack of common residence.

URBANIZATION AND MIGRATION

Two factors relevant to the distribution of population that also affect the potential availability of kin with whom contact may occur are urbanization and migration. Rapid urbanization has been a feature in the American experience since the early nineteenth century, and the twentieth century has witnessed an increasing concentration of population into large metropolitan centers. Kin, therefore, may be concentrated in areas in which fairly frequent contact is possible, contact that is easier to make (and harder to avoid) because of the expansion of the highway system and the widespread availability of automobiles, air travel, and the telephone.

Migration, a characteristic of American life both past and present, has often been used to explain the absence of kin contact among mobile populations, because the act of migration (particularly overseas migration) reduces the pool of potential kin available both to the migrant and the non-migrant. Furthermore, the process of internal (versus overseas) migration can also thin the ranks of kin with whom contact is possible. Here again, literacy and the technology of communication are important, for once a relative leaves a community, contact between family members depends on what modes of communication are available. But the impact of migration may also vary according to whether it occurs earlier or later in the historical development of an area.

In earlier generations, migrating family members often established themselves in places that did not include members of their own kin group. First-generation migrants would be most severely restricted in terms of the availability of ascendant kin. The likelihood that kin would be found in the destinations of the next generation of migrants, however, was increased by the very fact that earlier migration of family members had occurred. It has been shown that nineteenth- as well as twentieth-century migrants chose their destinations in part because of the presence of kin group members in the new area. Thus, migration, particularly under modern technological conditions, does not necessarily reduce contact among kin to the degree suggested by earlier authors, although it does, perhaps, make it more voluntary.[23]

To summarize, structural factors have created the potential for family membership to become a more salient feature of personal identity in the contemporary period than in the Western, preindustrial past, through their effect on socialization within the household, on the increased number of ascendant kin, and on the spatial distribution of kin group members. In addition, developments in the technology of contact and communication, and increased literacy, make it easier for family members to be in touch with each other whether or not they live close together. In the earlier period, the co-resident domestic group was less often confined to primary kin group members alone, while in the present more households contain nuclear family members only. Thus, within the home, non-kin are not so likely to be available to diffuse identification with a particular family, and greater numbers of ascendant kin outside the home, with whom contact can easily take place, are available to amplify the identification developed within it.

THE IDEOLOGY OF FAMILY LIFE

Beliefs about family life in contemporary American society tend to reflect and reinforce the intimacy and intensity that residential and demographic factors make possible. The early Puritan ideology in America emphasized the role of the family as guardian of the public as well as the private good. Not only did religion

23. For a discussion of American migration patterns, see Everett S. Lee, "Internal Migration and Population Redistribution in the United States," in *Population: The Vital Revolution*, ed. Ronald Freedman (Garden City, N.Y.: Anchor Books, 1964). For data on foreign immigrants, see U.S. Bureau of the Census, *Statistical History*, p. 112. For evidence on the effects of kin on nineteenth- and twentieth-century migration patterns, see Hareven, "Family Time and Industrial Time," and Llewellyn Hendrix, "Kinship and Economic-Rational Migration: A Comparison of Micro- and Macro-Level Analyses," *Sociological Quarterly* 16 (Autumn 1975): 534–43.

specify the approved type of relationships between family members, their duties and responsibilities to each other, but it also made it a sacred duty of members of the church to see that these edicts were carried out. It was not sufficient for people to be moral in public; they also had to be moral in private, and religion provided a legitimating ideology for minding other people's family affairs.

In contrast to these beliefs, the idea of the private family and the home as a personal sanctuary grew throughout nineteenth-century America. Family life began to be characterized as an oasis, a retreat, a haven from the uncertainties, immoralities, and strains of life in a rapidly changing society. Elder's suggestion that "the family as refuge" was one reaction of American families to the Depression of the 1930s indicates that this theme has continued into the twentieth century. Insecurities in public and occupational roles reinforced the belief that the family was the only place where meaningful relationships were possible.[24]

The theme of the family as a retreat can also be found in recent discussions of contemporary nontraditional family forms such as communes and open marriages. These alternative family forms are thought to provide the opportunity for deep and meaningful personal relationships to a greater extent than other types of family living. Thus the family continues to be seen as a haven from the larger society. The ideology of family living, even in its most avant-garde forms, still views the family as a refuge from the larger society. The belief still prevails that it is only within the family that one can find intimate relationships and a sense of control over one's own life.[25]

The relationship of the family to other social institutions reinforces this image of the family. One of the features that has been said to characterize modern industrial societies is an increase in the importance of achieved versus ascribed attributes. In the life

24. See Kirk Jeffrey, "The Family as Utopian Retreat from the City: The Nineteenth-Century Contribution," *Soundings* 55 (Spring 1972): 21–41; and Glen H. Elder, Jr., *Children of the Great Depression: Social Change in Life Experience* (Chicago: University of Chicago Press, 1974).

25. Marvin B. Sussman, ed., *Non-Traditional Family Forms in the 1970's* (Minneapolis: National Council on Family Relations, 1972); and Zaretsky, *Capitalism, the Family and Personal Life*.

of families in Andover, Massachusetts, in the seventeenth century, access to land was crucial to the adult life of sons, and the father's control over land affected many aspects of the son's adult behavior, including when he could marry.[26] The growth of an occupational system that emphasizes an individual's educational achievements and the increasing availability of public education have loosened the constraints that these authority patterns and practices were likely to impose. Family contacts may therefore seem less crucial to achieving one's place in the modern occupational world. But the very fact that family contacts may no longer play such an important part in placing individuals in their public roles, thus reducing the instrumental usefulness of kin contacts, may increase their socio-emotional importance. In a society whose ideology values individual achievement and where favors won on grounds of kin ties are not generally considered legitimate, family membership may be prized simply because it does not have to be earned. The ascribed character of family membership may be experienced as a positive attribute for the very reason that it can be "taken for granted."

The socialization that occurs in today's American family is likely to contribute to the "taken for granted" character of family relationships. As social institutions have become more specialized, differences between the family and other institutions have sharpened. The fact that the contemporary family is private in character, providing a "backstage area" where persons can relax from performing their public roles, contributes to an ideology that defines the family primarily in socio-emotional terms. What is frequently forgotten in these formulations, however, is that performers not only relax backstage, but they also prepare for—and sometimes rehearse—their public roles. Potentially contradictory and confusing messages, a central focus of the recent developments in communication theory as it has been applied to the family, may create considerable discrepancy between the ideology and the actuality of contemporary family life.[27]

26. See Philip J. Greven, Jr., *Four Generations: Population, Land and Family in Colonial Andover, Massachusetts* (Ithaca, N.Y.: Cornell University Press, 1970).

27. For discussions of privacy and the family, see B. Laslett, "The Family as a Public and Private Institution: An Historical Perspective"; Skolnick, *The*

Changes in economic organization within society in general may also have affected the emotional meaning of family relationships in other ways. In the past, when the family was the unit of production as well as the unit of consumption, work and family roles were intertwined. The systematic separation of home and work activities that began in nineteenth-century America, the decline in proprietorship in the contemporary period, and the increase in the salaried and bureaucratic sector of the economy meant that today fewer family members work together than before. In the past, relationships between employers and employees, between masters and servants or apprentices, and between parents and children had greater emotional similarity to each other than they do today. It is precisely the decline in the intertwining of what we now see as diverse social roles that permits the intensification of the emotional aspects of family relationships.[28]

A similar argument can be made in relation to the family as educator. Before public schooling became widely available, much of a child's education took place in the home. When education was removed from the home, potential conflicts arising from the parents' responsibilities for both the intellectual development and the psychological well-being of the children were reduced. This is not meant to imply that parents are less concerned now than in the past about their children's educational achievement. Quite the opposite may in fact be the case. Alice Rossi has suggested that in the absence of clear-cut standards for parenting, mothers and fathers often look to children's report cards and pediatricians' reports as ways of judging their own performance as parents. The availability of institutions to foster children's attainment of cognitive skills outside the home permits

---

Intimate Environment, esp. pp. 63–67, and Erving Goffman, *The Presentation of Self in Everyday Life* (Garden City, N.Y.: Doubleday, 1959).

28. For studies which indicate that work relationships and familial ones shared greater similarity in the past, see Paul H. Douglas, *American Apprenticeship and Industrial Education*, Studies in History, Economics and Public Law 91 (New York: Columbia University Press, 1921), p. 55; see also B. Farber, *Guardians of Virtue: Salem Families in 1800* (New York: Basic Books, 1972) and P. Laslett, *The World We Have Lost*, 2d ed. (London: University Paperbacks, 1971).

and encourages greater concentration on the affective character of the parent-child relationship within it. Children's educational and occupational attainments are likely to take on a deeper psychological meaning for their parents, to become reflections or extensions of parental fantasies and ambitions for themselves. Thus the socio-emotional intensity of parent-child relations is even further reinforced.[29]

Social contact outside the residential unit may help to confirm or diminish the importance of family membership for personal identity. Frequent interaction between extended family members provides a basis for the continuing reaffirmation of the sense of family membership generated within the residential group; many studies since World War II show the importance of contact between kin compared to non-kin in the United States.[30] Thus, the importance of kinship is not only theoretical; it is also real, since kinship appears to provide the most significant basis for interaction when options are available.

CONCLUSION

The preceding analysis suggests the increasing importance of family membership in the United States. Changes in household composition and the demography of kinship, in the technology of communication and the spread of literacy, in the ideology of family life and the relationship of the family to other social institutions have affected the process of socialization in ways that have increased the salience of the family in the formation of personal identity. The fears of early writers that urbanization and industrialization would weaken "the bonds of kinship" have not materialized. On the contrary, the historical changes that

29. See Lawrence A. Cremin, "The Family as Educator: Some Comments on the Recent Historiography," *Teachers College Record* 76 (December 1974): 250–65, for a discussion of the importance of the home as educator in earlier times. Other relevant features of modern parenthood are discussed in Alice S. Rossi, "Transition to Parenthood," *Journal of Marriage and the Family* 30 (February 1968): 26–39, and Flacks, *Youth and Social Change*.

30. See, for instance, John E. Lawson, Jr., "The Impact of the Local Metropolitan Environment on the Patterning of Social Contacts" (Ph.D. diss., University of Southern California, 1974).

have been described have resulted in an "intensified . . . weight of meaning [being] attached to the personal relations of the family."[31]

How, then, are the family problems and strains discussed at the beginning of this paper to be understood? Weigert and Hastings suggest that the contemporary family's "specialized function of affectivity and expressivity for the sustenance of emotionally charged personal identities" also makes it a particularly powerful source of pain and potential conflict.[32] In addition the specialized and bureaucratic organization of modern life has made the family one of the few places where the expression of strong feeling is felt to be legitimate, and thus the likelihood that emotionally charged interactions, both positive and negative, will occur in the family is increased.

Perhaps, then, the most important question to ask about the modern family is not whether it is "here to stay" but whether it can sustain itself under the weight of the expectations placed upon it. The contradiction implied by characterizing the contemporary family as "here to stay, but not well" may reflect real contradictions that the family faces in modern American society. We must begin to ask if the family does, or can, have the means, both material and emotional, to satisfy the multitude of urgent demands confronting it today. An answer to this question may require a change in our understanding of the family—a change that focuses on the reality of the resources available rather than simply on the intensity of our desires.

31. Fears that urbanization and industrialization would weaken family bonds were expressed by Louis Wirth, "Urbanism as a Way of Life," *American Journal of Sociology* 44 (July 1938): 3–24; but Zaretsky, *Capitalism, the Family and Personal Life*, p. 66, indicates that instead the bonds have intensified.

32. Weigert and Hastings, "Identity Loss, Family and Social Change," p. 1179.

I I

White Ethnic and Chicano Families: Continuity and Adaptation in the New World

ANDREI SIMIĆ

At a time when individualism, self-realization, and sexual liberation loom large in American social thought, the image of the ethnic family stands out in sharp contrast. There is little doubt that among the trend-setters and the so-called cultural elites this image is far from chic, and probably at best would be condescendingly dismissed as archaic or reactionary. Michael Novak, philosopher and spokesman for white ethnic causes, has gone so far as to suggest that in today's cultural atmosphere the deliberate creation of such a family has become a "political statement," and that to "love family life, to see in family life the most potent moral, intellectual, and political cell in the body politic is to be marked . . . as a heretic."[1]

When Novak speaks of traditional family life, he is undoubtedly drawing on the model that was brought to America by his own immigrant ancestors from their peasant, Catholic hearth in

1. The generalizations in this essay—the "images" of the white ethnic and Chicano families—represent a synthesis of a vast published and manuscript literature on immigrant society and culture in the United States, field work carried out by the author and his students among Euro-Americans and Spanish-speaking minorities in California, and a lifetime of personal familiarity with Southern and Eastern European immigrant life in this country. Michael Novak's remark comes from "The Family out of Favor," *Harper's* (April 1976), pp. 37–46.

Eastern Europe. It is from these, and similar Old World roots, that the term *ethnic* has taken on one of a number of restricted and very specialized meanings in American society. Increasingly ethnicity has come to signify something either in part *foreign* or otherwise outside the currents of the Anglo or Anglicized mainstream. For some, this concept refers almost entirely to racial minorities such as blacks, Chicanos, Asians, native Americans, and the like; for others, it is applied to the descendants of non–English-speaking immigrants, the majority of whom arrived at the end of the nineteenth and beginning of the twentieth century. It is to this latter group, the New Immigration, that white ethnics belong as the descendants and cultural inheritors of a Latin, Hellenic, or Slavic civilization. Their traditions of Mediterranean and Central European Catholicism and Byzanto-Slavic Orthodoxy injected into the American scene an element quite different from the older, entrenched Northern European Protestantism that had dominated the United States since its incipiency. Novak has facetiously labeled this new wave of immigration by the acronym PIGS: Poles, Italians, Greeks, and Slovaks. Though divided by language, divergent histories, centuries-old national antagonisms, and a deep-seated conviction by each group of its own superiority and cultural uniqueness, nevertheless white ethnics so closely resemble each other in their basic ideology and commonality of experience in the New World that they easily lend themselves to characterization as a whole. Similarly, as will be demonstrated later in this essay, many of the same traits that typify Southern and Eastern Europeans also pertain to the Mexican-Americans, who, though they differ in a number of important respects, including their partially Indian origins, are nevertheless the carriers of what is in its essence a Mediterranean cultural heritage.

SYNCRETISM AND CULTURAL MAINTENANCE

What then are the family image and the underlying ideology that transcend the boundaries of so many diverse national groups, and what has been the fate of this way of life in contemporary America? For the casual observer standing on the outside, socially distant from the ethnic communities, the answer has been obscured in two ways: first, by the tenacity in popular and academic thought of the doctrine of inevitable assimilation; and second, by the white ethnic's own reticence and relative invisibility within the greater white population. In the former case, assimilation is an undeniable historic fact, but it would be erroneous to believe that this has been the *only* process acting upon immigrant life. On the contrary, syncretism and cultural maintenance have occurred with equal or even greater vigor. For example, white ethnics in their incorporation over several generations into the lower-middle class have fused Old World traits devoid of their national specificity into a more diffuse, class-specific blue-collar culture. At the same time, others have built upon the legacy of their parents and grandparents, creating new meanings and functions within the American context. For evidence of the continuity of immigrant culture and society one need only observe the vitality of the many thousands of ethnically based voluntary associations, churches, and other cultural institutions. However, these often exist in our very midst unnoticed. The low profile of ethnic-Americans is due in part to the indifference of the society around them, and in part to the intensity of their own cliquishness, their heavy dependence on personal social networks composed principally of co-ethnics, and, above all else, their pride in family, group autonomy, and self-sufficiency. Thus, in times of crisis they have largely avoided the established routes of political influence and public welfare in favor of reliance on the integrity of their own kinship and ethnic ties. The ethnic world view has rested heavily on the pillars of nationalism, personalism, and tradition. Moreover, while there has been considerable sloughing off of members into ethnically undifferentiated American life, core values have been maintained over three or four generations by those descendants of the New Immigration whose principal source of identity has remained their *hyphenated* Americanism.

In seeking the antecedents of the ethnic family vision, one is tempted to cite those cases that most pronouncedly differ from the loosely organized, highly individualized, egalitarian view of family life held by many upper-middle-class Americans. For example, Italy, particularly in the south, provides a picture of a family united as a single moral entity in opposition to what is perceived as a "dangerous, pernicious, and predatory" external world. As Richard Gambino observes, the only system to which the southern Italian peasant paid attention was *l'ordine della famiglia*, the unwritten but all-binding rules governing relationships within, and responsibilities toward, one's family.[2] A similar ethic prevailed among the South Slav peasants of the Balkan Peninsula who contributed so many of their children to the mines and heavy industries of the American Midwest. In this case, however, the moral field was a more encompassing one including not only the nuclear family and household but also all of one's father's consanguine kin. Kinship obligations were so sacred and obligatory that men were sometimes called upon to avenge the killing of even very distant paternal cousins in the endless vendettas that raged throughout the Dinaric Mountains east of the Adriatic Sea. Such an ethic is not easily destroyed even in the vortex of the conflicting and ever-changing norms of contemporary American society. In the words of an aged Montenegrin writing from his village to a nephew in distant California whom he had never seen, "Forgetfulness creates separation, not time and space; and the passage of time has not succeeded in tearing one leaf from the tree of our family."[3]

FAMILY CORPORACY: ITS INTERACTION WITH NATIONAL IDENTITY AND AMERICAN LIFE

Two basic factors underlie the development of the ethnic family in the United States: the idea of *corporacy*, which provides the fundamental value structure upon which all elaborations are built, and the interaction of this value structure with the concept of national identity on the one hand and American life on the other. The relationship between family and ethnicity is an integrated one in that national origins are the product of birth and, by extension, ethnicity can be regarded as *kinship writ large*. Thus, it is not at all surprising that co-ethnics frequently address each other by such terms as "brother" and "sister." Ethnic con-

2. Richard Gambino, *Blood of My Blood: The Dilemma of Italian-Americans* (Garden City, N.Y.: Doubleday, Anchor Books, 1975).
3. Personal letter to the author.

sciousness is nourished from the child's earliest days at the side of the mother and father, and concurrently the very values that tie children to their parents by the strongest moral bonds are embedded in the traditional wisdom and customs of the national group. However, neither family nor ethnic enclave could replicate all of the institutions, functions, and services typifying the greater American society, and so the ethnic child was obliged to relate also to the outside world. Because of this, it was inevitable that a marriage take place between the two cultures, sometimes harmonious, sometimes turbulent. From this intertwining has emerged a new kind of dual, compartmentalized identity mirrored in such hypenized denominators as Polish-, Greek-, Slovak-, Armenian-, or Italian-American.

In no single area has the confrontation between American and old-country values been greater than in the realm of family ideology. For example, nothing could be more antithetical to the ethnic vision than the picture of the American family as seen through the eyes of a young Frenchman in Anne Morrow Lindbergh's novel *Dearly Beloved*: "They were all individuals . . . loosely but reluctantly tied together."[4] If the major tenets of the American ethos are unfettered personal freedom devoid of "demeaning dependence," atomistic individualism, unencumbered decision-making, and individual rather than familial fulfillment, then it was inevitable that Southern and Eastern European immigrants would experience a profound assault on the most basic premises upon which their lives were based. Similarly, it follows that their children in turn would be torn, sometimes irreparably, between the values pertaining to the hermetically sealed internal worlds of their natal homes and the exigencies and lure of American life. For some, the answer has been complete assimilation; for others, compartmentalization; and for still others, an almost total encapsulation within the ethnic enclave. These three options demonstrate an important fact about the nature of ethnicity, that is, ethnicity is not simply an *ascribed* characteristic, but also an *achieved* one, at least in American society. Thus, hyphenated ethnicity as it exists in this

4. Anne Morrow Lindbergh, *Dearly Beloved: A Theme and Variations* (New York: Popular Library, 1963).

country is not the product of the same kind of absolute either/or categorization that typifies the black-white racial dichotomy or the rigid ethnic boundaries that separate peoples in most other parts of the world. Rather, there is a spectrum of possibilities spanning the poles separating complete Anglicization on the one hand and what I will designate as *core ethnicity* on the other. In this sense a *core ethnic* is a person whose major social and psychological identity stems from his or her immigrant roots, and who participates consistently and actively in networks of co-ethnicity. They are the people who maintain the ethnic institutions and associations. The core ethnic is not likely to have large numbers of close friends outside of his or her own enclave, and will probably maintain an ethnic life style that includes a very special vision of the family.

If the white ethnic family ideal were to be realized (and there is every indication that it is at least often closely replicated), what would it be like? Stated simply, the stereotypic family is one in which roles are highly differentiated and complementary within the group, but solidary in the face of the outside world. This complementarity is based on the simple principles of generational and sexual differences, differences that are given expression uncritically as part of the "God-given" or "natural" order.

The Ideology of Family Corporacy

The development of corporate sentiments starts in the children's earliest years with a strong, constantly reinforced orientation away from their extra-familial age-mates and other nonfamilial, nonethnic influences. For example, boundaries against "outsiders" and "foreigners" are continually strengthened through parental authority, appeals to moral absolutes, and negative stereotyping, while at the same time family unity is emphasized as the primary bastion of obligation, fulfillment, and security. One manifestation of this mentality is de-emphasis of the concept of privacy and private property within the home, combined with a prevailing ethic of secrecy and rejection in respect to persons outside this tight-knit group. For the ethnic, the social universe consists of *we* and *they*. For example, a Sicilian-American related how once in her early childhood she was severely castigated by her mother for casually revealing to her playmates that her father had recently purchased a new jacket. In her family, one of the worst accusations was that of "blabber-mouth," since any bit of information no matter how trivial or seemingly inconsequential represented a possible chink in the family's protective armor, and thus a potential weapon in the arsenal of others.

The ideology of family corporacy also generates a sentiment of common reputation, as well as economic solidarity and inter-dependence. The concept of common reputation acts as a power-ful force preserving traditional values and insuring acceptance of family norms. Thus, one's behavior is never regarded as simply one's own concern, but rather that of the entire family group who will exert a variety of moral and social pressures to bring deviants back into conformity. Moreover, another correlate of this belief system is the firm expectation that each person will use his or her particular talents, position, or power to the advantage of the entire family, sometimes even that of more distant kin. Conversely, economic individualism is antithetical to the family ideal, and in many immigrant families even adult children con-tinue to contribute their earnings to a common coffer controlled by their mother or father. This reflects a more generalized con-cept whose guiding rule is that among close kin good fortune will be shared, and thus individuals will be constantly subjected to equalizing forces.

Internal Differentiation by Age and Sex

Though the ethnic family may appear as a homogeneous and solidary unit to the outsider, internally it is highly differentiated in terms of the loci of affection, power, and authority. Within the home the principle of *age* is dominant whether it corresponds to different generations or to the order of birth among siblings. Crosscutting the criterion of seniority is that of *sex*, with the male associated with authority, and the female with positive affect. From the constraints and prerogatives associated with age and sex, there emerges a logic that only *likes* may compete since those who differ in these respects also differ in terms of their contribu-tions, obligations, and privileges.

One of the points of greatest variance between the model of the ethnic family and that of the Anglo or Anglicized middle class is the view of what constitutes an ideal marriage. Among the most familiar American images is that of a husband and wife joined together by bonds of communication, affection, and sexual and ethereal love. In this all too frequently unrealized dream husbands and wives are pictured as companions and confidants. In contrast, such a concept would have surely seemed strange, and even indecent, to Southern and Eastern European immigrants at the turn of the century. For example, among the older generation of Serbian immigrants in the United States, as is even today the case in many parts of rural Yugoslavia, overt displays of affection between husbands and wives were considered socially unacceptable, and I can remember hearing more than once a man introduce his wife with the apologetic words, "if you will please forgive me, may I present. . . ." Thus, for them marriage was not a matter of personal predilection, but rather the product of an inevitable and pragmatic decision to create a reproductive and economic unit whose cohesiveness was based on the authoritative and affective links between generations. These ties were especially strong between mothers and sons, since mothers formed the affectual core of the family, and daughters "married out," and were in a sense lost.

The preceding model of the ethnic family, like all stereotypes, should not be attributed unwarranted reality or taken to be predictive of all actual cases. Clearly any single construct will ignore the very real differences that divide the various white ethnic groups: for example, the Greek and southern Italian stress on chaperonage and female premarital virginity, or the south Slav insistence on male dominance and overt displays of machismo. Nevertheless, it is also important to distinguish between what are simply superficial differences in custom and individual behavior and the deeper structure of more generalized ideology and relationships. In other words, what has been outlined here is an abstract set of ideas, a basic cultural plan according to which decisions and courses of action are formulated and evaluated. It is this set of guidelines interacting with other forces in American life that has determined to a large extent the historical development of the ethnic family in the United States.

ETHNIC NEIGHBORHOODS

The maintenance of traditional peasant life in Cleveland, Chicago, or Youngstown poses obstacles undreamed of in the villages of the Calabrian, Thracian, or Croatian countrysides. In the small, rural community of traditional Europe where a homogeneous body of public opinion and intimate highly personalized means of social control prevailed, it was exceedingly difficult, if not impossible, to deviate from the norms of propriety permeating every aspect of existence. There, to deviate was to be outside the moral sphere, to place oneself, as it is sometimes phrased in parts of Eastern Europe, "behind God's back." Nevertheless, immigrants did succeed in forming compact, village-like ethnic enclaves in some American cities where the weight of age-old custom and the fear of ostracism could still compel a degree of conformity. These were the so-called *ethnic neighborhoods* such as the Boston Italian community described by Herbert Gans in his classic work *The Urban Villagers*.[5] Today such neighborhoods are rapidly disappearing though their remnants still survive in such places as Chicago or Cleveland where a tour of the city will reveal the visible evidence of the boundaries that once firmly separated Slovene, Italian, Croat, Hungarian, Polish, and Jewish sections. One can still see the small shops with their appetizing offerings of native foods, the ethnic churches and meeting halls, and a few bars and restaurants where on Saturday nights polka and Gypsy bands still play into the early morning hours. But these neighborhoods are dying under the impact of suburban growth, ethnic occupational mobility, and the progressing social and physical deterioration of the inner city. Even during the florescence of such enclaves, immigrant children could not be hermetically sealed safely away from the "polluting" influences of American life. There was inevitable fraternization in the schools, and in the mixed multiethnic congregations that typified some Catholic churches. Although exposure to American ways and acculturation was inevitable, some groups have been more resistant than others. This has

5. Herbert J. Gans, *The Urban Villagers: Group and Class in the Life of Italian-Americans* (New York: Free Press, 1965).

been true for example of the various Eastern Christians such as the Greeks, Serbs, Bulgars, Romanians, and Armenians who have maintained their own national churches and a plethora of associated institutions. But even here, the use of English has gradually penetrated the rituals, replacing the ancient liturgical languages, and reflecting the at least partial assimilation of the faithful. Perhaps among all immigrant groups only the Gypsies, through their stubborn defiance of public education, their spatial mobility, and uncompromising exclusivity, have remained relatively untouched by the forces of Americanization.

THE CONCEPT OF GENERATIONS

From the process of assimilation has emerged the concept of *generations*, the idea that each succeeding generation descending from the original immigrants manifests its own particular relationship to Old World and American culture. For instance, the Serbs are similar to other groups in this respect, and among them the first immigrants are affectionately known as the "old-timers." These early settlers now occupy an almost sacred and mythological place even though many are still with us. It is they who established the first national churches and voluntary associations, and upon whose regional, rural culture future elaborations in the new homeland were built. Popular belief holds that no other generation in either the old country or America has exhibited their moral fiber: they were honest to a fault, their word was their honor, they worked tirelessly from dawn until late at night, they were thrifty and built a material basis for the mobility of future generations, and above all else, they were the guardians of the sanctity of the family. The old-timers attempted to maintain a way of life reminiscent of their impoverished but still cherished villages, but in doing so they encapsulated themselves in isolation from American life, partially out of pride in their own heritage and in part out of fear of rejection and ridicule.

In contrast to the original immigrants, the first-generation ethnics born in the United States frequently opted for assimilation with an enthusiasm and dedication that deeply distressed their parents. Nikitas became "Nick," Miroslav was transformed into "Mike," and Pietro was rendered as "Pete." Perhaps even more disturbing to the older generations was the loss of time-honored family and clan names, and the metamorphosis of Petrovich, Georgiades, and Simonovski into Peterson, George, and Simpson was a stinging rejection of ancestral heritage and a sign of conflict in generational values. Nevertheless, the break with old-country language and culture and the gulf separating parents and children were rarely irrevocable, and in many cases only superficial. Though first-generation Americans rarely mastered their ancestral languages totally, and their mothers and fathers frequently spoke only rudimentary English, a deeper more basic kind of communication had occurred and left its mark. This was on a profound instinctual level of human interaction, and it consisted of the implicit messages that link children and parents through the medium of authority and positive affect. Thus, it was a rare first-generation American who doubted the deep and lasting dedication of his parents to the ideal of family solidarity and welfare, and regardless of their new-found freedom and mobility in American society, immigrant children continued on the whole to regard the family as an entity spanning the generations in contrast to the more limited nuclear-family model current in the United States.

Sexuality and Marriage

Perhaps the area of most acute conflict between immigrants and their children was that of sexuality and marriage. On the one hand, the older generation attempted to control the selection of a marriage partner and to impose old-country standards of sexual morality, while on the other their children were attracted by the freedom that young people enjoyed in the United States to associate openly with the opposite sex and to choose their own husbands and wives. This certainly occurred among all Southern and Eastern European ethnic groups, but it was perhaps most pronounced among those with origins in the Mediterranean countries. In this respect, Gambino describes the desire of Italian-American parents to dominate their children:

Attempts by Italian immigrants to impose this system of courtship and wedding on their American-born children were strongly rejected and led to great conflict between generations. The second generation sought parental approval but insisted on free dating and personal selection of spouses in the American manner. The second generation usually won its way, but at the cost of breaking the cultural wellsprings of its own values.[6]

Gambino's contention clearly reflects one aspect of ethnic intergenerational relationships; however, there is also another reality in which parents have succeeded in at least partially imposing their own customs and standards on their children. It is interesting that the inculcation of sexual and filial values is inseparably tied to the perpetuation of ethnic sentiment, and those who are most alienated from their parents are also likely to be those most estranged from their national origins. Certainly, many individuals have been lost in this way to their ethnic communities, but at the same time there has always remained an uninterrupted core maintaining from generation to generation the integrity of ancestral identities. Perhaps among the most successful in this respect have been the Greek-Americans for whom the control of courtship has been central to the maintenance of both family and ethnicity. Consider, for instance, the following case:

Twenty-four-year-old Helen is beautiful in an almost classic Hellenic sense with flowing auburn hair, large grey eyes and a gently aquiline nose. Her parents, immigrants from an Aegean island, are "old-fashioned" even by the standards of the conservative Greek-American community. Nevertheless, as such they are seldom the brunt of malicious gossip, and are even openly admired for their conservative stance. Helen has never been on a "real date," though she did attend the senior prom with a Greek-American boy whose family were long-time friends of her parents, and whom her mother and father hoped she would eventually marry. However, the romance progressed too slowly, and he eventually married another Greek-American girl at his mother's instigation. On another occasion, Helen was a "debutante" at an Orthodox Church Ball, and was escorted there by her forty-two-year-old bachelor cousin, "so no one would talk." Helen has repeatedly requested permission to go out with boys, but her parents' answer is always the same, "Look at your older sister, she never dated, and now she is happily married to a wonderful Greek boy, and besides, we don't

6. Gambino, *Blood of My Blood*, p. 199.

want the whole community gossiping about you." For her parents, the entire social universe consists of their church congregation, and they harbor the omnipresent fear that Helen may lose her reputation in the tight-knit Hellenic colony, or worse, that she may marry a non-Greek or even a non-Orthodox.[7]

Fear of Losing "Communication" with One's Grandchildren

The attempt at control of courtship and marriages rests not only on the fear of alienation of one's children but also the potential loss of grandchildren and the disappearance of marriage as a social resource by which alliances are created. Immigrants who speak only Czech, Polish, or Italian fear with justification that if their children marry outside the ethnic group the parents will not only be unable to communicate with their new in-laws but also with their own grandchildren. In this case, *communication* is used in its broadest context including not only language but also culture as a system of shared values and ideas. Moreover, immigrants steeped in the mysticism of nineteenth-century European nationalism frequently harbor feelings of distrust and antipathy toward members of other national groups. Nevertheless, no matter how firm their commitment to such values, immigrant families have over the generations adapted and compromised.

First-generation Americans have often played a special kind of social role in respect to their parents, that of *culture brokers* negotiating relationships between the home and the outside world, and as interpreters of American life styles. It is in this function that we can discern the origins, at least in part, of what I call the "sacrificial child." By this I refer to an unmarried, adult son or daughter who does not leave the parental home until the death of both parents, if then. Certainly this occurs among every group, but among ethnic-Americans it assumes a particular meaning. In some cases, an older sibling assumes responsibility for his or her parents so as to "liberate" the younger brothers and sisters. Moreover, as the eldest, the child may take advantage of

7. This composite case history is based on work by Marie Marsis, my former student at the University of Southern California, who collected case histories among young, unmarried Greek-Americans in Los Angeles.

this authoritative position within the traditional concept of family roles to allow greater autonomy to younger and often more Americanized siblings. Perhaps the most poignant example of the sacrificial child acting as a culture broker is the case of the adult son with a widowed mother. Among immigrants, men because of their work-a-day lives usually acquired a better handle on the English language and American culture than did their wives who remained isolated in the home and in the exclusive company of family and co-ethnics. Thus, for a bicultural son to remain unmarried so as to respond to his widowed mother's needs in this manner was considered an entirely normal, and indeed expected, solution.

The Grandchildren's Quest for Their Heritage

For the grandchildren of immigrants, that is, for second-generation Americans, old-country ways have largely lost their stigma. What was overt rejection of "foreignness" on the part of their parents has turned for many into an exciting quest for a lost heritage. This has resulted in a revivalistic movement stressing the acquisition of ancestral culture particularly in the areas of music, folklore, language, and cuisine. This, of course, points to the romanticization that results from both distance in time and space. It also gives evidence of a certain kind of discontinuity between the generations, a discontinuity, however, that is largely superficial. In this respect, the loss of certain visible cultural characteristics has masked the perpetuation of a deeper structure of underlying values many of which relate to family solidarity. Certainly the kinship ethic has suffered a frontal attack in America, and as a result many of the descendants of the New Immigration have simply disappeared into the mainstream. However, old-country ideology has survived in two ways: first, in the context of families who have maintained their ethnic identity from generation to generation in spite of numerous accommodations to American life; and second, through the infusion of these same values into American culture as part of the assimilation process. For example, in this latter respect, Krickus speaks of what he terms "an immigrant working-class subculture" resulting from the fusion of beliefs and social patterns transplanted from the Old World with those existing in the new one.[8] Thus, we can observe that on the one hand ethnic communities and families have survived intact and that on the other many of their values have become part of the body of American tradition particularly as it pertains to the so-called blue-collar class.

THE CHICANOS

Much of what has been said about white ethnics also pertains to the Chicanos. By and large they are the products of a peasant, economic emigration from a non–English-speaking, traditionally Catholic culture whose dominant component is of Mediterranean origin. Moreover, one of the most common stereotypes of the Mexican-American is the association with a family ideal, *la familia*. However, at the same time there are salient differences that distinguish the Chicano from the white-ethnic. Chicanos are usually, though not always, identifiable by physical type which represents a synthesis of Indian, Hispanic, and sometimes black ancestry. Also, they are concentrated in the American Southwest contiguous to their country of origin, a fact tending to confer on them a status analogous to that of national minorities in other parts of the world. Finally, for a variety of reasons, Chicanos have not thoroughly integrated into the lower-middle class but rather have remained, for the most part, on its fringes confined largely to unskilled or semiskilled labor.

Although the Chicanos' vision of the family as the focus of the most basic human values closely parallels that of the white ethnic both in sentiment and form, what probably most differentiates them from the latter has been the difficulty in achieving this ideal, and thus the resulting disparity that exists between their values and their reality. In this respect, anthropologist Oscar Lewis notes that those living in what he has controversially labeled "the culture of poverty" frequently are aware of middle-class values but are unable to give them substance. For example, in his study of impoverished Puerto Ricans in San Juan and New

8. Richard Krickus, *Pursuing the American Dream: White Ethnics and the New Populism* (Garden City, N.Y.: Doubleday, Anchor Books, 1976).

York City, he observes that "to men who have no steady jobs or other sources of income, who do not own property and who have no wealth to pass on to their children, who are present-time oriented, and who want to avoid the expenses and legal difficulties in formal marriage and divorce, free unions or consensual marriage make a lot of sense."[9] Surely Lewis's comments apply to a minority of Chicano families but yet point out one of the many ways in which economic and social discrimination combined with poverty has made the realization of the Hispanic familial vision difficult.

The Male-Female Dichotomy: Machismo and Vergüenza

If the traditional Mexican-American image of the family and its incumbent roles differs from that of the white ethnic, the difference is more one of degree than quality. Stated simply, the ideology is one of a solidary family group stratified by age, and with husband and wife occupying antithetical roles of dominance and submission. Perhaps the key to this model is not so much the idea of corporacy as the stress on the male-female dichotomy which appears to be even more pronounced than among Southern and Eastern Europeans. This opposition has become almost a cliché in the familiar stereotypes of male prowess called *machismo* and those of female shame or propriety frequently referred to as *vergüenza*. According to this pattern a man must be independent, self-reliant, quick to take offense, and equally quick to defend his honor. He establishes the proof of his manhood through the seduction of woman, the fathering of many children, and the defense of his family's honor. This involves a moral dichotomization of the female world into the *sacred* and *profane*. The most sacred of all women is the mother, followed by daughters, sisters, and wives, all of whom occupy essentially equally revered positions. By definition, profane women are not members of one's household, and as such are subject to male aggression. On the other hand, the sacred female assumes a perfect counterpart to the male. She is unassertive, sexually passive, oriented away

9. Oscar Lewis, *La Vida: A Puerto Rican Family in the Culture of Poverty—San Juan and New York* (New York: Random House, 1966), p. xlvi.

266

from the outside world toward the home, and dedicated to the care and welfare of her husband and children. However, anthropologist William Madsen found that even in the conservative Mexican-American communities of south Texas over a decade ago this stereotype was rarely realized in its entirety, and he observes: "The conservative Latin wife is, in fact, a skilled manipulator of her lord and master. The weapons she uses in disguised form are his own self-esteem, his *machismo*, and his role as provider and protector."[10]

Not only does it appear that the machistic image has always been one difficult to actualize, but in contemporary America the growing impact of political and social activism has also been felt in the realm of Mexican-American family life, particularly as it applies to sexual stereotypes. Many young Chicanos, influenced by the Women's Movement and other recent ideologies, have sought new more egalitarian sexual models. Nevertheless, much of the old mentality lingers on, sometimes in overt manifestations, but perhaps more often as an underlying force channeling new forms of behavior and expectations. For example, although chaperonage has disappeared, and American-style dating has become the rule, nevertheless, many young women still value virginity and respect their parents' demands "to be home before midnight." Similarly, young men, although they espouse the values of equality, still believe that women are to be "conquered," and that true love can be commanded through bravado and force of personality rather than mutual sympathy and the development of common interests.

The Mother as a Quasi-Sacred Object

Another key to understanding the Chicano family lies in the idealized role of the mother, which is less ambiguous and more secure than that of the wife. The wife, who always carries some taint of sexuality and thus potential profanity, as a mother assumes the position of a quasi-sacred object to her own children, and as such possesses the power usually associated with holy

10. William Madsen, *Mexican-Americans of South Texas* (New York: Holt, Rinehart and Winston, 1964).

things. This power also rests on her focal position in the household as the affectual core of family life. Thus, paradoxically, as is also the case in the white ethnic family, the machistic ideal is embedded in what might be termed a *crypto-matriarchy*. Culture is, however, nothing if it is not paradoxical, and in dealing with its exhortations we learn to segregate its various functions and call upon them in situations where they promise utility. Therefore, the conflict between the role of adoring and respectful son, on the one hand, and the aggressive dominant male, on the other, is resolved by the segregation of behavioral modes, some appropriate in the home, and others outside its walls. The inevitable passage of time also mitigates these conflicts since with age women acquire increasing prerogatives in inverse relationship to their sexual attractiveness since their sexuality no longer threatens family honor. Conversely, as a man grows old his strength wanes, and with it there develops a growing dependence on his wife and children.

Children as the Inevitable and Desired Product of Marriage

Another central theme in the family life of Mexican-Americans, as in Mexico, is the firm expectation of children as the inevitable and desired product of marriage. It would not be an exaggeration or needless embellishment to state that young children are *adored*, and in this adoration is personified the solidarity and continuity of the Chicano family group. It is not coincidental that so many religious and family rituals focus on children. Commencing with baptism and confirmation children provide the rationale for the gathering of family and kin, and these occasions whether birthdays or a young girl's "coming out" party at the age of fifteen provide an opportunity for the expression of family unity and a device for socializing the children themselves into the dominant value system. Some large families, in fact, are so self-sufficient that there is little need of external stimulus in the form of non-kin friends or acquaintances. Where such extra-familial friendships do exist, the patterns of interactions are those based on the same model of intense reciprocity that typifies family ties. Moreover, close friendship is often transformed into a kind of kinship through the powerful medium of the ritual of godparenthood.

Conclusion

Both Mexican immigrants and those from Southern and Eastern Europe brought with them to the United States a concept of family life rooted in the small-scale, rural societies from which they emigrated. These ideas were the product of the intimate relationships and close cooperation that were both necessary and possible in the context of a subsistence agricultural life. In these distant and impoverished villages, generation had succeeded generation in a predictable and orderly way. However, it is remarkable that these images could have provided the basic framework for the building of a new kind of life in a very different sort of society, one based on a vast urban population and an industrial economy where change and social mobility were among the most widely accepted and revered values. The persistence of these familial ideologies in the United States constituted the basic plan for the establishment of new roots, and the subsequent acculturation, accommodation, and successful mobility of future generations. Moreover, the very persistence of these Old World values testifies to the adaptability and tenacity of traditional forms of family organization even in the face of concerted onslaughts against their central ethos. Finally, the evidence provided by these immigrant groups belies the inevitability of the "melting pot."

Images, such as those described in this essay, are seldom realized in their entirety, but nevertheless there are moments in life for all of us when we hold the warm illusion that indeed they have been. The ultimate significance of such ideologies lies, then, not in the frequency with which they are given expression but in their function as a guideline for making choices, as a measure to judge one's personal success or failure, and finally, and most significantly, as a personal and social resource assuring us of the ultimate reasonableness and meaningfulness of life.

12

Black Families: A Social Welfare Perspective

BARBARA BRYANT SOLOMON & HELEN A. MENDES

Black people do not have families—we have survival units. That is all that we are allowed to have. A family plays a specific role in the organization of any social system. A family in a viable society has a particular role and then they have little social units called children to be functional people to carry out the natural development of the groups. As oppressed people, we are not supposed to be maximally developed. . . . We hear a lot of discussion by black scholars . . . praising the strength of black families. Nonsense! You can't talk about strengths and then talk about oppression![1]

In these bitter words, a young black psychiatrist identifies the deep-seated pain felt by many blacks when the realities of their family life are compared to the "American ideal." Her response is perhaps exaggerated precisely because she is a helping professional and is exposed frequently to the most distorted lives and the most distressing losses. Under those circumstances, strength, adaptability, and resiliency can be obscured, and pain can take on a semblance of normality. Effectiveness in helping black families to deal with the characteristic problems they encounter requires, however, that the helping professional have a reasonably accurate knowledge of the forces that have created those facts. For example, it is well known that black family members are overrepresented as clients in many of our social delivery systems—43 percent of all public welfare recipients, 60 percent

1. "Conversation with Frances Welsing," *Essence* (October 1973), p. 51.

271

of all public housing residents, etc.[2] But *why* black families are overrepresented is a matter of considerable controversy and conflicting interpretation.

MODELS OF CAUSATION

The helping professions are based on a conviction that knowledge can lead to effective control of behavior. Therefore, if one is aware of the causes of a particular problem, then ways of eliminating these causes can be sought. When Comte introduced this positivistic social philosophy in the nineteenth century, it served to counter the prevailing notions of sin and fate and moral weakness as the roots of personal and social problems.[3] The unfortunate, the poor, the mentally ill, no longer needed to be seen as victims of fate or as carriers of inherent inferiority; instead they could be understood as victims of conditions external to themselves. Causality became the mainstay of professional thinking about problems and conditions and prevailed until recent years, when some theorists began to question whether true causes could be usefully or fully understood in view of the complex nature of human beings. The issue of causality has important implications for this review of recent social science research on the black family.

Since the profound influence of the late-nineteenth-century psychoanalytic movement on professional social work, psychiatry, and psychology, there has been a steady emphasis on the significance of the family as a source of problem behavior. This "blaming the family" for all sorts of personal and social problems has come about despite considerable evidence that there is no direct quantitative relationship between pathology in a parent and pathology in a child. Such evidence is especially pertinent to black families. These families have been given far less systematic study than have white, middle-class families but have been subject to even more sweeping generalizations about

2. U.S. Census, *General Social and Economic Characteristics*, 1971.

3. Auguste Comte, *A General View of Positivism* (1848), trans. J. M. Bridges, 2d ed. (London: Reeves and Turner, 1880).

the effects of their behavior on problems experienced by family members.

Many of the social science studies of black families in one way or another attempt to account for the overrepresentation of black families in problem categories, for example, among the poor, the unskilled, the uneducated, the poorly housed, and so forth. More specifically, why do black families and white families appear in these categories in different proportions? From a review of these studies, three major paradigms have emerged. In the first paradigm, black and white families are viewed as sharing the same essential cultural values and norms. But it is admitted that there are cultural differences based on socioeconomic class. Thus, cultural differences usually associated with "black culture" are deemed to be in reality aspects of "lower-class culture," in which blacks are overrepresented.

The second paradigm is somewhat more complex, since poverty or socioeconomic class is viewed as an *outcome* of culture rather than its determinant. Those who hold this view believe that poverty or socioeconomic class among blacks is overwhelmingly the result of the harsh and oppressive slavery which erased traditional African culture and developed behavior patterns that have persisted into the present where they effectively impair the family's ability for social functioning. Although there are socioeconomic differences among blacks, all blacks share to some extent the negative consequences of slave ancestry.

The third paradigm suggests that black culture contains elements of "mainstream" white culture as well as a black culture constructed of elements from traditional African culture, from slavery and reconstruction, and from a past and present history of racism and discrimination. Thus, there is a biculturalism which explains why both similarities and differences are noted when black families and white families are compared.

We will consider here some of the research that supports each of these paradigms. A wide variety of family behaviors are addressed by this research. But one must remember that, because of the very uniqueness of the family, the very intimacy that characterizes the interrelationship of its members, outsiders who want to study its transactions find the family difficult to penetrate, particularly when the outsider is not only outside the family but outside the racial or ethnic group to which the family belongs. As a consequence, research on the black family has not yet produced sharp, clear images but often only shadowy outlines of black family life.

BLACK FAMILIES, WHITE FAMILIES: THE NULL HYPOTHESIS

The differences observed when black families and white families are compared have been attributed to the influence of an intervening variable—socioeconomic class. Since blacks are overrepresented in the lower socioeconomic class, if socioeconomic class were "controlled," differences between social classes would hold, but differences between racial groups *of the same class* would not hold. This approximates a statement of a null hypothesis; that is to say, there is no significant relationship between race and family structure or behavior; moreover, any relationships that *are* found are spurious and can be explained by the relationship between race and socioeconomic class. This view is consonant with the concept of a "culture of poverty" which is self-perpetuating and transcends racial or ethnic differences. Thus, the poor, regardless of the ethnic or racial group to which they belong, share common cultural values, norms, attitudes, behaviors. In fact, those who favor this view hold that certain frequently cited characteristics are not elements of *black* culture, as many in our society *believe*, but of *lower-class* culture regardless of race or ethnicity. Such characteristics include female-centered or mother-focused households, informal and extralegal but effective adoption, support of fatherless families through other lines of kinship connection, little ability to defer gratification and plan for the future, tolerance for psychological pathology, and free unions or consensual marriages.[4] At the same time middle-class blacks do not reflect these characteristics but rather share the values, attitudes, norms, and behaviors of middle-class whites. A variety of research studies in areas of family behavior as diverse as child-rearing practices and social relations of widows have

4. Oscar Lewis, *Five Families: Mexican Case Studies in the Culture of Poverty* (New York: Basic Books, 1959), pp. xiv–xvii.

attempted to test the hypothesis that, within socioeconomic levels or social classes, differences between black and white individuals and families disappear.

In Miller and Dreger's edited compilations of reviews of comparative studies of blacks and whites in the United States, Jackson contributed a review of studies relating to family organization and ideology.[5] It comprised for the most part psychological and sociological studies reported from 1966 to 1970. The specific issues addressed were (a) dominance in the family; (b) father absence; (c) childbearing; (d) child-rearing; (e) familial, attitudinal, and behavioral relationships; and (f) age statuses and roles. Jackson's review indicated that although some researchers tended to support the idea that there are distinctive subcultures among family patterns of blacks and whites, there is weightier evidence that family patterns among blacks do not represent a distinctive subculture. There is not only considerable variation in family patterns among blacks, but blacks and whites in similar socioeconomic positions tend to resemble each other more than those of the same race in different socioeconomic positions. Jackson states: "In most major respects there are no significant differences between blacks and whites of similar education, occupations, employment, and income levels where similarities with respect to family background (e.g., family size) also persist. Perhaps those differences which do persist may be best explained by racism" (p. 440).

It should be pointed out that several times in her review Jackson says that she does not believe that blacks would necessarily follow the same patterns as whites in their family behavior if there were no differences in their educational, occupational, and income levels. Moreover, she states: "I do however believe that many of the so-called racial differences reported between black and white families can be more readily explicated by such variables as education, occupation, income, and employment" (p. 407). Researchers, increasingly sensitive to the manner in which the same data are often interpreted differently to suit different

5. Jacquelyne Johnson Jackson, "Family Organization and Ideology," in *Comparative Studies of Blacks and Whites in the United States*, ed. Kent S. Miller and Ralph Mason Dreger (New York: Seminar Press, 1973).

purposes, are often compelled to present findings which could be used to support diametrically opposed views. Although Jackson found little evidence that black families are more matriarchal, more permissive in child-rearing practices, or have lower aspirations for their children, she did not wish her readers to conclude that there were *no* significant differences in family behavior patterns. The evidence does not support the notion that the two groups are culturally identical, and many behavior patterns remain unstudied. Jackson points out that the general similarity of the picture is peppered with incidences of difference; for example, blacks who are alleged fathers of illegitimate children tend to be much more supportive of the mothers of these children than are whites; broken families appear to have a far more devastating effect upon white than upon black children; a larger proportion of aged whites than aged blacks are institutionalized.

Heiss came to similar conclusions in his secondary analysis of data collected in a national study supported by the U.S. Civil Rights Commission to determine the effects, if any, of attending integrated schools; the findings also included considerable data about the respondents' family life and life style.[6] Heiss was most interested in the consequence of various black family structures. With family structure as the independent variable, Heiss looked at several dependent variables including marital stability, fertility, aid from kin, and control of decisions. He summarized his findings as follows:

Taking all the dependent variables into account, we see an impressive degree of similarity between the dynamics of white and black families. Certainly they are not identical. Some variables do have different effects in the two groups. Usually, however, the patterns are unmistakably similar. It seems clear that black and white families work under similar principles, and the explanations which hold for one group hold for the other. At least this is so in the areas we have considered. And when there is a difference, it seems to be not so much a difference in principle *but rather a difference in the application of the principle.* [p. 227, emphasis added]

It is, of course, the manner in which groups develop different

6. Jerold Heiss, *The Case of the Black Family: A Sociological Inquiry* (New York: Columbia University Press, 1975).

ways to achieve what may be common goals—socialization of children, establishment of family support systems, and so forth—that defines their culture.

Staples also reviewed the research on black families, covering a much longer period than did Jackson, extending from the early thirties with the seminal work of Frazier and the other early black sociologists, to the late 1960s when Rainwater, Billingsley, Bernard, and Moynihan were publishing their studies.[7] His conclusions are quite different from those drawn by Jackson and Heiss. In essence, his major finding was that the bulk of the research whether done by black or white researchers found black family life to be deficient when compared to white family life. According to Staples, the research had uncovered true differences but had interpreted them as deviant because of a set of standards for normative behavior which was middle-class Anglo in origin. Staples wrote:

In an overall assessment of theories and research on black family life, their value is diminished by the weak methodology employed; the superficial analysis that ensues from the use of poor research designs, biased and low samples, and inadequate research instruments . . . [the] inferences drawn from data to theory on the black family is unjustified on the basis of the research evidence presented by most investigators of black family life. [p. 133]

Staples specifically rejects the notion that black culture is merely white culture distorted by poverty. He insists that an entirely different set of social forces determines its structure and dynamics; these forces have not been perceived, however, by some other researchers, who have concluded that black males' family-role performance in low-income black communities is a direct response to the failures represented by their unemployment, low income, and experiences of discrimination. According to Staples:

By asserting that the only difference between Afro-American males and other American males is that they are black and live under adverse conditions, they ignore the existence of a unique black culture with its

7. Robert Staples, "Toward a Sociology of the Black Family: A Theoretical and Methodological Assessment," *Journal of Marriage and the Family* (February 1971).

own beliefs, attitudes and rituals which constitute a life style that gives every culture its own distinctive character. [p. 132]

THE BLACK FAMILY AS PRODUCT OF SLAVERY

In 1959, E. Franklin Frazier wrote: "As a result of the manner in which the Negro was enslaved, the Negro's African cultural heritage has had practically no effect on the evolution of his family life in the United States."[8] Frazier goes on to contend that slavery and its practices regarding the sale and treatment of blacks produced a "deviant" family form in which the woman was dominant. This matriarchal structure was reinforced by the stresses of emancipation and urbanization of the black population. Although Frazier challenged the dominant racist arguments of the time that saw in the high incidence of female-headed households among blacks evidence of their moral looseness and depravity, he did not challenge the view that such households are pathological and destructive to development of a capacity for effective social functioning.

This point of view was expressed even more forcefully in 1965 by Kenneth Clark:

Because of the system of slavery in which the Negro male was systematically used as a stud and the Negro female used primarily for purposes of breeding or for the gratification of the white male, the only source of family continuity was through the female. . . . This pattern, together with the continued post-slavery relegation of the Negro male to menial and subservient status, has made the female the dominant person in the Negro family. Psychologically, the Negro male could not support his normal desire for dominance. . . . The pressure to find relief from his intolerable psychological position seems directly related to the continued high incidence of desertions and broken homes in Negro ghettos.[9]

Despite this long-standing and repeated indictment of slavery for its negative impact on black families, Moynihan's 1965 re-

8. E. Franklin Frazier, "The Negro Family in America," in *The Family: Its Function and Destiny*, ed. Ruth Nanda Anshen, rev. ed. (New York: Harper & Row, 1959), p. 65.

9. Kenneth B. Clark, *Dark Ghetto: Dilemmas of Social Power* (New York: Harper & Row, 1965), p. 70.

port, *The Negro Family: The Case for National Action*, which connected contemporary problems of family breakdown and dysfunction to slavery, brought controversy and bitter attacks, particularly from blacks.[10] Moynihan attributed the overrepresentation of blacks in problem categories to the deterioration of the social structure of the black community, most particularly to the deterioration of the black family. Furthermore, he saw this problem as deriving from the slavery experience; it was nurtured also, in his view, by the discrimination and racism of the Reconstruction period and later by the urbanization of the black population. Moynihan asserted that the family structure of lower-class Negroes is highly unstable and in many urban centers approaches complete breakdown, in contrast with white families, who have achieved a high degree of stability and are maintaining that stability.

The attacks on the Moynihan report centered on his apparent emphasis on family disorganization and chaos as *characteristic* of black families and the little emphasis given to factors in the social system, particularly the economic system which produced the behaviors and attitudes described as problems or problem-producing. Whatever the deficiencies in the report itself, it can be said without question that it stimulated scores of scholarly research projects aimed at testing its conclusions.

One such report, rivaling the Moynihan report in the controversy it stirred up, was Fogel and Engerman's *Time on the Cross: The Economics of American Negro Slavery*, published in 1974.[11] Although not a study of the black family per se but rather of the economic system in which all slaves were deeply involved, *Time on the Cross* had strong implications for judgments being made on the relationship between slavery and contemporary problems of American black families. Its authors' major thesis was that black slaves responded so well to the positive incentives devised by their masters to encourage nuclear families, caring for their young and working diligently, that they were in fact re-

---

10. Daniel Patrick Moynihan, *The Negro Family: The Case For National Action*, Office of Policy Planning and Research, U.S. Department of Labor, 1965.

11. Robert Fogel and Stanley Engerman, *Time on the Cross: The Economics of American Negro Slavery*, vols. 1 and 2 (Boston: Little, Brown, 1974).

sponsible for the smooth profitable operation of the system of slavery. The slaves had, moreover, internalized the Protestant work ethic as well as the mores of Victorian family life so that they were able to function within a market-oriented society and make a profit for their masters who after all depended upon their labor.

Since *Time on the Cross* was hailed upon its publication as "perhaps [the most] important book about American history . . . published in the last decade,"[12] it deserves some attention. Fortunately, Gutman in 1975 provided an amazingly detailed book-length review which identifies essential flaws in the analysis of the data in *Time on the Cross*.[13] Although its authors asserted that the data indicated that both moral convictions and good business practices led slaveowners to encourage stable nuclear families, that slaves had internalized sexual values resembling "Puritan," "Victorian" or "prudish" beliefs, Gutman's own analysis of the same data brought opposite conclusions. Gutman demonstrated that the model of slave socialization underlying *Time on the Cross* was not different from earlier studies of slave life in which the slave is "made over" by his owner: "The 'inputs' and 'outputs' differ, but the process does not. The enslaved live in a 'Skinner box.' The 'sanctions of the system' flow in one direction over time" (p. 166). Thus the criticism leveled at *Time on the Cross* was that, although its aim was "to identify black achievement in spite of adversity," it still did not see the slave as having any influence over what kind of person he was to become or having any influence on what his family structure, attitudes, norms, and so forth, would be. He was essentially the product of his owner.

In an article published in 1972 Szwed identifies nicely the problem presented by the kind of model of slave socialization projected in *Time on the Cross*:

From the beginning of slavery Afro-Americans exercised the capacity to perpetuate and create themselves out of what they found around

12. Peter Passell, review of *Time on the Cross, New York Times Book Review* (28 April 1974), p. 4.

13. Herbert Gutman, *Slavery and the Numbers Game: A Critique of Time on the Cross* (Urbana: University of Illinois Press, 1975).

them and create means of comprehending and dealing with the natural and social world surrounding them—they were cultural bearers and creators as well as receivers and learners. In other words, although slavery, poverty and racism have severely circumscribed the exercise of this capacity, even sometimes driving it underground, these constraints can in no way be seen as sufficient cause of Afro-American behavior. [14]

Thus, the questions regarding the impact of the slavery experience can be seen to require far more than the consideration of what the masters *did* to the slaves and how the slaves *responded*. According to Gutman it requires "the examination of the way the enslaved themselves accumulated historical experiences over time (culture) and the ways in which these accumulated experiences helped to shape slave belief and behavior" (p. 170). Moreover, the implication is that a culture rooted in slavery may be a more negative culture if perceived merely as the distortions created by oppressive slaveholders than if perceived as at least in some measure constructed by slaves themselves to meet, as effectively as could be done under the circumstances, their basic human needs.

The issue of whether or not there exists a black culture with its roots as far back as slavery is not merely academic. If indeed contemporary attitudes and behaviors which are associated with personal and social problems are *culturally* determined, the strategies for bringing about their change must necessarily be conceived as long-range strategies. Sarason suggests that it is a matter of time perspective; that is, one's conception of what human beings and society are determines one's time perspective about changing either. He has stated:

What combination of ignorance and arrogance permitted people to proclaim that if we delivered the right kinds of programs and spent the appropriate sums of money we could quickly undo what centuries had built up? When the expectations that powered these efforts were obviously not being fulfilled, what permitted some people to conclude that perhaps the victim was in some ways different from (less endowed than) those in the dominant society? Few things are as immune to quick

14. John Szwed, "The Politics of Afro-American Culture," in *Reinventing Anthropology*, ed. Dell Hymes (New York: Random House, Pantheon Books, 1972), pp. 166–67.

changes as the historically rooted, psychological core of racial and ethnic groups.[15]

Thus if loose family structures, weak and temporary family relationships encountered in many black communities, result from some culturally determined preference for such family form and dynamics, the message to practitioners is quite different than it would be if those same family forms and dynamics were perceived as a consequence of conditions existing in the present and experienced in the present.

Gutman, whose scholarly critique of *Time on the Cross* strongly suggested that Fogel and Engerman had not shown that slavemasters were successful in socializing slaves to internalize the Protestant ethic, Victorian morals, and capitalist economic principles, later demonstrated (1976) that they did develop strong culturally determined belief systems and behavior nevertheless.[16] Thus, slavery did not prevent the development of a viable black culture nor did it promote the development of an essentially distorted and pathological culture primarily in response to slaveholder treatment. Obviously, the facts show that certain behaviors or practices were encouraged by slaveholders, for example, having children. Thus, since a fecund female slave who had many children was viewed as valuable by a slaveowner, it was less likely that a couple actively producing children would be separated. It would be wrong however to project the economic reasons for having children upon the slave couple. It would be much more probable that their reasons were to strengthen the likelihood of the family's survival as a unit. It is interesting that the same projection occurs today. Black mothers on welfare are accused of having illegitimate children for *economic* reasons, specifically, to increase welfare payments rather than for *familial* reasons, to cement interpersonal relationship.

Even more interesting perhaps was Gutman's finding in the later volume that there were certain aspects of black family patterns that could not be perceived as merely imitation of the

15. Seymour Sarason, "Jewishness, Blackishness, and the Nature-Nurture Controversy," *American Psychologist* (November 1973), pp. 969–70.

16. Herbert Gutman, *The Black Family in Slavery and Freedom, 1750–1925* (New York: Random House, Pantheon Books, 1976).

white masters, but were necessarily related to black-created values. For example, Gutman provides strong evidence that marriage to first cousins were specifically taboo among black slaves regardless of region. On the other hand, such marriages were quite common among whites and were often entered into as a means of consolidating family fortunes (pp. 89–90). It is quite possible therefore for white practitioners today to underestimate the traumatic effects of the violation of this culturally derived taboo on black clients.

Gutman's most significant contribution to scholarly work on the black family may well be his voluminous documentary evidence of *the strength of the concept of family* among blacks despite the adversities of slavery. Furthermore, the strength of the family developed *not* as a consequence of the deliberate efforts of slavemasters to encourage it for the sake of economic benefits but in spite of slavemasters' callous and often deliberate efforts to deny its reality for "nonhumans" (as slaves had been defined). There were certain behaviors, such as naming sons after fathers (not daughters after mothers), the taboo against cousin marriages, and others, that were almost universal among slaves regardless of such variables as size of plantation, geographical region, etc., which suggest a genuine slave subculture that "blended together African and Anglo-American cultural beliefs and social practices, mediated throughout the harsh institution of enslavement" (p. 34) and was not merely a response to master-sponsored external stimuli.

Another of Gutman's valuable insights in regard to the black family's viability in the face of externally imposed stresses is the substantial evidence that families who were separated during slavery reconstituted themselves after emancipation (pp. 363–431). The implication is that the strength of the slaves' commitment to the family as a valued social unit overcame for many the blows imposed by the slave system itself. This reduces the power of Moynihan's argument that the contemporary breakdown of black families is somehow the reverberation of the contemptuous handling of black families by white slaveowners. Gutman's voluminous data also revealed no evidence to sustain the contention in Osofsky's *Harlem: The Making of a Ghetto* that "the slave heritage, bulwarked by economic conditions, continued into the twentieth century to make family instability a common factor in Negro life."[17]

Despite the meticulousness of his scholarship, the image Gutman draws of the black family in slavery is not without some important deficiencies. He demonstrates admirably the fact that some slave beliefs and values transcended region or type of owner, so that the concept of a slave culture *independent* of the type of treatment received or characteristics of the slaveholder could be supported. On the other hand, he makes no effort to identify characteristics of black slave life which were associated with these facts of region or type of enterprise. Blackwell suggests that there were enough differences to account for the diversity in black families today:

Although white disregard for the slave family seems to have been the norm, there were exceptions. In the South and Middle Atlantic states, for example, usually depending upon the size of the plantation, some slave owners did make valiant attempts to protect and preserve the sanctity of the institution of the family among slaves. Smaller plantation owners were often more diligent in this regard than larger owners, among whom a callous disregard for black family life was particularly characteristic.[18]

The implication is that, even though slaves were able to develop a slave-initiated set of beliefs, attitudes, and behaviors which transcended the specific condition imposed upon them by white slaveowners, there were other behaviors that were influenced strongly by those same specific conditions.

For the practitioner in the human service agency in this last quarter of the twentieth century, the most important question is which beliefs, attitudes, behaviors are a consequence of culture developed over time and relatively impervious to change and which are the consequence of "here and now" experiences of discrimination, exploitation, and racism and therefore quite likely to change with their elimination.

17. Gilbert Osofsky, "The Making of a Ghetto," in *The Black Ghetto: Promised Land or Colony*, ed. Richard J. Meister (Lexington, Mass.: D. C. Heath, 1972).

18. James E. Blackwell, *The Black Community: Diversity and Unity* (New York: Dodd, Mead, 1975), p. 37.

BEYOND LINEAR THINKING

The initial paradigm described earlier was drawn from a theoretical framework in which the core concept is a "culture of poverty." If accurate, it could be expected that there would be great similarity between black families and white families of the same socioeconomic status and great differences between black families of different socioeconomic levels. Instead, the evidence is decidedly mixed. In some instances, there were no significant differences between black families and white families regardless of socioeconomic level and in others, there were significant differences when white families were compared with black families even after controlling for socioeconomic status.

The second paradigm attempted to draw a similar linear relationship but this time not between socioeconomic level and family behavior patterns but between the experience of slavery and family behavior patterns. Slavery, however, was not merely a set of oppressive conditions imposed by slavemasters to which slaves responded. It was a constellation of transactions made between slaves and masters, each with personal as well as collective histories. Certainly, as Gutman so elegantly documented, it was not an assassination of a culture; blacks *in spite of* the harsh slave system were able to maintain the concept and the reality of the family. Furthermore, the typical black household between 1880 and 1930 (always a lower-class household) had in it two parents and was not "unorganized and disorganized."[19] Thus, this paradigm does not permit us to "explain" problems experienced by contemporary black families by reference to slavery or the period immediately following. It does permit us, however, to identify strong cultural values, attitudes which have persisted over time and which are present to some extent in our current black family behavior.

The necessity of a third paradigm is clear. Essentially it is one which attempts to integrate the others into a more accurate representation of the dynamics of black family life. However, it eschews the linear model and reflects instead a systems view-

19. Gutman, *The Black Family*, p. 433.

point. Black family behavior is considered to be a consequence of multiple influences that need to be identified and assessed if that behavior is to be understood. Admittedly more complex, this paradigm holds much more promise for the practitioner who must choose among alternative strategies for effecting change. It denies the validity of a generalization based on the first paradigm: "Middle-class blacks are no different from middle-class whites; i. e., what 'works' with middle-class whites will also 'work' with middle-class blacks." It also rejects a generalization based on the second paradigm: "Family instability is a consequence of limited commitment to family which is the cultural heritage of slavery; thus, any change in this cultural value will require long-term change efforts." Our third paradigm recognizes the essential power of the past and the present in determination of present family behavior patterns and the need for a much more complex assessment than is possible with linear thinking.

This complexity is no more clearly identified than in Stack's anthropological study of a low-income, urban black community in the Midwest.[20] She found an abundance of poverty, father-absent households, and welfare clients, all of these usually considered to be indicators of disorganization, instability, and pathology in ghetto communities. But she found much more. The black families she studied had evolved patterns of co-residence, kinship-based exchange networks linking multiple domestic units, elastic household boundaries, lifelong bonds to three-generation households, social controls against the formation of marriages that could endanger the network of kin, the domestic authority of women, and limitations on the role of husband or male friend within a woman's kin network (p. 124). Stack found these features of black urban family life to be highly adaptive to the realities of their social situation. For example, it was not uncommon for some "windfall" to be shared immediately with others in the kin network rather than saved. Instead of viewing this as an indicator of inability to "delay gratification," Stack observed it as a rational assessment by the

20. Carol B. Stack, *All Our Kin: Strategies for Survival in a Black Community* (New York: Harper & Row, 1974).

individual of the low probability that additional sums could be received to raise appreciably the family's standard of living. Given such a low probability, it was far wiser to strengthen the mutual obligational system that represented a major basis for survival (pp. 105–06). In fact, the definition of family which evolved for Stack reflects this collaborative network: ". . . the smallest organized, durable network of kin and non-kin who interact daily, providing domestic needs of children and assuring their survival" (p. 31). Certainly this is a more functional definition for the practitioner who is involved in problem-solving with black families than the more traditional definitions of family.

Stack suggests that these families are essentially bicultural. This has been suggested also by Valentine who found little evidence in his research in black communities for the notion of a single homogeneous black culture.[21] He speculated that black culture may comprise three derivations: (1) shared African cultural roots; (2) common influences from New World domination by the Anglo majority; and (3) an emergent Afro-American culture influenced most recently by Black Nationalism. More importantly, socialization into both the Afro-American and "mainstream" cultural systems begins at an early age with the family as primary transmitter of "ethnic cultural socialization" and mainstream enculturation coming from wider sources.

The concept of ethnosystem as proposed by Solomon also incorporates the notion of biculturalism as the primary force in the dynamics of black family behavior. "An ethnosystem is defined as (1) a collectivity of interdependent ethnic groups, (2) each in turn defined by some unique historical and/or cultural ties, and (3) bound together by a single political system."[22] An ethnic group is necessarily influenced by its own group as well as the larger social system of which it is a part. Solomon points out that black families share mainstream cultural values to the extent that in many cases their family forms and processes are indistin-

---

21. Charles Valentine, "Deficit, Difference, and Bicultural Models of Afro-American Behavior," in *Challenging the Myths: The Schools, the Blacks and the Poor, Harvard Educational Review*, repr. ser. no. 3 (1971), p. 5.

22. Barbara Solomon, *Black Empowerment: Social Work in Oppressed Communities* (New York: Columbia University Press, 1976), p. 45.

guishable from those of other American families. On the other hand, black families must deal with experiences that many other families do not have to deal with, for example, discrimination in the ways open to them to make a living, finding suitable housing and good schools for children, and helping children to understand how to deal with racism and the negative self-images it places in front of them.

Biculturalism if accepted as a functional adaptation to contemporary life for blacks in America may also influence the interpretations made by practitioners of black family structure and process. For example, black American families have traditionally been viewed in terms of a European-American family model in which family leadership lies primarily with the male, while females play only secondary roles, if any, as decision makers and economic providers. The fact that many black families do not conform to this model has been identified as a deviation caused by the effects of slavery, poverty, and/or racial oppression. Such a perception, however much validity it may have in some instances, nevertheless presents the more dominant roles played in some families by black females as an aberration from the "norm" as exemplified by white females. However, scholars such as Herskovits[23] and Nobles[24] suggest that black American families have retained more elements of the African matrilineal family system than is generally recognized. In matrilineal systems where descent is traced through the female line, males traditionally have leadership roles but females play far more crucial roles as decision makers and income supporters of their families than do females in either American or European patrilineal families. Stack's study, however, suggests that the Afro-American matrifocal system may vary considerably from African or European systems, reflecting instead the particular integration of several cultural forms to adapt to the realities of the urban, black experience. The extensive and cooperative involvement of fathers—even when nominally absent from the

23. Melville Herskovits, *The Myth of the Negro Past* (New York: Harper and Brothers, 1941).

24. Wade Nobles, "African Root and American Fruit: The Black Family" (Paper presented to the Charles R. Drew Postgraduate Medical School Conference on the Black Family, November 1972).

household—in the lives of families seems similar to the African matrilineal system described above. However, Stack points out that the cooperative life style represents only one dimension of a multivalued cultural system. "Employers, social service agencies, mass communication, televisions, advertising, and teachers and schools continuously reinforce the value system of the traditional middle-class white sector of American society."[25]

The paradigm in which black family behavior is perceived as a consequence of multiple influences is particularly useful to the practitioner since it serves to "explain" more diverse phenomena or situations than does class or the slavery experience or any other single causal factor. Moreover, the identification of behavior patterns as "lower-class" or a consequence of slavery will be almost automatically pejorative. The negative images of black families reflected in these conceptualizations are inevitably transmitted into the helping process and reinforce feelings of powerlessness and dependency rather than feelings of self-worth and competence. The multivalent model of black family behavior provides a theoretical framework for the practitioner which reflects its true complexity.

Building the Knowledge Base
for Practice with Black Families

The white social scientist has been accused of racist biases that have resulted in studies of blacks in which the problem formulation was irrelevant, the designs were inappropriate, and the interpretations were inaccurate or distorted. But the overview of research on black families presented here indicates that the race of the researcher is not necessarily associated with sensitivity to those issues of black family life most critical to study, and blacks and whites have proceeded from the perspective of predominantly white academic social science rather than from the perspective of the black community. The emphasis on deficiencies is clear, regardless of whether the research was initiated by black E. Franklin Frazier or white Daniel Patrick Moynihan. For practitioners interested in *why* black families experience prob-

25. Stack, *All Our Kin*, p. 125.

lems and *how* problem situations can be resolved, this research is of limited value. *Effective* practice with black families requires a much broader knowledge base. In order to make the practice of the helping professions more effective with black families, research must help to fill in the gaps in our knowledge base. It is apparent that an interdisciplinary approach might well be the most productive since it would insure that the influences on family behavior emanating from cultural, social, and psychological sources will receive attention.

We need to identify the adaptive responses that black families have made to an oppressive environment, particularly those which have functional value even after the oppression is removed. There are statistics which show that blacks' achievement was often higher in communities where oppression was greatest and the conflict more open than in other communities where there was a facade of equality and discrimination was more subtle. It may well be that the skills required to battle oppression and discrimination are valuable in the ordinary demands to achieve in our society. At least some studies of the coping strategies developed in families where discrimination has been reduced if not removed entirely would be highly important to those of us who are in the business of promoting and reinforcing effective coping behaviors.

There is a need to identify external and internal support systems utilized by black families to assist in coping with oppression, among them, religion and the dynamics of its utilization. For example, Billingsley has identified six opportunity screens that appear to be operative when black families are able to move beyond survival to stability and social achievement.[26] They are: a set of values accompanied by behavior consistent with those values, and a degree of independence and control of the forces affecting the lives of their members; strong religious convictions and behavior; education or educational aspirations of one or more members; economic security; family ties; and community-centered activities, offering associational ties, role models, and advocates for children.

26. Andrew Billingsley, *Black Families in White America* (Englewood Cliffs, N.J.: Prentice-Hall, 1968), pp. 97–121.

Scanzoni identified a similar list of factors that were associated with four hundred black families in Indianapolis.[27] These included economic advantage over the black population nationally, residence in and length of exposure to the urban milieu, strong family ties, support and aid from community figures, religious affiliation and involvement, positive school experiences, and positive self-image.

Although an association between these factors and family stability and achievement has been discovered, it is not clear *how* or *why* the association exists. For example, there is a possibility that instead of these factors constituting a set of independent variables associated with the single dependent variable, family stability, we might have instead a single independent variable, family stability, exerting a strong influence on the separate dependent variables represented by these factors. Or there may be any combination of associations between some of the factors as independent variables and others as dependent variables. Regardless of the particular pattern that exists, if it can be identified, it will illuminate considerably the nature of the strategies that will help black families to function more effectively.

Comparatively little research has been done on marriage and family organization. The existing data on marriage and family among blacks are sketchy and consist mainly of gross indicators that suggest a higher proportion of black than white households has a female head, that the incidence of marital dissolution is higher among blacks than whites, and that many black children do not spend their entire childhood in their families of orientation. The nagging statistics on female-headed households are particularly important to confront.

Mother-headed families which have been defined as "matriarchal" constitute a minority of black families. Indeed in terms of absolute numbers, white matriarchs head more families than do black matriarchs—of the approximately 4.4 million single-parent families headed by women in the United States, 3,038,000 are white and 1,216,000 are black.[28]

27. John H. Scanzoni, *The Black Family in Modern Society* (Boston: Allyn and Bacon, 1971).

28. U.S. Census, 1971.

291

An underlying pejorative assumption is made whenever the term "matriarchal" is used to describe a family, particularly a black family. Matriarchy is associated automatically with pathology, inadequacy, and deviance. The assumed superiority of the patriarchal family is easily definable as sexist from the feminist perspective so recently admitted into academic consciousness. The assumption that there are inherent deficiencies in woman-headed, single-parent families has not been derived from empirical evidence.[29] Poverty, racism, and all of their attendant ills emerged as the major contributory factors in the problems which members of *some* matriarchal families display.[30] It cannot be denied that some black matriarchs are poor. Some receive public assistance. Others struggle to maintain families on meager wages. The evidence is that their economic situation exists, in part, because of limited job skills, sporadic employment histories, and racial discrimination as well as inadequate or expensive child-care resources. These are powerful factors contributing to many of the problems often associated with matriarchal families. Thus, more research is needed which focuses on "healthy," "successful," matriarchal, and other types of single-parent families.

Some beginnings are discernible in the social science literature. In Jordan's[31] (1966) and Branham's[32] (1970) studies of adoptive single-parent families—the majority of whom are black women—it was found that the children were thriving. Mendes's study of thirty-two single fathers, fourteen of whom were black, also described some of the social and psychological factors which contribute to the viability of single-parent families.[33] More research needs to be done, however, on the social-psychological

29. Andrew Billingsley and Jeanne Giovannoni, *Children of the Storm* (New York: Harcourt Brace Jovanovich, 1972).

30. Alfred Kadushin, "Single Parent Adoption," *Social Service Review* 44, no. 3 (September 1970): 263–74.

31. Velma Jordan, "Early Comments on Single Parent Adoptive Homes," *Child Welfare* (November 1966), pp. 536–38.

32. Ethel Branham, "One Parent Adoptions," *Children* (May–June 1970), pp. 103–07.

33. Helen Mendes, "Single Fatherhood," *Social Work* 21, no. 4 (July 1976): 308–12.

support systems utilized by thriving matriarchal and other types of single-parent families. Such studies could identify the components of these support systems and uncover some of the important dynamics of the ways in which families interact under them. Since it is generally known that religion and religious institutions have historically played formative roles in the lives of many black families, we need to study the role which religious beliefs and affiliations play in promoting or hindering family stability. The findings from such studies could assist practitioners in assessing family strengths and weaknesses and may suggest effective ways of strengthening or modifying a family's use of social-psychological support. The need for this kind of research is strongly supported by the seminal work of Billingsley in developing a typology of black family structures, although it lacks empirical data on the range of the various types within black communities.[34] This has led, however, to efforts to gather such empirical data and to the identification of other kinds of black families not included in the Billingsley typology, for instance, the sizable number of black people who do not actually live in households where there are families but are intensely involved in family systems. Jackson describes elderly black men living alone but adopted by neighborhood families with whom they regularly had their meals in return for various support services such as baby-sitting.[35] There are also the consensual marriages which are frequently ignored as stable systems despite their endurance over long periods. Since there has been no research evidence that can substantiate a significant association between family structure and any particular personal or social problem, it may well be that the typologies of family structure utilized are too gross to be useful as an analytical framework. Certainly, the myriad studies of black families that have classified them simply as one-parent or two-parent hopelessly obscure the rich variation in family structure and suggest doubt as to the utility of that limited classification.

34. Billingsley, *Black Families in White America*, pp. 16–21.
35. Jacquelyne Johnson Jackson, "Sex and Social Class Variations in Black Aged Parent-Adult Child Relationships," *Aging and Human Development* 2, no. 2 (May 1971): 96–107.

At the same time, methods of collecting data have often had built-in biases. For example, Brody reported a study in which he found that black children often received conflicting cues from parents, for example, on the verbal level, "Your opportunities are good"; on the nonverbal, "You really don't have a chance." But Brody goes on to explain that the interviewers were white, which he concedes "poses an obvious methodological problem."[36] In fact, it is more likely that the mother's cue was misread by the white researcher but not by the child. Thomas and Sillen have placed another possible interpretation on these same findings: "The mother's apparently contradictory message may be an accurate transmission of the ambiguities of social reality. The black mother's danger signals may not be unconscious at all but quite deliberate."[37] At any rate, the lack of exposure of people in different racial or ethnic groups to each other in our society calls into question the ability of an interviewer from one culture to interpret responses from persons from another culture.

These differing interpretations of the determinants of behavior represent weak points in the knowledge base upon which professional practice supposedly rests. Certain surface priorities may be determined by whether you think that behavior (for example, perceptions of male-female roles) is a consequence of cultural tradition or a consequence of the manner in which major social institutions function. Yet, it must be considered that the purpose of academic and professional research is the search for truth from different perspectives.

The academic disciplines seek to identify regularities in the chaotic-appearing world we live in. Their generalizations furthermore are approximations of reality, based on the laws of probability. Yet practitioners have often lifted these generalizations from the research literature as explanations in an individual case when in fact they only refer to a set of probabilities based on infinite observations in the long run. Furthermore, the set of probabilities can be viewed most rationally by the practitioner as

36. E. B. Brody, "Social Conflict and Schizophrenic Behavior in Young Adult Negro Males," *Psychiatry*, 24 (November 1961): 344–45.

37. Alexander Thomas and Samuel Sillen, *Racism and Psychiatry* (New York: Brunner-Mazel, 1972), p. 95.

a set of alternative explanations, from most likely to least likely, with the practitioner still having the task of using practitioner skills—not research skills—to determine which possibility holds in the individual case. The generalizations made about matriarchal or mother-centered families as characteristic of black families are a prime example. No matter how one might fault the researcher's biases which led to an invalid generalization, the practitioner must take full responsibility for translating it into practice strategies that have routinely ignored black husbands and fathers in planning services to families. We need to consider the individual case, and we must use *the experience in the human encounter* as final determinant of what is reality.

13

Public Images, Private Realities: The American Family in Popular Culture and Social Science

ARLENE SKOLNICK

A few months ago, word was heard from Billy Gray, who used to play brother Bud in "Father Knows Best," the nineteen-fifties television show about the nice Anderson family who lived in the white frame house on a side street in some mythical Springfield–the house at which Father arrived each night, swinging open the front door and singing out, "Margaret, I'm home!" Gray said he felt "ashamed" that he had ever had anything to do with the show. It was all "totally false," he said, and had caused many Americans to feel inadequate, because they thought that that was the way life was supposed to be and that their own lives failed to measure up.
    "On and Off the Avenue," *The New Yorker*, December 12, 1977

Within the past hundred years, our lives have become immersed in images and messages. The technology of modern communications has created an "information-rich" society in which most of what people know is learned vicariously, rather than through direct experience.[1] Much of this vast flood of imagery deals with family life and is aimed at families. The mass media entertain us with endless dramatizations of family normality and deviance. Advertising exhorts us with glamorous visions of the good family life. A variety of advice-givers—in television, in print, and in

1. See James Coleman, "Children, Schools, and the Informational Environment," in *Computers, Communications and the Public Interest*, ed. Martin Greenberger (Baltimore: Johns Hopkins Press, 1971), pp. 115–48.

person—offer prescriptions for home management and family living. And, at the furthest end of the spectrum from commercial mass culture, social scientists and other scholars develop theories of family life that eventually find their way into the mainstream of the popular culture.

In this essay, I examine the interplay between family experience and the images of family life that permeate our culture. As Susan Sontag observes, the production and consumption of images in modern society revive ancient questions about the relations between truth and illusion; images have come to have "extraordinary powers to determine our demands upon reality."[2] They are "coveted substitutes for firsthand experience" and have become "indispensable to the health of the economy, the stability of the polity, and the pursuit of private happiness."

Few attempts have been made to assess this radical change in the social landscape in its entirety; discussions about the mass media and their effects usually consider each medium in isolation. McLuhan looks at television versus print, and others analyze the press, the movies, television violence, or advertising. Sontag finds the key to modern consciousness in photographic imagery; Stuart Ewen finds it in advertising.[3] As the German writer Hans Enzenberger points out, "hardly anyone seems to be aware of the phenomenon as a whole: the industrialization of the human mind."[4]

Even Enzenberger limits his discussion to the mass media, the "mind-making industry," as a means of social control. Such a definition omits the scholars, theorists, scientists, and writers whose work is transmitted in schools and colleges as well as by counselors, doctors, nurses, and other helping professionals. In an era of mass higher education and broad dissemination of ideas, the distinction between the high culture and popular culture becomes blurred. For example, psychoanalysis has

2. Susan Sontag, *On Photography* (New York: Farrar, Straus and Giroux, 1977), p. 153.

3. Stuart Ewen, *Captains of Consciousness: Advertising and the Social Roots of Consumer Culture* (New York: McGraw-Hill, 1976).

4. Hans M. Enzenberger, *The Consciousness Industry: On Literature, Politics, and the Media* (New York: Seabury Press, 1975), p. 4.

changed the way people think about themselves, but it is hard to specify how its ideas were spread. A broad understanding of life in an information-rich society would have to consider not only television and radio but books and magazines, not only the commercial media and advertising, but scholarship and theory, fiction as well as fact. And an understanding of modern family life surely requires some awareness of the informational environment that forms its cultural setting. If, as Sontag, Ewen, and others have argued, the images purveyed by modern communications are capable of usurping reality, the effects on the family can be powerful indeed. Certain features of the family—its elusiveness as a concept, the strong moral aura surrounding it, and the privacy of modern family life—make the family especially vulnerable to the confusion of "image" and "reality."

The Elusive Family

Despite its familiarity, the concept of the family is elusive; discussions of the family often become discussions of individuals or society. The current debates about historical changes in family structure—whether the family has become more or less nuclear, how to document and measure family change, and what a given set of findings can mean—reflect basic difficulties in conceptualizing the family. The protean nature of family life makes it difficult to create a framework for its study; efforts to establish a single definition of the family, or a clear and simple analysis of its functions, run the risk of distortion and artificiality.[5]

Until recently many social scientists, reluctant to acknowledge variations in family life, insisted upon the reality of a universal form of the family. "The family" was treated as a Platonic essence of which the real families in the world were only imperfect shadows. The tendency to treat the family as an abstract essence has been exacerbated by the norm of family privacy. In contemporary Western society, the family is a "backstage" area,

5. See E. Anthony Wrigley, "Reflections on the History of the Family," *Daedalus* 106, no. 2 (Spring 1977): 71–85.

to use Goffman's term, where people are free to act in ways they would not in public.[6] Family privacy has strong effects on family life and individual family members—and it makes research difficult. Privacy results in pluralistic ignorance—we have a backstage view of our own families, but can judge others only in terms of their public presentations. The gap between public norms and private behavior can be wide; marital relationships tend to be even more private and "invisible" than those between parents and children. Waller observes that the true nature of a couple's interaction is hidden from even close friends.[7] More recently, Berardo notes that "the impulse to maintain a public facade of solidarity persists even in those marriages which are deteriorating . . . once the marital difficulty is made public, the processes of deteriorating may be accelerated."[8]

The strong moral and legal norms surrounding family life have also blurred the distinction between image and reality. Judges and clinicians are likely to evaluate the families that come before them in terms of an ideal standard; ethnographers have often written descriptions of family life in terms of the rules for family behavior, a tendency which idealizes and camouflages family processes.

Not only may the outside observer apply inappropriate categories to the families under study, people themselves may not be accurate informants about their own families. Anthropologists often find discrepancies between observable behavior and the accounts people give of their family lives. Marvin Harris, for example, observes that there is "a vast literature in anthropology and related disciplines which indicates that norms and events never quite match and that, not infrequently, the main function of the norms is to obscure the reality."[9] Lévi-

6. Erving Goffman, *The Presentation of Self in Everyday Life* (Garden City, N.Y.: Doubleday, 1959).

7. Willard W. Waller, *The Family: A Dynamic Interpretation* (New York: Dryden Press, 1951).

8. Felix M. Berardo, "Marital Invisibility and Family Privacy," in *Man-Environment: Evaluations and Applications*, vol. 6, ed. Daniel H. Carson (Milwaukee, Wis.: University of Wisconsin, Environmental Design Research Associates, 1974).

9. Marvin Harris, *The Rise of Anthropological Theory* (New York: T. Y. Crowell, 1968).

Strauss and others have taken discrepancies between imagery and behavior as the starting point for theoretical analysis. Robert Murphy argues that, rather than being signs of social crisis, contradictions between ideology and behavior are pervasive features of any society.[10]

The fact that images are incongruent with behavior does not mean that they are unimportant. Indeed, for the anthropologists noted above, the investigation of the imagery surrounding kinship and marriage becomes an important professional preoccupation. Images may not correctly represent the social order, but they influence what people do, what they think they are doing, and what they say they are doing.

While gaps between norms and behavior may be the rule rather than the exception in the world's cultures, such discrepancies seem to be particularly disturbing to contemporary Americans. In traditional societies, there exists what Keniston has called the "institutionalization of hypocrisy";[11] customary violations of cultural rules are justified by a set of customary rationalizations or denials that violations are in fact taking place. In a rapidly changing modern society such as ours, new cultural norms emerge without an accompanying set of rules to justify deviations. For example, modern parents trying to follow the latest expert advice on child-rearing have no new rationalizations to sustain them when they fail to live up to the new principles.

The privacy of modern family life distinguishes it in another even more crucial way from family life in the past. In traditional cultures and our own past, much of daily life within the family was visible to outsiders.[12] Besides regulating family life through observation and the threat of gossip, the premodern community could often intervene directly. Perhaps the most dramatic example of community intrusion into family life was the practice called the "charivari" or several other names, prevalent in Western Europe and America until the nineteenth century. Charivari

10. Robert Murphy, *The Dialectics of Social Life* (New York: Basic Books, 1971).

11. Kenneth Keniston, *Youth and Dissent: The Rise of a New Opposition* (New York: Harcourt Brace Jovanovich, 1971).

12. Edward Evans-Pritchard, *The Position of Women in Primitive Societies and Other Essays in Social Anthropology* (New York: Free Press, 1965), p. 49.

were noisy public demonstrations used to discipline wayward family members by humiliating them: "Sometimes the demonstration would consist of masked individuals circling somebody's house at night, screaming, beating on pans, and blowing cow horns. . . . On other occasions, the offender would be seized and marched through the streets, seated perhaps backwards on a donkey or forced to wear a placard describing his sins."[13] The sins that attracted such punishment were unusual sexual behavior, marriages between people of grossly discrepant ages, deviations from proper sex roles, or simply "household disorder." Although this extreme form of community regulation did not persist far into the nineteenth century, the degree of family privacy we know today is relatively recent. Barbara Laslett's analysis of the family as a public and private institution shows that "the private family . . . is a modern development which has occurred only within this century in the United States."[14]

Ironically, the external influences on family life did not disappear with the emergence of the private family; they merely became more shadowy. Instead of regulation by gossip and the direct intrusion of neighbors, family life came under the guidance of images and prescriptions derived from the mass media, and from a vast literature of books, magazines, pamphlets, as well as from doctors, educators, and other professional "experts" and social reformers.

The removal of family life from public scrutiny seems to have pushed family ideals and realities in opposite directions. As Merton has pointed out, the more behavior is immune from observability, the more deviation from the norms is likely to occur.[15] Laslett observes that the private family lacks both social control and social support, except in the unusual situation where family behavior comes to the attention of the community—

13. Edward Shorter, *The Making of the Modern Family* (New York: Basic Books, 1975), p. 219.

14. Barbara Laslett, "The Family as a Public and Private Institution: An Historical Perspective," *Journal of Marriage and the Family* 35 (August 1973): 480–92.

15. Robert K. Merton, *Social Theory and Social Structure* (Glencoe, Ill.: Free Press, 1957).

people are no longer censured for departing from the norms, nor are they supported by the community for fulfilling them.

While family *behavior* has acquired the potential for greater deviance, family *norms* have become more demanding. One reason, as noted earlier, is that privacy allows families to overestimate how much other families conform to ideal norms, since we have access only to other families' public performances. Moreover, the images and prescriptions for family life that began to be promoted by the new mass media of the nineteenth century were both vague and perfectionistic. Instead of avoiding violations of family decorum, the modern family came under pressure to live up to elusive and abstract standards. Having internalized such standards, the modern middle-class spouse or parent was confronted with a superego far more severe and scrutinizing than the traditional community had been. As one father put it, "Every time I yell at my kids, I have the feeling I'm being reported to some secret psychiatric police force."[16]

Traditional and Modern Images of Family Life

The family has always been a pervasive theme in Western literature, but before the nineteenth century many of the most vivid portrayals of family life had been negative or at least ambivalent. In what could be called the "high tragic tradition"—including not only the dramas of the Greeks and Shakespeare, but the Bible, fairy tale literature, and the novel—the family is portrayed as a high-voltage emotional setting, laden with dark Freudian passions of love and hatred. Freud himself was fond of stating that the essential themes of his theories could be found in the works of poets, novelists, and playwrights. While to the psychoanalyst such figures as Cain and Abel, Oedipus and Medea, Hamlet and Lear, and the witches and ogres of fairy tales present disguised versions of the emotions of ordinary family life, to the audiences such figures serve in Durkheimian fashion as horrible examples, deviants whose actions go beyond the boundaries of permitted behavior.

16. Eda Le Shan, quoted in Nancy P. Weiss, "Mother, the Invention of Necessity: Dr. Benjamin Spock's *Baby and Child Care*," *American Quarterly*, in press.

Another tradition is that of low comedy—the world of hen-pecked husbands and tyrannical mothers-in-law. George Orwell once pointed out that this kind of humor is as traditional a part of Western European consciousness as Greek tragedy.[17] Among the conventions he finds in this brand of humor are the following: (1) Marriage benefits women only; every woman is plotting marriage, and every man, seduction; (2) there is no such thing as a happy marriage; and (3) no man ever gets the better of a woman in an argument. This imagery, like that in the tragic tradition, presents negative examples of family behavior. The stock figures of low comedy were, in fact, once used (as in the charivari) to humiliate publicly those who had violated community norms. For many in the audience, such negative imagery of family life probably served a cathartic function, draining away some of the tensions that could not be expressed in daily life. For others, buried passions might be stirred to awareness. Yet no one watching either tragedy or comedy would experience an idyllic image of family perfection that would make their own family life seem flawed by contrast.

But the new "sentimental model"[18] of the family, which arose in response to massive social changes, introduced impossible ideals that did indeed make normal family life seem flawed. As other have pointed out—Philippe Ariès and John Demos among them—when production moved from home to factory, the family was no longer a group of interdependent workers. Men went out into the world and became "breadwinners"; wives and children became dependents. The home was placed in an ambiguous position outside the realm of economic necessity. The new ideology of the family filled the void by idealizing the home and the woman's role in it. Many of our traditional notions about femininity and family life were emphasized by industrialization: the idea that woman's place is in the home; the idea that the essence of femininity lies in ministering to the personal and psychological needs of husbands and children; the idea that mothers have a Pygmalion-like influence on their children.

17. George Orwell, "The Art of Donald McGill," in *A Collection of Essays* (New York: Harcourt Brace, 1953).

18. Ray L. Birdwhistell, "The American Family: Some Perspectives," *Psychiatry* 29 (1968): 203–12.

THE SENTIMENTAL MODEL AND ITS VARIATIONS

Over the course of a century and a half, the new ideology of the family took several forms. The earliest and most saccharine form appeared in the new mass media that proliferated during the second quarter of the nineteenth century—the novels, tracts, newspaper articles, and ladies' magazines that represented the beginnings of modern mass culture. Middle-class women and liberal Protestant clergymen, both newly disenfranchised by the development of an aggressively materialistic society, became the custodians of femininity and domesticity. They elaborated a "cult of true womanhood" with religious piety, submissiveness, and domesticity as the core of virtuous femininity.[19] Women were placed on a pedestal and made into objects of almost religious worship. Here, for example, is a quotation from *The Lady's Magazine* of 1830:

See, she sits, she walks, she speaks, she looks—unutterable things! Inspiration springs up in her very paths—it follows her foot-steps. A halo of glory encircles her, and illuminates her whole orbit. With her, man not only feels safe, but actually renovated.[20]

Later in the century, science replaced religion as the justification for domesticity. Child care and housework were seen not as woman's "special mission" or "beautiful errand," but as a full-time career. The professionalization of the housewife took two different forms. One was concerned with motherhood and the socialization of children according to the scientific understanding of their physical and emotional needs. The other was the domestic science movement, which focused on the woman as full-time homemaker, applying "scientific" and "industrial" rationality to housework.[21] The new ideology brought about a series of cultural splits that have remained ever since. The world was divided into man's sphere and woman's sphere. Toughness, competition,

19. Barbara Welter, "The Cult of True Womanhood: 1820–1860," in *The American Family in Social-Historical Perspective*, ed. Michael Gordon (New York: St. Martin's Press, 1973), pp. 224–50.

20. Quoted in Ann Douglas, *The Feminization of American Culture* (New York: Alfred A. Knopf, 1977), p. 46.

21. Barbara Ehrenreich and Dierdre English, "The Manufacture of Housework," *Socialist Review* 26 (1975).

and economic expansion were the masculine values that ruled the world outside the home. But the softer values banished from the larger society were worshiped in the home and the church. The clergymen and middle-class women who promoted the cult of true womanhood disdained the materialistic, competitive forces in the larger world from which both were excluded. As Ann Douglas observes, sentimentality "asserts that the values a society's activity denies are precisely the ones it cherishes . . . [it] provides a way to protest a power to which one has already capitulated."[22] Despite this "capitulation," the sentimental model of the family contained a profound critique of the social and economic order that had spawned it.

Kirk Jeffrey argues that in many ways this ideology presents the family as a utopian community, analogous to the communes that sprang up during the same historical period. He notes that the same three themes appear in both sets of writings: a retreat from urban chaos into idyllic rural settings, conscious design of the physical setting of everyday life, and perfectionism.

Our ancestors thus were encouraged to nurse extravagant hopes for the domestic realm. Whether they regarded home as an utter and permanent retreat from life in a shocking and incomprehensible social order, or as a nursery and school for preparing regenerate individuals who would go forth to remake American society, they agreed that domestic life ought to be perfect and could be made so. Through careful design of the home as a physical entity, and equally painstaking attention to the human relationships which would develop within it, the family could actually become a heaven on earth.[23]

By separating work and family, industrial capitalism both undermined the home and at the same time increased its attractions as the only place where security and emotional release could be found. The home came to be seen as both the mainstay of the social order and, at the same time, a precarious enterprise in need of constant shoring up. Any challenge to the prevailing ideology provoked an angry response. The woman was held in

22. Douglas, *Feminization of American Culture*, p. 12.

23. Kirk Jeffrey, "The Family as a Utopian Retreat from the City: The Nineteenth-Century Contribution," in *The Family, Communes and Utopian Societies*, ed. Sallie TeSelle (New York: Harper & Row, 1972).

the home as hostage to the values that men both cherished and violated in their daily lives. In Barbara Welter's words:

In a society where values changed frequently, where fortunes rose and fell with frightening rapidity, where social and economic mobility provided instability as well as hope, one thing at least remained the same—a true woman was a true woman, wherever she was found. If anyone, male or female, dared to tamper with the complex of virtues which made up True Womanhood, he was damned immediately as an enemy of God, of civilization, and of the Republic.[24]

What is striking as one looks at the writings of popular moralists and advisers of the nineteenth century—the physicians, clergymen, phrenologists, and "scribbling ladies"—is how little their essential message differs from that of the sociologists, psychiatrists, pediatricians, and ladies' magazine writers of the twentieth century. The language has become less flowery, and the whole framework of analysis and justification has become scientific, rather than religious or moral, but the ideas remain the same. The idealized family of the nineteenth century has become the "normal" family of the twentieth century. Until recently, most family studies accepted the sentimental family as reality. As Birdwhistell notes, statistics are made of units derived from this model, anecdotes are collected, and formalistic abstractions are drawn from it.[25] Instead of men's and women's spheres, sociologists speak of "instrumental" and "expressive" functions and roles. The idea of the family as retreat from and regenerator of the outside social order reappears in the form of the sociological concept of "functional differentiation"—the family has become a specialized agency ministering to the psychological needs of its members: preparing adjusted, well-socialized children to take their places in the social order, and soothing the tensions acquired in the competition of the office or factory.

Even studies of presumably pathological families have reinforced rather than challenged the sentimental model. As Ruesch and Bateson point out, clinicians tend to construct norms by assuming the general population is marked by the exact opposite

24. Welter, "The Cult of True Womanhood," p. 225.
25. Birdwhistell, *The American Family.*

of the features they find in their patients.[26] The result of this kind of thinking is the assumption that there are two distinct types of families—the normal and the deviant—with little in common, and that the deviant type is responsible for all our ills. Like the nineteenth-century utopians who believed that society could be regenerated through the perfection of family life, twentieth-century social scientists have looked at the pathological family as the source of all social problems, poverty, crime, mental illness, and all forms of deviant behavior.

Academic theories and popular writings on the family spoke to the same social problems—the place of women, children, and the home in industrial society, and the contradictions between the values and beliefs cherished in the family and those that apply in economic life. To deal with the void left when work was removed from the home, both academicians and popular writers elaborated the woman's role as child-bearer, housekeeper, and soother of the husband's work-related strains. Above all, the sentimental ideology of the family in all its forms assumed the family must compensate for the harsh realities of life outside the home.

Although sociological theory replicated many of the ideas of nineteenth-century sentimentalism, it omitted one important element—the implicit or explicit critique of the dominant social values. The leading intellectual model of sociology, until recently, has been structural functionalism. The key assumption of functionalism is that social institutions work like body organs, contributing to the functioning of the whole (thus, the popular image of the family as the backbone of society). Functionalism emphasizes stability, consensus, continuity, and social control as the goals of social life. Individuals fulfill their social roles because the needs of the social system become their own. The family fits into this functional system in two ways. As a small society in itself, it embodies the principles of harmony, consensus, and an identity of individual and group needs. Second, the family performs vital functions: it reproduces the social order from one generation to the next, and soothes tensions in adults.

26. Jurgen Ruesch and Gregory Bateson, *Communication: The Social Matrix of Psychiatry* (New York: Norton, 1968).

PARADOXES OF PERFECTIONISM

None of those who formulated the modern ideology of the family considered the ironic possibility that the idealized images of family life they presented could introduce new tensions into the home. By either denying that daily family life is inevitably punctuated by tension and ambivalence or suggesting that all problems are easily solved if the proper methods are followed, the sentimental image of the perfect, happy family makes failure inevitable. The molehills of ordinary troubles become magnified into mountains of pathology. As family therapist John Weakland observes:

There are countless difficulties which are part and parcel of the everyday business of living for which no known ideal or ultimate solutions exist. Even when relatively severe, these are manageable in themselves but readily become "Problems" as a result of the belief that there should, or must, be an ideal solution for them.[27]

If we choose to avoid the pain and stigma of failure to live up to the ideal image by sweeping problems under the rug, we open ourselves to a deeper kind of trouble: ". . . the husband and wife who insist their marriage was made in heaven, or the parents who deny the existence of any conflicts in their children . . . are likely to be laying the groundwork for some outbreak of symptomatic behavior."[28]

An example of the kind of everyday difficulty that can be made into a problem through exaggeration or denial is provided by marriage counselor David Mace. He reports that the single biggest cause of the marital troubles he has witnessed is the spouses' failure to deal with anger. Although anger is an inevitable component of intimate relations, most people think that something is wrong with their spouse or their marriage if angry conflict occurs. Eventually, the angry feelings in both parties may crowd out the positive ones, and the result is a corroded relationship full of bitterness.

Another example of the sentimental ideology leading to its

27. John Weakland, R. Fisch, Paul Watzlawick, and A. M. Bodin, "Brief Therapy: Focused Problem Resolution," *Family Process* 13 (1974): 141–68.
28. Weakland, *et al.*, p. 148.

own contradictions is given in a recent article on child abuse[29] which theorizes that some of the incidence of violence toward children on the part of middle-class parents can be attributed to child-rearing theories that rule physical punishment out of bounds. In the past, a parent could spank a child for misbehavior and, because it was socially approved, could do it in a controlled manner. Now, parents try not to spank their kids, but when they almost inevitably do, it is outside any context of approved parental behavior. The parent's guilt is likely to increase his or her outrage, and may result in an out-of-control attack.

By prescribing inner states rather than behavior, modern standards of family perfection make success almost impossible to achieve. They are like religions of faith, rather than religions of deeds. Family members, if their family is to be regarded as normal, healthy, adjusted, and so forth, are supposed to experience emotional states such as love, happiness, joy, fun, and good orgasms. Martha Wolfenstein, in her discussion of "fun morality," has argued that such a concern for inner experience may paradoxically increase the strain on family relationships.[30] In former days, the proper performance of family roles was a matter of duty—carrying out tasks properly. If your child was clean and reasonably obedient, you had no cause to look further into his or her psyche. By contrast, the modern mother's self-evaluation can no longer be based on whether she is doing the right and necessary things, but involves nuances of feeling that cannot be controlled voluntarily. It is little wonder that surveys of middle-class mothers (such as that conducted by Sears *et al.*) reveal widespread guilt and anxiety over child-rearing.[31]

It is not only "fun morality" that has made modern child-rearing difficult, but also the fact that the goals of parenthood

---

29. R. D. Parke and C. W. Collmer, "Child Abuse: An Interdisciplinary Analysis," in *Review of Child Development Research*, vol. 5, ed. M. Hetherington (Chicago: University of Chicago Press, 1975).

30. Martha Wolfenstein, "Fun Morality: An Analysis of Recent American Child-Training Literature," in *Childhood in Contemporary Cultures*, ed. Margaret Mead and Martha Wolfenstein (Chicago: University of Chicago Press, 1955), pp. 168–78.

31. Robert Sears, Eleanor E. Maccoby, and Harry Levin, *Patterns of Child Rearing* (Evanston, Ill.: Row, Peterson, 1957), p. 33.

have become elusive and psychological. Around the turn of the century, a mother's concerns about feeding her child were physical ones—was the food clean and nourishing? Was the child chewing it properly? By the time of Dr. Spock, feeding a child became embroiled in issues of personality development. As historian Nancy Weiss observes: "Checking the bread and milk a child eats and seeing that he or she chews it well are concrete labors mothers can complete. The permissive tasks of enjoying a child at the table, and considering the learning element in feeding, are by their nature less susceptible to being finished. These are tasks that linger, and ones of Sisyphean proportions."[32]

The task of twentieth-century parents has been further complicated by contradictions in the advice offered them. The experts disagree with each other, and they often contradict themselves. The kindly Dr. Spock is full of double binds. In a detailed analysis of Spock's advice, Michael Zuckerman observes that the doctor tells mothers to relax and trust their instincts, while at the same time warning them that they have an "ominous power" to destroy their child's innocence and make him discontent forever; Spock presses them again and again to "ask the doctor."[33] However contradictory the advice offered them, parents seem to have acted upon it. A review of child-rearing research by Bronfenbrenner revealed that middle-class parents reflected in their actual child-rearing practices the swings in expert opinion. During the first half of the twentieth century, middle-class parents tended to be more strict with their children than working- and lower-class parents, but by the fifties they had crossed over and become more permissive. Attributing these changes to the great sensitivity of middle-class parents to expert opinion, Bronfenbrenner observes that child-rearing practices are likely to change most quickly among those who have closest access to the agencies or agents of change such as public media, clinics, physicians, and counselors.[34]

32. Nancy P. Weiss, "Mother, the Invention of Necessity."
33. Michael Zuckerman, "Dr. Spock: The Confidence Man," in *The Family in History*, ed. C. W. Rosenberg (Philadelphia: University of Pennsylvania Press, 1975), pp. 179–207.
34. Urie Bronfenbrenner, "Socialization and Social Class through Time and

Not only did parents internalize expert advice and the sentimental image of the family, but children did as well. For example, consider the beliefs that parental love is necessary for the proper development of the child, and that disastrous consequences result from its lack. Jerome Kagan observes that non-Western cultures, and Western society before the seventeenth century, did not recognize parental attitudes as a source of physical or mental illness. These beliefs can act as self-fulfilling prophecies: parents believe they will harm their children if they fail to love them enough. Children and adolescents learn of scientific and popular theories relating lack of parental love to unhappiness and psychological illness; and adults interpret their emotional problems as delayed reactions to a lack of love during childhood, rather than, say, fate, witchcraft, or evil spirits.[35]

AN END TO THE SENTIMENTAL MODEL?

After a century and a half, the web of beliefs and attitudes that made up the sentimental model of the family appears to be unraveling. The postwar era of togetherness and the feminine mystique, of the baby boom and the rise of suburbia, seemed to represent its fullest realization. Yet both the prosperity and the social tranquillity of the period turned out to be fragile and illusory. The tensions simmering just below the calm surface of the fifties were later to erupt in the youth revolts of the sixties and the rebirth of feminism.

The sense of malaise about the family today, the widespread feeling that it is falling apart, may be seen as a response not only to rapid and profound social change, such as the steep rise in the divorce rate and the increase in women working, but also to the weakening of the sentimental model. Many people, faced with the obvious discrepancy between the realities of today's family life and the model, refuse to give up the dream of domestic

---

Space," in *Readings in Social Psychology*, 3d ed., edited by Eleanor E. Maccoby *et al.* (New York: Holt, Rinehart and Winston, 1958).

35. Jerome Kagan, "The Child in the Family," *Daedalus* 106, no. 2 (Spring 1977): 33–56.

perfection, and project it back into the past. A fierce nostalgia for some lost golden age of the family afflicts a large segment of the public and a few family scholars as well. For most contemporary students of the family, however, there is a growing awareness that the image of the stable, harmonious family is a myth or, at best, a half-truth. Within the social sciences there has been a rebirth of theories that see conflict and change as inherent aspects of social life, not perturbations arising from outside the system. Also emerging from a number of fields is the view that family problems arise out of the processes of family life itself—not necessarily from quirks of the individual psyche. In many ways, we are witnessing a resurrection of the tragic view of the family, a return to the kind of models of family life suggested by Freud and Simmel around the turn of the century. Rather than viewing the family as a haven of perfect peace and tranquillity, we have begun to realize that intimate relations inevitably involve antagonism and hostility as well as love. Indeed, the two aspects are inseparable—intimate relations provide more occasions for conflict than less close relationships, and conflicts between intimates are usually more intense than those between non-intimates.

Recently, a number of sociologists have turned their attention to family violence—not only child abuse, but husband and wife violence as well. Researchers such as Straus, Steinmetz, and Gelles remind us of well-established facts that family scholars have tended not to think about very much, such as the fact that more policemen are killed in action on family fight cases than in any other situation, and that in most murder cases the victim and the murderer are either relatives or involved with each other in some intimate way.[36] These scholars are also turning up new findings, such as the fact that family violence is much more widespread in the middle class than anyone thought, and that pregnancy is a likely time for wife-beating to occur. Most significantly, these scholars do not approach family violence as a product of deranged minds, or as a product of uniquely

36. Suzanne K. Steinmetz and Murray A. Straus, *Violence in the Family* (New York: Dodd, Mead, 1974).

violence-prone families, but rather they see violence as a "normal" part of family life. That is, they see violence arising out of stresses and strains that may be found in most if not all families.

The point of the studies of family violence is not that all families are violent, but that the emotional dynamics in families that are violent are not unique to them. For these researchers, the focus on force and violence is one way of understanding the family, and a more revealing way than a focus on consensus and harmony. On the theoretical side, William Goode recently wrote on the topic of force and violence in the family.[37] Explaining why people conform to prescribed roles, Goode argues that family structures are maintained not only by solidarity and love, but also by force, both personal and social.

The revised view of family life emerges also in the work of researchers trying to locate the sources of schizophrenia in the interactional patterns of the patient's family. These researchers started out trying to discover the pathological family but ended up, as Jules Henry observes, discovering the family.[38] Such family processes as the double bind, mystification, invalidation, family myths, secrets and alliances, and so forth, first found in the families of mental patients, were later found in a variety of "normal" or nonclinical families. Lennard and Bernstein observe that, compared to other kinds of groups, families are difficult interactional environments.[39] As Jules Henry remarks, many families are "Greek tragedies without heroes."[40] This view of families as difficult environments creates problems for the notion that family conflict and trauma inevitably damage children. There are many more seemingly schizophrenogenic families than there are schizophrenics, for example. We need to rethink the role of stress and trauma in development. Retrospective studies of the backgrounds of "normal" or high-achieving adults reveal as

37. William J. Goode, "Force and Violence in the Family," *Journal of Marriage and the Family* 33 (1971): 624–36.

38. Jules Henry, *Pathways to Madness* (New York: Random House, 1971).

39. Henry L. Lennard and Arnold Bernstein, *Patterns in Human Interaction* (San Francisco: Jossey-Bass, 1969).

40. Henry, *Pathways to Madness*, p. xx.

much "pathology" as does the study of the backgrounds of hospitalized patients.[41]

Although researchers in a variety of areas of family study are dismantling the old sentimental model of family, new ones are appearing to take its place. Thus, in recent years we have seen communes and open marriages presented as routes to individual salvation, social regeneration, or both. Recent works on sex have opened up whole new areas in perfectionist standards. At the same time, many people still hold to the traditional notions about family. Given the uncertainty of family norms and family life, plus their private character, illusions can flourish and be sustained here more readily than in other areas.

To conclude, I would like to consider briefly the social consequences of the sentimental model of the family. From the nineteenth-century commune to the suburban exodus to the hippie commune, the sentimental model has encouraged the American frontier tendency to deal with social problems by running away from them. As Jeffrey observes, "When middle-class Americans increasingly opted for retreat rather than active engagement in the life of their society, they thereby ensured that the abuses they perceived would be perpetuated and that their reasons for despairing about their society would grow ever stronger."[42]

Thus, I see in the current disillusion with family life some hope for the future. Lowered expectations of family life may increase our ability to cope with the strains and irritations of marriage and child-rearing. Further, once we are no longer convinced that we may find heaven by withdrawing from the world, we may try harder to change it.

41. See W. Schofield and L. Balien, "A Comparative Study of the Personal Histories of Schizophrenics and Nonpsychiatric Patients," *Journal of Abnormal and Social Psychology* 59 (1969): 216–25, and H. Renaud and F. Estess, "Life History Interviews with One Hundred Normal American Males: 'Pathogenicity' of Childhood," *American Journal of Orthopsychiatry* 31 (1961): 786–802.

42. Jeffrey, "Family as a Utopian Retreat," p. 37.

IV. RESPONSIBILITIES

Law, Politics, and Ethics

14

Family Law in Transition: From Traditional Families to Individual Liberty

STEPHEN J. MORSE

In our democratic society the law is an excellent indicator of social reality, for the law both expresses fundamental values and sets limits to social evolution. For example, the United States Supreme Court has affirmed often that the family is one of our fundamental and most precious social institutions. Recently the Court had the following to say about the family as an institution:

> Our decisions establish that the Constitution protects the sanctity of the family precisely because the institution of the family is deeply rooted in this Nation's history and tradition. It is through the family that we inculcate and pass down many of our most cherished values, moral and cultural.[1]

For the law, the family is a crucial social institution, but what is the law's vision of the family? This essay will examine the changing American family as it is reflected in family law during the last hundred years and especially during the last two decades, when extensive legislative and judicial shifts have occurred. Focusing mainly on the United States Supreme Court, we shall examine legal trends in the following areas: the definition of the family, procreative freedom, spousal relations, child-parent-state relations, and family dissolution.[2]

1. Moore v. City of East Cleveland, 431 U.S. 494 (1977).
2. I shall not attempt a comprehensive, analytic overview of American

I would like to argue that traditional family values and expectations may conflict with current conceptions of liberty and autonomy. Although families may be a source of love and acculturation, they may also stifle liberty, especially the liberty of women and children. For instance, parents are traditionally entitled legally to control the upbringing of their children. What should be the result, however, if the parents oppose their minor pregnant daughter's wish to have an abortion? In this case traditional family values conflict with the young woman's rights to privacy and to choose whether to become a parent herself. Who should prevail—the parents or the daughter? To take another example, if divorce is hard to obtain, many marriages that would otherwise be ended may be preserved in legal name. But what is the human cost to spouses who wish to be free of an unhappy and perhaps destructive relationship? Here legal attempts to preserve traditional family stereotypes ("till death do us part") inhibit the liberty of spouses and children buffeted by an unhappy home.

Until the past twenty years or so, the tension between liberty and autonomy and traditional family life was usually ignored or resolved in favor of the latter. But the last two decades have witnessed a social revolution whereby the rights of various

---

family law but rather will highlight important cases and trends in an effort to portray descriptively the law's view of the family. The discussion will focus on the results of the decisions rather than on the Court's judicial craftsmanship or the persuasiveness of its reasoning. This emphasis should not be taken to mean that only the result in a case is important. Indeed, the Court has a duty to develop rational and consistent principles for its holdings, a duty which the Court often fails to fulfill in the area of family law. Nevertheless, intensive, critical discussion of the Court's reasoning would go beyond the scope of this essay, and we must therefore content ourselves with examining the ultimate outcome of the cases. Cases decided after February 1, 1978, are not included, except for two decisions reported at the end of this essay, pp. 359–60. Readers who wish to pursue family law in greater detail may consult any standard casebook such as H. Krause, *Family Law* (Minneapolis: West Publishing, 1976); H. Clark, *Cases and Problems on Domestic Relations*, 2d ed. (Minneapolis: West Publishing, 1974), or C. Foote, R. Levy, and F. Sander, *Cases and Materials on Family Law*, 2d ed. (Boston: Little, Brown, 1976). An excellent treatise, now somewhat out-of-date, is H. Clark, *Domestic Relations* (Minneapolis: West Publishing, 1968). A concise, excellent current overview is H. Krause, *Family Law in A Nutshell* (Minneapolis: West Publishing, 1977).

groups including women and children have been enhanced. Whereas the law formerly proclaimed that husband and wife were one and the husband was "the one," this view is now considered outrageous, an affront to the dignity and autonomy of women. And it is no longer possible to view children as objects who can be regulated without regard for their wishes and liberty.

Political-legal change has occurred simultaneously with a de-mythologizing of family life. The conception of the family as a relatively harmonious group headed by a wage-earning husband attended by a homemaking wife and two children is simply untenable as a reflection of past or current reality. Examinations of family life, especially since the Second World War, have made it clear that many families are not intact, that wives work, parents beat children, spouses beat each other, and often there can be serious conflicts of interest between spouses and between spouses and children. I am not implying that the Hogarthian profile just drawn is the dominant one. Rather, I am suggesting that the Norman Rockwell vision does not apply to large numbers of families, and in recent decades this fact has been recognized (and much lamented, as if it were a surprise).

Thus two trends have emerged in recent years: the liberty and autonomy interests of women and children have been recognized and furthered and the costs of family life have been exposed. Together these movements have fostered the dominant modern shift in family law—increasing autonomy for family members in relation to one another.[3] Throughout our exploration of family law, our consistent focus will be on the relationship between liberty and traditional family values. We shall see that older conceptions of family roles and behavior have given way to a new sociolegal regime of enhanced autonomy. Of course, this does not mean that the family is "dead." It simply means that the law

3. The autonomy of the family in regard to the state has increased and decreased simultaneously. In many ways the state interferes less to allow family members more freedom as in no-fault divorce. But, conversely, the state plays a greater role because it provides the enforcement mechanisms whereby family members can vindicate their newly won autonomy in regard to one another. For instance, the state has increasingly intervened in family life to insure that children are protected and given opportunities the state believes every child should have in order to fulfill his or her potential.

has recognized and ratified the social, political, and economic changes that have occurred since the Second World War. The law comports better now with social reality, although there has been much opposition from those who believe that enhancing liberty at the expense of traditional family values is misguided and that the law should have exerted a more restraining influence.

THE DEFINITION OF THE FAMILY

Many legal rights and duties flow from family status. If we examine what relationships lead to those rights and duties, much can be learned about our society's view of what a family is and should be. The Supreme Court has made it quite clear that biological relationship (or its equivalent by legal adoption) and marriage are the touchstones of family status.

In *Moore* v. *City of East Cleveland*,[4] Ms. Moore challenged a municipal ordinance that limited occupancy of a dwelling unit to a single family and defined "family" so as to exclude Ms. Moore who lived with two grandsons who were first cousins. Previously, in *Boraas* v. *Belle Terre*,[5] the Court had upheld the constitutionality of a zoning ordinance that prohibited more than two *unrelated* persons from living together in one dwelling unit. *Belle Terre* thereby upheld legislation that would effectively prohibit a family-equivalent, the commune, from establishing itself in towns that passed such ordinances. The Supreme Court found the East Cleveland ordinance unconstitutional, however, because it intruded on highly protected freedom of choice about family living arrangements. Although the East Cleveland ordinance had the same general type of objectives as the permissible ordinance in the *Belle Terre* case, the two situations were distinguished because the latter involved individuals unrelated by blood, marriage, or adoption.

The Court affirmed that there is "a private realm of family life which the state cannot enter" and went on to hold that the constitutional protection given to the sanctity of the family and

4. 431 U.S. 494 (1977).
5. 416 U.S. 1 (1974).

its internal choices had to be extended to Ms. Moore's type of family group. The Court said,

Ours is by no means a tradition limited to respect for the bonds uniting the members of the nuclear family. The tradition of uncles, aunts, cousins, and especially grandparents sharing a household along with parents and children has roots equally venerable and equally deserving of constitutional recognition. . . . Even if conditions of modern society have brought about a decline in extended family households, they have not erased the accumulated wisdom of civilization, gained over the centuries and honored throughout our history, that supports a larger conception of the family.[6]

In another important case, *Stanley* v. *Illinois*,[7] the Court invalidated a state statute which provided that on the death of the mother, her nonmarital children became wards of the state. In this case the biological father, who had lived with the children and contributed to their support for many years, wished to retain custody of the children. As is often true in the family law area, the case was not reasoned crisply, but drawing on the Court's recognition of family integrity, the strong interest of parents in their children, and the fact that parent-child responsibilities exist without a marriage ceremony, the Court held that "Stanley's interest in retaining custody of his children is cognizable and substantial." Thus, Stanley, like mothers or married parents, could not have his children taken from him without a finding that he was unfit to be a parent.[8]

A last and more recent case, *Smith* v. *Organization of Foster Families*,[9] emphasizes the importance of biological traditional

6. Moore v. City of East Cleveland, 431 U.S. 494, 504–06 (1977).

7. 405 U.S. 645 (1972).

8. *Stanley* should be compared with a case just decided, Quillon v. Walcott, 98 S.Ct. 549 (1978). In *Quillon* a biological father sought to veto the adoption of his child by the mother's husband (with whom the child and mother lived in a family unit). Prior to the adoption filing, the natural father had not sought or had custody of the child, nor had he sought to legitimate the child. The Court held that the father was not denied equal protection or due process when, without a finding that he was an unfit parent, he was denied standing to veto the adoption. This case is distinguishable from *Stanley*, of course, because the father here had considerably less interest in and contact with his child prior to the time when parental rights would be lost.

9. 431 U.S. 816 (1977).

relationships as the foundation for family status. The plaintiffs in *Smith* challenged on due process grounds New York procedures that gave foster parents substantial but limited means of redress when the state sought to take away their foster children. Distinguishing foster families from traditional families, the Supreme Court held that the procedures were constitutionally adequate to protect caretaker-child relationships. And the Court used the occasion to comment once again on its definition of the family:

The usual understanding of "family" implies biological relationships. . . . But biological relationships are not exclusive determination of the existence of a family. . . . [T]he importance of the familial relationship, to the individuals involved and to the society, stems from the emotional attachments that derive from the intimacy of daily association, and from the role it plays in "promoting a way of life" through the instruction of children, . . . as well as from the fact of blood relationship. No one would seriously dispute that a deeply loving and interdependent relationship between an adult and a child in his or her care may exist even in the absence of blood relationship. At least where a child has been placed in foster care as an infant, has never known his natural parents, and has remained continuously for several years in the care of the same foster parents, it is natural that the foster family should hold the same place in the emotional life of the foster child, and fulfill the same socializing functions as a natural family. For this reason, we cannot dismiss the foster family as a mere collection of unrelated individuals. . . .

But there are also important distinctions between the foster family and the natural family. . . . In this case, the limited recognition accorded to the foster family by the New York statutes and the contracts executed by the foster parents argue against any but the most limited constitutional "liberty" in the foster family.[10]

The Court noted that granting greater recognition to foster parent-child relationships would disadvantage natural parents who had not finally given up their right to their child:

It is one thing to say that individuals may acquire a liberty interest against arbitrary governmental interference in the family-like associations into which they have freely entered, even in the absence of biological connection or state-law recognition of the relationship. It is quite another to say that one may acquire such an interest in the face of

10. 431 U.S. 816, 843–46 (1977).

another's constitutionally recognized liberty interest that derives from blood relationship, state-law sanction, and basic human right.[11]

The definition adopted by the Supreme Court seems to fit the definition that nearly all Americans would accept: The contours of the legal family seem to depend on marriage and biological or equivalent legal relationships. Relationships that do not have these bases are not considered families, even though they may be functionally equivalent to traditional families. Still, the recognition that "family-like associations" may have some family-like rights, especially where the best interests of children may be involved, reflects a concern for the rights of children and for the autonomy of adults who may obtain some family rights in nontraditional ways.

THE FORMATION OF FAMILIES—PROCREATIVE FREEDOM

In this section we shall discuss sterilization, birth control, and abortion. After all, the most basic biological means of forming a family is procreation, whether or not it is sanctioned by the state. We shall see that in this area there have been revolutionary legal changes, all of which have increased procreative freedom of choice, especially for women.

In *Skinner* v. *Oklahoma*,[12] the Supreme Court termed the right to procreate one of the "basic civil rights," a "basic liberty." Even so, compulsory sterilization laws are constitutional, but only if there are allegedly important state interests behind the need to sterilize[13] and those interests cannot be served by less restrictive means. Furthermore, the necessity for sterilization must be proved by the state in judicial proceedings that provide weighty procedural safeguards. As a result, compulsory sterilization is infrequent and freedom to procreate is nearly unlimited.

Like most freedoms, the freedom to procreate is not without costs. For a variety of reasons some persons cannot parent adequately at all or with more children than they already have.

11. 431 U.S. 816, 846 (1977).
12. 316 U.S. 535 (1941).
13. Buck v. Bell, 274 U.S. 200 (1927), upheld a compulsory sterilization law that applied to retarded persons.

In such cases the freedom to procreate leads inevitably to the neglect and dependency of many children, and to economic and social burdens on the state. Further, the dangers of overpopulation, while more remote, are real, according to many responsible commentators. Educating persons about contraception and the responsibilities of parenthood and motivating them to employ contraception may ameliorate the personal and social costs of free procreation to some degree; ultimately, however, these will be partial solutions. Nevertheless, there has been little attempt to restrict free procreation in the United States. The right to procreate is too fundamental to be restricted.

The most controversial legal issues in family formation involve family planning—the right of both sexes to have access to contraception and the right of women to have abortions. Perhaps no other area of family law has created such intense debate about moral issues and the appropriate role of law in regulating behavior. Questions about the right to life, the definition of a human being, the quality of life, and the right to control one's own sexual activity and body are enormously controversial and have vast social and legal implications. But despite the complexity of the issues and the powerful opposition to change, legal change in the area of family planning has been revolutionary.

The bellwether case that signaled a shift in judicial attitude was *Griswold* v. *Connecticut* (1965).[14] Appellants, the executive and medical directors of a family planning agency, challenged a criminal statute that prohibited the use of contraceptives and aiding or assisting others to use them. Appellants had been charged and found guilty as accessories to contraceptive use because they gave information, instruction, and medical advice to married persons and they examined the wife and prescribed the best contraceptive for her. The Supreme Court ruled the statute unconstitutional, holding that it violated a right to privacy found in the penumbra of the specific guarantees of the Fourth, Fifth and Ninth amendments to the United States Constitution. Concurring justices agreed with the result but used different constitutional theories to justify it. What was clear,

14. 381 U.S. 479.

however, was that a large majority of the Supreme Court believed that the freedom of married persons to make decisions about family size is a primary right of liberty and privacy that cannot be abridged by the state without powerful reasons for doing so.

After *Griswold*, the interesting question was how far the Court would carry the implications of that case. The next important contraception case, *Eisenstadt* v. *Baird* (1972),[15] reached a result consistent with *Griswold* but evaded the issue of whether the right to contraception was fundamental. *Eisenstadt* held that the state could not constitutionally bar the right of access to contraceptives of *nonmarried* persons. The Court said, "If the right of privacy means anything, it is the right of the individual, married or single, to be free from unwarranted governmental intrusion into matters so fundamentally affecting a person as the decision whether to bear or beget a child." Although the preceding language sounds like a fundamental rights analysis, the Court decided the case on equal protection grounds, arguing that it was irrational to distinguish married from unmarried persons for purposes of allowing access to contraceptives. Still, whatever the rationale, it was now clear operationally that states could not restrict access of adults to contraceptives.

The Court did not discuss in *Eisenstadt* the changing sexual mores of the 1960s and early 1970s, but the existence of the case itself and its decision are evidence of a profound shift in public attitudes toward sexual behavior and child-begetting. The Supreme Court gave adults, married or unmarried, unrestricted control over the reproductive repercussions of their sexual activity. Some might argue that the Court's decision encouraged sexual permissiveness by adding strength and moral prestige to the view that sex was appropriate outside as well as inside marriage, thus undermining traditional views that associated sexuality with marriage. But *Eisenstadt* was a realistic response to the growing social acceptance of nonmarital sexual behavior.

Finally, in 1977, in *Population Services International* v. *Carey*, the hint in *Eisenstadt* that the right to procreative freedom was

15. 405 U.S. 438.

fundamental was explicitly recognized. The Court declared unconstitutional a New York law that allowed only licensed pharmacists to sell non-prescription contraceptives to persons over sixteen. [16] The Court held that New York's restriction on permissible sellers violated a citizen's constitutional right to privacy because it placed too much burden on individual freedom of choice about contraception.

Population Services International was no surprise because in 1973, one year after *Eisenstadt*, the Supreme Court decided the landmark abortion case, *Roe* v. *Wade*, [17] probably the most controversial Supreme Court decision of the 1970s. The question in *Roe* was the extent to which a state could regulate the abortion process. The Court relied on the *Griswold* case and a vaguely defined Fourteenth Amendment right to privacy in order to grant a limited right to abortion. Although the doctrinal basis for the decision is dubious and oft-criticized, the Court's practical ruling laid down reasonably clear guidelines for the state regulation of abortion. The Court held that during the woman's first trimester of pregnancy there is no compelling state interest that justifies limiting the woman's fundamental right to privacy. Therefore, the state cannot prohibit abortion where the mother and her physician decide in its favor. In the second trimester, however, when abortion is more medically complicated, the state may regulate the abortion process in ways that promote the health of the mother because the state does have a compelling interest in maternal health. At the point of fetal viability (approximately the third trimester), the state has a recognizable interest in promoting the potential life of the fetus and thereafter abortion may be regulated or even prohibited except where it is necessary to preserve the life or health of the mother. In sum, a woman has an absolute right to terminate pregnancy during its early stages so long as she can find a sympathetic physician and the funds to pay for the abortion. And even after the fetus is viable, she may terminate the pregnancy by finding a physician who will agree that abortion is necessary to preserve maternal health.

16. 431 U.S. 678 (1977).
17. 410 U.S. 113 (1973).

The *Roe* decision was indeed revolutionary. Abortion horrifies many people on moral and religious grounds because they believe it embodies a lack of reverence for life and family. For many persons a fetus is a human being and abortion is tantamount to criminal homicide. But, prior to the Supreme Court's decision, it was clear that enormous numbers of women, the majority married, were using abortion as a means of birth control. Women with means found it relatively simple to secure a safe abortion, but poor women faced hazardous conditions that led frequently to disease or death. By the time of the *Roe* decision, these facts were well known, and unwanted pregnancy was still common despite the relative ease of access to contraception. Consequently, the continued use of illegal abortion, which was hazardous in many cases, could be predicted unless the law permitted abortion under medically acceptable conditions. More importantly, the woman's rights to privacy, to control her body and to have a life she could manage without undue hardship or anxiety, and the children's right to adequate parents who wanted them were rights that needed to be balanced against the right of the fetus to come to term. Abortion is an enormously difficult issue, but abortion will take place with or without legal permission, and there are strong moral arguments on both sides of the question.

By 1973 some state legislatures, such as those of Colorado and New York, had passed liberalizing abortion legislation in response to the realities of abortion practice and the shift in public attitudes toward it. It was likely to be a long time, however, before such legislation would be passed in all states. Although there was a change in public attitudes toward abortion, the practice still faced strident political opposition. An opinion by the Supreme Court was probably the only means then possible to insure the right to procreative choice for all American women. In this area, therefore, the Court led the country and gave powerful impetus to growing social acceptance of abortion. By a single decision, the Court immeasurably increased the liberty and autonomy of women in regard to the fundamental right of privacy and control of their bodies.[18]

18. The *Roe* decision raised the issues of whether the consent of a spouse or

The abortion decision led predictably to enormous outcry and political reaction by those opposed to abortion. And indeed, on questions involving access to abortion, the Court and legislatures have not been willing to follow the arguable implications of the *Roe* case. In a series of three cases decided in spring 1977, *Beal* v. *Doe*, [19] *Maher* v. *Roe*, [20] and *Packer* v. *Doe*, [21] the Court made the following rulings respectively: that the portion of the Social Security Act which provides for joint federal-state medicaid programs does not require participating states to fund non-therapeutic abortions as a condition of participation in the program; that a Connecticut welfare regulation limiting state medicaid benefits for first trimester abortion only to those abortions that are medically necessary is constitutional; that a city hospital's refusal to provide publicly financed hospital services for nontherapeutic abortion while providing such services for childbirth is constitutional. And, as the newspapers constantly remind us, there is a pitched battle in the U.S. Congress as abortion foes have so far successfully sought to prevent federal medicaid funding for abortion except under extremely limited circumstances.

In one sense the Court and Congress appear to be returning to the pre-*Roe* era: relatively affluent women have easy access to safe, medical abortions, whereas poorer women in many places must either forego abortion or seek it from unqualified practitioners, often under very hazardous conditions. Although the Supreme Court has demonstrated no inclination whatsoever to review the *Roe* decision, leaving intact the fundamental right to

---

the parent of a minor child was necessary before a pregnant spouse or minor could have an abortion. In Planned Parenthood of Central Missouri v. Danforth, the Supreme Court decided both these questions in the negative, 428 U.S. 52 (1976). Although the biological father has a strong interest in the fetus and parents have an equally strong interest in controlling important decisions concerning the life of their child, the woman's right to privacy was not outweighed by the father's rights in the fetus, the need for family harmony, or the parents' traditional right to control their child. In any case, these are surely not the types of family decisions in which the law can intervene effectively.

19. 432 U.S. 438 (1977).
20. 432 U.S. 464 (1977).
21. 432 U.S. 519 (1977).

bodily privacy and consequently to have an abortion, it seems difficult to reconcile the access decisions with *Roe*. Of course, simply because there is a right to abortion does not mean the state should have to pay for it. But by effectively allowing a distinction in access to abortion on the basis of wealth, the Court seems to be undermining the spirit of *Roe* by implicitly undercutting the importance of the right to bodily privacy and procreative choice. Still, the right to abortion is the law of the land and to that extent the Supreme Court has continued to uphold the principle of enhanced liberty for women.

As the Supreme Court said in *Griswold* and thereafter, the freedom to reproduce is older than the Bill of Rights and has its source in intrinsic human rights. The Court's clear recognition and affirmation of this freedom are a reflection of historically evolving and emotionally held attitudes. The Court has extended the freedom to control procreation beyond traditional limits, undermining strongly and widely held religious and moral views, and it has done so in keeping with an evolving conception of personal liberty and autonomy. The Court's views on contraception and abortion have wide support because they reflect a shift in social attitudes; the Court's stance is also a strong impetus to the continuing acceptance of the newer view.

THE FORMATION OF FAMILIES—MARRIAGE

Writing for the Supreme Court in *Griswold*, Mr. Justice Douglas expressed the opinion:

Marriage is a coming together for better or for worse, hopefully enduring, and intimate to the degree of being sacred. It is an association that promotes a way of life, not causes; a harmony in living, not political faiths; a bilateral loyalty, not commercial or social projects. Yet it is an association for as noble a purpose as any involved in our prior decisions.[22]

The Supreme Court has held repeatedly that marriage is a fundamental right; indeed, it has written that "the freedom to marry

22. 381 U.S. 479 (1965).

has long been recognized as one of the vital personal rights essential to the orderly pursuit of happiness by free men."[23] American regulation of marriage is thus relatively minimal.

Regulation of marriage is entirely under state control; the only typical restrictions are against bigamous, consanguinous and homosexual marriages, and those contracted by parties legally incapable of giving consent such as infants or insane persons. Because these restrictions are of limited applicability and most are rarely enforced, few persons are barred from getting married. Further, in some states, marriage can be accomplished by simply living together as man and wife (so-called common law marriage). To date there have been few serious suggestions for further state-imposed screening to insure that only compatible and mature persons marry or the like.[24]

The Supreme Court has decided only three cases concerning who may marry. The first case, *Reynolds* v. *U.S.*,[25] involved a claim by Mormons that state prohibition of polygamy was unconstitutional because it infringed the Mormons' First Amendment right to the free exercise of their religion. The Court seemed to rely on tortured distinctions to deny the Mormons' claims and held the prohibition constitutional, but the true basis of the holding was that polygamy, even if compelled by religious belief, was simply too deviant from dominant cultural moral standards. The second major case, *Loving* v. *Virginia* (1968),[26] involved an attack on the constitutionality of anti-miscegenation laws which were still prevalent in the South. In *Loving*, the Court affirmed the broad power of the states to regulate marriage but also noted, as it had in the past, that "marriage is one of the 'basic civil rights of man,' fundamental to our very existence and survival." The Court went on to hold that this freedom could not be denied on the flimsy basis of a racial classification that clearly

23. Loving v. Virginia, 388 U.S. 1, 12 (1967).

24. There have, however, been many suggestions that marital life education courses be given in schools or to persons planning to marry. But these suggestions have not borne fruit in any way that seriously compromises the ability of persons freely to marry whom they choose when they choose.

25. 98 U.S. 163 (1878).

26. 388 U.S. 1.

violated the principle of equality embodied in the Fourteenth Amendment and thus deprived affected citizens of liberty without due process of law.

The most recent case, *Zablocki* v. *Redhail* (1977),[27] concerned a Wisconsin statute which provided that Wisconsin residents who were legally obligated to support a minor not in their custody could not marry in Wisconsin or elsewhere without a court order. Court permission would not be granted unless the marriage applicant furnished proof that he or she was in compliance with the support order and that the children covered by the support order were not then nor likely to become public charges. The Court affirmed that reasonable regulations which did not significantly interfere with the decision to marry were permissible. In this case, however, the State's purposes that supported the regulation were not sufficiently weighty to overcome the individual's fundamental right to marry.

The importance of marriage and the freedom to marry are well recognized. Although most Americans take this state of affairs for granted, some might question whether so little regulation is the wisest course for the law to pursue. Much disharmony is certainly the result of the mismatching of spouses, and the costs are high, but should the state regulate more intensively the decision to marry? Would such regulations truly improve marriage and subsequent family life? Although some commentators bemoan the fact that marriage is "too easy to get into" (and "so hard to get out of"—although less so at present), the great freedom to marry is surely the wisest social policy. Freedom to marry is viewed as such a fundamental right in our society that any major legal infringement on that right would lead to widespread evasion and disrespect for law. Furthermore, the decision to marry is so powerfully motivated by emotional factors that more than minimal regulation would almost certainly fail. Although "mismatches" and their consequences interfere with the goals of traditional family life and are costly to society, these are costs that should be borne because freedom to marry the person of one's choice is too precious to abandon.

27. 434 U.S. 374.

Husbands and Wives

Legal regulation of spousal relations deals mainly with two areas: support obligations and the legal-economic autonomy of women. Of course, the law does not intervene in the day-to-day affairs of marriage, and spouses are left to regulate their relationships as they see fit. Compared to intrafamilial negotiation, the law is simply not an efficient and workable means to order spousal relations or to remedy "ordinary" family difficulties. Indeed, most of the legal standards concerning spousal relations are not tested until significant disharmony occurs and breakup is threatened. Still, the law has announced various standards that reflect social values and serve as moral precepts to guide family behavior.[28] As we shall see, legal standards for regulation of spousal relations are quite traditional and conservative, albeit presently undergoing substantial legislative and judicial changes.

Husbands and wives are traditionally obligated by law mutually to support each other, but in different ways: husbands are responsible for the financial support of the family and wives are responsible for domestic services.[29] Such legislation obviously discriminates against both sexes, theoretically locking individuals into roles they neither prefer nor perform. For example, well over 50 percent of married women are in the work force. But the law is not an obstacle to families creating their own support regimes. Legal support rights become important if families dissolve. For the going family then, the dictates of support law are of little consequence. Still, the law on the books is discriminatory, and various legislatures have reformed support laws to make financial support a mutual responsibility.

The Supreme Court has not taken a clear position on sexual equality under the Equal Protection Clause, and one cannot predict with certainty what the Court would do if faced with a challenge to traditional support laws or other laws that reflect traditional sex roles and stereotypes. This is a convenient place, however, to explore a series of Supreme Court decisions dealing

28. See H. Clark, *Domestic Relations*, Section 6.1 (1968).

29. If the husband is unable to work, then his wife incurs the primary financial support obligation, but otherwise the traditional relationship is upheld by law.

with spousal equality. The Court has reached somewhat incon-
sistent results, but the thrust of the decisions clearly points
toward greater equality and thus liberty and autonomy.

Kahn v. *Shevin* (1974)[30] involved a challenge to a Florida statute
that granted a tax break to widows but not to widowers. The
Court upheld the discrimination because it was rationally related
to the social reality that men are the dominant wage earners in
our society and women need more financial assistance. The
second case, *Weisenfeld* v. *Weinberger* (1975),[31] concerned an attack on a sex-based distinction in the Social Security Act that
provided a widow benefits based on her deceased husband's
earnings but did not provide corresponding benefits for a
widower. Although the Court recognized that men are more
likely to provide primary support for families, this generalization
could not justify denigrating the efforts of women who work and
contribute significantly to supporting their families. The Court
thus invalidated the distinction and allowed widowers to obtain
benefits based on a deceased wife's earnings.[32]

In *Frontiero* v. *Richardson* (1973),[33] a female member of the
armed services challenged the service-person's dependent's
benefit provisions. Wives of male members of the armed services
were automatically deemed dependent and entitled to benefits,
whereas the dependence of the husband of a female member had
to be proven specifically. The Court invalidated this procedural
distinction on equal protection grounds. *Frontiero* is not good
precedent for equality in support rights, because there was no
inequality in the rights themselves—only in the proof of those
rights. The case is nevertheless interesting because the Court
found the procedural distinction unconstitutionally discriminatory even though it *is* more likely that the spouse of a male
service-person is truly dependent. Another case striking down

30. 416 U.S. 351.
31. 420 U.S. 636.
32. It is hard to reconcile *Kahn* and *Weisenfeld*. Perhaps the difference is that
the former involves a benign distinction that benefits one class, whereas the
latter disadvantages men as well as denigrates women without giving them any
benefit.
33. 411 U.S. 677.

sex-based discrimination is *Reed* v. *Reed* (1971).[34] There the Court invalidated on equal protection grounds an Idaho statute that gave mandatory preference to males in the choice of administrators of estates.

Weisenfeld, Frontiero and *Reed* together demonstrate that the Court is forging new law in the realm of sex-based discrimination, even if it has not demonstrated a complete willingness to invalidate laws that reflect traditional assumptions and rules and that arguably protect women who occupy traditional roles. Neither *Weisenfeld, Frontiero*, nor *Reed* deprives women of traditional protections, but they do recognize that some forms of inequality are invalid and they do increase the autonomy and power of women.

Many sex-based discriminatory laws remain in force. The law thus reflects traditional and perhaps still dominant cultural views while allowing married couples full autonomy to work out their own arrangements. And in more progressive states, legislatures are amending the law to reflect newer and perhaps emerging majority attitudes. Newer laws may end traditional protections for traditional wives, but they enhance the dignity of all women and do not prevent traditional couples from creating traditional arrangements.

A second area of legal regulation of spousal relationships concerns the economic and legal autonomy of wives. Until the mid-nineteenth century, women lost their legal autonomy when they married: the husband controlled property that the wife had previously owned, any earnings during the marriage became the husband's, and wives could not sue or be sued. About the middle of the nineteenth century, various state legislatures began to pass what are known as the Married Women's Property Acts which tried to provide women with legal-economic autonomy.[35] Conservative courts interpreted these acts quite restrictively, however, and the legislatures were engaged in a constant attempt to enact specific measures that would "overrule" the courts' restrictive decisions. Today there are almost no such disabilities re-

34. 404 U.S. 71.

35. See, for example, N. Y. *Domestic Relations Law* (McKinney's) Section 50; N. Y. *General Obligations Law* (McKinney's) Sections 3-301 to 3-315; Clark, *Domestic Relations*, chap. 7.

maining. Women can own and manage separate property, retain their earnings, contract, make wills, and sue and be sued separately. Some vestiges remain, such as interspousal tort immunity and the inability of spouses to contract concerning marital obligations such as support, but even these, especially the former, are being abolished or called increasingly into question.[36]

It is mild irony that, when the Married Women's Property Acts were passed, few women had separate earnings or strong inclination to lead autonomous legal-economic lives. On the frontier, the realities of life probably made such acts or their lack irrelevant, and traditional role patterns dominated in more developed areas. Today, of course, many women work and assume even greater autonomy. But at a time when the acts have taken on new meaning, there is an increasing movement in non-community-property states to pass laws that create joint marital property, thus decreasing to some extent the autonomy of women in regard to their own property and earnings. And various property rules still do allow a spiteful spouse (typically the dominant wage earner, who is still usually the husband) to disadvantage his or her partner in one way or another. Still, spouses can make gifts to each other, contract, and in various other ways achieve the marital property regime that they wish, whether or not they live in a separate- or community-property state. The law is for the most part no bar to economic negotiation between spouses who wish to cooperate in a going marriage.[37]

Related to the theoretical grant of autonomy to married women is the law's attempt systematically to end discriminatory practices that inhibit the economic equality of women in fact.

36. See H. Clark, *Domestic Relations*, Section 7.2; also, L. T. Weitzman, "Legal Regulation of Marriage: Tradition and Change. A Proposal for Individual Contracts and Contracts in Lieu of Marriage," *California Law Review* 62: 1169 (1974).

37. It is a truism, however, that having separate property and good earnings increase one's autonomy and the ability to avoid the possible negative actions of a spiteful spouse. Although the law generally grants equality to the spouses, the richer or higher wage earner is favored in fact. Thus, until women achieve economic equality with men, as a practical matter they will be somewhat economically disadvantaged in their marriages, especially if the marriage dissolves.

Title VII of the Civil Rights Act of 1964[38] prevents discrimination in the labor market on the basis of sex. In a very recent case, for example, the Supreme Court held that employers could not deny accumulated seniority to women returning from a pregnancy leave even though the seniority policy appeared "neutral" in its treatment of the two sexes.[39] In fact, the policy burdened only women and the Court held that, because there was no business necessity for the policy, it constituted an unlawful, discriminatory employment practice under Title VII.

In another case, *Cleveland Board of Education* v. *La Fleur* (1973),[40] the Court invalidated municipal school board regulations that forced pregnant teachers to take pregnancy leaves quite early in pregnancy and to remain out of work for a substantial length of time after childbirth. The Court held that it was unconstitutional to presume that pregnant teachers were incapable either of teaching after the early months of pregnancy or of returning to the classroom soon after childbirth. Such incapacity might exist in some cases, but it was unfair to presume that it existed in all cases and thus to discriminate against all pregnant teachers. Although the doctrinal basis for the Court's discussion was much criticized, the Court was again willing to limit employment disabilities based on pregnancy. Thus, constitutional decisions and federal legislation (implemented by Court decisions and Equal Employment Opportunity Commission guidelines) have made it increasingly possible for women to enter the labor force on a basis of equality with men and at the same time to bear children.[41]

38. 42 U.S.C., Section 2000 (e) (1) *et seq.*
39. Nashville Gas Co. v. Satty, 431 U.S. 936 (1977).
40. 414 U.S. 632.
41. It should be pointed out, however, that the Court has upheld worker's disability benefit plans which cover all disabilities except pregnancy and childbirth. Geduldig v. Aiello, 417 U.S. 484 (1974); General Electric Co. v. Gilbert, 429 U.S. 125 (1976). Of course these decisions make it harder for women to have children, but they do not in any way discourage women from working. In fact, such discussions place a premium on taking minimum time off from work for pregnancy and childbirth, and indeed they may discourage pregnancy altogether in those families where the wife's income is an economic necessity. Thus these decisions decrease the autonomy of women by limiting their ability both to work and bear children.

338

It is clear that women are becoming increasingly autonomous even though some traditional laws remain on the books. Further, the law does not ban spouses from creating almost any kind of relationship that satisfies them. The law allows much freedom within marriage and is providing women greater employment equality, increasing the power of women both in and out of marriage. Thus, the laws of spousal relationships reflect emerging social attitudes that favor spousal and sexual equality.

Many of the issues discussed in this section involve laws that discriminate against women, a result that would be terminated by passage of the Equal Rights Amendment to the United States Constitution by the requisite number of states. Some opponents of the ERA believe that laws which treat the sexes differently are proper, especially those that "protect" traditional women. Opponents may not realize, however, that most discrimination is already prohibited by Supreme Court and lower court decisions based on equal protection doctrine and by state and federal legislation. But a constitutional amendment is less likely to be repealed than a particular statute, and the Equal Rights Amendment strongly reinforces the theory that sex discrimination is presumptively unconstitutional. Its importance lies partly in its highly significant symbolic effect on our society; it makes the principle of equality between the sexes an explicit part of our nation's highest law, rather than a result of interpretation of other principles.

CHILDREN, PARENTS, AND THE STATE

The Supreme Court has consistently recognized that parents have a fundamental right and duty to exercise custody, care, and control in the upbringing of their children.[42] The state may limit this right and duty only if parental conduct seriously endangers the health and safety of the child or if the limitation is necessary to avoid significant social burdens. Thus, parents cannot physically abuse their children and must educate them according to

---

42. Meyer v. Nebraska, 262 U.S. 309 (1923); Pierce v. Society of Sisters, 268 U.S. 510 (1925); Wisconsin v. Yoder, 406 U.S. 205 (1972).

minimal governmental dictates, but beyond such limitations the power of parents over their children is near absolute.

On the other hand, children are not chattels, and recently the Court has emphasized that children have constitutional rights. In *Planned Parenthood of Central Missouri* v. *Danforth* (1976),[43] the Court reaffirmed a decade-old line of cases granting juveniles greater rights and wrote: "Constitutional rights do not mature and come into being magically only when one attains the state-defined age of majority. Minors as well as adults are protected by the Constitution and possess constitutional rights."[44] As juvenile law has evolved in this century, the role of the state in child control has increased at the same time that the rights of children vis-à-vis their parents and the state have also increased. The autonomy of families has been decreased thereby, but the autonomy of children has increased markedly. We shall begin with an analysis of the increasing role of the state and then turn to the growing liberty of children.

The turn of the century was marked by the growth of both compulsory schooling and the juvenile court, the first systematic and large-scale state intrusions in child-rearing. In the state's view, an educated citizenry was necessary for the orderly functioning of a democratic, advanced society, and families were simply not adequate to insure this outcome. Thus for the first time the transmission of fundamental values and skills became the normal responsibility of the state. Although this was an enormous intrusion upon family autonomy and privacy, it was considered socially necessary, and, of course, it widened the outlook and options of children. In addition, compulsory schooling provided parents, especially women, with more free time. All in all, compulsory schooling balanced its intrusion on the traditional parental prerogatives by a corresponding increase in autonomy for individual family members. At the same time, the Supreme Court has upheld the rights of parents to educate their children in private religious schools,[45] and to educate them in

43. 428 U.S. 52.
44. 428 U.S. at 74.
45. Pierce v. Society of Sisters, 268 U.S. 510 (1925).

part in a foreign language[46] and even in special circumstances to abbreviate the required amount of compulsory schooling.[47] Thus schooling might take place largely outside the home, but a large measure of parental control was allowed so long as the schools met certain state requirements.

Compulsory schooling was required for all normal families and children, but the juvenile court was established to furnish state aid to troubled children and their families. This is not the appropriate place to chronicle the background of the juvenile court movement.[48] It is sufficient to note that many juveniles were neglected or delinquent, and had problems that their parents were seemingly incapable of correcting. The juvenile court was to function as a "good parent" to save those children whose parents were unwilling or unable to do so: the state would intervene to insure minimally adequate parenting. The court would remove neglected children in order to provide adequate care; the court would also take jurisdiction of delinquent children to provide the guiding hand of therapy or benevolent, firm discipline, rather than to punish them as criminals.

Aided and abetted by a panoply of benevolent and social science–oriented probation officers, counselors, and the like, the juvenile court established itself as a superparent.[49] The movement viewed itself as guided only by the best interests of parents and children and thus did not cast itself as an adversary to its "clients," families in trouble. Reflecting this view, the procedures of the juvenile court were extremely informal, theoretically analogous to procedures whereby a parent disciplines a

46. Meyer v. Nebraska, 262 U.S. 390 (1923).

47. Wisconsin v. Yoder, 406 U.S. 205 (1972), upholding the right of Amish parents to terminate the secular schooling of their children two years earlier than non-Amish children. In a partial dissent, Mr. Justice Douglas argued that mature children have a right to religious freedom separate from the right of their parents, and thus the children's views should have been canvassed before the children were removed from school.

48. An excellent, albeit critical, history is A. Platt, *The Child Savers: The Invention of Delinquency* (Chicago: University of Chicago Press, 1969).

49. For a provocative analysis of the "discovery" of the family by social scientists and consequent intrusion by the state into family life, see C. Lasch, *Haven in a Heartless World: The Family Besieged* (New York: Basic Books, 1977).

child or a friendly counselor "disciplines" a parent. Children needed to be saved and the state knew how to do it. No formalistic, anachronistic legal rules, it was argued, should be allowed to stand in the way.

And so it was, for approximately six decades. Allegedly neglected and dependent children were removed from their families and placed in institutions or foster homes. On occasion, the state would decree that parents were so bad that they should be deprived permanently of their parental rights, freeing the child for adoption into supposedly more suitable homes. All sorts of misbehaving children, ranging from truants and those who associated with bad company to those who committed serious crimes, were labeled as delinquent and placed under onerous conditions of probation or were sent to institutions that were simply prisons for young persons.

There were at least two major troubling aspects to these developments. First, the informal benevolent procedures of the court tended to be quite unfair both to parents who wished to avoid the state's kindness and to youngsters who wished to avoid being labeled delinquent and subjected to the "discipline" of the juvenile court. The second difficulty with the juvenile court movement was that the services theoretically to be provided were not available or did not nearly meet the ideals of juvenile court proponents. Foster care was an unfortunate expedient, and little technology for fixing dysfunctional families was available or applied. There were too many unwilling subjects, too little knowledge, and too few resources. Similarly, little could be done to straighten out delinquent youths. Reformatories, instead of being therapeutic communities, often warehoused under brutal conditions many juveniles who were hardly very bad or dangerous. Despite the best motives, the juvenile court turned out to be as deficient as the real parents it sought to augment or replace.

After the Second World War, increasing recognition of the failure of the juvenile court movement occurred simultaneously with the growing sophistication of adolescents as a group and the social emphasis on civil rights. It is difficult if not impossible to obtain "hard" measures of the greater social sophistication of an age group, but it is a commonplace that since the late 1940s adolescents have become more worldly, independent, and, unfortunately, dangerous. Simply put, it is harder to conceive of modern adolescents as children who are still subject to the complete or near complete control of their parents. Far more independent and peer group—oriented than they were in previous times, adolescents can no longer be treated as easily manipulable by their parents, the schools, or the legal system.

The many sociocultural trends bearing on children's rights coalesce in the landmark juvenile rights decision, *In re Gault*,[50] decided by the Supreme Court in 1967. Because the case is so important and its facts are so representative of prior legal treatment of children, we shall present it in some detail. Gerald Gault, a fifteen-year-old boy with a minor history of juvenile court difficulties, was accused of making indecent phone calls and arrested by the local sheriff. His parents learned that he was in custody, made inquiries, and were told that a hearing would take place the next day. The following day a juvenile probation officer filed a delinquency petition with the court. Gerald and his mother appeared in the judge's chambers for the hearing, but they received no copy of the petition which, in any case, detailed no factual basis for the request that Gerald should be judged a delinquent. Also present at the hearing were two juvenile probation officers.

At the hearing no witness was sworn, nor was a record made. Afterward no formal record or memorandum was prepared. Indeed, all knowledge of the proceedings comes from testimony given by the judge at later hearings when Gerald sought his freedom. The hearing was brief and produced contradictory testimony about the alleged telephone calls. The judge later testified that Gerald admitted making one lewd call. At the conclusion of the hearing, the judge decided to think about his decision and sent Gerald back to the detention center where he remained for two or three more days until he was allowed to go home. On the day of his release, Gerald's mother was given a note on plain paper signed by one of the probation officers which informed her that the judge had scheduled further hearings in three days.

The second hearing was attended by Gerald's father, and

50. 387 U.S. 1.

Gerald's alleged accomplice and his father, in addition to all those who were present at the first hearing. Again there was conflicting testimony, but Gerald now admitted only to dialing the complainant's number and not to making lewd remarks. Mrs. Gault requested that the complainant be present to identify accurately the alleged caller, but the judge ruled that the complainant's presence was not necessary. (In fact, the only contact with the complainant after the initial complaint was one phone conversation, on the day of the first hearing, between her and one of the probation officers.) Also, at the second hearing the probation officers filed a "referral report" with the court, but it was not disclosed to Gerald or his parents. At the conclusion of the hearing the judge found Gerald delinquent and committed him to the State Industrial School for the remainder of his minority—that is, for about *six years* until he was twenty-one. Under state law, no appeal was allowed in juvenile cases.

In effect, Gerald was found delinquent because he violated a section of the state criminal code that prohibited using "vulgar, abusive or obscene" language in the presence of a woman or child. Adults convicted under this statute could be fined five to fifty dollars or imprisoned for not more than two months. The judge also claimed that he acted under a statute that defines a delinquent child as one "habitually involved in immoral matters." Evidently the basis for the latter conclusion was the judge's memory of an earlier referral concerning Gerald that had received no formal adjudication for lack of a material foundation. The judge also noted that Gerald had admitted making other nuisance phone calls.

Gerald appealed his case through the state courts and finally to the Supreme Court of the United States. He claimed that the due process clause of the Fourteenth Amendment was violated by his commitment to a state institution pursuant to proceedings wherein the Court has near unlimited discretion and the juvenile is denied basic rights such as notice of the charges, right to counsel, right to confrontation and cross-examination, and the privilege against self-incrimination.

The Supreme Court agreed with Gerald and in a far-ranging opinion changed markedly the intellectual climate and practical working of juvenile courts around the country. Although the

344

case was limited to issues arising from delinquency determinations where commitment to a state institution was a possible consequence, it detailed the juvenile court's history of failure and abuse. Admitting that the juvenile court movement had proceeded from the best of motives, the Supreme Court still recognized, first, that under the guise of benevolence, young persons were deprived of their liberty in hearings like Gerald's that were a mockery of fairness; second, that these juveniles were then provided with little or no treatment but only incarceration, often for terms far longer than adults would receive for the same behavior. The Court noted that the name of the institution made no difference—a State Industrial School is in fact a prison. Under these conditions, the Court wrote, ". . . it would be extraordinary if our Constitution did not require the procedural regularity and exercise of care implied in the phrase 'due process.' Under our Constitution, the condition of being a boy does not justify a kangaroo court."[51]

To protect the juvenile from the massive deprivation of liberty involved in commitment to a reformatory, the Court held that the gulf between the protections granted to adults and those granted to children should be narrowed substantially. More specifically, the Court held that during delinquency determination proceedings, the juvenile is entitled to notice of charges, the right to counsel, the right to confront and cross-examine opposing witnesses, and the privilege against self-incrimination. The issue was not whether the proceedings were denominated civil or criminal. The crucial fact was that substantial liberty would be lost, and consequently the juvenile was constitutionally entitled to meaningful protections before liberty could be taken away. Put another way, in terms of procedure, alleged delinquents were now to be treated much like adult criminal defendants.

There has been much rhetoric and a fair amount of research on the actual changes in juvenile court proceedings following *Gault*.[52] Certainly the myriad juvenile courts across the nation did not reform overnight. But over the years there have been

51. 387 U.S. at 28.
52. See, for example, L. Teitelbaum and W. Stapelton, *In Defense of Youth* (New York: Russell Sage Foundation, 1972).

substantial practical changes, and perhaps more importantly, the proposition that children have real constitutional rights as independent beings was affirmed by the highest court in the land. At the same time, the failures and hypocrisies of the state's superparent, the juvenile court, were publicly proclaimed by the High Court. In all future cases concerning juvenile rights, claimants would now have a strong precedent on which to base their claims and arguments. Moreover, although *Gault* itself involved a family united against state intrusion, some of the underlying rationales about juvenile rights might very well apply when the child's antagonist was his or her parents and not the state. Although parents have enormous power over their children, that power might very well be limited when the child's independent, fundamental liberties were in question.

In the decade since *Gault* the Supreme Court has decided a large number of cases that have extended the constitutional rights of minors. In 1969 the Court decided that school children have First Amendment rights and could not be prohibited from wearing black armbands to school as part of a political protest.[53] In 1970, the "beyond a reasonable doubt" burden of proof applied in adult criminal cases was also applied in delinquency determinations—no child could be found delinquent unless the facts underlying the delinquency determination were proved beyond a reasonable doubt.[54] Consequently, it has been considerably more difficult for the state to prove allegations of delinquency.

A later case extended the protections of double jeopardy to juveniles, holding that a state could not try a juvenile as an adult criminal after it had begun a juvenile adjudicatory hearing to determine if the juvenile was delinquent by virtue of having violated a criminal statute.[55] Finally, the Court extended the protections of due process into the public schools, ruling that due process required some sort of regularized adequate procedure whereby a child could defend himself or herself against charges

53. Tinker v. Des Moines Independent School District, 393 U.S. 503 (1969).
54. In re Winship, 397 U.S. 358 (1970).
55. Breed v. Jones, 421 U.S. 519 (1975).

346

that would lead to suspension from school.[56] The procedure did not have to be so formal as a delinquency hearing, but some protections needed to be afforded.

Despite the clear thrust of *Gault* and its progeny, not all decisions extended the rights of juveniles. But those decisions that refused to enlarge juvenile rights were few and did not impose major substantive restrictions on juveniles. For instance, in *Ginsberg* v. *New York*,[57] the Court upheld a state statute that prohibited the sale to minors of material deemed obscene to them even if it might not be obscene to adults. The materials in question were rather tame, but the Court ruled that it was constitutionally permissible to restrict the rights of minors, more than adults, to judge and determine for themselves what sex material they might read or see. The Court explicitly held that the statute did not invade constitutionally protected rights of minors.

The second major decision that distinguished juveniles from adults, limiting the right of the former, was *McKeiver* v. *Pennsylvania*,[58] wherein the Court held that juveniles were not constitutionally entitled to a jury determination on the issue of whether they were delinquent. Previously the Court had ruled that the right to a jury trial for adults in serious cases was a fundamental right implicit in ordered liberty in our system of jurisprudence.[59] I believe the reasoning of *McKeiver* was singularly unpersuasive. The Court admitted that the juvenile court experiment with delinquents was generally unsuccessful, but retreated from further equating the juvenile process with that for adults. Indeed, *McKeiver* may be read as the Court's last indication of hope that the juvenile court might still fulfill its lofty goals.

Finally, in a summary opinion, *Ingraham* v. *Wright*,[60] the Court upheld the right of schools to apply corporal punishment to misbehaving students. The Supreme Court ruled that the Eighth Amendment ban on cruel and unusual punishments did

56. Goss v. Lopez, 419 U.S. 565 (1975).
57. 390 U.S. 629 (1968).
58. 403 U.S. 508 (1971).
59. Duncan v. Louisiana, 391 U.S. 145 (1968).
60. 430 U.S. 651 (1977).

not apply to disciplinary paddling of children in public schools. But it held that the right of schoolchildren to be free from corporal punishment is a constitutional liberty interest, thus raising the question of what procedural protections were due schoolchildren before they could be corporally punished. The Court noted that teachers were traditionally privileged to apply corporal punishment when necessary, with prudence and restraint, and held that common law remedies such as a suit for damages were adequate protection against abuse. Consequently, schoolchildren were not entitled to notice and a hearing prior to being punished. The Court recognized that school disciplinary problems are increasing in frequency and severity, and noted that speedy punishment was desirable.

In sum, the state intruded heavily into the privacy of parent-child relations in the twentieth century, usurping or augmenting child-rearing tasks that were traditionally left to parents and informal community disposition. The state's intrusion leads to a number of pertinent observations. First, it is clear that the state often is not skilled at providing the training or experiences that families are allegedly not fully capable of providing; indeed, state intrusion may be harmful in many cases. Second, provision of those services may conflict with the desires of parents and children, thereby rendering the state the adversary of the family. Consequently, there has been a growing tendency to grant legal protections to the possible recipients of state intervention in order to allow them to challenge the necessity for intervention.

At present, there is an uneasy tension between the state and families concerning state intrusion into child-rearing. The juvenile court apparatus still exists and the state continues to believe it should provide various therapeutic services through the schools (e.g., the current practice in some schools of compelling parents to accept drug treatment for allegedly hyperkinetic children and then administering the drugs through the schools). But the state's desire to intervene is now clearly balanced, first, by the recognition that state intrusion often unhelpfully invades family privacy and, second, by enhanced procedural protections for the family.

A series of Supreme Court cases dealing with the rights of illegitimate children deserve mention here because they also bear

348

on the Court's view of the liberty and protection of children and state regulation of family life. Prior to these cases, state law could constitutionally distinguish legitimate and illegitimate children, always to the disadvantage of the latter. Then, in a line of cases beginning with *Levy* v. *Louisiana* in 1968,[61] the Supreme Court systematically struck down as unconstitutional almost every state or federal disability imposed on illegitimate children. Except in extremely limited situations, the government cannot prevent an illegitimate child from receiving whatever benefits a legitimate child would receive. For instance, a dependent, unacknowledged nonmarital child must be given death benefits under workers' compensation equivalent to those for legitimate children.[62] Except in a few circumstances, the Court recognized that it is unfair and inhumane to punish innocent children for the misbehavior of their parents.

I have reserved until last what seems to me the most far-reaching recent decision concerning the relationship of parents, their children, and the state. In *Planned Parenthood of Central Missouri* v. *Danforth*[63] the Supreme Court considered the constitutionality of a Missouri statute that permitted unmarried minor women to have abortions only if one parent consented or a physician certified that it was necessary to save the woman's life. Missouri defended the statute on the grounds that states traditionally place greater limitations on minors than on adults in order to protect minors. The State claimed that allowing a child (some of whom were as young as age ten or eleven) to have an abortion without the counsel of an adult responsible or concerned for the child "would constitute an irresponsible abdication of the State's duty to protect the welfare of minors." In response, appellants argued that minors were allowed to obtain medical services for pregnancy, venereal disease, and drug abuse

61. 391 U.S. 68. See also Glona v. American Guarantee and Liability Insurance Co., 391 U.S. 73 (1968); Weber v. Aetna Casualty and Surety Co., 406 U.S. 164 (1972); Gomez v. Perez, 409 U.S. 535 (1973); Jiminez v. Weinberger, 417 U.S. 628 (1974); Mathews v. Jiminez, 427 U.S. 912 (1976); Trimble v. Gordon, 430 U.S. 762 (1977); *but see*, Labine v. Vincent, 401 U.S. 532 (1971); Mathews v. Lucas, 427 U.S. 495 (1976).

62. Weber v. Aetna Casualty and Surety Co., 406 U.S. 164 (1972).

63. 428 U.S. 52 (1976).

without parental approval, and that the abortion law "is the ultimate supremacy of the parents' desires over those of the minor child, the pregnant patient."

The Court recognized the power of the state to protect minors, but held that the "State does not have the authority to give a third party an absolute, and possibly arbitrary veto over the decision of the physician and his patient to terminate the patient's pregnancy, regardless of the reason for withholding the consent." *Danforth* reaffirmed that minors have constitutional rights that must be respected and protected. The right to privacy recognized in *Roe* v. *Wade*, the abortion decision, was too fundamental to allow veto by a third party, even a parent. Nor was it likely, the Court reasoned, that permitting parental veto would promote family harmony or parental authority "where the minor and the nonconsenting parent are so fundamentally in conflict and the very existence of the pregnancy already has fractured the family structure." The justices continued, "Any independent interest the parent may have in the termination of the minor daughter's pregnancy is no more weighty than the right of privacy of the competent minor mature enough to have become pregnant."[64] The Court concluded by noting, however, that not *every* pregnant minor, regardless of age or maturity, is competent to give effective consent.

The decision to abort is clearly a crucial matter involving moral, social, psychological, and medical concerns. Few decisions can be as important in the life of a young woman. Such matters traditionally have been subject to the control of parents or the state. This decision seems far more revolutionary than granting juveniles First Amendment rights to wear armbands to school, or due process protection in delinquency proceedings and school suspension cases. Now the nation's highest court has ruled that parents cannot veto the child's abortion decision (nor, certainly, compel one), and it is not clear that parents would be entitled to an indefeasible right to be informed of the abortion decision or to counsel their pregnant daughters about it.[65]

64. Planned Parenthood of Central Missouri v. Danforth, 428 U.S. 52, 75 (1976).
65. Questions raised by *Danforth* are whether a state can compel a pregnant

Although the *Danforth* decision may be revolutionary, there is much compelling logic behind it. Bearing a child is arguably the most irrevocable action a person can take in life—an action whose consequences typically will extend until the mother's death. The pregnant minor's parents will not have to bear the child or be responsibile for it for the rest of *their* lives. Although the decision upsets fundamental expectations about children-parent-state relationships, minors have rights that are increasingly recognized, and the Court has ruled that the right to decide about procreation is too fundamental and private to be entrusted to others.

The interesting question raised by the children's rights cases is how far they are likely to be extended. How autonomous will children become, how free from parental and state control? Although one can only speculate about individual situations, general principles that will probably guide future decisions may be discerned. When the right in question is deemed fundamental or basic (e.g., liberty, procreation) and the question arises in a situation in which the interests of children may conflict with those of their parents or the state, we may expect the Court to scrutinize very carefully absolute or near absolute parental or state control. Further the Court will be more willing to admit that under certain conditions children can be adversaries of their parents or the state.

A useful example of future trends concerns a minor's rights when the parents wish to place the youth in a mental hospital but the minor does not wish to go. In the past, parents had an absolute right to place their minor children in mental hospitals. This practice was consistent with near absolute parental control over health care decisions. It has been recognized, however, that

minor to seek her parents' advice and consent or the consent of a court before abortion. Recently the Supreme Court has granted review in two cases which test the constitutionality of a Massachusetts law which prohibits a physician from performing an abortion on an unmarried female under the age of eighteen unless the minor has obtained parental consent or, if parental consent is refused, the consent of a superior court judge. Hunerwadel v. Baird; Bellotti v. Baird, 4 FLR 2845 (1978). The lower court ruled that the statute was unconstitutional because it impermissibly burdened the exercise of the mature minor's rights. Baird v. Bellotti 450 F. Supp. 997 (D. Mass. 1978).

placement in a mental hospital, often for extended periods of time, is a substantial and frightening deprivation of the child's liberty right. Further, psychiatric science is too imprecise to assure that only appropriate children will be accepted by the hospital, even if the doctors are exercising their utmost skill in good faith. Finally, it is clear that parents who have trouble with their children may sometimes act in ways not consonant with the child's best interests. Thus they may seek hospitalization of a child they find troublesome not because the child needs a psychiatric hospital but because they wish to be rid of the child.

This issue has reached the courts only in the last few years and represents a merging of concerns about children's rights and mental patients' rights. Lower federal courts and a state supreme court have held that minors are entitled to hearings that provide many of the procedural protections ordered by the *Gault* decision.[66] A lower federal court decision, *J. L.* v. *Parham*,[67] was argued before the Supreme Court in the fall of 1977 and was reargued in the fall of 1978. If past decisions are a guide, we may expect that the Court will rule that children will be entitled to some protection against parental commitment—the power of parents will not be absolute—but children will have fewer safeguards than when the State seeks to commit adults to mental hospitals.

Decisions concerning children mainly have increased their autonomy from both their parents and the state. This trend is clearly in opposition to the traditional view that granted parents and the state enormous power over children, but it is equally clearly consistent with modern views about civil liberty and the increasing sophistication of children. It must be recognized that these cases do not arise from the course of normal, relatively harmonious family relations, but rather in instances where family unity already is greatly disrupted. The pregnancy of an unmarried minor, the criminal behavior of a juvenile, or the extrusion

66. Bartley v. Kremens, 402 F. Supp. 1039 (E.D. Pa. 1975), vacated as moot and remanded, 97 S.Ct. 1709 (1977). In re Roger S., 19 Cal. 3d 921 (1977).

67. 412 F. Supp. 112 (N.D. Ga. 1976); probable jurisdiction noted, Parham v. J. L. 431 U.S. 936 (1977).

of a child from the home into a hospital are not modal family experiences. The vast range of everyday family experience has not produced legal decisions because weighty value-conflicts concerning liberty and autonomy do not arise in that context (at least not to date). Normal family life is still probably governed, as it always has been, by strong parental authority or by a model of parent-child interaction that individual families find acceptable.

THE DISSOLVING FAMILY

Family dissolution, like family formation, is regulated largely by the states. The grounds for divorce, rules about custody and support, and the like are all matters of state law. Indeed, the Supreme Court has decided only two major cases dealing with family dissolution, neither of which was a substantial intrusion on the state's power. As we shall see, the trend in dissolution clearly has moved from heavy restrictions to greater autonomy for the parties.

Let us first consider premarital agreements that concern the disposition of marital property upon divorce. Antenuptial arrangements concerning divorce have been disfavored until quite recently because it was believed such agreements were conducive to divorce. Years ago, when the myth was that marriage vows were to last until death parted the spouses, there may have been something unseemly about persons contracting about rights at divorce even before they were married. It is unlikely, however, that such agreements really would be conducive to divorce. In any case, marriage is still taken seriously, but it is apparent that divorce is a high likelihood for all marriages. Now that the stigma attending divorce is steadily decreasing, the law is finally moving toward approval of antenuptial agreements. After all, they are worked out when the parties are not hostile toward one another and are inclined to be reasonable, and they save the parties and the legal system the costs of having to settle these matters at the time of dissolution, hardly the moment for optimally reasonable and cooperative negotiations.

One leading state, California, has gone even further and decided a precedent that may indicate a possible future trend in family law. In *Marvin* v. *Marvin*,[68] the California Supreme Court decided that when couples living together out-of-wedlock break up, they may be entitled to a legally enforceable dissolution of their property, depending on their agreements and expectations concerning their relationship and property. Although the Court might have used many theories to justify its decision, it basically relied on a theory of contract. Thus, if the man agreed to cook, clean, and shop in return for material support by the woman with the further understanding that everything accumulated during the relationship belonged to both, then the principles of community property would apply to the relationship. In sum, couples living together could obtain all the economic benefits and consequences (in California) of marriage simply by agreeing to do so, and courts would enforce the contract. This decision gave couples living together more freedom to arrange their economic affairs than is usually given to married couples.

Marvin was a revolutionary case because it treated some couples living together much as if they were married, a result previously achieved only by common law marriage, a disfavored institution that had been abolished in California. In a sense, *Marvin* discourages traditional marriage because many of the rights and obligations traditionally accompanying marriage can now be achieved without it. Although those who favor encouraging marriage and discouraging nonmarital relationships see *Marvin* as an unfortunate decision, there is much logic behind it. Large numbers of couples now live together without a marriage ceremony, many of these relationships proceeding on the same basis as traditional marriage—mutual support and affection, and often the begetting and raising of children.

When nonmarital relationships dissolve, the question for the law is whether the party who furnished inputs other than money should be completely disadvantaged financially. After all, unless the law is willing to treat these relationships like marriages for at least some purposes, the financially dependent party will be the loser. At a time when so many couples are living together non-

68. 18 Cal. 3d 660, 134 Cal. Rptr. 815 (1976).

maritally, it seems unfair to punish either party based on perhaps outmoded social or moral theories.

The questions remaining are the extent to which other states will adopt the *Marvin* decision and to what other areas its rationale will apply. It is hard to estimate the answer to the first question, but we may speculate a bit about the second. If a couple have lived together for life in agreement that all property accumulated is to be treated as common property, then on the death of one of them without a will, should not the rules applying to marital couples also apply to them? Such changes would indeed be revolutionary and would have considerable ramifications for federal tax laws and policies, but they do seem the logical conclusion to the rationale of a case like *Marvin*.

The preeminent change in American family law in the last decade has been the shift from divorce based on fault to so-called no-fault divorce. Under traditional law, a spouse was entitled to divorce only if he or she could prove against the other spouse one of the statutorily specified fault grounds such as adultery or extreme cruelty. If the defendant-spouse could prove that the complainant-spouse was also guilty of behavior constituting divorce grounds, then neither guilty party was entitled to divorce. If the marriage was totally unsatisfying to one or both partners but no specific grounds were met, or if both partners furnished provable grounds for divorce, no divorce could be had. This arrangement was clearly illogical but it had the virtue of upholding the traditional ethos of cohesive marriage by making divorce difficult and costly.

Explanation of why divorce has become more acceptable is complex, and definitive explanation may forever elude social scientists. There can be not doubt, however, that by the 1960s much of the stigma had disappeared. Marriages were no longer viewed as ends in themselves; if they did not satisfy the partners, there was little reason to continue them. In such a social climate, the costs of traditional divorce law were unacceptable, and by the late 1960s, legislatures began to pass no-fault divorce legislation.[69] Generally these laws provide that a

69. For example, California Civil Code, Section 4506.

divorce can be obtained if one partner avers that the marriage is irretrievably broken down because of irremediable differences. This standard is terribly vague but commonsensical: if the parties feel the marriage is over and beyond repair, it is over. There may be "cooling off" periods provided for during which the divorce is not final, but there are no defenses. If one party wants the marriage to end, the divorce occurs.

No-fault divorce has not been adopted in every state, but it clearly is the dominant model for divorce reform. And residents of those states that maintain restrictive divorce laws may avoid them by moving to a more tolerant state. The only restriction on "migratory" divorce is the common residency requirement whereby a state will not divorce someone unless he or she has been a resident of that state for a specified time. The constitutionality of these requirements was tested in one of the two major Supreme Court cases dealing with divorce, *Sosna* v. *Iowa*. [70] The Supreme Court upheld the residency requirement. This decision restricts the ease with which some Americans can obtain a divorce, but it is only a slight hindrance in the movement toward unrestricted divorce. If one lives in a no-fault state such as Iowa or California, the Court's decision is no obstacle to divorce at will.

The other major Supreme Court case concerned with divorce is *Boddie* v. *Connecticut*, [71] which considered a challenge to Connecticut's requirement that divorce plaintiffs had to pay the state a filing fee before they could gain access to the court to obtain a divorce. The Court declared the fee a violation of due process of the law. The accessibility of divorce was then eased for the poor.

Divorcing couples do not usually fight primarily over the divorce itself; instead, the true battleground is the incidents of divorce—property disposition and child custody. In the past, property and custody laws were written in conformance with cultural expectations. Women were entitled to alimony and mothers were preferred as custodians, especially for young children. Further, property and custody awards were tied to some degree to marital fault. Thus, a needy woman who would make a fine custodian for the children might obtain considerably lower

70. 419 U.S. 393 (1975).
71. 401 U.S. 371 (1971).

alimony and even lose a custody fight with her husband if she was being divorced on grounds such as adultery which involved moral turpitude. Finally, alimony payments typically lasted until the payee remarried. Of course, such laws are sex-biased and carry a heavy overlay of judgmental morality.

Like many restrictive family law provisions that reflected traditional cultural roles and morality, these laws could not withstand cultural and moral changes. Either legislatively or judicially, the legal system has rendered divorce-related property and custody law increasingly sex-neutral. Moreover, considerations of fault have decreasing importance as courts look more to need or to whether a parent has the capacity to act in the best interests of the child. Indeed, the easing of divorce requirements has meant that partners can no longer easily use the divorce itself as a bargaining chip in negotiations over custody and property. Finally, even where alimony is justifiable, the law is beginning to disfavor long-term arrangements, preferring instead that where possible the supported party should become self-supporting. Courts have ordered supporting spouses to pay for further education and training for the supported spouse in order to help the latter become self-supporting. Although these laws are intended to be sex-neutral and perhaps logical, they may economically disadvantage a homemaker spouse who has always been supported and who cannot easily learn new skills, and such spouses should be protected.

In the area of family dissolution, then, the law reflects changing mores, giving individuals far more autonomy and power over their lives than ever before. At the same time, of course, traditional expectations are being upset and it is easier to end one's marriage with decreasing cost. What the final costs and benefits will be is impossible to determine, but it is clear that the law is not fomenting a revolution in family affairs. Rather, it is reflecting, often belatedly, those changes that have already occurred in the consciousness and behavior of society.

CONCLUSION

The thesis of this essay is that the law reflects and sometimes significantly promotes changes that occur in social attitudes and

357

behavior. In the family law area, this has meant that the law has followed a trend of increasing autonomy for individuals at the cost of some traditional family values. After all, individual liberty and autonomy have been primary values of the past two decades: the law has mirrored accurately social and moral changes that were readily perceivable.

Legal articulation of social change has most often been a ratification of that change, a recognition by the usually conservative opinion leaders of our society that the change has truly occurred. Occasionally, as in the epochal school desegregation case, *Brown* v. *Board of Education*, [72] and perhaps in the equally epochal decision, *Roe* v. *Wade*, the Court will lead a social movement already firmly begun but not well recognized. In a few cases, such as the one outlawing anti-miscegenation laws, the Court's decision will leave one with a sense of *déjà vu*; one can hardly believe that the offensive laws were still on the books awaiting this *coup de grâce*.

Many bemoan the decisions and criticize the courts that made them. The Supreme Court in particular is sometimes the object of severe and vitriolic attack. But these criticisms are misplaced. For one thing, the family as an institution is not dead and the law has no intention of killing it. Clearly the Supreme Court is not a collection of radicals seeking to remake American society in accord with its unique sociopolitical views, but is instead a group of rather conservative gentlemen who see their mission as proper interpretation of the Constitution in light of changing social values. The Court is not the sole or even an important cause of increasing sexual activity, the desire for civil rights, the striving for autonomy and privacy, or the growing sophistication and power of children. To the contrary, many of these attitudinal changes have occurred in spite of the preferences or rear-guard actions of the Court. Rather, the Court's decisions, like the art of an era, are an indication and reflection of the attitudes and behavior of the people to whom the decisions apply.

72. Brown v. Board of Education, 347 U.S. 483 (1954).

RECENT DEVELOPMENTS

In the 1978 Term, the Supreme Court decided two cases of interest, one dealing with alimony and the other with the rights of nonmarital children.

In *Orr* v. *Orr*, 5 FLR 3065 (March 6, 1979), the Court finally considered the constitutionality, under the Equal Protection Clause, of state statutes that provided for divorcing husbands to pay alimony to wives but prohibited such husbands from *receiving* alimony. Because the Alabama statute in question discriminated on the basis of sex, the Court reaffirmed that to withstand scrutiny, such a classification by gender "must serve important governmental objectives and must be substantially related to achievement of those objectives." Alabama suggested three governmental objectives to sustain its statute: first, to reinforce a State preference for an allocation of family roles in which the wife plays a dependent role; second, to help needy spouses, using sex as a proxy for need; and, third, to compensate women for past discrimination during marriage, which has left them unprepared to adapt to the working world after the termination of marriage.

The Court summarily rejected the first goal as illegitimate: prior cases had already determined that "old" notions, such as that males were primarily responsible for "providing a home and its essentials," could not justify a statute that discriminated on the basis of gender. To support their position, the justices cited *Stanton* v. *Stanton*, 421 U.S. 7 (1975), wherein the Court had held that a state distinction in the age at which males and females attained majority was unconstitutional under the Equal Protection Clause. Recognizing that the other two objectives were legitimate, however, the Court turned to an analysis of whether the statute was substantially related to achieving them. Even if sex were an accurate proxy for need, and marriage did discriminate against women, the Court reasoned that these factors would not adequately justify the Alabama statute. Individualized hearings on need were already a feature of alimony hearings: thus, the needs of men as well as women could be considered with little additional burden on the State. Such hearings could also determine when either party had been a victim of discrimination and needed compensatory support. The majority therefore concluded that the statutory gender distinction was gratuitous. (Indeed, the scheme produced perverse results in the case at hand, where the financially secure wife received alimony from a needy husband.) Finally, noted the Court, gender-based classifications "carry the inherent risk of reinforcing stereotypes about the 'proper place' of women and their need for special protection," and thus must be "carefully tailored." Where gender-neutral classification would serve state purposes equally well, gender-classifying statutes, with their risks of stereotypes, are constitutionally impermissible.

The *Orr* case is a significant step in abolishing sexual discrimination in the marital relationship. Although the case deals with a postmarital situation, its clear implication is that traditional support law and other sex-stereotyped family laws will be upheld only if the state can make a powerful showing that the gender classification is substantially related to legitimate governmental objectives and is tailored carefully to them. Thus, the continued validity of many traditional gender classifications under the Equal Protection Clause is seriously in question.

In a much less significant plurality opinion, *Lalli* v. *Lalli*, 99 S.Ct. 518 (1978), the High Court retreated slightly from its attack on statutes which discriminate against illegitimate children. Under attack was a New York statute which allowed an illegitimate child to inherit from his or her intestate father only if there had been a judicial declaration of paternity prior to the father's death. Although in *Trimble* v. *Gordon* (see note 61 and accompanying text, pages 348–49 above) the Court had invalidated a somewhat similar restriction of an illegitimate child's ability to inherit from an intestate father, the Court distinguished the *Lalli* case on the ground that the New York statute in question was a more substantial means to further the related legitimate governmental interests of accurately determining the paternity of the deceased, preventing spurious claims, and thus insuring the orderly administration of estates. Although *Lalli* is a setback in the quest for equal rights for nonmarital children, it is a rather limited case.

15

Government and the Family: Justice and Acceptance

JUDITH HICKS STIEHM

Analogies have often been drawn between governments and families.[1] Aristotle described governments as being composed *of* families. Others have noted similarities between a nation's governmental structure and its family structure, a favorite comparison being that between the popularly supported Nazi regime and the authoritarian German family. Still others have argued that government begins when and where the family ends; thus, some anthropologists date "government" to the substitution of ties of contiguity for those of consanguinity. The state comes into being, then, when citizenship assumes more importance than tribal membership, when actions are judged and rules are made by people organized by geography rather than genes, when the ruler can be someone other than the senior, usually male, member of an extended family. Indeed, in Plato's extreme but ideal state described in the *Republic*, the elimination of all family ties was seen as a necessary precondition for justice.

Plato's republic has had few proponents; most individuals are happy to have governmental justice tempered by familial acceptance—to benefit from compassion as well as from fairness. Indeed, perhaps that is just how governments and families differ.

1. Thomas Hobbes drew one; but Robert Filmer's *Patriarcha* (which John Locke took such pains to refute) is one of the most elaborate. For discussion of these, see Peter Laslett's introduction to *Patriarcha* (Oxford: Basil Blackwell, 1949).

Both judge, both direct, both teach and sometimes make rules. But a government succeeds when it acts dispassionately, avoids nepotism, and treats all citizens in the same way. Conversely, a family succeeds when it acts lovingly, favors its own, and accepts each member without reservation.[2] The one institution, then, provides justice, while the second offers acceptance.

In this country, intrafamily relationships are a private rather than a governmental concern. The state does establish a legal basis for the family's existence, but this defining function is exercised principally when families are either being founded, as in marriage and adoption, or dissolved, as in divorce and death. Even then the state's role is minimal unless property is involved. The government is only too happy to avoid having either to forbid or to require particular interpersonal behavior. It is loath to become involved in cases of child abuse, spouse abuse, adultery, or incest; even to investigate such cases is costly, delicate, and embarrassing, and the possibility of resolving them is doubtful. Nevertheless, government policies affect families indirectly, especially in economic matters. A particular policy may enlarge or diminish family resources or simply alter dependency relations. In Germany, for example, the state affords more benefits to women than in the United States. German women are no more independent than American women, but instead of benefiting individually from their husbands, they benefit collectively from the state.[3]

One obvious way government affects families is by supplying services once provided by the family, for example, education. A second way is by supplementing family efforts to care for its own, as in providing health care for those who cannot afford it. The family is also affected by decisions on social security entitlements, tax deductions, and eligibility for housing loans; even zoning ordinances affect family life, for they usually separate residence and work place. Sometimes the impacts on families are intended, but more often they are not. The family as a whole

2. The state's tolerance of, or resignation to, the family's special obligation to its own is shown in such rules as the one which provides that spouses need not testify against one another.

3. Judith Hicks Stiehm, "The Pursuit of Equality: German and American Women," *Frontiers* (Winter 1976), p. 65.

may be affected, or its members may be differentially affected so that the child-husband-wife equipoise is disturbed. To illustrate, a major welfare experiment guaranteeing a minimum income to poor families resulted in an almost 60 percent increase in marital breakups among black and white families (but not among Mexican-American families).[4] The opposite effect was intended. What may have happened is that the attempt to provide external assistance to a family unit in fact disturbed established intrafamily roles.

SOVEREIGN CITIZENS AND CITIZEN-FAMILIES

When a government that is selected by its citizens *individually* then treats those same citizens as members of *groups*, a problem arises. American democracy has two central individualistic myths: individual (inalienable) rights and popular sovereignty. The one emphasizes the sanctity of each separate individual and his or her immunity to wrongful governmental action. The second emphasizes the power of agreeing individuals; it suggests that ordinary citizens can collectively direct and control their government. In reality, citizens' participation in government has been limited. At first, voting was restricted to propertied, white, male adults, who were understood to act on behalf of themselves and their dependents. In the last century, however, the franchise and eligibility for office have been continually extended. Unpropertied white males were the first to join the electorate; next were nonwhite males, then women, and finally eighteen-year-olds.[5] It is no longer assumed that the "head of the house"[6] should or even can act in the best interests of the varied but interdependent members of the household. Each individual now speaks to the government for himself or herself.[7] The govern-

4. *Los Angeles Times*, 2 May 1978, sec. 1, p. 2. Further analysis can be obtained from Robert Spiegelman of the Stanford Research Institute.

5. Extension of the right to vote has been related to military service. There seems to be a homely assumption that one who risks death for his or her country can be trusted with a ballot.

6. In the 1980 census this value-laden category will finally be dropped.

7. As late as 1841, Catharine Beecher, sister of Harriet Beecher Stowe, noted that "in a truly [and "fully developed"] democratic state each individual is

363

ment, however, does not always treat its citizens as individuals. When it does not, as for instance, when it defines some as "minorities" and treats that group differently, our individualistic assumptions are assaulted. Programs and policies using such categories are frequently met with suspicion. For example, affirmative action programs seem just, if viewed historically and in the context of a society composed of a number of groups. Support for such programs erodes rapidly today when the ideal is one of equal opportunity for *all* individual citizens.

"Family" is another category to which the government sometimes assigns individuals before dealing with them. On the one hand this is realistic, for citizens do live, think, and act in relation to others. On the other hand, public policy based on a "normative" family (the kind whose image appears in countless advertisements), may ill serve the majority of the nation's citizens inasmuch as only 9 percent of the families in the United States are composed of a husband, a nonworking wife, and two children under the age of eighteen. In fact, only 15 percent of all families fit the two-parents-with-two-children-under-eighteen stereotype. Fully 52 percent of all American families differ from the "typical" family of two-parents-plus-children (in any number).[8] It should be evident that a policy which assumes a single-family pattern cannot begin to provide an adequate "public" policy.

Also, policy may systematically disadvantage certain citizens even if they live in "normal" families. For instance, at a time when unemployment rates were highest among teenagers and

---

allowed to choose for himself, who shall take the position of his superior. No woman is forced to obey any husband but the one she chooses for herself"; and also "in this country it is established . . . that women have an equal interest in all social and civil concerns; and that no domestic, civil or political institution is right, that sacrifices her interest to promote that of the other sex. But . . . it is decided that, in the domestic relation, she takes a subordinate station, and that, in civil and political concerns her interests be intrusted to the other sex, without her taking any part in voting, or in making and administering laws."

8. These data are based on the 1970 census figures given in U.S. Bureau of the Census, *Census of Population: 1970, Subject Reports, Final Report PC (2)-4A, Family Composition* (Washington, D.C.: Government Printing Office, 1973), p. 121. Figures for today would be somewhat different, but if anything, they would show an even larger percentage of "atypical" families.

women, President Jimmy Carter expressed concern about unemployment. However, when he announced a new program to create one million jobs, he did so in these words: "Our goal is for every single family to have a guaranteed job by the government."[9] The plan was to control eligibility for the program by having a low limit on total family income for the previous year. Since the adult male is usually the most employable family member, the two groups with the highest unemployment rates, women and teenagers, were blocked from competition for the one million new jobs, at least for as long as the husband/father remained within the family. Thus, even though it is individual citizens who vote, and it is individual citizens who are qualified for and wish to work, many of them are denied access to a government-sponsored job solely because they have relatives who are working.

Again, the government subsidizes the college education of many students. Following the above logic it could limit advanced degrees to one per family. The issue is further complicated by the fact that two salaries are becoming a new norm. Forty-six percent of married women now work, and 47 percent of the families with $15,000 or more income have two persons contributing to that income.[10] The surest way out of poverty, then, is not to get one exceptional child into pro football or medicine but for two people to work. Carter's plan, which essentially makes one ineligible for a government job if another family member is working, blocks the surest way most families have of lifting themselves out of poverty. Moreover, the effect of such policies is actually to pit family members against each other.

FUNCTIONS OF THE FAMILY

The family can be understood as a legal, a biological-emotional, and an economic unit. Generally, as Stephen J. Morse has

9. *Los Angeles Times*, 25 July 1977.

10. U.S. Bureau of the Census, *Statistical Abstract of the United States: 1977*, 98th ed. (Washington, D.C.: Government Printing Office, 1977), p. 391; and U.S. Bureau of the Census, *Current Population Reports, Series P-60, no. 105, Money Income in 1975 of Families and Persons in the United States* (Washington, D.C.: Government Printing Office, 1977), p. 36.

shown,[11] recent legal changes have made divorce easier and the responsibilities of women and men more similar and more equal. One hundred fifty years ago, John Stuart Mill argued that the "no divorce" policy of his era represented a step in the direction of women's emancipation. At that time the denial of divorce seemed to protect women as compared to an earlier period when they had little choice in mate selection and could be divorced by their husbands at will. Mill also looked forward to the day (today?) when women would not require such protection because decisions would be shared and competence would be equal. Much of today's resistance to the Equal Rights Amendment comes from women who feel they still need protection. Many do not realize that legal protections are rapidly being eroded in the courts (even in Mississippi, a judge recently held that women have no "right" to alimony). Further, such rights as alimony and child support, even if granted, are rarely enforced. Ironically, too, the principle of spousal equality is often more successfully litigated on behalf of a male than a female client.[12]

What is important here is that not long ago one had the sense that marriage was irrevocable, that commitment was permanent, that by definition one accepted and was accepted by one's relations. This is no longer the case. Today in an age of "nonbinding commitments,"[13] inevitability is gone from the marital relationship. For this reason the oppression of some marriages can be felt more keenly. Jean-Jacques Rousseau explained it well. Laws of nature, such as the law of gravity, he said, cannot be violated; therefore, they are not experienced as oppressive or constraining. After all, none of us expect to be able to fly and none of us are made miserable because we cannot. However, those laws that *can* be violated, and that some people *do violate*, weigh heavily on our minds and can make us feel unfree. Thus if

11. See the preceding chapter.

12. Ruth Bader Ginsberg of the Columbia University law faculty and the Women's Rights Project of the American Civil Liberties Union closely monitors this new area of judicial activity.

13. See Christopher Lasch, *Haven in a Heartless World: The Family Besieged* (New York: Basic Books, 1977), p. 139. Lasch borrows the phrase "nonbinding commitments" from Nena and George O'Neill's *Open Marriage* (New York: Avon, 1973).

the continuation of a marriage is not assumed, one begins to evaluate it. When a negative evaluation is made, termination becomes a possibility. Termination or divorce is very costly in terms of emotional stress. "Acceptance" is annihilated.

Inevitability in contemporary marriage is diminished in another way, for today we no longer assume reproduction of the biological family. Birth control and access to abortions give women of today a choice—but they also add to some women's feelings of oppression, and these feelings may, in turn, make men apprehensive. When babies "happened" to couples (as they occasionally did even when contraception was used), a woman could complain about the accident and at the same time enjoy the positive aspects of motherhood: her ambivalence could be expressed. With "free choice" a woman is supposed to be unreserved in her joy, rather than "coping so well" with having been "caught." For men the situation is different, too. If a man wishes to be a father, he must now not only find a marriage partner but must find one who actively agrees to bear and raise a child for him, and stay with him for an extended time. Because he cannot have children himself, he must depend on a woman for the opportunity to become a parent. Those who support abortion legislation refer to a woman's right "to control her own body." Such a right must be threatening (even if only unconsciously) to a man not supremely confident about his desirability.

At the present time parents cannot forbid their child to have an abortion, nor can a husband forbid his wife to do so. The rights of the male partner are now being asserted, however, in several court cases. It is hard to believe that men will ultimately permit women to have "control of their own bodies" and, therefore, of the reproduction decision and incidentally of the genetic selection process. The limiting sex in reproduction is, after all, women not men. In a stable monogamous system, most men may obtain mates. In a system of serial monogamy, however, all young women may mate (and therefore keep their genes in the genetic pool); older women may be left to provide for themselves while highly desirable men mate a second time, but the less desirable or shy men may well end up with no opportunity to mate at all. Unless cloning becomes a realistic option, such men cannot easily make the decision some feminists are making here and abroad—using artificial insemination, they are becoming parents without becoming spouses.

It is interesting to note that it was the House of Representatives that insisted on restrictive abortion legislation. The Senate did not. The House with its smaller districts and frequent elections often claims to be more in tune with the thinking of the "common *man*," and its action may reflect just that.[14] Senators, on the other hand, may move in a more rarefied atmosphere. They may have fewer doubts about the acceptability of their genes, and thus can afford to back selective birth legislation. Nevertheless, the bottom line is that women can have babies and men cannot, and that men hold social and governmental power and women do not. Women would be foolish to believe that men will permit them to exercise unilateral control over such a fundamental function as reproduction. Men will use their government power long before women win that control.

The responsibilities inherent in parenting are of three kinds. First, procreation is shared by a man and a woman, but the man's role is brief and his personal responsibility cannot easily be proved. Second, a moral obligation exists in a social context, and men are probably more able to rationalize away such obligation, especially if physically separated from the children. Women, however, find few justifications for reducing or abandoning their moral commitment; ill health and lunacy are almost the only ones. Third, responsibility means capacity—ability. This aspect has a variety of manifestations. The capacities a family demands of women and of men are often quite different. Moreover, they vary both according to the family's economic position and the development level of the country. In general the man is expected to provide cash income, the woman time and attention.[15] Before

14. "Pro-life" groups do, of course, include active female members, many of them religiously oriented. Minorities are cross-pressured on this issue. Their women often find childbearing and child-rearing onerous for they lack economic resources. However, their men fear being cut out of the gene pool and argue that birth control, sterilization, and abortions lead to (racist) genocide.

15. See Theodore W. Schultz, ed., *Economics of the Family* (Chicago: University of Chicago Press, 1975).

we explore these contributions further, however, several other points must be made about the biological family.

First, the biological family plays a crucial integrative role in society. It is the one institution in which the sexes participate in something approximating a fifty-fifty ratio. It is also the one institution in which there is little age segregation—indeed, in the extended family the whole age range is represented;[16] even different economic classes may meet at family gatherings,[17] although zoning rather strictly segregates residence by income. Families also bring together people with different capacities, something that many of our educational institutions do all they can to prevent. Indeed, the family almost uniquely fosters the social connectedness so important to an increasingly specialized society. (The one cleavage it bridges poorly is that between races.)

Political scientists regularly describe this nation as a collection of competing homogeneous groups each intent on achieving its own interests. Various rationales have been developed to explain how a system driven by self-interest can be benevolent or even "just" in its outcome. Strong arguments are made about "natural harmony," a "common cause," or "the public interest." Little reference is made, however, or discussion offered, as to the connectedness provided by families. Perhaps it is an institution that is simply too important to notice in this regard.

Biology also anchors individuals in history, bringing meaning both to the past and to the future. It gives the individual definition, and a history to rise up from (or live up to) and one to make; it offers a human-resource base, too, by assigning each a status, a locus, and a social network that does not have to be earned or deserved. The family provides an instant community where human interaction and material support are available without condition or justification. Justly or not, acceptance lies at the heart of kin relationships.

16. It is easier to take the needs of senior citizens seriously when one has living parents and grandparents, and it is easier to care about day care if one is a single parent or the parent of a single parent.

17. The Kennedys are an exception not the rule. Imagine Carter, Ford, Nixon, and Johnson family reunions. All would include a broad range of class identifications.

THE FAMILY AS ECONOMIC UNIT

The most likely governmental impact on the family is economic, for the family is and always has been an economic unit, both a producing and consuming "pool" in which individuals participate. But in recent years children are no longer economic assets, and specialization within the family has created a new alienation. Once the family was a production-consumption unit and the larger the family, the more workers, the better. Being a mother was by definition to be productive, not just reproductive. Now, however, the cost of raising a child has become so high that, for many families, children are a luxury.[18] On the other hand, some families continue to have children even though they cannot afford them. In these cases, the government provides subsistence. Middle-class families often expect to provide for their children, but their economic margin is so thin that a grave illness, an automobile accident, a divorce, or any of many regular occurrences reduces the family to poverty and dependency.

Equally important is the specialization that has developed within the family. Our culture applauds work and its rewards and, for many persons, production and consumption are linked and satisfying. Yet within the family the husband's role has more and more become one of production of income, while the wife and children have more and more become consumers; both specialized roles tend to be partial and alienating. Interdependence may make them bearable, and if *within* the family each contributes according to his or her abilities and receives according to his or her needs, the relationship may be equitable. But when a family dissolves, two things become evident: women are more easily replaced as far as economic contribution is concerned and, although many women can earn their *own* way, few can assume the male role of providing enough income to support others. In part this may be a matter of deficient skill and will. In part it is a matter of discrimination and of men's protection of the productive role as "manly." It is also a matter of structure and of government support for working conditions designed for adult males and *not* for the young, the old, the female. Organized

18. See Schultz, *Economics of the Family*.

labor, corporate management, and government administrators have structured work within a framework that includes a minimum wage, veterans' and pension benefits, seniority, and required full-time work. By so doing, they have made it difficult for women and young people to participate in the world of work. In spite of such obstacles, almost half of all married women do work outside the home. Society cannot afford to have more than half of its adult population not producing. In addition, the burden of supporting a family is really too heavy for any single producer; thus a wife rightly assists her husband, either by working herself or by participating in his "two-person career." The plight of the single parent, male or female, demonstrates the family's need for two adults. More and more, the government attempts to fulfill the function of the missing parent, and a good many parents *are* missing: currently 16 percent of families in the United States are headed by a single adult.[19]

THE FAMILY AND GOVERNMENT

How can a government dedicated to "justice" participate in the family's unique function, "acceptance"? One thing policy makers have done is to base policy decisions upon what they see as the needs of children. This kind of justification works politically because children are credible as innocent victims and therefore are seen as deserving recipients of tax-supported programs. Often such proposals are both racist and sexist. It is important to remember, however, that adults are essential to the family, and adults need the family and acceptance as much as children do. One recent study funded by the Carnegie Council on Children emphasizes children but also makes the compelling point that children are best served by helping parents to be effective.[20] The first two of the council's five proposals stress the need for full and

19. U.S. Bureau of the Census, *Current Population Reports, Series P-20, no. 313, Household and Families by Type: March 1977 (Advance Report)* (Washington, D.C.: Government Printing Office, 1977), p. 6.

20. Kenneth Keniston and the Carnegie Council on Children, *All Our Children: The American Family under Pressure* (New York: Harcourt Brace Jovanovich, 1977).

fair employment and for flexible working conditions. Other recommendations, also aimed at enhancing parental effectiveness, include a minimum income, and access to services, along with parent education and "preventive" assistance. The goal is to give parents "enough power so that they can be effective advocates with and coordinators of the other forces that are bringing up their children." The point is: give parents the wherewithal, the *capacity* to be responsible.

Once monarchies were unquestioned. In the same way the family was assumed: marriage was for life, children were accepted, and production and consumption took place at home. In short, habit, nature, and interest all reinforced family ties. Later, however, the American "take charge" approach to life spilled over into even our most personal relationships. Government came to be understood as a willful creation, and marriage and children became a matter of choice. At the same time, the division of labor led to a division between production and consumption, and this increased alienation. As the bonds of law and need have loosened, a family's staying together has become more and more contingent upon personal attachments. The family's crucial role, then, has become that of emotional nourishment, a role government cannot directly influence. If people begin to see "even better" relationships as possible, we must hope they will remember that families provide more than an intense relationship for two adults; they also provide "a place" for everyone and bring intersection to the sexes, to various ages and classes, and to diverse competencies.

As governments develop family policies, then, they must consider adults as well as children. If policy is in fact neutral when it professes to be, they must ask whether it is possible to "forbid" or better only to "discourage," and what can actually be "required" rather than just "encouraged." Governments may have to do more in the way of providing emergency help, and they should probably continue their assistance in areas like education and health. In developing new policies, there are three directions the government might move. One is to enable the family to function again as a communal economic unit. This means the *whole* family. It is not enough to provide a job for the "head of the house." *Each* member of the family must have the chance to be productive, and the family as a group must be able to produce enough surplus so that they can support an ill, aged, or dispirited family member. Second, it means assisting people in making various kinds of living arrangements viable, if those arrangements foster familial functions—even when they are original and willful creations. These could include communes or groups like old-age homes. Third, it means seeing to it that no individuals end up in isolation—that widows, the mentally ill, and alcoholics, for instance, find a way of living in relationship with others, and that their relationships, even if unconventional, are encouraged. Plato's meritocracy was an exercise in carrying logic to an illogical, anti-family conclusion. Aristotle's, and the medieval, sense of complexity and interconnectedness may at first seem more realistic, but older forms of relatedness no longer suffice. Interdependency has replaced an older, hierarchical dependency.

To make the family more satisfying, male parent–child bonds will have to be strengthened so that parenthood does not change a happy pair into a non-isosceles triangle, one in which the social distance between mother and child is less than between father and child.[21] Also the mother, given an opportunity to share in production, must feel free to move about in public without seeking a male protector (whose role has been to preserve her from the male predator who in turn protects other women from the first woman's protector!).[22]

Even the most committed couples find it difficult to have a fifty-fifty marriage. In the United States, because women tend to marry men with more income, more education, and higher oc-

---

21. Society provides men with few images or models to encourage parenting. Reasons for this are discussed in Dorothy Dinnerstein, *The Mermaid and the Minotaur* (New York: Harper & Row, 1976); and Alice S. Rossi, "A Biosocial Perspective on Parenting," *Daedalus* 106, no. 2 (Spring 1977): 1–31.

22. Susan Brownmiller neatly describes the double role of men as ravishers and protectors and of women as victims and motivators in *Against Our Will* (New York: Bantam Books, 1976). Charlotte Perkins Gilman noted the same irony. See *The Living of Charlotte Perkins Gilman: An Autobiography* (New York: Harper Colophon Books, 1975), p. 72.

cupational status, women often experience an invidious comparison in their personal relationships. "Invidious intimacy"[23] (a
marriage in which the man has more income, education, and
status than the woman) is basic to many of our social and political
assumptions. Further, equally shared parenting is more the fantasy of the depressed than it is a possible choice. It is realized
only by sacrifice, ingenuity, willingness to depart from the conventional, and probably a dash of luck. Government could encourage changes in family arrangements, but because government proposers are so overwhelmingly male their vision is likely
to be partial and their will weak.[24] Fortunately, many experts on
the family are female. What is called for, then, is integration of
women into government and men into the family. But women
are better schooled in the "acceptance" that characterizes the
family and men in the "justice" between equals that characterizes
government. Thus, just as women must learn to exercise public
power, men must learn private interaction. Just as women must
learn to perform before a critical audience, men must learn to
perform without an audience. The results of such change would
be radical. Versatility and flexibility would be valued over either
"virility" or "femininity." Twice as many individuals would be
nurturing children as before, and twice as many individuals
would be producing and making public judgments. Most importantly, the role of "provider and protector" (which has long
justified vile economic exploitation as well as every known war)
would be diminished. Those who now allegedly benefit from
men's protection would no longer grant men license (as at present) either out of ignorance or feelings of helplessness. Instead,

23. Judith Hicks Stiehm, "Invidious Intimacy," *Social Policy* 6 (March–April
1976), pp. 12–16.

24. Any program which seems to lead to an increase in divorce is anathema
to public officials. They do not usually consider the "quality" of existing
marriages, nor do they consider the effect of the most meliorating change on an
existing relationship. The fact is that people find it very difficult to change an
existing intimate relationship, probably because it implies criticism of what has
gone before. Thus, when a woman moves toward increased independence and
equality within a marriage, the husband may not accept the change in *their*
relationship even if he is quite comfortable in an equal relationship with a *new*
wife after divorce from the first. The change is too stressful even if the principle
is acceptable.

the former observers would be participating in their own protection and helping to provide as well. Then the behavior of all adults would be justified by a single moral standard. It may be that the strain between the "justice" of government and the "acceptance" of families can never be resolved, but surely women and men can participate in both institutions, and surely they can cherish and be measured by the same moral standard.

16

The Changing Family: A Social Ethical Perspective

JOHN B. ORR

Most of the essays in this volume are far from neutral. Their preoccupation with changing images and forms of the family bears witness to an underlying liberal assumption that, after all, the family is a social construction—something that has been made by human hands and not by the lawful forces of nature. The assumption, I suppose, involves correlates: that by achieving self-awareness of the images that shape our family experience, the possibilities for taking control are enlarged; ultimately, that we *ought* to intervene via public policy, education, family counseling, or moral preachment to nurture the family climate we desire.

These have been my assumptions also. So when I was assigned the task of providing a social ethical perspective on the changing American family, of pronouncing on the subject of what we should be seeking in our family life, naturally my mind turned to define the options open to us. It was to be a Herculean task, but I had accepted the assignment as a legitimate project. The ethicist's task had always been to do just that—to dream utopian dreams without having to grovel too deeply in empirical realities. In my own private reality, I shared with almost every observer of American culture the feeling that the American family has been in crisis for some time. But, as a liberal spirit, I assumed that crisis breeds institutional creativity. The assignment by the editors to dream dreams, then, was a call to the practical business of dealing with a crisis that could be overcome.

In reviewing the essays prepared for this volume, though, I was also, albeit incongruously, reminded that it may be foolhardy simply to spell out blueprints for tomorrow's family. In spite of all their liberal assumptions, a number of writers here (and elsewhere) are suggesting that there has been a kind of iron logic to the evolution of the American family—that we are moving into a new era which entails a number of serious problems and also dictates the limits of reasonable hope. What is being drawn into question is the degree to which various forms of intervention are capable of addressing our situation. Social psychologists like Philip Rieff, for example, have argued for some time that it may already be too late for the American family. The new era, he claims, is one in which we are losing control of our institutions. The American family, like the church and educational institutions, may already have been subjected to lethal strains. The problem is not one which calls for heroic social intervention, as if—if we could just figure out what is going amiss—we could devise realistic levers for change. The problem is spiritual: a matter of values, cultural revolutions, and altered expectations which have arrived on the American scene and over which, apparently, we have little control. Rieff himself ends in being frightened. He does not know where this new era will take us, and he cannot imagine how we can live in an environment of decaying institutions. In fact, in *Fellow Teachers*, Rieff becomes a conservative; he dedicates himself to the battle for stability, apparently because he does not know what else to do.

In this essay, I want to analyze and evaluate this dour hypothesis, which at least among scholars is undermining hope for the American family. My suggestion, finally, will be that the hypothesis is suffused with myth. It ends in being one more form of the Garden of Eden story, which encourages a belief that our trek is always away from an ideal state of affairs toward a future so impossible that we can hardly imagine it. At best the hypothesis arbitrarily structures our collective family history, and it is simply not productive. Although this era is obviously filled with dangers for family stability, it is also filled with

378

interesting possibilities. This may well become a time of important creativity, both in raising issues about the legal rights of family members and in experimenting with legislative supports for a satisfying family life. It is far too soon to give up on the traditionally conceived American family. The situation is not so dire that we ought to despair of the possibilities of the public imagination in approaching the current threats to family stability.

THE MYTH

Although myths often take the form of a supposedly objective rendering of the history of a collectivity, they are nevertheless stories that purport to set forth "the truth" about that collective's past. They relate what *really* happened, and in so doing, they reveal that which is most important about the collective's identity.

The Garden of Eden described by historians of the American family (such as John Demos) is one that had its setting in colonial America—a place where the family existed in harmony with the larger community. In this vision, the home was described as one institution among many, each functioning within God's design for the total well-being of man. Thus, the building of the family was of a piece with the search for every other kind of salvation—economic, political, as well as spiritual. Translated into political terms, this was a Whiggish understanding of the family. Although Puritan saints were fond of dramatizing the devastating effects of the fall of man from grace, the family was not singled out for special treatment. Like every other institution, it was fallen; and like every other institution, it was redeemable. The family had no particular mission that placed it in tension with the "outside world."

Sometime during the waning years of the nineteenth century, the myth continues, the American family was expelled from its harmonious Garden. Dominant images of the family (especially images of the family as a refuge from "the jungle," or as a sphere of intimacy in the midst of a depersonalized world) now suggested the home was an ideal world developed over and against the larger society. It was a domain of ideal human

379

relations—a utopia—that compensated for and was in contrast to the tedium, the impersonality, the harassment, the exploitation, the pretension, and the boredom of life in the outside world. No longer merely one among many institutions, each reflecting the reasonable design of its Creator, the home assumed greater significance. At its best, the home was now seen as a kind of judgment on other institutions, or at least a haven in the midst of institutions from which regular experiences of escape seemed necessary.

During the last part of the twentieth century, according to a number of contributors to this volume, careful observers have become aware of a further shift in the shared perception of American family life. Arlene Skolnick, for example, says that she sees a more biblical understanding of the family emerging—a view which emphasizes that the home is a locus for the clash of interests, temperament, and passions. John Demos, speaking self-consciously as a participant-observer, refers to the emergence of the family as a kind of encounter group, where mutuality in self-realization has become the dominant value. Others refer to a new, pervasive sense of crisis, where the very survival of the family unit seems to have become an issue.

These new images of the family appear to gather around the therapy theme: sickness-health, repression-liberation, pain-pleasure, self-fulfillment, satisfaction. If the family is viewed as somehow a "natural" social group, essential to the human condition, then nature is no longer the same God-given harmony of interests envisioned by the colonial forefathers. It is a post-Darwin, post-Freud nature, marked by conflict, passionate forces, and the possibility both for health and destruction. If the family is interpreted, as it usually seems to be, in utopian terms, it is no longer seen as a compensatory institution, but as a community whose end is the support, the fulfillment, and the health and satisfaction of its individual members. To borrow Philip Rieff's vocabulary, the family no longer serves mainly to nurture the citizen, the religious person, or even the economic person. It is there to serve "psychological man"—persons who are "born to be pleased."

If this assessment proves to be accurate in any significant sense, the Garden of Eden must be considered as far, far away.

Therapeutic values are privatistic values, and they are probably even anti-institutional. This may well be an era, according to some observers, when individuals will be experiencing their families increasingly as a burden—as a network of responsibilities, roles, and traditions that can be tedious, boring, and inhibiting. Consequently, the largest problem we face may well be the fundamental one of keeping the family interesting enough and satisfying enough to generate commitment. The fact that activities outside the home often are experienced as more interesting and satisfying makes them strongly competitive with family loyalties; the family is placed in competition with the marketplace.

Those who make use of this Garden of Eden myth betray habits of historical interpretation which almost inevitably nurture a serious pessimism about the family and which run counter to their otherwise liberal assumption that political intervention is always possible. They assume, for example, that the history of the family is linear, in the sense that it always moves from era to era with an inner logic—an essential story-in-the-making. The family has come from somewhere and it is moving down a road that will take it someplace, that is, it makes sense to inquire about "where we are going." To discern the future of the family merely requires that one be able to read the map. This spatial image of our collective family's development, of course, suggests that over time certain points on the road are passed, and that it is probably not possible to return. We are coerced to value newness—new vistas, new possibilities, change; or at least we *feel* coerced to give up our nostalgia for the old ways in the interest of adjusting creatively to the new places to which our family trek takes us. If we are uneasy with these new places, that is our fault. We need to see these places with different eyeglasses. The road leads forward, not back.

This linear view of family development in American society is itself pessimistic only in the sense that it reinforces the notion that not all options (including the past ones) are open to us. The view suggests at least that only a limited number of options are realistically available at any given time, and that what once were possibilities have now disappeared from sight. What is indeed pessimistic, however, is the correlative belief that the process is one of progressive radicalization of family forms—that each era brings the American family closer and closer to a form of anarchy. The colonial era views the family in solidarity with all the rest of society; the late nineteenth and twentieth century pits the family against the world; the late twentieth century (so the suggestion goes) pits the individual against the family and the rest of the world. This hypothesis about our collective trek is truly frightening. It is not just another description of America's mild appropriation of individualistic behavior patterns; it is a description of a therapeutically oriented cultural revolution, whose end is a new era of self-fulfillment where norms do not count and where sacrifices for the common welfare no longer seem attractive. From almost any perspective, if the hypothesis holds, we would appear to be at the end of the road. The logic of development would take us straight into an era in which the family would lose its ability to generate commitment and energy—a period of decadence, marked by rising divorce rates, the breakdown of discipline, and extreme tolerance for experimentation with alternatives to traditionally conceived family patterns.

An Alternative Vision

From my point of view, this dour Garden of Eden myth deserves to be analyzed with a great deal of seriousness because it currently has an enormous ability to shape the perceptions we hold of our shared family situation. It is a powerful vision of what is going on in America—a plausible story about American family life, one that suggests with conviction which courses of action can or cannot be taken. This is the moral power of the myth: the description of our situation implies prescription. The myth provides the dramatic context within which we consider the moral choices that are open to us. In an important sense, moral reflection is little more than the process of trying to determine what is the fitting action in a given setting, so the vision we hold of what is happening in that setting cannot be separated from the principles or the images of virtue that we cherish. We inevitably consider the latter in terms of the former, that is, we always consider our moral choices in terms of how they help us to complete a particular story in our lives.

The American Garden of Eden myth, then, does not simply tell us a story about our collective family life. It also suggests what we ought to be doing about the situation. Most important, it is suggested that we ought to decide whether to struggle against the fates of family misfortune or to surrender to them. We ought to decide whether "the family can be made to work," or whether one must face up to modernity and accept the unhappy fact that the extended or even the nuclear family is dead. Those who take the family seriously are called to accept the rigors of heroism, whatever course they choose. The Garden of Eden is forever behind us; the times are tough now. Thus, family life enters the realm of the problematic, wherein the possibility of defeat is imminent and wherein, frankly, people often become weary trying to work matters out. Although the myth is capable of inspiring the most intense forms of labor, either in preserving family intimacy in the face of destructive tides or in shaping new family relationships that appeal to a changing sense of justice, it is also self-defeating. The myth demands a continual flow of energy on behalf of the family, and people soon start to long for relationships that are not so problematic.

There is no question that some form of the American Garden of Eden myth is dominant in the minds of large numbers of people at this time. But one of the major contributions of this volume has been to place this myth in perspective, and thereby to suggest that it is unnecessary to be passive and uncritical in the face of it. Billie Joyce Wahlstrom, for example, does just that: her essay on family iconography in mass media points to the complexity, the contradictions, and the mutually exclusive visions within our common-sense interpretations of family life, and thus she suggests that there are far more ways than one of viewing what is happening to the American family. In deciphering mass media icons, she suggests that the American public views its home life as a refuge and as a high form of human fulfillment. But it also views the family as a prison, where the loss of male power is the badge of freedom surrendered. The

family is utopia, but it is also the arena for neurosis and schizophrenia. The family is a support for the blossoming of individuals; the family is also an impediment.

Wahlstrom encourages us, then, to be wary of any form of
reductionism in describing the state of affairs in American family
life, simply because our commonsensical experience of the family does not appear to be expressible in a wholly systematic and
coherent fashion. The myths we make use of to articulate our
experience of the family are not dramatic "translations" of
philosophical statements, where the rules of formal logical discourse can be applied. They are more like a collection of dispa-
rate stories, all of which seem necessary for an adequate expression of human experience.

This propensity to assert contradictory things about the family is, we must admit, simply the normal state of affairs. No society
is entirely systematic in its values or in its modes of perception.
But, to some extent, the pluralism of our images and myths of
the family must be regarded as the peculiar fruit of a historical
era in which no single institution has assumed the power to
impose its vision of the good life as the supremely authoritative
vision. For example, Ariès is undoubtedly correct in his observation that churches in America have become "private clubs." The
churches no longer provide a collective conscience for the community; they are among a variety of public consciences, embodied in a variety of institutions. Wahlstrom is also correct in
her observation that the mass media in America have assumed
many of the functions of the churches in providing religiously
potent family icons. In the modern world the need for religious
meaning has not disappeared, but the purveyors of religious
meaning are legion. The religious scene is fragmented, hardly
recognizable as such.

Conversely, Ariès is undoubtedly wrong in his claim that the
family is the heir of the church in providing religious meaning,
that is, as the new center from which visions of the good life
flow. And Wahlstrom undoubtedly needs to be corrected in her
suggestion that mass media have become the primary arena for
interpreting the religious meaning of our collective experience,
including our family experience. The fact is that no single institution or network of institutions is able to command human

loyalties to such an extent that it has the power to bring about any kind of widespread agreement. In our family life in America, we are not the inheritors of a new set of doctrines of the family, expounded in new Holy Roman Empires. We are surrounded by a multiplicity of visions, and our aspirations for family life reflect this diversity.

We are not, for example, exclusively in a new therapeutic era of family life, where Freud's understanding of human relations provides the most authoritative interpretation of the tension experienced between the collective and the individual. Nor are we exclusively in a Marxist era, where those who have been exploited by traditional images of the family are in a position to rectify previous power imbalances, for example, between husband and wife, parent and child, or even between persons who participate in conventional marriages and those who participate in homophile or other nonconventional unions. We are in a number of eras simultaneously, because the myths through which we interpret our experience are fragmented and plural and limited in their power to attract adherents. Thus in our family life we may be in a period when it is important simultaneously to protect the family as a refuge of intimacy, to acknowledge that role differences have unjustly created differences in rights and privileges and to compensate for these, to assert individuality, to fight narcissism, to experiment with alternative forms of family life, to reaffirm the values of traditional American forms of family life, to oppose parental totalitarianism, to reassert parental authority. The agenda appears to be endless, and the coherence of the agenda is, to say the least, sometimes questionable.

Thus, the social ethicist who is asked to dream utopian dreams about the future of the American family has an important choice to make. He or she must decide whether to speak out of a private, sectarian vision, which is vulnerable because of its very particularity, or to comment critically on what all of us should do about our shared, but pluralistic, family environment. I choose the latter course here, simply because one of the largest problems we face is, undoubtedly, our confusion in knowing what kind of moral stands we ought to be taking in a pluralistic society, where one is virtually coerced into assigning a relativity even to his or her own moral principles. Our danger, in short, is moral impotence, the loss of moral nerve, the tendency to lapse into a flabby morality of "different strokes for different folks."

I believe it is important, however, to affirm the integrity of a pluralism of family life styles within the American environment. There are probably limits as to what can be tolerated at any given time, but these limits should be loosely delineated and expansive. Ours is a society that measures freedom in terms of the proliferation of choices, and I see no reason why we should not liberally extend our passion for expansive choice to include family patterns which at first blush may appear to be utterly shocking as well as patterns which are conventional, but which have been excluded by social and economic conditions.

Thus my bias is toward policies and procedures that insure the civil rights of conventional and deviant families, and that insure as broad a choice of life styles as can be included within the bounds of democratic society. We need, for example, to liberalize laws that relate to nonconventional households and to define more carefully the legal rights and responsibilities of persons who enter into nonconventional family experiments or simple "living-together" arrangements. Choices that should be open to traditionally conceived families need to be extended and protected as well. We need to consider, in addition, such matters as: (1) the way in which banking policies currently exclude large numbers of persons from the experience of home ownership; (2) the manner in which welfare and social security practices coerce persons (particularly the elderly) into undesired family arrangements; (3) the ownership of pension funds, the nontransferability of which often precludes movement from one job to another or from one geographical area to another; (4) the manner in which inflated property taxes often drive the elderly from their homes into unfamiliar neighborhoods and undesirable living conditions. The list could easily be extended. The point, however, is abstract: the environment which supports the extension of family choice is an incredibly complex system of economic, social, and legal structures which must be considered one by one as well as collectively in their impact upon families. The process of expanding choice, and thereby of protecting the health of the American family, is a laborious, pragmatic, and highly politicized one. It is not mainly a process of heroically fighting a "predicament" in which a Garden of Eden myth has placed us. The need is rather for a careful, skilled delineation of the conditions that affect the quality of our family life, for political and legal imagination, and for the political ingenuity necessary to effect change. Perhaps most important, the need is for patience enough to sustain political energies.

There is a considerable difference between the search for political and legal justice (which in our society includes the maximum feasible extension of choice) and the approval of life styles that appear as unhealthy or unjust. The former is morally obligatory; the latter is not. To advocate the extension of the right to choice in family life styles is not to say that all choices are healthy. Indeed, one of the skills we should cultivate in a pluralist society is the ability to advocate justice and at the same time to voice a sense of disapproval or outrage concerning choices that seem negatively to affect the quality of our shared environment. This is tricky business. Collectively we have a right to a humane environment too, and firm lines cannot easily be drawn between life style options which can be tolerated and those which are so destructive of our shared ethos that they should be barred. The bias, I believe, should be toward toleration, but it is also important that we build a political arena in which the quality of our environment is always an issue for open debate and for political maneuvering.

Needless to say, we also have the right to point out the hypocrisy of experiments or movements that champion a rhetoric of pure principles (e.g., equality of the sexes, self-determination, mutual encouragement toward self-realization, sexual liberty), but which end in forms of dogmatism, totalitarianism, and inconsistency that seem worse than the options they oppose. Pluralist society at the minimum needs an ethic that stresses the responsibility to live up to the social covenants into which various groups have entered. Granted the inevitable inconsistencies of group life, generally speaking, do you live up to your rhetoric? Do you honor your own convenants? Have your new covenants issued in new forms of exploitation? These are the moral questions of pluralism.

If it is true that in the minds of large numbers of persons the Garden of Eden myth is the dominant force shaping their perceptions of the American home, it is also true that the cause of justice may well be served by that very fact. The sense of crisis breeds concern, and concern, among the hearty, breeds political energy. Thus this may be a period when the dominant myth exhausts and discourages us, but at the same time a period when that myth opens up possibilities for extending the rights of choice. In the therapeutic era, dramatized as a departure from Eden, values flow in the direction of self-determination and self-fulfillment, and in this atmosphere the rights of persons (and classes of persons) emerge as subjects for public debate. I expect that the next several years will be such a period of debate. And I expect that that debate will be associated with intense legal and legislative activity. Thus, ironically, the liberal dream that we can and should intervene on behalf of a more humane society is both encouraged and discouraged by that dominant myth. To many, our family problems seem so large that it appears foolhardy to pretend that an erector-set mentality can be of much help at all. But the therapeutic air also promotes interest in possibilities for choice. That is an air that energizes the continuing search for justice.

Suggested Readings

Although books are listed here only once, a number of them are of course relevant to more than the one chapter under which they are grouped.

CHAPTER 1

Ariès, Philippe. *Centuries of Childhood: A Social History of Family Life.* Translated by Robert Baldick. New York: Alfred A. Knopf, 1962.

Goode, William J. *World Revolution and Family Patterns.* New York: Free Press, 1970.

Laslett, Peter. *The World We Have Lost.* New York: Charles Scribner's Sons, 1965.

Laslett, Peter, ed., assisted by Wall, Richard. *Household and Family in Past Time.* Cambridge: Cambridge University Press, 1972.

Shorter, Edward. *The Making of the Modern Family.* New York: Basic Books, 1975.

Stone, Lawrence. *The Family, Sex and Marriage in England 1500–1800.* New York: Harper & Row, 1977.

CHAPTER 2

Demos, John. "The American Family in Past Time." *The American Scholar* 43 (1974): 422–46.

Kett, Joseph. *Rites of Passage: Adolescence in America, 1790 to the Present.* New York: Basic Books, 1977.

Lasch, Christopher. *Haven in a Heartless World: The Family Besieged.* New York: Basic Books, 1977.

Laslett, Barbara. "The Family as a Public and Private Institution: An Historical Perspective." *Journal of Marriage and the Family* 35 (August 1973): 480–92.

Morgan, Edmund S. *The Puritan Family: Religion and Domestic Relations in Seventeenth-Century New England.* Rev. ed. New York: Harper & Row, 1966.

Wishy, Bernard. *The Child and the Republic: The Dawn of Modern American Child Nurture*. Philadelphia: University of Pennsylvania, 1972.

CHAPTER 3

Demos, John. *A Little Commonwealth: Family Life in Plymouth Colony*. New York: Oxford University Press, 1970.

Greven, Philip J., Jr. *Four Generations: Population, Land and Family in Colonial Andover, Massachusetts*. Ithaca, N.Y.: Cornell University Press, 1970.

Lockridge, Kenneth. *The New England Town: The First Hundred Years*. New York: W. W. Norton, 1970.

Powell, Sumner C. *The Puritan Village*. Middletown, Conn.: Wesleyan University Press, 1963.

CHAPTER 4

Cott, Nancy. *The Bonds of Womanhood: "Woman's Sphere" in New England, 1780–1835*. New Haven and London: Yale University Press, 1977.

Greven, Philip J., Jr. *The Protestant Temperament: Patterns of Child-Rearing, Religious Experience, and the Self in Early America*. New York: Alfred A. Knopf, 1977.

Keniston, Kenneth, and the Carnegie Council on Children. *All Our Children: The American Family under Pressure*. New York: Harcourt Brace Jovanovich, 1977.

Zaretsky, Eli. *Capitalism, the Family and Personal Life*. New York: Harper & Row, 1976

CHAPTER 6

Houghton, Walter E. *The Victorian Frame of Mind*, chapter 13, "Love," pp. 341–93. New Haven: Yale University Press, 1957.

Lane, Margaret. "Dickens on the Hearth." In *Dickens 1970*, edited by Michael Slater, pp. 153–72. New York: Stein & Day, 1970.

Mayhew, Henry. *London Labour and the London Poor*. Vol. 1. New York: Dover Publications, 1968.

Quennell, Peter. *Victorian Panorama: A Survey of Life & Fashion from Contemporary Photographs*, chapter 3, "Victorian Family Life," pp. 43–51. London: B. T. Batsford, 1937.

Wilson, Angus. "Dickens on Children and Childhood." In *Dickens 1970*, edited by Michael Slater, pp. 195–227. New York: Stein & Day, 1970.

CHAPTER 8

Baum, Charlotte; Hyman, Paula; and Michel, Sonya. *The Jewish Woman in America*. New York: Dial Press, 1976.
Glazer, Nathan, and Moynihan, Daniel Patrick. *Beyond the Melting Pot: The Negroes, Puerto Ricans, Jews, Italians, and Irish of New York City*. 2d ed. Cambridge, Mass.: M.I.T. Press and Harvard University Press, 1970.
Guttmann, Allen. *The Jewish Writer in America: Assimilation and the Crisis of Identity*. New York: Oxford University Press, 1971.
Herberg, Will. *Protestant-Catholic-Jew: An Essay in American Religious Sociology*. Garden City, N.Y.: Doubleday, 1955.
Howe, Irving. *World of Our Fathers*. New York: Harcourt Brace Jovanovich, 1976.
Rich, Adrienne. *Of Woman Born: Motherhood as Experience and Institution*. New York: W. W. Norton, 1976.
Rose, Peter I., ed. *The Ghetto and Beyond: Essays on Jewish Life in America*. New York: Random House, 1969.
Zborowsky, Mark, and Herzog, Elizabeth. *Life Is with People: The Jewish Little-Town of Eastern Europe*. New York: International Universities Press, 1952.

CHAPTER 9

Cox, Harvey. *The Secular City: Secularization and Urbanization in Theological Perspective*. Rev. ed. New York: Macmillan, 1966.
Fishwick, Marshall, and Browne, Ray B., eds. *Icons of Popular Culture*. Bowling Green: Bowling Green University Popular Press, 1970.
Gerbner, George. "Violence in Television Drama: Trends and Symbolic Functions." In *Television and Social Behavior*, edited by George A. Comstock and E. A. Rubenstein, *Content and Social Control*. Vol. 1. Washington: Government Printing Office, 1972.
Jewett, Robert, and Lawrence, John Shelton. *The American Monomyth*. Garden City, N.Y.: Anchor Press, 1977.
McLuhan, Marshall. *Understanding Media: The Extension of Man*. New York: McGraw-Hill, 1964.
Panofsky, Erwin. *Studies in Iconology: Humanistic Themes in the Art of the Renaissance*. New York: Oxford University Press, 1939.
Window Dressing on the Set: Women and Minorities in Television. A Report of the United States Commission on Civil Rights. August 1977. Washington, D.C. Free.

CHAPTER 10

Modell, John, and Hareven, Tamara K. "Urbanization and the Malleable Household." *Journal of Marriage and the Family* 35 (August 1973): 467–79.

Skolnick, Arlene. *The Intimate Environment: Exploring Marriage and the Family.* Boston: Little, Brown, 1973.

Slater, Philip. *Footholds: Understanding the Shifting Sexual and Family Tensions in Our Culture.* New York: E. P. Dutton, 1977.

Sussman, Marvin B., ed. *Non-Traditional Family Forms in the 1970's.* Minneapolis: National Council on Family Relations, 1972.

CHAPTER 11

Lopreato, Joseph. *Italian-Americans.* New York: Random House, 1970.

Ludwig, Ed, and Santibanez, James, eds. *The Chicanos: Mexican-American Voices.* Baltimore: Penguin Books, 1971.

Moore, Joan W., with Cuellar, Alfredo. *Mexican-Americans.* 2d ed. New York: Prentice-Hall, 1976.

Novak, Michael. *The Rise of the Unmeltable Ethnic: Politics and Culture in the 1970's.* New York: Macmillan, 1972.

Sinclair, Upton. *The Jungle.* New York: New American Library, 1960 (first published in 1906).

Wheeler, Thomas C., ed. *The Immigrant Experience: The Anguish of Becoming an American.* Baltimore: Penguin Books, 1971.

CHAPTER 12

Blackwell, James E. *The Black Community: Diversity and Unity.* New York: Dodd, Mead, 1975.

Gutman, Herbert G. *The Black Family in Slavery and Freedom, 1750–1925.* New York: Random House, Pantheon Books, 1976.

Heiss, Jerold. *The Case of the Black Family: A Sociological Inquiry.* New York: Columbia University Press, 1975.

Jackson, Jacquelyne Johnson. "Family Organization and Ideology." In *Comparative Studies of Blacks and Whites in the United States*, edited by Kent S. Miller and Ralph Mason Dreger. New York: Seminar Press, 1973.

Solomon, Barbara. *Black Empowerment: Social Work in Oppressed Communities.* New York: Columbia University Press, 1976.

Stack, Carol B. *All Our Kin: Strategies for Survival in a Black Community.* New York: Harper & Row, 1974.

CHAPTER 13

Jeffrey, Kirk. "The Family as Utopian Retreat from the City: The Nineteenth Century Contribution." In *The Family, Communes, and Utopian Societies*, edited by Sallie TeSelle, pp. 21–41. New York: Harper & Row, 1972.

Laing, R. D. *The Politics of the Family*. New York: Random House, 1971.

Murphy, R. F. *The Dialectics of Social Life: Alarms and Excursions in Anthropological Theory*. New York: Basic Books, 1972.

Schneider, D. M., and Smith, R. T. *Class Differences and Sex Roles in American Kinship and Family Structure*. Princeton: Princeton University Press, 1973.

Steinmetz, S. K., and Straus, M. A., eds. *Violence in the Family*. New York: Harper & Row, 1974.

Wolfenstein, Martha. "Fun Morality: An Analysis of Recent American Child-training Literature." In *Childhood in Contemporary Cultures*, edited by Margaret Mead and Martha Wolfenstein, pp. 168–78. Chicago: University of Chicago Press, 1955.

CHAPTER 14

Clark, H. *Domestic Relations*. Minneapolis: West Publishing, 1968.

Glendon, M. *State, Law and Family: Family Law in Transition in the United States and Western Europe*. Amsterdam: North-Holland, 1977.

Katz, S., ed. *The Youngest Minority I & II. Lawyers in Defense of Children*. Chicago: American Bar Association, 1974, 1977.

Krause, H. *Family Law*. Minneapolis: West Publishing, 1976.

Mnookin, R. *Child, Family and State*. Boston: Little, Brown, 1978.

Platt, A. *The Child Savers: The Invention of Delinquency*. Chicago: University of Chicago Press, 1969.

Rheinstein, M. *Marriage Stability, Divorce, and the Law*. Chicago: University of Chicago Press, 1972.

CHAPTER 15

Dinnerstein, Dorothy. *The Mermaid and the Minotaur*. New York: Harper & Row, 1976.

Firestone, Shulamith. *The Dialectic of Sex*. New York: Bantam Books, 1972.

Mill, John Stuart. *Essays on Sex Equality*. Edited by Alice S. Rossi. Chicago: University of Chicago Press, 1970.

Rossi, Alice S. "A Biosocial Perspective on Parenting." *Daedalus*, Spring 1977, pp. 1–31.

Schultz, Theodore W., ed. *Economics of the Family*. Chicago: University of Chicago Press, 1974.

Stiehm, Judith. "Invidious Intimacy." *Social Policy* 6 (March–April 1976): 12–16.

CHAPTER 16

Bellah, Robert N. *Beyond Belief: Essays on Religion in a Post-Traditional World*. New York: Harper & Row, 1970.

Lifton, Robert J. *Boundaries: Psychological Man in Revolution*. New York: Random House, 1970.

Orr, John B., and Nichelson, F. Patrick. *The Radical Suburb: Soundings in Changing American Character*. Philadelphia: Westminster, 1970.

Rieff, Philip. *Triumph of the Therapeutic: Uses of Faith after Freud*. New York: Harper & Row, Torchbooks, 1968.

Sennett, Richard. *The Fall of Public Man*. New York: Alfred A. Knopf, 1978.

Contributors

PHILIPPE ARIÈS is a French social historian, former visiting professor of history at Johns Hopkins University, now Directeur d'Études at the École des Hautes Études en Sciences Sociales, Paris.

BEVERLY GRAY BIENSTOCK is a lecturer on American Jewish literature at Hebrew Union College, Los Angeles, and a freelance writer.

RALPH J. CRANDALL is a historian and editor of *The New England Historical and Genealogical Register*.

JOHN DEMOS is professor of history at Brandeis University.

DAVID KUNZLE teaches art history at the University of California, Los Angeles.

BARBARA LASLETT is associate professor of sociology at the University of Southern California.

SYLVIA MANNING is associate professor of English and director of the Freshman Writing Program at the University of Southern California.

HELEN A. MENDES is assistant professor of social work at the University of Southern California.

STEPHEN J. MORSE is professor of law and psychiatry at the Law Center and the School of Medicine, University of Southern California.

JOHN B. ORR is professor of religion and social ethics and director of the School of Religion, University of Southern California.

DEMETRA PALAMARI is associate professor of French language, literature, and culture at California State University, Los Angeles.

ANDREI SIMIĆ is associate professor of anthropology at the University of Southern California.

ARLENE SKOLNICK is a research psychologist at the Institute of Human Development, University of California, Berkeley.

BARBARA BRYANT SOLOMON is professor of social work at the University of Southern California.

DAVID E. STANNARD is associate professor of American studies and history at Yale University.

JUDITH HICKS STIEHM is associate professor of political science at the University of Southern California.

BILLIE JOYCE WAHLSTROM is assistant professor of English and women's studies at the University of Southern California.

Index